The Dolphin Smalltalk Companion

A hands-on guide to building complete applications

The Dolphin Smalltalk Companion

A hands-on guide to building complete applications

Ted Bracht

Addison-Wesley

An imprint of PEARSON EDUCATION

Boston ■ San Francisco ■ New York ■ Toronto ■ Montreal ■
London ■ Munich ■ Paris ■ Madrid ■ Cape Town ■ Sydney ■
Tokyo ■ Singapore ■ Mexico City

PEARSON EDUCATION LIMITED

Head Office:
Edinburgh Gate
Harlow CM20 2JE
England
Tel: +44 (0)1279 623623
Fax: +44 (0)1279 431059

London Office:
128 Long Acre
London WC2E 9AN
Tel: +44 (0)20 7447 2000
Fax: +44 (0)20 7240 5771
Website: www.informit.com and www.aw.com/cseng

First published in Great Britain in 2002
© Pearson Education Limited 2002

The right of Ted Bracht to be identified as the author of this work has been asserted by him in accordance with the Copyright, Designs and Patents Acts 1988.

ISBN 0-201-73793-0

British Library Cataloguing-in Publication Data
A catalogue record for this book is available from the British Library.

Library of Congress Cataloging in Publication Data
Applied for.

All rights reserved; no part of this publication may be reproduced, stored in a retrieval system, or transmitted in any form or by any means, electronic, mechanical, photocopying, recording, or otherwise without either the prior written permission of the Publishers or a licence permitting restricted copying in the United Kingdom issued by the Copyright Licensing Agency Ltd, 90 Tottenham Court Road, London W1P 0LP.

The programs in this book have been included for their instructional value. The Publisher does not offer any warranties or representations in respect of their fitness for a particular purpose, nor does the publisher accept any liability for any loss or damage (other than for personal injury or death) arising from their use.

Many of the designations used by manufacturers and sellers to distinguish their products are claimed as trademarks. All products and company names are trademarks or registered trademarks of their respective owners. Pearson Education Limited has made every attempt to supply trademark information about manufacturers and their products mentioned in this book. A list of trademark designations and their owners appears on p. x.

10 9 8 7 6 5 4 3 2 1

Typeset by Mathematical Composition Setters Ltd, Salisbury, Wiltshire.
Printed and bound in Great Britain by Biddles Ltd, Guildford and King's Lynn.

The Publisher's policy is to use paper manufactured from sustainable forests.

Contents

Preface xi

1 Introduction 1

1.1　The Smalltalk language 1
1.2　The Dolphin Smalltalk environment 4
　　1.2.1　The file setup 4
　　1.2.2　The Launcher 6
1.3　The workspace 7
1.4　Playground 9

2 The application 17

2.1　What we are going to build 17
2.2　How we are going to build the application 18
2.3　A standard pattern for the components 19

3 The first application component: the Team 21

3.1　The Team model 22
　　3.1.1　The class hierarchy browser 23
　　3.1.2　Creating our first class 26
　　3.1.3　Summary 31
3.2　The Team presenter 31
　　3.2.1　Summary 35
3.3　Creating a view 35
　　3.3.1　The view composer 36
　　3.3.2　The Team view 38
　　3.3.3　Testing the Team view 42
　　3.3.4　The finishing touch 43
　　3.3.5　The Microsoft look 44
　　3.3.6　Summary 46

3.4 Some basic maintenance work 47

4 The Driver component 50

4.1 The Driver model 51
- 4.1.1 The abstract RacingActor class 51
- 4.1.2 Modifications to the Team class 53
- 4.1.3 The Driver class 55
- 4.1.4 Summary 61

4.2 The Driver presenter and view 61
- 4.2.1 The Driver presenter 61
- 4.2.2 The Driver view 63
- 4.2.3 Testing the view 66
- 4.2.4 Summary 68

4.3 The driver's gender 68
- 4.3.1 The 1-of-n variable in the model 69
- 4.3.2 Presenting 1-of-n variables 70
- 4.3.3 Radio buttons 71
- 4.3.4 List presenters 77
- 4.3.5 Summary 83

4.4 Some loose ends 83
- 4.4.1 The caption 83
- 4.4.2 A picture paints a thousand words 85
- 4.4.3 Summary 88

5 The Season component 89

5.1 The Season model 89
- 5.1.1 The Collection classes 90
- 5.1.2 The score definition 93
- 5.1.3 Summary 95

5.2 The name of an object 95

5.3 The Season presenter and view 96
- 5.3.1 The SeasonDialogPresenter definition 97
- 5.3.2 The Season view 99
- 5.3.3 Copy and deepCopy 100
- 5.3.4 Summary 104

5.4 Multi-column lists 104
- 5.4.1 A virtual list 105
- 5.4.2 The multi-column ListView 107
- 5.4.3 Summary 109

6 The RaceCar component 110

- 6.1 The RaceCar model 110
  - 6.1.1 *The RaceCar class definition* 110
  - 6.1.2 *The starting number* 112
  - 6.1.3 *The Team association* 116
  - 6.1.4 *The default driver* 120
  - 6.1.5 *The link with the season* 121
  - 6.1.6 *Summary* 122

- 6.2 Error handling and the debugger 122
  - 6.2.1 *Error handling in Dolphin Smalltalk* 122
  - 6.2.2 *The debugger* 124
  - 6.2.3 *Debugger playground* 125
  - 6.2.4 *Another way of writing Smalltalk* 127
  - 6.2.5 *Our own error handling mechanism* 128
  - 6.2.6 *Summary* 131

- 6.3 The RaceCar presenter and view 132
  - 6.3.1 *The lists of teams and drivers* 132
  - 6.3.2 *The RaceCarView as subclass of the Shell class* 134
  - 6.3.3 *Building the view for the race cars* 137
  - 6.3.4 *Summary* 140

7 The Circuit component 141

- 7.1 The basic Circuit model 142
  - 7.1.1 *The length of the circuit* 142
  - 7.1.2 *The lap record* 145
  - 7.1.3 *Summary* 150

- 7.2 The Circuit presenter and view 150
  - 7.2.1 *The milliseconds TypeConverter* 154
  - 7.2.2 *The length of the circuit* 156
  - 7.2.3 *Summary* 160

8 The Race component 161

- 8.1 The Race model 161
- 8.2 The Race presenter and view 166
  - 8.2.1 *The Race dialog* 167
  - 8.2.2 *The main Race view* 170
  - 8.2.3 *Entering the results* 174
- 8.3 Sorting the starters 179
- 8.4 Summary 184

9 Bringing the components together 186

- 9.1 The basic racing application model 186
  - 9.1.1 The model 186
  - 9.1.2 The race application presenter 192
  - 9.1.3 The application framework view 193
  - 9.1.4 Summary 196
- 9.2 Maintaining items 197
  - 9.2.1 The maintenance methods 197
  - 9.2.2 Context menus and menu bars 198
  - 9.2.3 Enabling and disabling commands 200
  - 9.2.4 Toolbars 201
  - 9.2.5 Summary 208
- 9.3 Integrating the season-dependent components 208
  - 9.3.1 The tree model 208
  - 9.3.2 Add branches for the Race and RaceCar 220
- 9.4 Tidying up the race application components 225
  - 9.4.1 Global variables revisited 225
  - 9.4.2 Opening a race for the results 228

10 The results 230

- 10.1 The results for the season 230
  - 10.1.1 Collecting the results 230
  - 10.1.2 A presenter for the results 231
  - 10.1.3 Showing the results in the application shell 233
  - 10.1.4 Dynamic resizing of multi-column lists 236
  - 10.1.5 Summary 238
- 10.2 A graph of the results 238
  - 10.2.1 A short information requirement analysis 239
  - 10.2.2 The LineGraph view 240
  - 10.2.3 A user-definable graph 246
  - 10.2.4 Summary 254

11 Saving and importing the race data 255

- 11.1 Saving object data 255
  - 11.1.1 Modifications to the presenter and the view 256
  - 11.1.2 Modifications to the models 258
  - 11.1.3 Save data on exit 259
  - 11.1.4 Summary 261

11.2 Importing comma-separated data 261
    11.2.1 A generic import class 262
    11.2.2 The data import wizard 268
    11.2.3 Summary 276

11.3 Importing from the Web 276
    11.3.1 The HTML import model 277
    11.3.2 The Web data import wizard 283
    11.3.3 Summary 289

11.4 XML data 289

12 *Application deployment* 292

12.1 Making an executable 292

12.2 Web deployment 293

12.3 Summary 294

Appendix A Other Smalltalk resoures 295

Appendix B Overview of the main classes 297

Appendix C Additional tools 306

Appendix D Date and Time field formatting 311

Appendix E The CD 312

Index 315

TRADEMARK NOTICE

Java™ is a trademark of Sun Microsystems, Incorporated.
Windows 95®, Windows 98®, *Microsoft ME*, *SQLServer*™, and Windows NT4® are registered trademarks of Microsoft Corporation.
Apple Macintosh® and *Apple Lisa* are registered trademarks of Apple Corporation.
Oracle® is a trademark of Oracle Corporation.
Dolphin™ is a trademark of Intuitive Systems Ltd
Unix is a registered trademark of X/Open Company Ltd.

LICENSING AGREEMENT

This book comes with a CD-ROM software package. By opening this package you are agreeing to be bound by the following.

The software contained on this CD-ROM is, in many cases, copyrighted, and all rights are reserved by the individual licensing agreements associated with each piece of software in the CD-ROM. THIS SOFTWARE IS PROVIDED FREE OF CHARGE, AS IS, AND WITHOUT WARRANTY OF ANY KIND, EITHER EXPRESSED OR IMPLIED, INCLUDING, BUT NOT LIMITED TO, THE IMPLIED WARRANTIES OF MERCHANTABILITY AND FITNESS FOR A PARTICULAR PURPOSE. Neither the book publisher, author nor its dealers and its distributors assumes any liability for any alleged or actual damage arising from the use of this software. The software on the CD is subject to the conditions of Object Arts' licence agreement and any problems with the performance of the software should be directed to Object Arts http://www.objects-arts.com

Preface

When I tried to learn Smalltalk, it took me a long time to work out how to use it to build real applications. I could see how to execute snippets of code, and even how to make those snippets of code permanent. I bought a couple of books, and they helped me to understand more of the language, how to become a better object-oriented designer, how to make better use of the standard classes, but I still couldn't see how to build a complete application in Smalltalk.

This book will therefore take you through the creation of a complete application with Dolphin Smalltalk. Thus this book differs from most other books on Smalltalk, which typically explain the language and show you some examples. This book will not cover all the ins and outs of the Smalltalk language – there are too many good books around to compete with. See Appendix A for a number of suggested additional reads. But as we will be writing quite a lot of Smalltalk code throughout this book, Chapter 1 gives a brief introduction to the Smalltalk language and the Dolphin Smalltalk development environment. Appendix B contains some additional explanation on the major Dolphin Smalltalk classes.

One of the most difficult choices to make in a tutorial is which domain (business case) to use to illustrate the material. The domain has to have something recognizable for readers so that they can translate the examples into their own environment. It also has to have enough aspects so that a wide variety of the available functionality of the programming language can be demonstrated and it has to allow us to start simply. The tutorial used in this book is built around an application which we can use to maintain the scores for Formula One (F1) motor racing. The marginal notes show which aspects of the Smalltalk language will be discussed in that section.

We start the tutorial with simple building blocks which we will later glue together in an application framework. Then we will build some more advanced components that allow us to import data and show data in graphical form. We will come across some issues that are specific to Formula One racing, but much of the functionality that we will be building can easily be adapted for other sports. Formula One racing is about teams and drivers. Most other sports have equivalents, for example football where it is all about teams and the players within the teams. In F1 a driver scores points, which also make up the team's points. In football the player scores, and the end result defines the points scored by a team.

Stretching the example a bit, you can even think of similarities with a business application such as a bank account application, where you have "static data" like the bank account which bears similarities to the team, and "dynamic data," the transactions, which bear similarities to the results of races.

As Smalltalk is an object-oriented programming language, we will approach the design of the application by trying to find the objects in the domain and build the functionality around those objects which together make up the application.

This book comes with a CD. This CD contains the Dolphin Smalltalk development system and the code for all the chapters. Appendix E describes how to install Dolphin Smalltalk and how to use the code for the individual chapters.

Acknowledgments

First, I want to thank Debbie Griffiths for her patience and support while I was writing this book. Even though she didn't and surprisingly still doesn't have any interest at all in the subject, she was always willing to listen to whatever I wanted to explain to her in order to marshal my thoughts.

I would also like to thank Blair McGlashan and especially Andy Bower from Object Arts, for their encouragement to produce this book and of course for bringing Dolphin Smalltalk to market. Furthermore, I want to thank Peter Kriens for enthusiastically introducing me to Smalltalk back in the 1980s. Thanks to Till Schümmer, Roel Wuyts and Stephane Ducasse for help in shaping the book's structure and contents. Finally I want to thank Steve Waring and Ian Bartholomew for their coding suggestions and everybody else in the Dolphin Smalltalk newsgroup community who supported me with coding issues and other suggestions. Susan Harrison deserves to be ackowledged as well after the amount of energy she put in to get the book looking like it does.

Ted Bracht
September 2001

In essence, Smalltalk is a programming language focused on human beings rather than the computer.

Alan Knight

Introduction

1.1 The Smalltalk language

The Smalltalk language was originally developed during the 1970s by a team at the Xerox Palo Alto Research Center. Their aim was to build a computer with a programming language that could be used by children (the Dynabook). Smalltalk was the first programming language with overlapping graphical windows and a pointing device, the mouse. Today we are all used to the graphical user interface and the mouse, but in those days they were revolutionary. It took another ten years before Apple copied these ideas and made them available to a larger public through the Lisa and the Macintosh. The language itself had to have as few fixed elements as possible, so that it could be expressed in itself. The designers came up with the structure that you can still find in every Smalltalk environment; objects, classes, messages, and methods. These are the basic building blocks of Smalltalk.

Smalltalk was the first and still is one of the purest object-oriented languages. In Smalltalk everything is an object. You will find this sentence in virtually every book and article about Smalltalk. But what does it mean? What are those objects? This is the most crucial question in every object-oriented design. The simplest answer is that the objects are those things that you are interested in, or for which you are building an application. If you are building a card game, then the cards and the players are the objects. If you are building a simulation of a factory floor, then the machines on the workfloor, the people that operate the machines, the raw materials, and the finished products are the objects.

So why are we interested in those objects? What is the advantage of object orientation (O-O)? The main thing about O-O development is that we can do it as though those objects live in our application. They all have knowledge about themselves and interact with each other. The objects and interactions between objects form our application, which is a mirror image of the real world. This means that we don't have to make a mental translation from the real world (the "problem domain") into data structures, libraries, and subroutines like you have to do with other development approaches.

Let's take a card game as an example. In a card game you've got cards and players. Each player has got a hand of cards and each card knows its suit and value. Therefore, each card knows with which cards it can be combined based on the rules of the game. This means that a card can ask another card something like: "Can you be combined with me?". The other card can then answer: "Yes, we would form a pair" or "No, I can't be combined with you."

What would be needed to make this work in a development environment? First, objects need to have knowledge of themselves; a card needs to have knowledge of its suit and value. This knowledge is stored in the instance variables of an object. We will come back to the term instance shortly. Secondly, objects need to be able to receive messages and to send a reply to the senders of the messages. For this ability, objects need to be able to find the code that needs to be executed for the message and then execute that code. This can be compared to calling a subroutine in traditional programming. The difference is that such a piece of code can only be called by those objects for which it is meant. In Smalltalk this "subroutine" is called a **method**, and its name is called the **selector**.

In the card example one of the cards sent the message "Can you be combined with me?". This message contained a parameter (in Smalltalk terms an **argument**), namely the sender of the message itself ("me"). The receiver needs that argument for the evaluation of the method. This is not always the case: sometimes methods don't need any arguments, sometimes they need more than one argument.

When an object sends a message to another object, the sender waits until it receives an answer from the receiver, so the receiver *has* to give an answer. This can be seen as a "contract" between the sender and the receiver. The answer is not always of interest to the sender. Sometimes the sender just wants the receiver to do something like writing data to a file or setting a status. Even though the sender might not be interested in the answer, it cannot continue with its own processing until it has received an answer from the receiver.

Objects in Smalltalk are called "safe". By this we mean that whatever is held in the instance variables of the object can only be read and changed by the object itself. If another object wants to know the contents of the instance variables, it has to send a message to the object. For example, in our card game an object might want to know the suit and value of a card object. Only if that card object has a method that reveals that information will it impart it to the sender. You could imagine that the card object has an instance variable "visible", which indicates whether the card is lying face down or not. Based on the value of that instance variable it would then either answer with its suit and value or it would answer that it is not allowed to reveal that information as it is lying face down. Changing instance variables of objects works in the same way; if an object has a method that allows an instance variable to be changed, then other objects can send a message to change the instance variable. If the object doesn't have such a method, then other objects cannot change the instance variables. This "protection" of the instance variables is called **encapsulation**.

INTRODUCTION

Considering our card game, if we have a game with a full pack, then we have 52 objects for the cards. All 52 card objects have the same instance variables, albeit that they store different information, and all 52 card objects have to be able to understand the same messages and react to them in the same way. It would be very inefficient if we had to define the behavior (the combination of all methods and instance variables of an object) for each object individually. That is why classes were introduced. A **class** is a factory where you can create an object of a specific type. In the above example you would have a factory for cards and a factory for players. The class holds the definition of the objects it can create and each object knows to which class it belongs. As a result, the objects don't need to hold their methods themselves; they can be stored in the class and each object of that class can make use of them. When a class creates an object, that object is called an **instance** of that class. That is why the variables of the individual objects are called **instance variables**.

This structure of classes and instances opens another possibility, namely subclassing. Each class can have subclasses which are specializations of their superclass. If you don't change anything, a subclass has exactly the same behavior as its superclass; it **inherits** the behavior. But by changing the behavior, you can specialize it. Going back to our card game example, we could have a class for card games in which we would define the general structure of a card game. Then we could give it two subclasses, one for Poker and one for Bridge. In the Poker subclass we would add the rules for the Poker game and in the Bridge class we would add the rules for Bridge. There are several ways to play Poker, which are extensions to the standard Poker rules. These would form subclasses of the Poker class. In this way you could build a whole inheritance tree of card games.

The superclass of the Poker and Bridge classes is different from the other classes, in that it only holds behavior on behalf of its subclasses. It will never have an instance of itself, therefore it is called an **abstract** class. Not all superclasses are abstract classes; for example, you could still have a Poker instance, even though you have defined the Poker variants in subclasses underneath it.

The superclass-subclass relationships are also called "A-Kind-Of" relationships. Poker is A Kind Of (AKO) card game, and so is Bridge. The Poker variants are AKO Poker games. Make sure that you don't mix these relationships with "parent-child" relationships or "bill-of-material" relationships. Parent-child relationships are typically aggregations of instances of one and the same class, like a family tree. In a family tree all the members of the tree are of class "person", and based on the parent-child relations the tree is built. Bill-of-material (BOM) relationships are also aggregation-type relationships, but of a mixture of instances from different classes. A BOM for a car would have four wheels, a chassis, an engine, bodywork, and so on. The engine would have cylinders, pistons, a crankshaft, and so on.

The specialization in subclasses typically has a combination of two forms: it can extend the behavior of the superclass and it can *override* the behavior of the superclass. Theoretically subclasses could have less functionality than their superclass, but that is very rare. On those occasions you could wonder whether the subclass is really a subclass or whether the superclass and the subclass should both be subclasses of a shared superclass. In our application later on in this book we will come across that situation and learn how to deal with it.

Extensions to inherited behavior are simple: the subclass just has methods that the superclass doesn't have. In the standard Smalltalk class hierarchy you can see many examples of this. For example, the numbers in Smalltalk form part of the Magnitude class hierarchy. The Number class holds the generic behavior for all kinds of numbers. You can use the definition of negated both for the number 6 and the number 5.413. However, a message like #factorial (messages are typically preceded with a #) can only be sent to integers; therefore it is defined in the Integer class, which is a subclass of Number.

Examples of overriding can also be found in the Number subclasses. For example, rounding is defined differently for an integer and a float. In case of an integer, the answer is the integer itself, and in case of the float, a proper rounding has to be executed. When you look in the class hierarchy (which we will do later in this chapter), you will find that Float doesn't have a method #rounded, as it inherits it from its superclass. Integer does have a method #rounded, which overrides the superclass's definition.

This is a simplistic example of **polymorphism**, which means that you can send the same message to objects of different classes, which results in different code being executed for the different objects. Polymorphism does not only apply to subclasses of a certain superclass. It can also be applied to objects of classes that are not related to each other; for example, if you ask a string and a triangle to #print themselves, those objects know how to do that even though they are totally unrelated in the class hierarchy.

Let's have a look at how this all works in Dolphin Smalltalk.

1.2 The Dolphin Smalltalk environment

In this section we are going to explore the Dolphin Smalltalk development environment. If you haven't yet installed Dolphin Smalltalk, now is the time to do that. From this section onward we will do lots of hands-on work with the Dolphin Smalltalk system.

1.2.1 *The file setup*

When you look in the Dolphin Smalltalk directory, you will find a file setup completely different from development environments in other languages. This is because the Smalltalk development environment *is* completely different from other languages. Every Smalltalk development environment consists of three development files and a couple of supporting files. The three development files are the Image, the Source and the Changes.

The **Image** is the file that contains all the compiled code in your development environment in binary format. This is not only what you have coded yourself, but also all the "libraries" that come with the development environment. In Smalltalk you don't have separate steps for linking and compilation – you don't have to do linking, everything is already there. When you create your own classes and methods, they are added to the Image. In Dolphin Smalltalk this file is normally called Dolphin.img.

The **Source** file contains the source code of the Image at the time that you installed it. It is used to show you the source code of the methods that come with the standard system. In Dolphin Smalltalk this file is normally called Dolphin.sml. This file is in a readable format; however, you should never manually edit it, as the image maintains indexes to the methods in this file.

The **Changes** file is a log of everything that you have done with Dolphin Smalltalk. Whenever you create a new method, it is added to the Changes file. When you modify existing methods (even system-provided methods), the new definitions are added to the Changes file. Even when you evaluate '6 negated', the evaluation is added to the Changes file. The Changes file can be seen as an extension to the Source file. If you want to view the source code of a method that you wrote, Dolphin Smalltalk will look up the latest definition in the Changes file. The same applies when you want to view the definition of a system-supplied method that you have changed. In Dolphin Smalltalk this Changes file is normally called Dolphin.chg.

You can picture those files as shown in Figure 1.1.

These three files should always be kept together, as the compiled methods in the Image file maintain pointers to the Source and Changes files for their latest definitions. When you make a backup you always have to back up these three files together.

You can imagine that the Changes file grows rapidly when you are developing an application. If you create a new method and save it, it is added. When you make a modification, it is added again. As you will do this

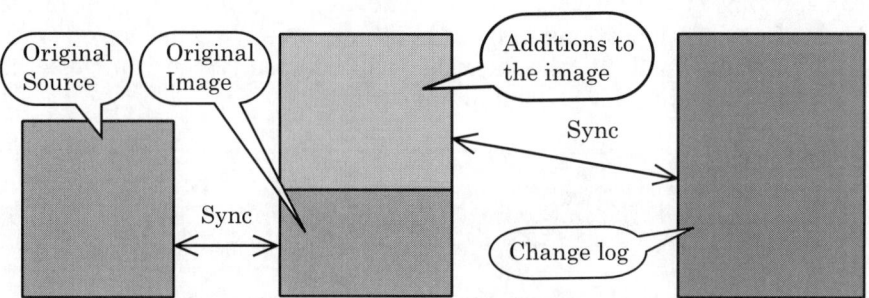

Figure 1.1

The Smalltalk file organization

very frequently, you will have many definitions of the same method in your Changes file. This has the big advantage that you can "roll back" changes that you have made to the previous state. When the file becomes too big, you can get rid of all these multiple definitions with a simple menu command (File – Compress Changes in the class hierarchy browser). You should only do this when you are really happy with the latest changes that you have made, because after that you can't roll back to the previous definition anymore, unless you have made a backup.

> As Dolphin is able to handle big Changes files (files of several megabytes haven't caused me any problems), in practice it is hardly ever necessary to compress the changes.

The other files, Dolphin.exe and Dolphin*.dll, are the files to run the Image. One of these (DolphinVMxxx.dll) is the virtual machine. The idea behind a virtual machine is that you can run Smalltalk code on any computer as long as you have a virtual machine for that computer platform. When Java was developed during the 1990s, the designers copied this idea; Java applets run on the virtual machine that is provided with most Internet browsers, independent of whether you have an Internet browser for a Unix machine, an MS-Windows machine, an Apple Macintosh or any other platform. Even though Dolphin Smalltalk only runs on MS-Windows platforms, it still benefits from the concept of a virtual machine in that the virtual machine provides the interface to the low-level operating system functions. The virtual machine also contains so-called "primitive" functions, which typically are performance-critical functions that would be too slow if they were written in Smalltalk.

1.2.2 *The Launcher*

When you start Dolphin, the Launcher window is the one window that is always opened (Figure 1.2). Depending on how you last saved the image, other windows might be opened as well. The Launcher is the main application window in the development environment. From the Launcher you can start any of the development tools and, as we will see at the end of the book, also the applications that we build ourselves. Whenever you work with Dolphin Smalltalk, the Launcher will be open. When you close the Launcher, you shut down Dolphin Smalltalk.

> Note, however, that almost all functionality that can be started from the Launcher can also be started from menus in the other development tools. Therefore I typically have the Launcher minimized and just ignore it.

INTRODUCTION 7

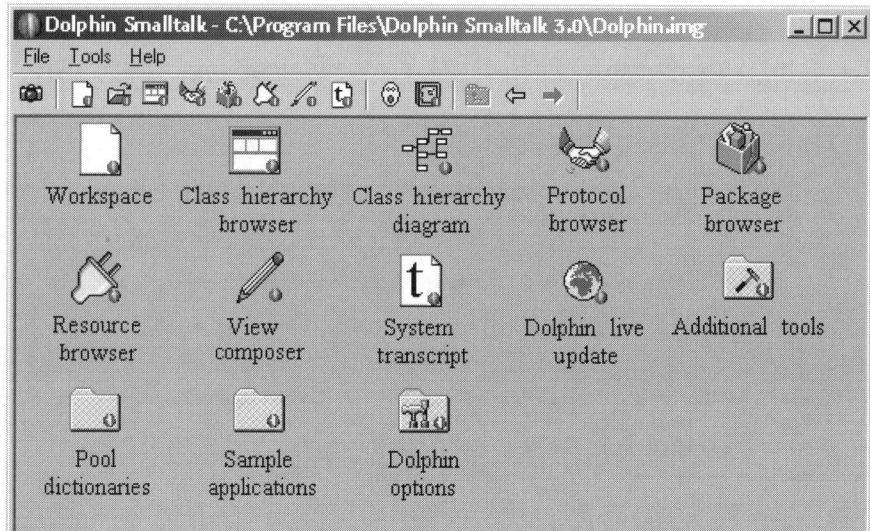

Figure 1.2
The Launcher

1.3 The workspace

The workspace, and especially Dolphin Smalltalk's version of it, is one of the most useful tools in the development environment. In the workspace you typically try out some code before you add it to your class. It is a great test environment. When you start Dolphin Smalltalk for the first time, a workspace is opened with a number of examples in it that you can execute (Figure 1.3). As the example shows, the workspace can open existing text files (including Rich Text) and you can create new text files with it. But the best is yet to come. The Dolphin Smalltalk workspace has its own "pool" of variables. Whereas in some Smalltalk environments you have to declare either temporary or global variables, here you just name the variable and append an object to it. You will learn to appreciate this functionality more than I can tell you here. Another "Dolphin special" is that whereas in other Smalltalk environments you have to select explicitly the code that you want to evaluate, in Dolphin, if the expression is just a one-liner, then you only need to have your cursor on that line.

> I typically have two or three workspaces open. First, one for test data in which I create objects of the classes that I am working on. From here I also open the self-made views on those objects. We will see the benefit of that when we create our first model and the view-presenter pair that goes with it. Furthermore, I use the

Figure 1.3

The workspace

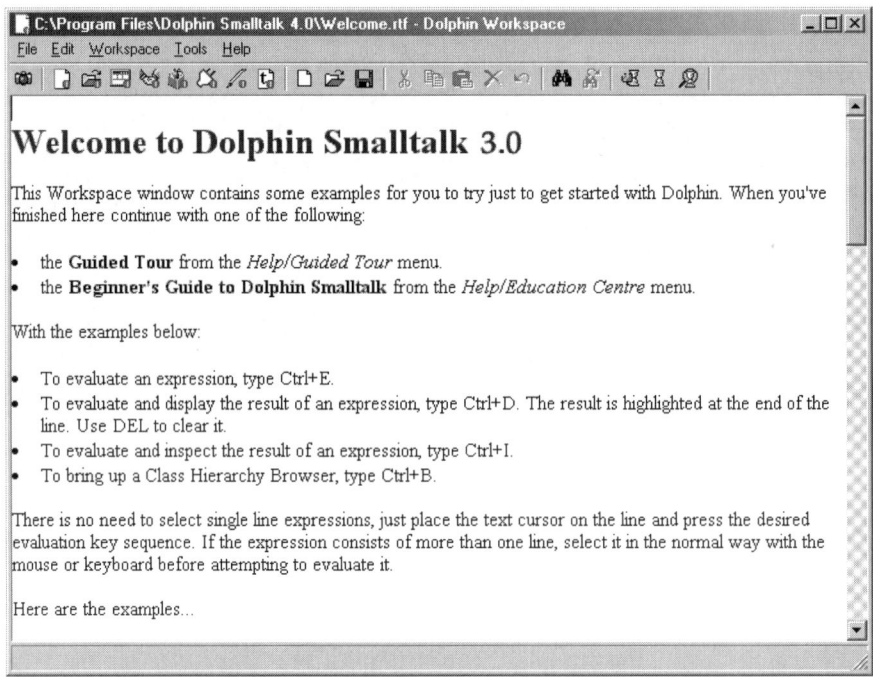

> workspaces to test snippets of code before I add the final version to the classes. I do that in different workspaces to avoid "cluttering up" the test data workspace. I normally don't save these workspaces as separate files, except the one with the test data.

Because of the pool of workspace variables, the workspace has a menu to maintain that pool; Workspace – Variables. This option opens an inspector (see Section 1.4) in which you can change the variables and remove them. You can re-create the variables by just re-evaluating the definition.

There is a special version of the workspace, called the system transcript. This is used as a logging screen. Whenever you install or uninstall packages (see Section 3.4), a message is written to the system transcript. You can also write messages to the system transcript yourself, for example when you want to see the value of a certain variable during a looping process. We will see an example of that in the playground. The system transcript can be used in the same way as all other workspaces, with the difference that you cannot save your test code in a file as easily as with ordinary workspaces and you don't have the automatically declared variables like you have in normal workspaces.

1.4 Playground

Now that we have Dolphin Smalltalk running, I can imagine that you want to start doing something with it. Well, here we go.

Our playground will be a workspace, therefore double-click on the Workspace icon in the Launcher or select Workspace from the Tools menu or from the toolbar.

Evaluating and displaying expressions   When you enter a line of code in the workspace (Figure 1.4), you can just put the cursor anywhere on the line and then select the menu option Workspace – Display it. This command executes the line and displays the result. As you are going to use this very often, there is a shortcut, Ctrl + D.

Types of messages   Type in the following lines and display the result (Ctrl + D) one at a time:

```
6 negated
6 + 2
'a string' at: 6
```

The above three examples show the three different types of messages within Smalltalk. The first one is a **unary** message. A unary message does not have parameters; it just consists of a *selector* (the name of the method). The second line is an example of a **binary** message, and the third line is a **keyword** message. Both binary messages and keyword messages use parameters; these are called the *arguments*. Binary messages can have exactly one argument and the selector is typically a special symbol, like <, >=, /. Note that the "," (comma) is a binary message as well; see the example below.

```
'a ', 'concatenated ', 'string'
```

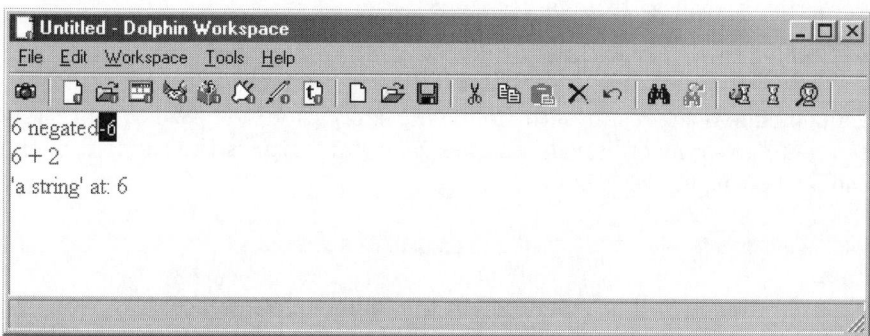

Figure 1.4

A workspace

The line `'a string' at: 6` is an example of a *keyword* message. A keyword message has a selector with one or more arguments. Each argument is preceded by a colon. An example of a keyword message with more than one argument is:

```
'a string' midString: 5 from: 3
```

The order of message evaluation Messages are evaluated in a strict order, which is applied very consistently; the unary messages are evaluated first, then the binary messages, and finally the keyword messages. Therefore the next line:

```
'a string' midString: 6 + 2 negated from: 3
```

is evaluated as follows:

```
2 negated >> -2
6 + -2 >> 4
'a string' midString: 4 from: 3 >> 'stri'
```

Within this order of precedence everything is evaluated from left to right. For example:

```
6 + 2 * 3 >> 24
```

You might have expected that the result is 12 instead of 24, but it is consistently evaluated from left to right. You can enforce the order evaluation by using brackets:

```
6 + (2 * 3)
```

To summarize, the order of precedence is:

- Unary ≫ Binary ≫ Keyword
- Within a level ≫ from left to right
- Change the order with ()

Can you guess the result of the following expression? (The # is a quick way to create an array of literals; the message #at: returns the element at the indexed position.)

```
#(5 4 3 2 1) at: 2 + 6 negated printString size / 2
```

This expression will be evaluated in the following sequence:

```
6 negated >> -6
-6 printString >> '-6'
'-6' size >> 2
2 + 2 >> 4
4 / 2 >> 2
#(5 4 3 2 1) at: 2 >> 4
```

You can evaluate and display parts of the expression by just selecting the part. For example, if you select the part `6 negated printString` on the above line and DisplayIt, it will show the result right after the selection. The result is conveniently selected so that you can delete it easily.

Blocks The receiver of the previous expression was an instance of the class Array. You can do something with every element in an array with the message #do:. This message has to be followed with an expression in a **block**. This block is then executed for every element of the array. The block is defined as everything in between square brackets. The next example prints all the elements on the transcript. Open the transcript to show the result.

```
#(5 4 3 2 1) do: [ :each | Transcript cr. Transcript show:
    each sqrt printString ]
```

In this case the block has two parts, split by a vertical bar. In the first part you define the temporary variable. Each element of the array is fed into the block through this temporary variable. Note that there is a colon in front of the name. This makes Smalltalk recognize it as the variable name. The second part consists of the expression that is executed with every element. In this case we first send the message "cr" to the transcript, which makes the current position in the transcript move to the next line. After sending the message cr, we end the message with a full stop. This tells Smalltalk that what follows is a new expression, not related to the previous expression. In the above example the next expression prints the square root of the current value of "each" on the transcript.

The return value If you evaluated the above expression with DisplayIt, then the workspace would have shown the original array. This shows that the return value of #do: is the original array. If you want the return value to be an array of the new values, you use #collect:. Evaluate the following with DisplayIt:

```
#(5 4 3 2 1) collect: [ :each | each sqrt ]
```

You can also use blocks to postpone evaluation. If you evaluate the next line with DisplayIt, it just displays the block.

```
[ 6 + 2 negated ]
```

But if you send that block the message #value, it is executed and returns the result:

```
[ 6 + 2 negated ] value
```

This can be combined with temporary variables that are fed into the block.

```
[ :temp | 6 + temp negated ] value: 2
```

or even:

```
[ :first :second | first + second negated ]
    value: 6 value: 2
```

Variable assignment   You can assign objects to variables with :=. Then you can send messages to the variable, just like you did with the string.

```
firstname := 'Bob'
firstname size
firstname reverse
firstname at: 1 put: $R
```

This last expression returned the character R. That might not have been what you expected, but if you select the variable firstname and then DisplayIt, you will see that the string has changed. This shows that you must be wary of the return value of a message. Every message returns something, but it might not always be what you expect.

The inspector   Instead of displaying the result, you can open an Inspector window on the result. An Inspector window allows you to look at more complex objects; all variables of an object are shown separately and can themselves be inspected as well. You can open an Inspector window on an object or the result of an expression by selecting the command "Inspect it" (Ctrl + I). Alternatively you can send the message #inspect to an object.

Enter the following in the workspace and evaluate it (Ctrl + D):

```
'Dolphin Smalltalk' inspect
```

This will open an Inspector window as shown in Figure 1.5. The left-hand panel shows a list of what the object is made of. If the object contains instance variables, the instance variables are shown here. A string consists of a number of characters, so in our example we see a list of numbers, representing the positions of the characters. If you select one of the lines, you see the value of that position in the workspace panel on the right. If the

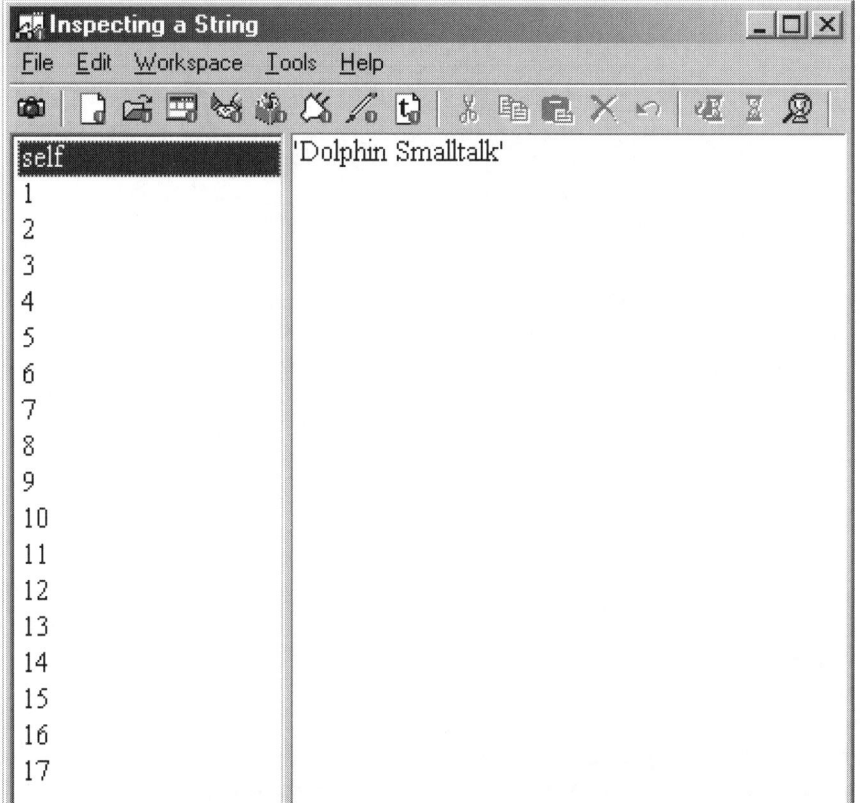

Figure 1.5
The object inspector

object had a variable containing a string, then the right-hand side would show the string. Double-clicking on an item in the list opens a new inspector on that object.

If you select the object itself (the "self" line), you can send messages to it. With the "self" line selected, evaluate the following message in the right-hand side of the inspector (just overwrite the existing text):

```
self at: 9 put: $s
```

When you evaluate this and then look at what is stored in position 9, you will see that the uppercase "S" is replaced by a lowercase "s". Selecting the "self" line again, you will see the whole object again, with the lowercase "s".

Error handling The expression below shows you what happens if you send a message to an object that it doesn't understand:

```
'Dolphin Smalltalk' reversed
```

Figure 1.6
The Error dialog

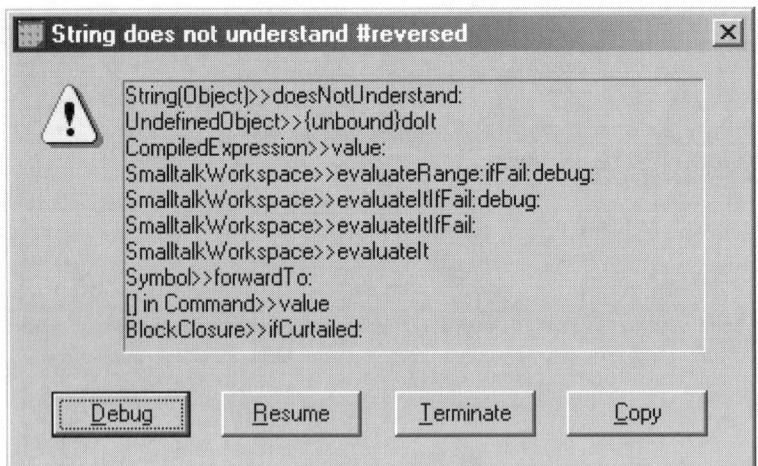

This shows you the error dialog (Figure 1.6). The error dialog contains some very valuable information, so don't press one of the buttons straight away. First, look at the caption. Most often this already gives a clue as to why the error occurred. In our case it was because instances of the class String don't understand the message #reversed. The list shows the message stack that was evaluated before the error occurred. Based on this information you can decide what to do with the dialog. In some cases you might just want to continue (Resume), in some cases you understand the problem and might just want to stop and correct it (Terminate), and in other cases you want to go into the debugger (see Section 6.2.2) either to investigate the problem further or to correct the code straight away and continue processing.

For now we just close it with the Terminate button.

Objects containing objects As we've seen so far, objects almost always contain other objects. For example, a point consists of two numbers, combined with the "@" character. Therefore, you can do calculations with points. A rectangle consists of two points, the origin and the corner. As you can do calculations with points, you can also do calculations with rectangles (as long as the rectangle exposes the points – remember the discussion about encapsulation). Try the following lines with DisplayIt (Ctrl + D).

```
rect := Rectangle origin: 0@0 extent: 200@300.
rect origin: rect origin + 2.
rect corner: rect corner / 2.
```

On the first line we create a new object of class Rectangle, and give it an origin of point 0@0 and a size 200@300. On the next line we move the origin by adding 2 to the origin point. Adding a value to a point means that you add it to both dimensions of the point. Therefore the new origin is 2@2. On the next line we divide the corner by 2. Again, the division is executed on both dimensions, which results in a corner of 100@150.

Combining multiple messages   The next example consists of multiple lines. If you send multiple messages to the same object, you don't have to repeat the object; instead, use the semicolon to separate the messages. (We want the variable to be returned, therefore we just repeat the variable.) Select all the lines and evaluate them with DisplayIt.

```
testString := 'dolphin smalltalk'.
testString at: 1 put: $D;
     at: 9 put: $S.
testString
```

You might wonder why we still repeated the testString variable. In the first line we assigned the string to it, in the second and third lines we manipulated the string, and in the last line we returned the contents of it. If you try to combine all these messages, you have to be aware that the assignment to the variable takes place after all the message sends, so the return value of the last message is assigned to the variable. Therefore, if we do:

```
testString := 'dolphin smalltalk'
     at: 1 put: $D;
     at: 9 put: $S.
testString
```

then the result of the last message is assigned to the variable testString. In the above example the last message is `'dolphin smalltalk' at: 9 put: $S`. The return value of that message is $S, therefore $S is assigned to the variable. To avoid this problem, we can send the message #yourself to the string. This makes sure that the object itself is returned and therefore assigned to the variable.

```
testString := 'dolphin smalltalk'
     at: 1 put: $D;
     at: 9 put: $S;
     yourself.
```

Hello World As virtually every tutorial for virtually every programming language contains a "Hello World" example, we will build a proper window showing the text neatly centered.

```
shell := ShellView new
    create;
    layoutManager: BorderLayout new;
    extent: 300@100;
    yourself.
text := StaticText new
    create;
    parentView: shell;
    arrangement: #center;
    beCenterAligned;
    value: 'Hello World!';
    show.
shell show.
```

In the first line a new ShellView object is initialized. The ShellView object is an object that contains all the information to build a window on the screen. On the next line we create it in memory so that we can modify it. Then we attach a layout manager to it, which controls the layout of the contents of the window. With the #extent: message we set the size to the point 300@100. After having created the ShellView object and manipulated it, we assign it to the variable shell.

On the next line we initialize a new StaticText object; we create it and tell it that it is a child of the shell. With the arrangement we tell the layout manager where this object should be placed on the parent. We want the text within this StaticText object to be centered as well (which is different from this StaticText object being centered in the shell), and we want to show a text string in this object. The last line tells the shell to show itself.

Summary

These examples are typical of how you can code and test in Smalltalk. You create an object of a certain class and assign it to a variable. This variable can then be used to send messages to the object and see what the result is. We are going to do this frequently during the remainder of the book, both to prototype our methods and to test the classes that we've created.

The application

2.1 What we are going to build

In this book we are going to build a complete application in which you will be able to maintain the results of Formula One racing, import data from files and from the Web, and view the objects and the score tables in different ways. Figure 2.1 shows some of the screens of the finished application.

You might think that this application is not very useful, especially if you don't have any interest in Formula One racing. However, the way in which we are going to build the application lends itself to being easily adapted for

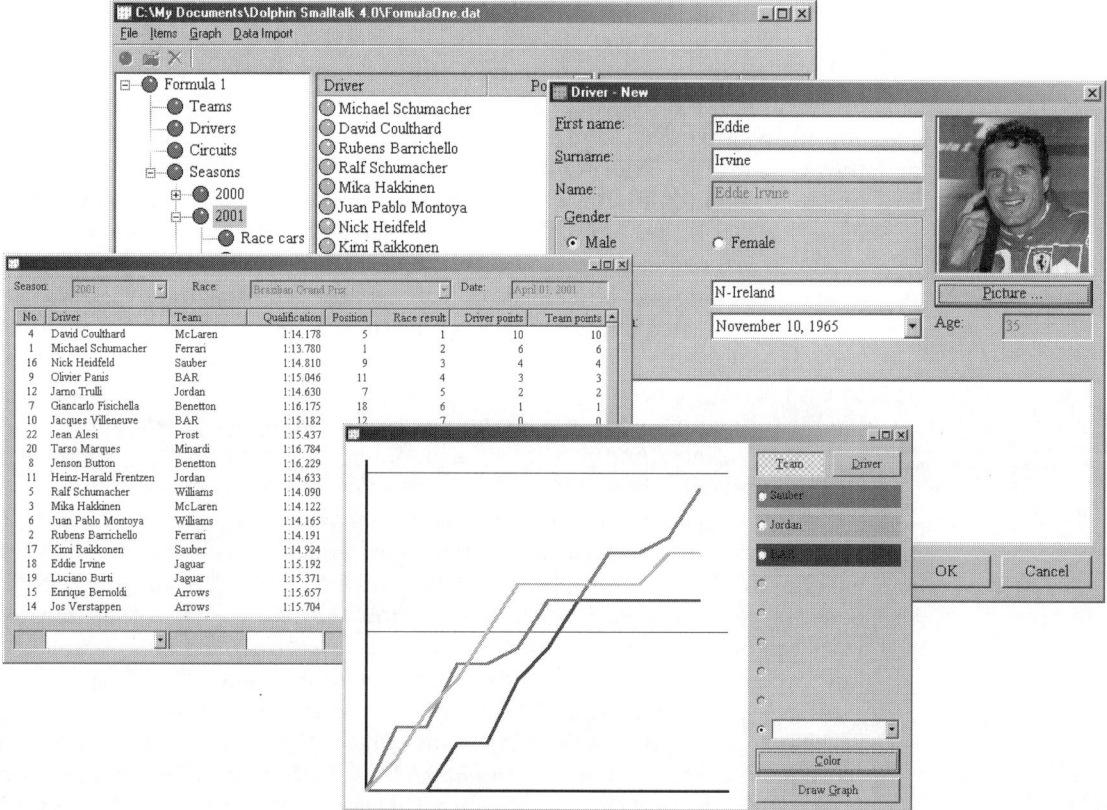

Figure 2.1   *The finished application*

other sports. Most sports consist of similar components: You have teams and players. The teams have some kind of competition going for a season and they score points per match. The contents of these components might be different, but the underlying structure is the same.

If you are not interested in sport at all, you can stretch the model a bit further and use the approach that we take in this book to build business applications. Most often business applications have a number of static components against which we want to record the result of dynamic components. Probably the most often used example in object-oriented tutorials is a bank account. The bank account is the static component like the team or the driver. The balance is what we want to record against it, like the points that we record against the team and the driver. The transaction forms the dynamic component, which is similar to the result of a race.

2.2 How we are going to build the application

The traditional approach to building an application is to investigate the problem, build the data structure, and build some screens to manipulate and display that data structure.

In object-oriented development, a different approach is taken. You start by looking at the objects in the "problem domain". For each of these objects, we investigate what they do, what they (need to) know, and what they understand. Once we understand that, we can build a factory (a class) for such an object and build the methods that give the objects the ability to have interaction with other objects. After testing the objects we can build a user interface for them.

We don't have to build all the objects and the factories in one go; we can build them as components of the application. This has the advantage that we can start with the simplest component and gradually build in more complexity.

Our first component will be the Team. This component will allow us to create new teams and modify existing ones. The next component, which will be similar to the team, is the Driver. We will try to make use of some of the work that we have done in the Team, as we will see that the Driver bears similarities to the Team. Then we will build a Season component in which we define how points are allocated. Once we have those three components, we can build the RaceCar component, which has a relationship with the other three components. The last "static" component that we have to build for this application is the Circuit component.

All these components are brought together in the Race component. This is where we can maintain a race and where the teams and drivers can score points. The next step is to put an "application shell" or "application framework" around the components, this application framework will host the individual components. We could say that we are finished at that point, as we have an application in which we can gather all the information required. The only problem is that we are not yet able to present the results in a usable format, therefore we concentrate on the presentation of the results next. We will not only present the results in tables, but also build a graph. After that we will focus on making life a bit easier for our users by building import functionality so that they don't have to type in all the data. In the last chapter we will discuss how we can deploy this application to the users.

While we build the components we will visit many of the standard Smalltalk classes and see how we can make conscious decisions to use them.

2.3 A standard pattern for the components

Dolphin Smalltalk supports a standard pattern for building components with a user interface. This pattern consists of the following (Figure 2.2):

- The **model**. This represents the domain, or business logic.
- The **presenter**. The presenter is responsible for communication between the model and the view. It links each of the fields in the view with the variables in the model and it defines the actions that can be taken from within the view. The presenter is also responsible for monitoring changes in the view and performing the appropriate actions.
- The **view**. The view is the actual window with fields and buttons and other controls that shows the model or part of the model.

We start by looking at the model of the component. This includes looking at how this component integrates with what we have already built. The model doesn't know about the presenter, therefore the line between the model and the presenter contains only a single arrow.

After building the model, we build a user interface for it, consisting of a presenter and a view. The presenter is the software that sits between the model and the view. It controls what the view can show of the model. The view can be seen as a simple window with a couple of fields and some buttons on it. The presenter is responsible for showing the right data, and

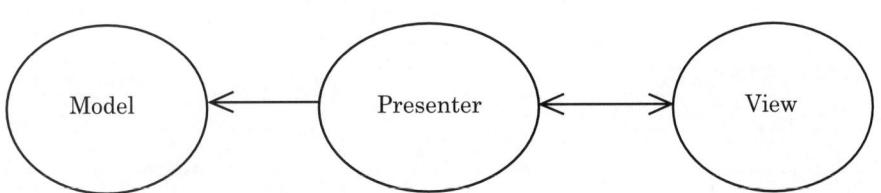

Figure 2.2

The Model-Presenter-View (MPV) paradigm

the view is responsible for showing the data in the right format. The fields and buttons on the view are linked to presenter variables and presenter commands. The presenter then communicates with the model in order to show the model's data, edit it, and do other commands. As the presenter and the view are split, we can easily create multiple views based on a single presenter, which is ideal for the purpose of this book as we are going to do that frequently to try out different options in the view area.

The first application component: the Team

In this chapter we are going to build the first component of our application, the Team. A component is a complete set of functionality that can be used on its own. In this case it consists of all three elements introduced in the previous section: a model, a presenter, and a view. By the end of the chapter it will look like Figure 3.1.

We will introduce a standard way of thinking about our design and how to approach the actual building of a component. This approach will be used throughout the book.

In the last section of this chapter we will discuss how to maintain our application source code.

Figure 3.1
The Team component

3.1 The Team model

How to build a class using the class hierarchy browser, what instance variables are, how to access them and how to set default values.

Each sport is team work; even though some sports look to be about individuals, there's almost always a team behind them (think of trainers, coaches, and so on). Therefore, if you want to record performance in a sport, you will most often find that the team is the starting point. In sports like football this is obvious: the team scores the points. But even in a sport like tennis, the team is a better starting point for the model – not only can we use the same model for singles and doubles, but we might also want to keep track of the change in the performance of a tennis player after a change of coach.

In Formula One the team is more obvious, even though the individual drivers are more in the spotlight than the teams. Using the team as the point of focus allows our model to handle changes like drivers getting injured and being replaced by other drivers. So what does a Formula One team consist of?

First, a team consists of two racing cars, or rather, two starting numbers. Each time the team arrives at a race track, they arrive with three or even four cars. And quite often the cars have undergone so many modifications since the last race that you can hardly call them the same cars.

Secondly, a team consists of people: drivers, technicians, trainers, directors, and so on. All these people have different roles. We are interested in some of these people, but not in others. Those we are interested in can form part of our model, each in their own role.

Then there might be additional information about a team that we are interested in, such as year of foundation, country of origin, and so on.

And finally, of course, their result!

Most of this information about a team is season-dependent. The car in 1985 had a different specification from the 1997 model. The people that make up the team are likely to have changed as well, and it would be a coincidence if the result happened to be the same. This forms the dynamic part of the model. Let's first focus on the easy part: the static part of the model.

This is a good starting point, as it is very simple. A team has a name, a country of origin, a year of foundation, and some general remarks. So those are the properties of a team (for now). What do we want to do with a team? Well, we want to be able to create and maintain a team. We might also want to be able to delete a team if it is not referenced, typically if you created a team that you didn't really want to create. Here you'll see one of the beauties of Smalltalk. Just remove the references and the team will become garbage, which is automatically collected by the garbage collector. So as we don't have any references, we don't have to worry about deletion.

THE FIRST APPLICATION COMPONENT: THE TEAM 23

Before we can start building our first application component, we have to learn a bit more about another tool in our Smalltalk environment, the class hierarchy browser (or CHB).

3.1.1 The class hierarchy browser

The class hierarchy browser (CHB) is probably the most important tool in every Smalltalk environment. Not only is this the tool used to view virtually all the source code, it is also the most convenient way to create and maintain your own classes and methods.

The CHB is divided into the following areas (Figure 3.2).

Class hierarchy tree This area shows you all the classes and their relative position in the hierarchy. This is the place where you create new classes. You first select the class that you want to be the parent of your class, and then you select New from either the context menu, the class menu, or the yellow icon with a "C" in it. If you want to see only part of the hierarchy, you can make a subset of it. Select the class that you are interested in, for example Number, and then press the white icon with a "-" in it. This will remove all classes that are not part of the Number hierarchy from the currently shown tree. As there is a vast number of classes, the Find Class function is also very useful. This can be accessed through the

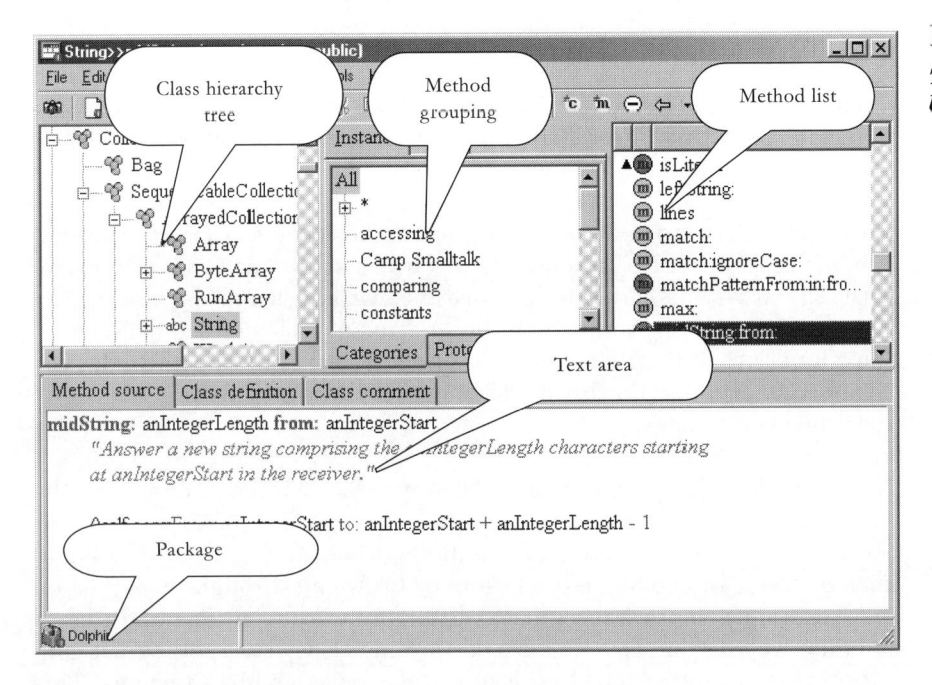

Figure 3.2

The class hierarchy browser

class context menu, the Class menu on the menu bar, or the binoculars icon. Note that for the latter to work, you have to have the cursor in one of the areas in the upper half. If the cursor is in the text area, the icon will bring up a text finder.

Method grouping   I haven't found a better name for this area yet, but as it actually does group the methods, it is appropriate. First, you have to make a decision about whether you are interested in the class methods or the instance methods. Class methods are those methods which can be executed against the class itself, as opposed to the instance methods which can only be executed against instances of a class. You typically find methods to create new instances on the class side, as you can't send a message to an instance that doesn't exist yet. In the tabs below the list you can switch between category grouping, protocol grouping, and variables grouping.

- *Category* grouping allows you to select a category and will then show you all the methods that belong to that category. The purpose of a category is to find methods more easily. Methods can belong to multiple categories. You can create your own categories and then add your methods to those categories or add your methods to existing categories.

- The second tab is *Protocols*. Protocols are a means of forcing a class to have a number of methods. By selecting this tab you can select a protocol to which this class conforms. The method list will then show you the methods that are enforced by this protocol. For more information about protocols, see Appendix C.

- The third tab is *Variables*. This tab shows you the list of instance variables for this class (if the instance tab is selected above the list). It allows you to show the methods that make use of the selected instance variable. Note that it shows not only those instance variables that are defined in the class itself, but also those that are inherited from the superclasses. When you select the Class tab above the list, it will display the class instance variables and the instance variables of the class in which the selected class is defined (see the explanation on the Behavior class and subclasses in Appendix B). To be honest, though, in this mode the list isn't as useful for grouping as the other modes.

Method list   The method list shows you the methods based on the method grouping as described above. As a learning aid I would suggest not bothering with subselections of the method list. Most often a class contains between 10 and 50 methods, and by browsing through them all, you will find that you start recognizing the naming conventions and understanding why certain classes have certain methods. The method list consists of three columns. The first column can contain a black triangle. This

THE FIRST APPLICATION COMPONENT: THE TEAM

means that the method overrides a method definition in the superclass. The second column can have a green icon, a red icon, a yellow icon with a red triangle in it, or a yellow icon with a red cross in it. These icons have the following meaning:

- The green icon is the general icon, and is shown if the method doesn't fall into any of the other categories.
- The red icon means that the method is categorized as private. Categorizing a method as private means that the method should not be used other than by the instances themselves, so they are not supposed to be used as messages from other objects to an object of that class. Smalltalk does not enforce it like other object-oriented languages do, it is just a convention.
- The red triangle means that the method is "deprecated", which means that it is likely to be removed in a future version. Therefore, don't use it! Most of the time the description of the method shows which alternative to use to get the same result.
- The red cross means that the method contains an error. This can happen when, for example, you remove an instance variable that is used in this method.

The icons are a result of putting the method in a certain category. If a method is in the category Private, it will have a red icon. If it is in the category Deprecated (which is a subcategory of *), it will have the deprecated icon.

Text area   The text area has three tabs:

- The first tab, *Method source*, shows you the source of the method. Here you can see, for example, how a number interprets the message "negated" (actually, Number doesn't have its own definition, it uses the definition of its superclass – ArithmeticValue), and how Integer overrides it. LargeInteger overrides it again. The definition in LargeInteger is a special one. It is one of the few methods that is not fully defined in Smalltalk itself, but in a so-called Primitive. There are two possible reasons to use a primitive method, either for performance reasons or as a low-level function that cannot be expressed in Smalltalk. These primitive methods are typically written in C or even in assembler. Such a primitive method, which sits outside the Smalltalk image, is called by the code <primitive: *number*>. If the primitive fails, then the Smalltalk code after the primitive is executed so that either the result is calculated with lower performance or an appropriate error message is raised.
- The second tab shows the *Class definition* or, in case the Class tab is selected above, the class instance variables.

- The third tab shows the *Class comment*. Many of the classes in the development environment come with very useful class comment. It typically tells you what the use of the class is, the meaning and purpose of the instance variables, and, in case of an application class, a one-liner to demonstrate the class.

Note that the text field in the text area is exactly like any other workspace, so if you suddenly want to know what the result of `6 negated` is, you can just evaluate and display it in any of these text areas. As they are really like workspaces, they even have that same ability to have local variables without declaring them.

> When I'm building applications, I typically have loads of browsers open, at least one on the model that I'm working on, at least one on the presenter that goes with it, typically one or two on subclasses of often used classes like Magnitude and Collection, a browser on the view that I'm working with, a browser on the class that defines the view, and so on. As far as I'm concerned, you can't have too many browsers open (as long as you still can find your way round it). I think there is some "useful" maximum of 10 to 12. Above that, you lose track of where you've seen what you need. I use the "local" hierarchy button a lot, especially on my own model class, my own presenter class, and on the big hierarchies like Collection and Magnitude. Some books suggest that you have to worry about code not being updated between browsers. In Dolphin Smalltalk you don't, as all browsers are automatically updated when code changes. That is, of course, as long as you accept the code. If you are building the same method in two different browsers, you will have a problem, but Dolphin Smalltalk will notify you of it. If it finds that you have modified something in a browser and you try to accept something in another browser on the same method, then during the attempt to update the first, it will notify you that there are unsaved changes in the other browser. Therefore, it is pretty safe to have many browsers open in Dolphin Smalltalk.

3.1.2 *Creating our first class*

The first thing to consider when you want to add a class to your Smalltalk system is which class is the best choice to be the superclass of your class. That is, which class provides you with as much behavior that you want to inherit as possible. When you are starting a completely new application, it is quite likely that there won't be much to inherit. However, there is one thing in a typical Dolphin Smalltalk application that you do want to inherit, and that is the Model-Presenter-View (MPV) paradigm. This paradigm doesn't really force you to use certain superclasses, but if you do, you will benefit from it. Within that paradigm, you create your business logic classes as subclasses of the Model class and the presenter classes as subclasses of the Presenter class or one of the Presenter subclasses. This makes communication between your Model classes and your Presenter classes inherit some handy features that are defined in the Model and Presenter classes.

Because of the above, we create our Team class as a subclass of the Model class. Open a CHB, open the hierarchy tree, select the class "Model" and select the menu option Class – New. Enter the name "Team" in the New dialog. We give Team its instance variables by editing the class definition as shown below. Accept the changes with Ctrl + S.

```
Model subclass: #Team
        instanceVariableNames: 'name origin foundationYear
        comment'
        classVariableNames: ''
        poolDictionaries: ''
```

As it is a good habit (and to make our development self-documenting), we add a class description to it, describing the purpose of the class and the instance variables (Figure 3.3). After entering the class comment you have to accept it with Ctrl + S.

All instance variables in our model need so-called getters and setters. The getter is used to read the contents of the instance variable, and the setter allows the instance variable to be set to a certain value. The getters and setters are required to let the subpresenters (the presenters that control the individual fields on the screen) talk with the instance variables of the model. There is a lot of discussion about these accessors, as they "open up" the contents of the object, and therefore go against the encapsulation of the inside of the object. This is the reason why the accessors are seen as "sort of" private methods. The presenter has to talk to them, but

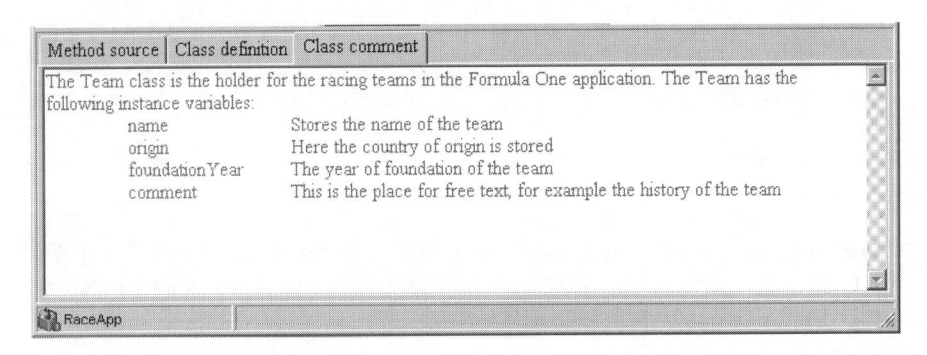

Figure 3.3

Class comment

other objects shouldn't directly use these methods. You can generate the getters and setters for the instance variables via the menu option Class – Generate Accessors. This presents you with a list of the instance variables that do not yet have accessors. In this specific case we want to have getters and setters for all our instance variables, therefore we select them all. If you now look in the list of methods you will see two methods for each variable. Selecting the methods will show you the definition.

You can see that the definition is very simple; for the getters the definition consists of the name of the method, which is the same as the name of the variable, and the actual code, which just returns the contents of the variable with the caret symbol (^).

The setter method consists of the name of the variable with a colon, so that it can receive a parameter. This parameter is what we want to store in the variable. Therefore the code is doing just that, assigning anObject to the variable with the assign symbol, := (colon and equal sign).

When you generate the accessors, Dolphin Smalltalk generates some standard comment with it. As the comment does not add real value to the code, I've removed the comment from the example code.

```
Team>>name
    ^name

Team>>name: anObject
    name := anObject

Team>>origin
    ^origin

Team>>origin: anObject
    origin := anObject

Team>>foundationYear
    ^foundationYear

Team>>foundationYear: anObject
    foundationYear := anObject

Team>>comment
    ^comment

Team>>comment: anObject
    comment := anObject
```

These are some of the methods we need – the maintenance methods. Do we need to do something extra to create a new team? Each class automatically has a way to create new instances, so we can already create new teams. (The #new and #basicNew methods are defined in the Behavior class, which is the class of which the classes themselves are instances.) However, quite often you want to initialize certain variables when you create a new instance. In our case, we want the year of foundation to be numeric and the name to contain a string. When we create a new team, all instance variables are nil. This might cause problems when we want to display them or do validations on them, so we have to initialize those variables with an "initialize" method. This method is called automatically straight after the new object is created without you having to do anything about it.

You can create your own methods by selecting "New" from the context menu in the methods list or by pressing the yellow button with the "M" in the toolbar. This moves the cursor to a blank Method source field, in which you can enter the method. As we have seen with the generated methods, the first line is the method name, possibly with arguments (parameters). You can make the method name as long as you want; there are no limitations. If you require many arguments, a method name can become quite long. (There is no physical limit to the number of arguments in a method: however, there are conventions which suggest that if you need more than four arguments, you should consider moving the required functionality into a separate class.) When you accept the method, the compiler checks the name by selecting all the words that end with a colon. All words directly following the colons are seen as arguments, and if the word after an argument does not end with a colon, the compiler knows that the coding starts there.

A lot has been written about standards for formatting, and there are even formatters that can be used to do the formatting automatically. The standard that I follow is to have the comment directly under the method selector, indented with one tab, and to have the code also indented with one tab. Nested code is indented even further. I insert one blank line between the comment and the code. Note that this blank line is removed in the code listings for readability. As a standard documentation method the class name and two arrows are added for instance methods. For class methods the word "class" is inserted between the class name and the arrows (like in Team class ≫ new). When you define the methods, you have to leave the class prefix out. When we add whole lines to an existing method, we normally don't repeat the other lines in the method listing, but replace them with three dots. When we insert or replace part of an existing line, we underline the inserted code in the method listing. And finally, comments are in italics and the class name and the method selector are in bold.

```
Team>>initialize
    "Initialize the receiver"
    self name: String new.
    self foundationYear: 0.
```

After you've entered the above three lines, you have to accept the method (Ctrl + S). This tries to compile the code. If it fails, the code is shown in red and the status bar shows why it didn't compile. If it does compile, the method name is shown bold in blue, the comment is shown in green italics, messages to objects are shown in blue, objects are shown in black, and values are shown in brown.

In the code that we've written, we send the messages #name: and #foundationYear: to something called "self". Here we come across one of the very few reserved words in Smalltalk. If you use "self" like in the context above, you want to send the message to the object that is actually sending the message, so it sends the message to itself.

Let's test what we've built so far. (Throughout this book we use workspaces to test our application. Instead of using workspaces, you can create a separate test class where you store the methods that create and test the instances. In that way they become part of your development environment and are available for later extensions. Kent Beck [http://www.xprogramming.com/testfram.htm] has written a paper on testing using classes, based on which a standard Smalltalk testing extension is built. This is available at the following web site: http://ansi-st-tests.sourceforge.net/SUnit.html.)

Open a workspace, and create a variable team1, a new instance of Team (Figure 3.4). Then inspect team1 (either send the message #inspect or select the line and Ctrl + I). You will see that it exists as you can inspect it. It is an instance of class Team, so it should be able to execute the methods that we've defined for Team objects. In the inspector you can also see that the name is an empty string and the foundationYear is set to 0, like we defined in the initialize method. All other instance variables are still nil.

Now let's go back to our workspace, leaving the inspector open. Set the name to, for example, Ferrari by sending the message `team1 name: 'Ferrari'`. Go back to the inspector. If you check the name now, it will show `'Ferrari'`.

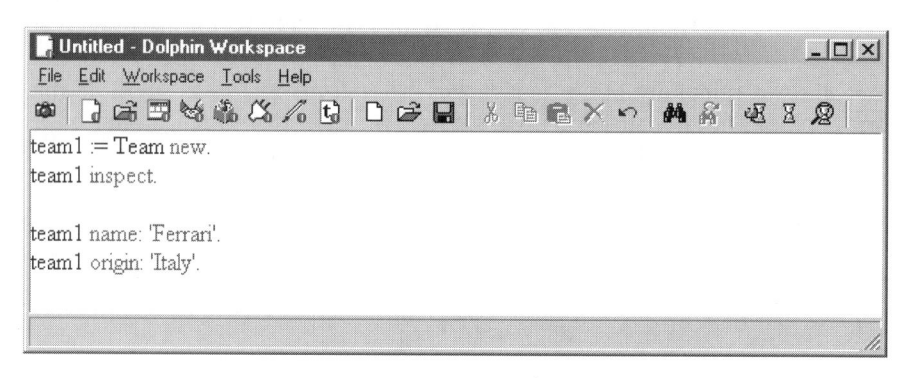

Figure 3.4

Team test workspace

```
team1 := Team new.
team1 inspect.

team1 name: 'Ferrari'.
team1 origin: 'Italy'.
```

> Note that if you had the cursor on the name variable in the inspector, then you have to select something else in the inspector list first to have the workspace updated.

That is all that we have to do for the Team class for now.

3.1.3 Summary

In the previous subsections we've introduced the class hierarchy browser and created a class with instance variables. We created accessors for these instance variables and initialized the variables as required. And finally we tested the class by creating an instance of the class, inspected it, and modified some of the instance variables.

3.2 The Team presenter

Now that we have finished building our first model, we can make a presenter and a view for it.

Just like the models are almost always subclasses of the Model class, presenters are almost always subclasses of the Presenter class, and more specifically, of the Shell class. Let's have a look at what we have in the Presenter class. The subclasses of Presenter can be split into two categories; on one hand we have the subclasses that can be seen as tools which we will be using to create the other category, the actual "application" presenters. The first category contains the ListPresenter, the TreePresenter, and all the ValuePresenter subclasses. Later in this book you will see that we will use these classes most often without knowing it. Still, it is good to know where they are, so that we can find the messages which are understood by these presenters. Note also the subclasses of the ValuePresenter class. These all use the ValueModel paradigm, which means that they have the ability to show seemingly permanently updated data through the events mechanism.

The other category is the category in which we build our presenters. Simple, single "field" presenters are typically subclassed directly off the Presenter class, like the workspace and scribble. As soon as you require more fields, buttons, or other widgets, you have to create your class as a subclass of CompositePresenter, or more specifically, of the class Shell. The class Shell makes the presenter into a proper window, by adding the usual window widgets to your subclass, like a window frame, a caption,

The difference between elementary presenters and composite presenters, how to choose between the different window types, and how to link the presenters to the model.

and a close button. Within Shell you have to make a choice between the following three options:

1. When you want a modal window, which is a window that continues to have focus until you close it, then you subclass Dialog or one of its subclasses. You typically use this when you want to force the user to do something with that window before continuing.

2. If you require a window that has file handling, then you subclass DocumentShell. This comes with all the functionality to open and save the model that it contains, either in binary or as text.

3. If the required window doesn't fall into the above two categories, it can be subclassed directly off the Shell class.

Taking this knowledge to our racing team, we could create a DocumentShell presenter for it. That would mean that we could save each team individually. However, it would cause problems if we want the teams to compete against each other. We would have to open all the individual files. Not really convenient.

What about Dialog? That seems a good choice, especially if you consider that if you are not happy with the changes that you have made to a team, you can just cancel them and the team remains in its original state. How does that work, when we have just learned that when using the MPV framework all the changes that you make are directly communicated to the underlying model? Well, when a dialog is opened on an object, it actually copies the object and shows you the copy. You can then make changes, and when you click OK on the dialog the values of the instance variables in the copy are copied to the original model. If you cancel the changes, the copy is just thrown away.

Dialog sounds like a good candidate to maintain our race teams, so let's create the TeamDialogPresenter class as a subclass of Dialog. Go into the CHB, find and select the class Dialog, and select New Class. Enter the name TeamDialogPresenter.

It requires instance variables for all the fields that we want to present: namePresenter, originPresenter, foundationYearPresenter, and commentPresenter. Modify the class definition as below:

```
Dialog subclass: #TeamDialogPresenter
    instanceVariableNames: 'namePresenter originPresenter
    foundationYearPresenter commentPresenter'
    classVariableNames: ''
    poolDictionaries: ''
```

Enter class comment, explaining that this presenter is the maintenance presenter for the Team model, and that the instance variable names are

THE FIRST APPLICATION COMPONENT: THE TEAM

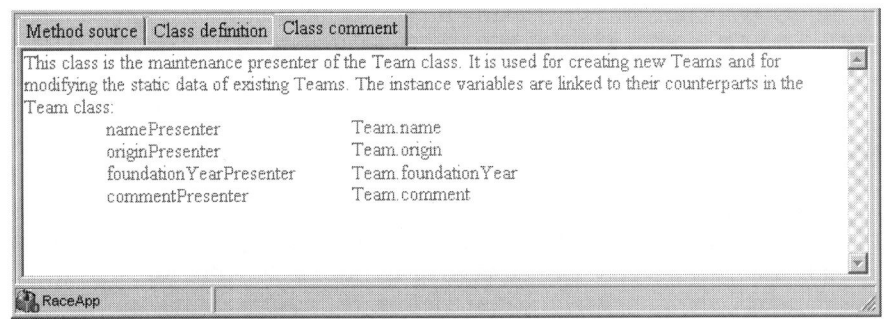

Figure 3.5

TeamDialogPresenter class comment

linked to the instance variables of the Team instance variables (Figure 3.5).

Now we have to create the components to link the presenter and the view and then make a link between the model and the presenter.

In the link between the presenter and the view we have to create and name presenters for each individual field that we want to show in our view.

```
TeamDialogPresenter>>createComponents
    "Create the view components"
    super createComponents.
    namePresenter := self add: TextPresenter new name:
        'name'.
    originPresenter := self add: TextPresenter new name:
        'origin'.
    foundationYearPresenter := self add: NumberPresenter
        new name: 'foundationYear'.
    commentPresenter := self add: TextPresenter new name:
        'comment'.
```

In the first line of actual code (`super createComponents`) we say that whatever is defined in the superclasses of our class is applicable to this class as well. Remember that we are overriding a method of the superclass of our class. Therefore, if we didn't include this line in our definition, we would lose functionality that is defined in one of the superclasses.

In the next lines we add a presenter to "self". What is that all about? In Section 3.1 we saw that when you want to send a message to the instance that is executing the message, you have to use "self"; therefore, in this case "self" is a presenter. So far, that presenter doesn't have anything to present, so we have to add presenters that do know how to present something. Remember the split in the two types of presenters that we made at the beginning of this chapter? We are building a CompositePresenter, and we are using the "tool" presenters to do the actual work of presenting information to us. Therefore we have to add instances of these "tool" presenters to each instance of the presenter that we are defining here.

In the Team class we only have text variables and a number variable, so we use the TextPresenter and NumberPresenter.

The names we attach to these objects are only by coincidence the same as the variable names in the Team model. We could have named them anything we liked, but as they represent whatever is stored in the instance variables of the model, it makes sense to give them the same name. We will use these names when we build our view in the next section.

The link to the model is made via the method #model:. In this method you not only link the model with the view, you also link the required instance variables of the model to the instance variables of the view.

```
TeamDialogPresenter>>model: aTeam
    "Create the link between the model and the presenter"
    super model: aTeam.
    namePresenter model: (aTeam aspectValue: #name).
    originPresenter model: (aTeam aspectValue: #origin).
    foundationYearPresenter model: (aTeam aspectValue:
        #foundationYear).
    commentPresenter model: (aTeam aspectValue: #comment).
```

Here again we start by calling the same method in the superclass (`super model: aTeam`).

In the following four lines we connect the instance variables to their counterparts in the team. We do that with the method #aspectValue:. We haven't defined this method in our Team class, but inherit it from the Object class. This method wraps the Team instance variables in ValueAspectAdapters. ValueAspectAdapters form the basis of the MPV framework, which standardizes communication between the model and the presenter by using the accessors to read and write the model's variables. For example, to read the foundationYear variable the message #foundationYear is used, and to set it the message #foundationYear: is used. By standardizing the communication, the ValueAspectAdapter can also "keep an eye" on changes in the variables and update views of those changes. This means that if you have two views on the same instance, then changing the model in one view will automatically update the other view.

This is the minimum we have to do for a presenter. We can now create the view, and then create and show objects using that view.

An alternative approach   Note that we don't have to create instance variables for every presenter, it just makes referencing the presenters a bit easier. If we didn't have instance variables for the presenters, the #createComponents and #model: methods would look like this:

```
TeamDialogPresenter>>createComponents
    "Create the view components"
    super createComponents.
    self add: TextPresenter new name: 'name'.
    self add: TextPresenter new name: 'origin'.
    self add: NumberPresenter new name: 'foundationYear'.
    self add: TextPresenter new name: 'comment'.

TeamDialogPresenter>>model: aTeam
    "Create the link between the model and the presenter"
    super model: aTeam.
    (self presenterNamed: 'name') model: (aTeam
         aspectValue: #name).
    (self presenterNamed: 'origin') model: (aTeam
         aspectValue: #origin).
    (self presenterNamed: 'foundationYear') model: (aTeam
         aspectValue: #foundationYear).
    (self presenterNamed: 'comment') model: (aTeam
         aspectValue: #comment).
```

This does preserve some memory as the memory is not allocated up front when initializing the object, so in the end this is a more efficient way. On the other hand, using the instance variables makes the model easier to understand. Therefore I will use the approach with instance variables throughout this tutorial.

3.2.1 Summary

In this section we discussed the difference between composite presenters and elementary presenters ("tool" presenters). We've discussed the main composite presenters and when to use each one. We've built a composite (dialog-) presenter for our first model and made links between the model and presenter through ValueAspectAdapters, which help standardize the communication between models and presenters. And finally we discussed two ways of creating presenters, either by making use of instance variables or without instance variables.

3.3 Creating a view

For the team we want to build a view that looks like the window shown in Figure 3.6, but before we can do that, we first have to explore the tool with which we can build views, the view composer.

How to work with the view composer and how to modify aspects of a subview.

Figure 3.6
Team dialog

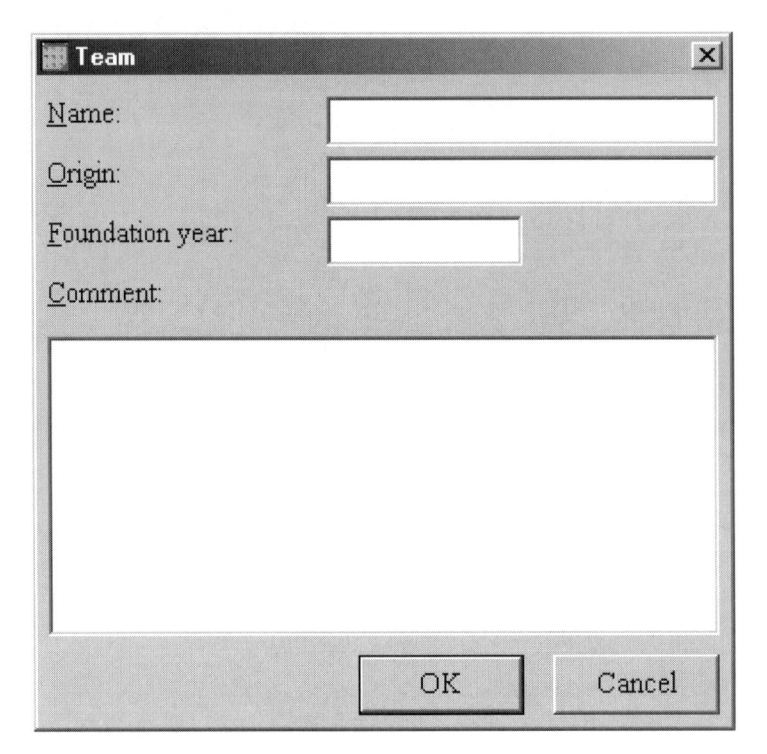

Even though you can start the view composer by selecting it from the Tools menu and from the toolbar menu, the best way to start it is by selecting the presenter class for which you want to make a view and then selecting from the right-click menu option "New view ... ". In this way you link the view and the presenter right at the start; the view knows to which presenter it belongs. In our case it automatically creates an OK/Cancel dialog, as the presenter is a subclass of the Dialog presenter class. If we had opened the view composer separately, we would have had to choose the right resource ourselves, and when saving we would have had to link the view to our TeamDialogPresenter.

3.3.1 The view composer

The view composer (Figure 3.7) is the most complicated tool in the Dolphin Smalltalk toolset. The reason for this is that it is the main interface with the Windows user interface widgets, also called Windows controls, like buttons, text fields, drop-down list boxes, and so on. These widgets typically have many settings. When you want to use such a widget, you want to be able to modify those settings to the situation.

The top half of the screen is the view that you are building. You can drag widgets on the view from the Resource toolbox (see below). These widgets are then shown on the view and in the view hierarchy, the

THE FIRST APPLICATION COMPONENT: THE TEAM 37

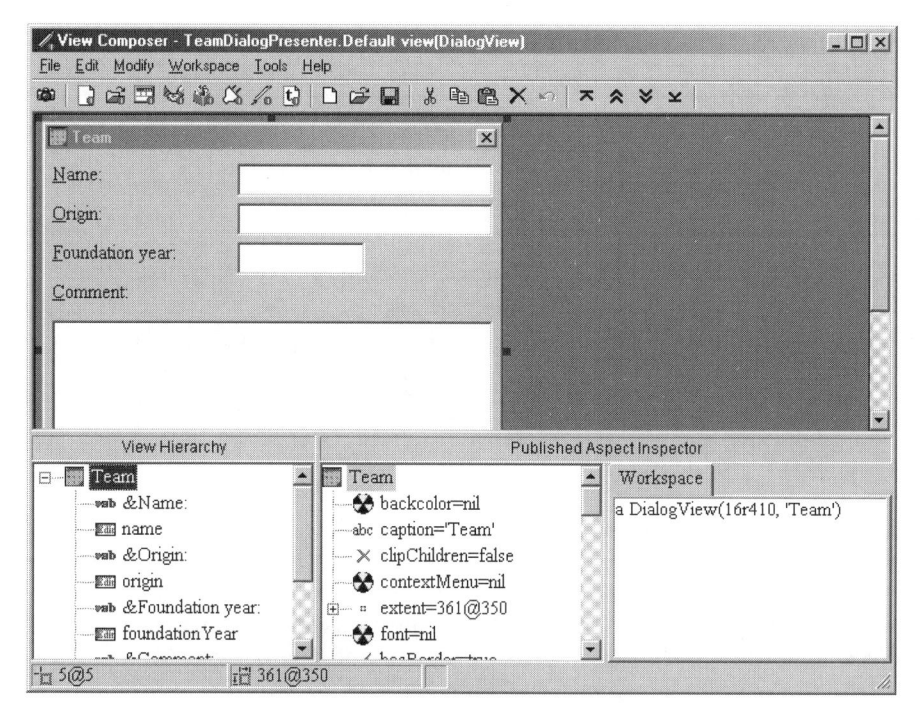

Figure 3.7

The view composer

leftmost panel on the bottom half of the screen. As views can contain other views, the view hierachy is a true hierarchy.

A window can contain widgets, but also view containers. Those view containers can contain widgets and other view containers, and so on.

When you select a view in the view hierarchy or in the view that you are building, the Published Aspect Inspector is updated, showing you all the aspects (properties, settings) of that view. The left-hand column shows you the aspects, and when you select one of the aspects you see the value to the right.

Most often the value is shown in a workspace, but sometimes it is shown in a different way, depending on the type of aspect. When the value is shown in a workspace, it can be changed by entering the new value and accepting (Ctrl + S) it.

In some cases the value is shown in a Value box. The tab then has the title "Value". In that case you can just enter the value and exit the box, for example by selecting another aspect.

In some cases the value can be changed by double-clicking on the aspect itself, for example when you want to change the font or the background color. This brings up a dialog in which you can change the setting.

This might all sound confusing at the moment, but trust me, you will get used to it before you know it.

The Resource toolbox (Figure 3.8) is a floating window belonging to the view composer. It can be opened with the menu option Edit – Show

Figure 3.8

The Resource toolbox

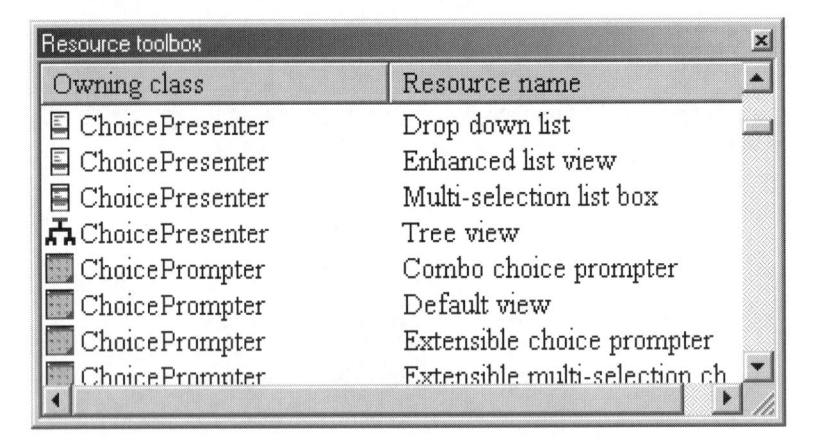

Toolbox. It consists of the list of widgets that you can put on your view. At first sight this list looks very confusing, as it not only contains the widgets that you would expect, like a check box, a radio button and a pushbutton, but also complete views, like the CHB and the view composer itself. The reason for this is that the "basic" widgets and the composite views are treated in exactly the same way. This means that you can build building blocks that can be used in other views. The toolbars are an example of this; there are a number of standard toolbars. These are defined like any other view, but are used in other views.

With the view composer you can, and during the course of this book you will, build your own basic widgets, just like you can build complete application windows. This also allows you to build composite view components and use those components on different application windows.

3.3.2 The Team view

As we opened the view composer with the context menu for our TeamDialogPresenter, we already see a half-built dialog view. We only have to add a couple of labels and fields to it and do some formatting and resizing.

First we will create the labels that we need for the fields (Figure 3.9). If the Resource toolbox is not visible, select it from the Edit – Show Toolbox menu (Ctrl + T).

The labels are static text resources of the TextPresenter class. Put four labels on your dialog by just selecting the Static Text resource and dragging it onto your dialog. As the Static Text box has the same backcolor as the dialog, you won't see the box on the dialog. Don't worry, you'll find them in the list of resources on the view (the view hierarchy). Once you've put the four text boxes on the dialog, select the first resource in the view hierarchy (Figure 3.10).

THE FIRST APPLICATION COMPONENT: THE TEAM

Figure 3.9
Resource toolbox

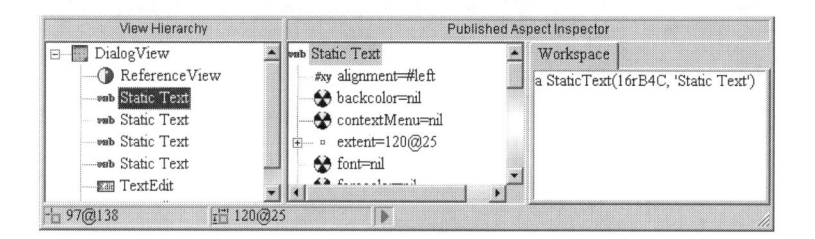

Figure 3.10
View hierarchy

On the right-hand side you can now see most of the available aspects (parameters) of this resource. Let's change some of them: Scroll down to the "text" aspect, select it, and then enter "Name:" (without quotes) in the workspace next to it. Ctrl + S saves it and you'll see the text appear on the dialog. Change the "position" aspect to "5@10". Modify the other labels in the same way. You'll find that 30 pixels between the labels are needed for the text boxes, as they are 25 pixels high. Therefore the vertical positions of the other labels will be 40, 70, and 100.

Now we start putting some data fields on the dialog. Drag two default text presenters on your dialog (for the name and origin), an integer number presenter (for the foundation year), and a multi-line text presenter (for the comment). In our TeamDialogPresenter we created a TextPresenter with the name "name", so we have to tell our system that we mean this field by that line. This is done by setting the name-aspect to "name" (Figure 3.11).

While you're here, change some of the other aspects as well (Table 3.1); position: 150@10, extent: 200@25. Do the same with the other fields (note the caption on the name aspect):

It is starting to look like a proper dialog now, even though the buttons are only half visible. Change their position to 265@290 for the Cancel button and 165@290 for the OK button. By the way, you don't have to scroll down to the "position" aspect. You can change aspects by entering them with their value in the workspace next to the list of aspects (Figure 3.12). Just enter "self position: 265@290" and "Evaluate it" (Ctrl + E). Note that this only works in the workspace of the control itself

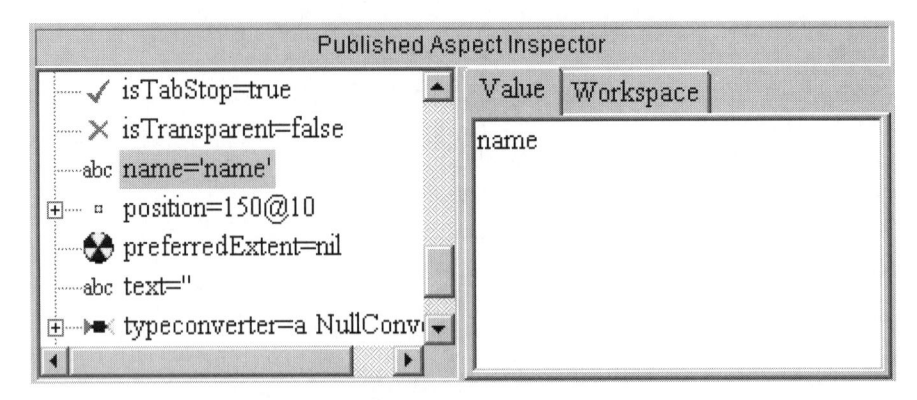

Figure 3.11
Published Aspect Inspector

[Published Aspect Inspector showing: isTabStop=true, isTransparent=false, name='name', position=150@10, preferredExtent=nil, text='', typeconverter=a NullConv...; Value/Workspace pane with "name"]

Table 3.1
Field aspects

Name	Position	Extent
origin	150@40	200@25
foundationYear	150@70	100@25
comment	5@130	345@150

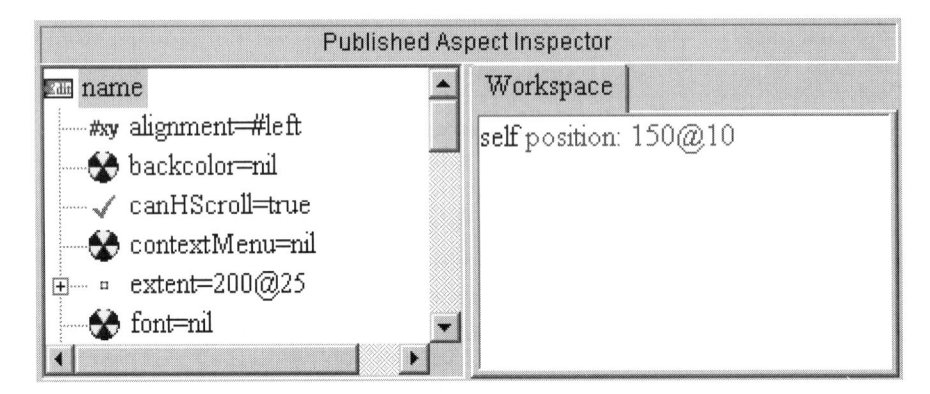

Figure 3.12
Set position

[Published Aspect Inspector showing: name, alignment=#left, backcolor=nil, canHScroll=true, contextMenu=nil, extent=200@25, font=nil; Workspace pane with "self position: 150@10"]

(the one with the text "a PushButton(..)" in it). You have to be a bit cautious: don't do it on the "text" aspect in static text fields and the "name" aspect in all other fields, as when you set these, other aspects are set at the same time. Therefore these aspects should only be changed through the aspect field itself.

We're almost there, we just have to change some of the dialog aspects. Set the caption to "Team" and the extent to 365@355. By now it should look like Figure 3.7 at the beginning of this section.

Now it's time to test it. For a first test on how it looks, go to the File menu in the view composer and select Test. This already gives you a good impression of what your dialog looks like. As you can see, the OK button is disabled. As the dialog isn't linked to anything, Dolphin doesn't know what to do with OK, so it disables it. Cancel, however, is enabled. As Cancel doesn't do anything more than closing the window, Dolphin knows what to do. Well, it's not so much Dolphin that knows what to do, but the dialog itself, being an instance of the class DialogView. Have a look in the class DialogView – you'll find a method "Cancel", but not a method "OK".

Before we can do some more realistic testing, we first have to save the dialog. When saving a view, we do two things: we say to which presenter class the view belongs and we give the view a name (Figure 3.13).

When we create a view from a presenter like we did here (using the right-click menu on a presenter class name), the view already knows to which presenter it belongs. So when you save a view, it has the right presenter selected. What about the name? We can give it any name we like, but there's one name that makes life a bit easier. Let's look in the class methods of the class Presenter. You will see a method called #defaultView. This method returns the string "Default view". This means that if we call our view "Default view", that is assumed to be the default, so if we want to open a view for our TeamPresenter class and we're not too picky on which view to open, we can open the default without specifying it. Note that as it is a string, you have to get things like caption and spaces

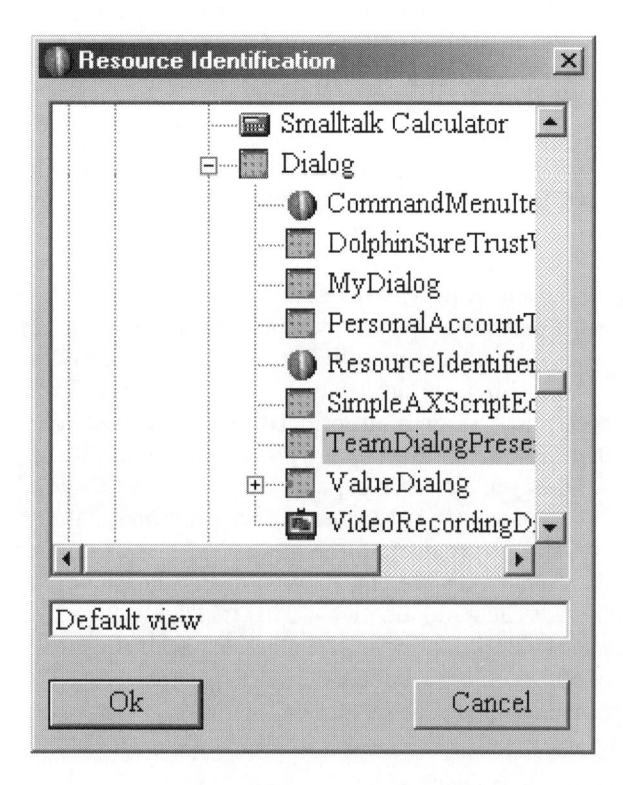

Figure 3.13
Naming the view

right. Of course you can name your default view for a certain presenter differently, but then you also have to override the class method #defaultView in your presenter subclass. Let's choose the easy option and name our dialog "Default view".

3.3.3 *Testing the Team view*

How to test the Model-Presenter-View triad together and how to make use of the dialog's aspect buffer.

Now we can do some testing on a proper model. Go back to your workspace and enter the following lines:

```
team1 := Team new.
team1 name: 'Ferrari'.
team1 origin: 'Italy'.
TeamDialogPresenter showOn: team1.
```

OK, let's now change some of our object's data, and give it a foundation year (the Ferrari racing team was founded in 1929) and some comment. Press the OK button, which should close the dialog. Back in the workspace, let's open an inspector on the variable team1. As you can see in the inspector, the instance variables have changed according to what you've entered. Now reopen the dialog by evaluating the above line again. Change the name from Ferrari to something else. When we now press the Cancel button (or the Close button or <esc>), we would expect the change to be canceled. This is one of the reasons why we used a dialog in the first place. Close the dialog in one of these ways and inspect our team1 again. Oops, the name has changed. How is that possible?

Let's have a look at what happened here. We pressed the Cancel button (or any other way to close the dialog), which closed the dialog. If we go to the Dialog class, we can see that the method "cancel" does just that. It doesn't update a model or anything. So this method can't be held responsible. What about the other way round then? Does OK do what it is supposed to do? OK calls the method #apply. This method tries to apply the changes from the buffer to the original object, just the way we want it to be. So that side works the way we want it as well. But are we talking to the buffer when we change something in our dialog? We made the link between the original object and the presenter in the method #model:. There you can see that each field is connected to the instance variable of aTeam, instead of some kind of buffer. This explains why it doesn't work as expected; when we change something on our view, we immediately update the model, which is the original instance instead of the buffered copy. Therefore, it doesn't matter how we close the view, as the model is already updated! Have a look at the #model: method in the Dialog class. In this method the model is set to an instance of the class AspectBuffer (via the method #bufferedModelFor:). So we have to set the instance variable "model" (see the Presenter class), and then instead of linking each presenter directly to aTeam, we have to link them to the "model" instance variable. We can do that using the expression "self model". The required changes are underlined.

```
TeamDialogPresenter>>model: aTeam
    "Create the link between the model and the presenter
    via the Dialog buffer"
     super model: aTeam.
     namePresenter model: (self model aspectValue: #name).
     originPresenter model: (self model aspectValue:
         #origin).
     foundationYearPresenter model: (self model
         aspectValue:
     #foundationYear).
     commentPresenter model: (self model aspectValue:
         #comment).
```

Now it should work as expected.

3.3.4 The finishing touch

Are we happy with our dialog? Not just yet. When we open the dialog, the OK button has the cursor, and when we tab from field to field, it feels like it goes at random. We are also missing shortcuts to the fields. So if you have closed the view composer, reopen it on the dialog (right-click on the TeamDialogPresenter has the option "Edit view").

How to set the tab order, shortcuts and other UI aspects.

The tab sequence is defined by the sequence of the fields in the hierarchy. By moving the name field to the first position, this becomes the field that has the cursor when the dialog opens. The shortcuts can be created by putting the "&" character in front of the character on the label that you want to be the shortcut character and moving the field that we want to access via that shortcut right after that label in the hierarchy of fields. So the right sequence of fields is as shown in Figure 3.14.

When we now open the dialog, we will be able to tab in the correct sequence and by using the Alt button in combination with the shortcut characters we can jump straight to a field. Note that the OK and Cancel buttons don't have a shortcut option. Why? Well, why would they? You can do OK by pressing Enter, and you can do Cancel by pressing Escape. Shorter than that you won't get.

There is one problem remaining. Try to tab through all the fields. You will notice that once you're in the comment field, you can't get out other than by using the mouse, a shortcut key combination or Escape, which closes the dialog and cancels the changes. The Tab key creates a tab in the text, and the Enter key brings you to the next line in the text box. Have a look at the aspects of the multi-line text box. At the bottom you will find "wantReturn" and "wantTab". They are both set to true, which means that both keys are seen as part of the text. Normally you don't use the

Figure 3.14

Modified view hierarchy

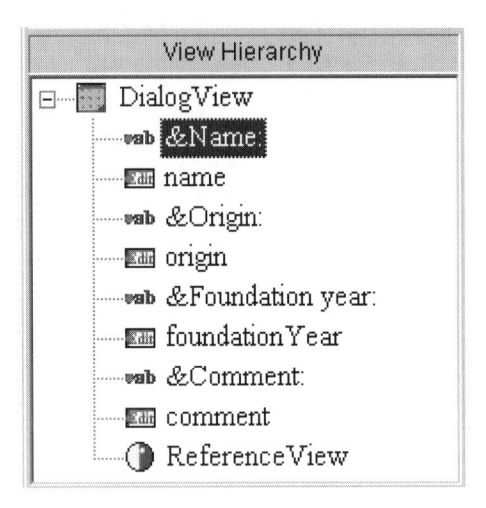

Tab key in this kind of text box, so in our case we set the "wantTab" aspect to false. If we now test the Dialog we will see that it behaves as expected.

3.3.5 The Microsoft look

How to build multiple views for the same presenter, how to change the default font, and how to create your own style.

A lot of people complain that applications developed in Smalltalk don't have the look and feel of Microsoft products. Well, as Dolphin Smalltalk uses the Win32 controls we should be able to overcome that problem. It is just a matter of creating the same dialog with a different font and different field sizes. The font that is used in Microsoft development kits is MS Sans Serif 8 pt and the fields are 20 pixels deep (or the nearest equivalent). We can of course change the standard font for Dolphin into MS Sans Serif 8 pt, so that everything is shown in that font. We can do that in the Dolphin Options view (Figure 3.15).

The problem with this solution is that everything will be shown in the font selected here, including all the text in the CHB. Unfortunately, the readability of the italics version of MS Sans Serif is rather poor, which makes comments in Dolphin methods hard to read.

For now, we will just create a new dialog where we set the individual fields to the right font and the right size. So from the TeamDialogPresenter we create a new view. To make life easy for us, Dolphin Smalltalk creates a copy of the default view as it assumes, rightly, that we won't make too drastic changes. It gives us a good basis to work from. Modify each field as described in Table 3.2, and modify the font of each field to **MS Sans Serif 8 pt**.

Note that you don't have to change the font of the dialog, which is used for the caption. Dolphin Smalltalk uses the Windows settings here.

Save this view as "MS view".

THE FIRST APPLICATION COMPONENT: THE TEAM

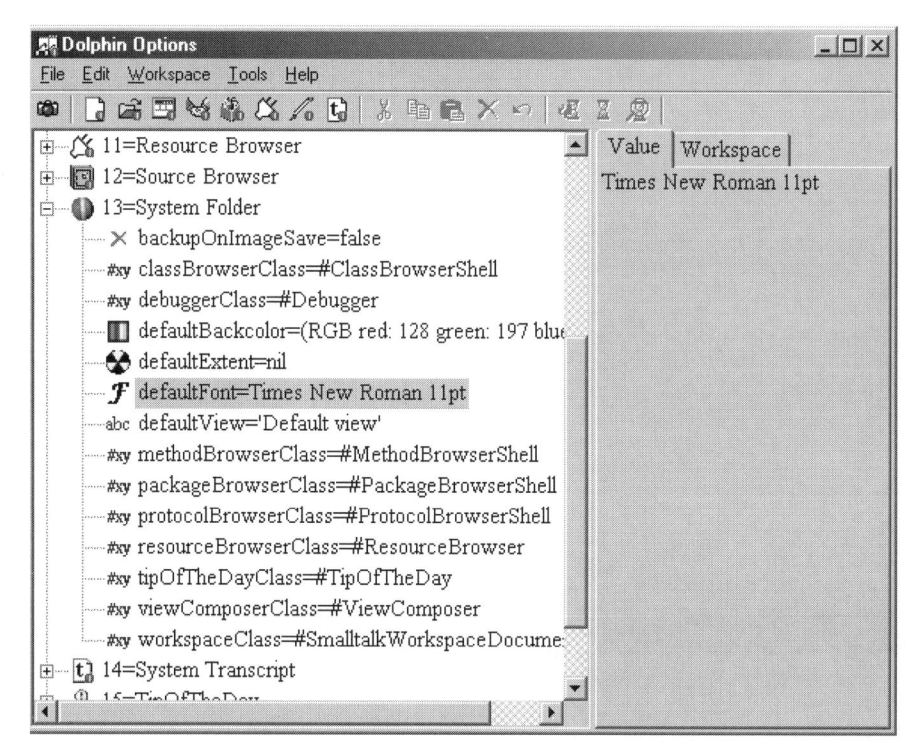

Figure 3.15
Dolphin Options

Name	Position	Extent
Name:	5@5	85@20
name	95@5	155@20
Origin:	5@30	85@20
origin	95@30	155@20
Foundation year:	5@55	85@20
foundationYear	95@55	60@20
Comment:	5@80	85@20
comment	5@100	245@150
ok	95@260	75@23
cancel	175@260	75@23
Team dialog		261@315

Table 3.2
Field aspects

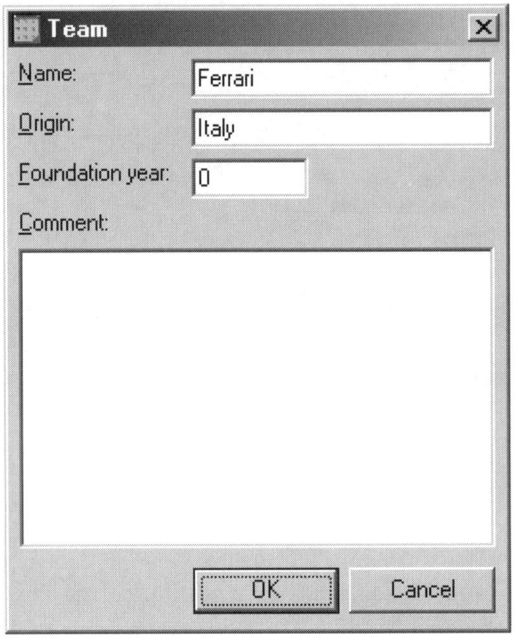

Figure 3.16

Microsoft look

You can now show the test data with the following line in the workspace:

```
TeamDialogPresenter show: 'MS view' on: team1
```

Does that look Microsoft-ish enough for you (Figure 3.16)?

Without changing a single bit of code, we created a new view on the presenter. You can imagine the benefits of this approach – one person wants to look at the data in one way, another wants to look at it in another way. It's just a matter of creating different views.

If you regularly have to make MS-style windows, you can make copies of the resources (text field, static text, button, and so on) with the preferred font and size. In the same way you can develop your own style; say you like the **Verdana 8 pt** font and the teal backcolor, then you copy the default resources with the settings as you like.

3.3.6 Summary

In the above subsections we've introduced the view composer, the view resources, resource hierarchies, and resource aspects. We've built multiple Dialog views for the Dialog presenter that we built in the previous section. We've learned that the view resources are linked to a presenter and that they have a name. Via a class method in the presenter we can define a default view. We've also learned that Dialog presenters update their model through aspect buffers so that changes can be canceled.

3.4 Some basic maintenance work

Before moving on to the next component, we will first organize our development environment. First, create a directory called FormulaOne in your data directory. Here we are going to save everything that we are using in our application. Save the workspace that we use for testing in this directory via the workspace menu option File – Save. Give the file a name like "test data". If you don't explicitly enter an extension to the filename, it will get the extension "st".

The next step is to create a package in which we are going to store all classes with their methods and all views that we are going to create for our application. Packages are the main method of storing applications. They are maintained through the package browser (Figure 3.17). You would typically create a package for each application that you build.

How to use the package manager and how to store your coding in your own package.

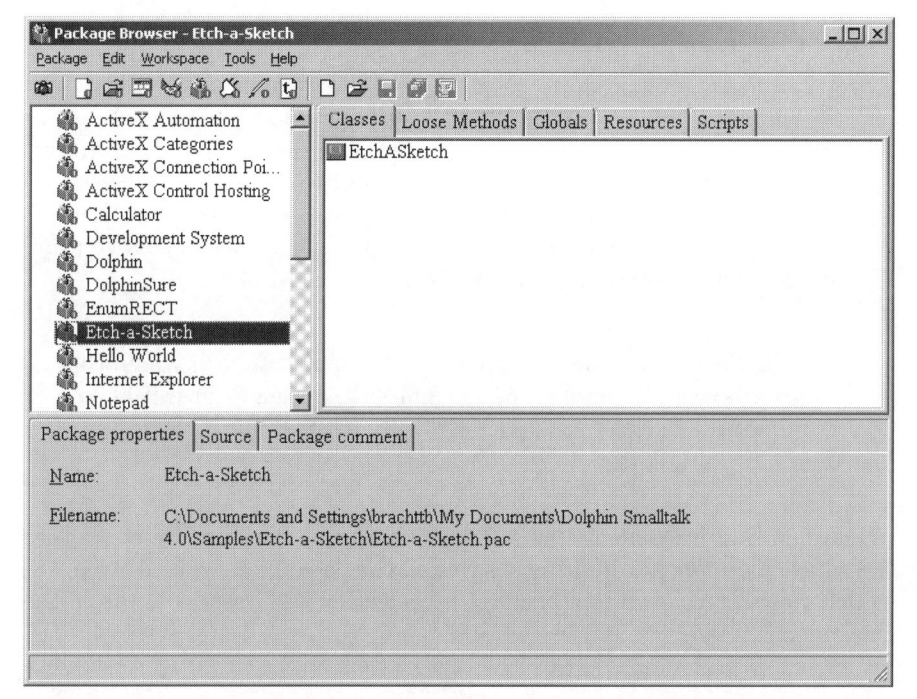

Figure 3.17

The package browser

If you want to install your application in another Dolphin Smalltalk image or upgrade to a later version of Dolphin Smalltalk, then you just copy the package and install it in the other image.

The left column shows the currently installed packages. A package can contain classes, individual methods of classes that belong to other packages, global variables, and forms (resources). Each of these can be shown through their individual tabs. On the Scripts tab you can set up expressions that are run before installing the package, after installing the package, before removing the package, or after removing the package. You would use that tab, for example, to add certain settings to shared resources (pool dictionaries).

In the Inspector tab you can set additional information about the package in the form of an "About" string or expression and add a version to the package.

We create our Formula One package through the following steps:

1. Go into the package browser, and create a package called "FormulaOne" via the menu option Package – New. After creating the package, go into the Package Comment tab and explain that this package is going to contain an application on which the scores for Formula One racing can be maintained. Save your comment with Ctrl + S. Later on we will add a line to the comment with which the application can be started.

2. Add the Team and TeamDialogPresenter classes to the package. You can do this in a number of different ways. In the package manager, you can use the menu option Package – Add Uncommitted – Class. This will show all classes that do not yet belong to a package. You have to have a package selected for this option, and then it is just a matter of selecting the "loose" classes that you want to add to the selected package. Another option is to go into the CHB, select the class that you want to put in a package and select the required package from the Package drop-down on the menu bar.

3. Save the package to disk with the Package – Save As menu option. By using the Save As option you can change the directory in which the package is saved. If you use the normal Save option after initial creation of the package, the package will be saved in the default Dolphin Smalltalk directory.

When you add a Presenter class to a package, any views linked to that Presenter class are automatically saved in the package as well. You can see which views are stored in a package by selecting the Resources tab in the package browser.

For convenience you can change the default package in the class hierarchy browser to FormulaOne (Class – Default Package). Now whenever you create a new class, it will automatically be put into the default package.

> Make it a habit to have each class belong to a package and save the packages regularly.
>
> Even though the package system is a convenient way to store your application code externally, the main working store is the image. Whenever I add a class and whenever I add or change some significant code, I save my image (the camera icon that is available on most tools).

4 The Driver component

In this chapter we are going to build the second component for our application, the Driver. We will create an abstract superclass for both the Team and the Driver classes that holds the commonalities between these classes. While we build the Driver class we will have a look at what we can do with dates, both in terms of calculations with them and in terms of presenting them. We will also do some string manipulation and update fields as a result of changes to other fields. In Section 4.3 we will investigate what kind of solutions we can find for 1-of-n fields, in this case the gender of the driver. In the final section (Section 4.4.2) we will learn how we can attach a picture to our model and display it in our view. By the end of this chapter we will have a window that looks like Figure 4.1.

Figure 4.1
The Driver window

4.1 The Driver model

How to make use of inheritance.

Focusing on the driver after having built the team, it appears that there are quite some similarities between them. Both have a name, albeit that the driver's name is made up of a first name and a surname (and, if you wish, middle name and so on). You might also want to store comments against the driver in the same way as we did with the team. And, even though we're not covering that here yet, drivers collect points in the same way as teams do. So it would be silly to set up the driver separately from the team; we can share some behavior between the two by making Driver a subclass of Team. Long live inheritance! However, as Driver and Team share only part of their behavior, it would be better if they were both subclasses of another class. This superclass should not be used as a normal class – it shouldn't have instances. Such a class is called an **abstract** class. In other languages you can explicitly say that a class is an abstract class, in Smalltalk you can't. There are ways to guarantee that a certain class doesn't have instances though, which effectively says that a class is abstract. As the only way to create an instance is by sending its class the message #new, you can override the #new method and say that it shouldn't be used. However, as the subclasses inherit this #new method, they have to override it again. In the code in the next sections you will see how we can do this. Using the abstract superclass allows the Team class to be extended without affecting the Driver class, and the other way round. If they both have to be extended in the same way, you just extend their joint superclass.

Figure 4.2 shows the abstract class and the Driver and Team classes as subclasses of the abstract class. When you model an abstract class, the name is usually shown in italics.

Based on this model we can create the RacingActor class, move the Team class and create the Driver class.

4.1.1 The abstract RacingActor class

We first create the RacingActor class and add the instance variables:

How to create an abstract class.

```
Model subclass: #RacingActor
    instanceVariableNames: 'name comment'
    classVariableNames: ''
    poolDictionaries: ''
```

When you create an abstract class, it is common practice to say in the class comment that it is an abstract class, so that other developers can see your intention.

For both the instance variables we generate accessors with the menu option Class – Generate accessors. As we want to be sure that the name

Figure 4.2

Inheritance class model

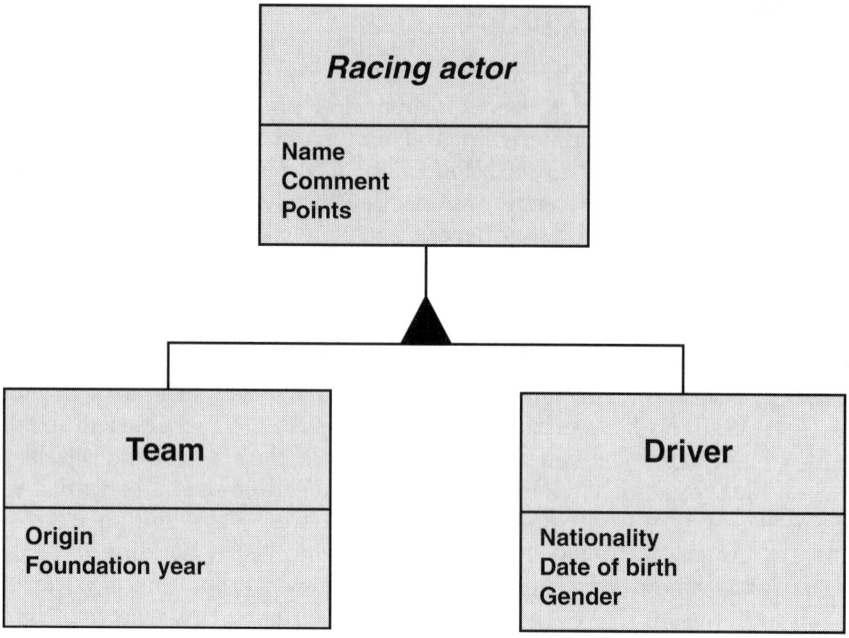

variable is initialized to an empty string, we have to move that part of the #initialize method to this class:

```
RacingActor>>initialize
    "Initialize the receiver"
    super initialize.
    self name: String new.
```

To make sure that nobody creates instances of this class, we create a class method that overrides the standard #new method. Select the Class tab to tell the system that you want to create a class method. Then select New Method and enter the following method:

```
RacingActor>>new
    "This class should not have instances as it is an
    abstract class"
    ^self shouldNotImplement
```

Now try to create an instance of this class by evaluating the following line in a workspace.

```
abstract := RacingActor new.
```

This brings up the dialog in Figure 4.3, showing in the header that even though there is a #new class method, it should not be used.

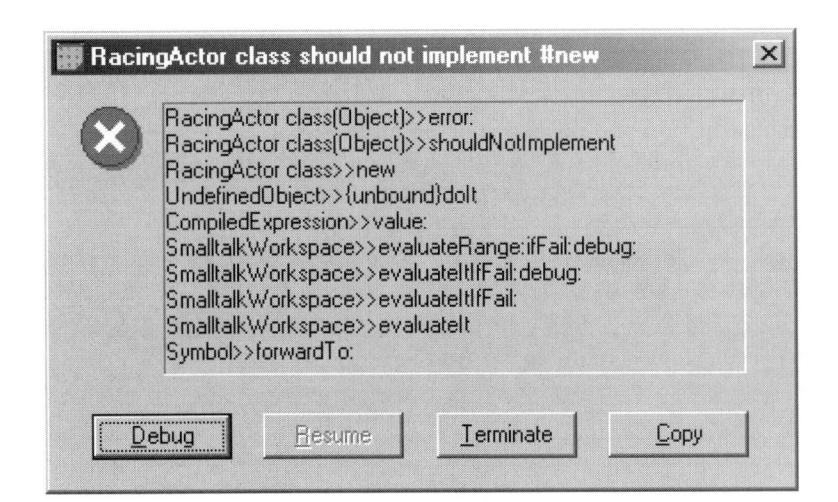

Figure 4.3
"Should not implement" dialog

4.1.2 Modifications to the Team class

Now that we have this "working," we concentrate on getting the team working again. First we remove the name instance variable and the comment instance variable from the team, as we inherit them in our abstract subclass. You can do this by selecting the instance variables in the class definition and deleting them, and then accepting the new definition (Ctrl + S).

How to change the superclass of a class and how to use #basicNew.

```
Model subclass: #Team
     instanceVariableNames: 'origin foundationYear'
     classVariableNames: ''
     poolDictionaries: ''
```

If you now look at the accessor methods for the name and comment, you will see that they are in red, as they try to access variables that do not exist anymore. We can remove these methods as we are going to inherit them from our abstract superclass. You can delete a method by selecting the method in the method list and using either the context menu option "delete", the cross on the toolbar, or the delete option from the edit menu. The #initialize method appears to be red as well, as it tries to initialize the name variable. We still want it to initialize the year variable, so we just remove the line where it initializes the name:

Team>>initialize
```
    "Initialize the receiver"
    super initialize.
    self foundationYear: 0.
```

After you have made these modifications, we are going to move the class so that it becomes a subclass of our new RacingActor class. Select the class and drag and drop it onto the RacingActor class.

The class definition should now look as follows:

```
RacingActor subclass: #Team
    instanceVariableNames: 'origin foundationYear'
    classVariableNames: ''
    poolDictionaries: ''
```

Now try to create a new team as we did before:

```
testTeam := Team new.
```

This brings up the same error dialog as for the RacingActor, as Team uses the same #new method. So we have to write a #new method specifically for the Team class. But how are we going to do that? We can't use the "trick" that we used in the previous chapter where we called the definition of the superclass with the `super` keyword, as that would call the #shouldNotImplement message again. The solution for this situation is to use the message #basicNew. This message calls the fundamental definition for creating new objects. As it is the fundamental method, it doesn't do anything other than create the new object. In our original solution in Section 3.1 we took it for granted that when you create a new instance the #initialize method is called automatically. Now we have to do that ourselves. The following would do (remember that this is a class method):

```
Team class>>new
    "Override the abstract superclass"
    ^self basicNew initialize
```

The placing of #initialize might look a bit strange at first, as we don't have a class method initialize. But if you recall the ordering from the playground (Section 1.4), you can see that it is executed as follows:

- `self basicNew` creates a new instance of Team;
- this new instance of Team is the receiver of the message #initialize;
- the result of the initialized instance of Team is returned with the caret.

In this kind of situation it quite often helps just to read it aloud. Now see if everything is working again as before. Try to create a new team and open one of the views on it.

```
team2 := Team new.
TeamDialogPresenter showOn: team2.
team2 name: 'Jordan'.
team2 inspect.
```

If you still have the original workspace open that we used for testing in Section 3.1, you might want to try to open the original team again. If you do so, you will see that the name that we entered has disappeared, and if you entered comment, then that will have disappeared as well. This is because we removed them from our original class definition and even though we replaced them with the new definitions in the abstract class, the original values were assigned to the original variables. Therefore, when you do reclassifications, you have to be aware that you might lose information in the existing instances.

Now, after this sidestep of the abstract class and getting the Team working again, we can concentrate on the Driver.

4.1.3 The Driver class

In the class definition for the Driver we just have to define the additional instance variables, as we inherit the others from RacingActor:

```
RacingActor subclass: #Driver
    instanceVariableNames: 'firstname surname nationality
    dateOfBirth gender'
    classVariableNames: ''
    poolDictionaries: ''
```

We create the standard accessors for all the instance variables with the menu option Class – Generate Accessors.

Driver>>dateOfBirth
```
    ^dateOfBirth
```

Driver>>dateOfBirth: anObject
```
    dateOfBirth := anObject.
```

Driver>>firstname
```
    ^firstname
```

Driver>>firstname: anObject
```
    firstname := anObject.
```

Driver>>gender
```
    ^gender
```

```
Driver>>gender: anObject
    gender := anObject

Driver>>nationality
    ^nationality

Driver>>nationality: anObject
    nationality := anObject

Driver>>surname
    ^surname

Driver>>surname: anObject
    surname := anObject.
```

Some string manipulation and the use of a temporary variable in a method.

The Driver's name   So now we are able to create drivers with a first name and a surname. But, as the Driver is a subclass of RacingActor, the Driver also has a name. As we don't want to have to enter the name twice, we let the name update automatically from the first name and the surname. We want the name to be a concatenation of the first name and the surname, with a space in between. We've seen in the playground that we can concatenate strings by putting a comma between them, therefore the following code should do the job:

```
self name: self firstname, ' ', self surname
```

Can we just enter this after the setter methods for firstname and surname? Well, we have to cater for the situation where we don't know the first name. In that case we don't want an annoying space in front of the surname. Furthermore, if a variable isn't initialized, then concatenation doesn't work, which would bring up an error message even though our users haven't done anything wrong. Therefore we have to capture the situation where either string is nil or has a length of zero. We can of course write some code to capture all the situations after updating the first name, and then write virtually the same code for the #surname: method. That doesn't sound very Smalltalkese! Why not write a method that is called from both update methods that checks the contents of the two variables and then updates the name variable? Like this:

```
Driver>>setName
    "Create the name from the first name and the surname.
    This method is called when either of them changes"
    | nameString |
    nameString := String new.
    self surname notNil ifTrue: [nameString := self
        surname].
```

THE DRIVER COMPONENT

```
    (self firstname notNil and: [self firstname notEmpty])
        ifTrue: [nameString := self firstname, ' ',
            nameString].
self name: nameString.
```

In this method we first create a temporary variable (between the two vertical bars), which we assign to a new string. Then we check whether we have a surname. If so, we set the temporary string to the surname. We then check if we have a first name. If that is the case, we combine the first name and the surname with a space in between. In the final line we set the name to the temporary variable.

Both the set methods for firstname and surname now have to call this method.

Driver>>firstname: anObject
    firstname := anObject.
    self setName.

Driver>>surname: anObject
    surname := anObject.
    self setName.

We can help the user a bit more by automatically capitalizing the first letter of the name. How would we do that? Using the same approach, we would have to create a method that has just that responsibility. This method can then be called by both the #firstname: and the #surname: methods. It is not enough just to capitalize the first letter; how would you cope with a name like Heinz-Harald? Therefore, we have to check all the words in the name. Open a CHB and select the String class. Then scroll through the methods to see if we can find a usable method. Have a look at the method #subStrings, which divides the string into separate strings of words. Once we have that, we can make sure that the first letter is capitalized. Then we stick it all together again with spaces in between. This sounds OK, but look what happens if you send the #subString message to the string "heinz-harald frentzen":

```
'heinz-harald frentzen' subStrings >> #('heinz-harald'
'frentzen')
```

This separates the first name and the surname, but it doesn't separate the two name elements in the first name. This is because the dash is not in the standard list of separators for words. We could go through our collection of substrings again with the message #subString: and then specify each character that we can think of to be used as a separator, but this leaves us with another problem. If we remove the dash when making the collection of substrings in the same way as we remove the spaces, how do we know when to use a space and when to use a dash when we put it all back together?

Why don't we just turn it round? Can we ask whether the character after a non-letter character is capitalized and, if not, just capitalize it? Then we don't have to worry if there are names with separators other than spaces and dashes.

The steps involved are:

1 for each character, check if it is not a letter;

2 if the character is not a letter, check if the next character is a letter;

3 if the next character is a letter, check if it is capitalized;

4 if it is not capitalized, capitalize it.

If we do it this way, we leave the string intact, so we don't have to put it all back together afterwards. You can do this kind of checking by walking through a string, as a string is just a collection of characters, so each character is indexed. However, in Smalltalk there is a far easier way to do this, namely with streams. A stream has very good support for walking through and maintaining its position, exactly what we want to do here. Let's try this in a workspace:

```
in := ReadStream on: 'heinz-harald frentzen'.
out := WriteStream on: String new.
capitalizeNext := true.
[ in atEnd ] whileFalse: [ | char | char := in next.
    capitalizeNext
        ifTrue: [ out nextPut: char asUppercase ]
        ifFalse: [out nextPut: char ].
    char isLetter
        ifTrue: [ capitalizeNext := false ]
        ifFalse: [ capitalizeNext := true ]
    ].
out contents
```

The next question is, where would we put this method? As we use it in the Driver class, you might think that that's where it belongs. But if you build another class in the future, also handling names, then you might want to reuse it. Why not put it in the String class? Then it is available to any string. We will name it #capitalizeEachWord, as that clearly reveals what it does.

String>>capitalizeEachWord
```
    "Change the first letter of each word to uppercase"
    | in out capitalizeNext |
    in := ReadStream on: self.
    out := WriteStream on: String new.
    capitalizeNext := true.
```

```
    [ in atEnd ] whileFalse: [ | char | char := in next.
        capitalizeNext
            ifTrue: [ out nextPut: char asUppercase ]
            ifFalse: [out nextPut: char ].
        char isLetter
            ifTrue: [ capitalizeNext := false ]
            ifFalse: [ capitalizeNext := true ]
    ].
^out contents
```

We are conveniently making use of the fact that #asUppercase checks whether the character is a lowercase letter. If that is the case, the uppercase version is returned, otherwise the original character is returned. Therefore we don't have to do the third and fourth tests, as they are done automatically by the #asUppercase method.

> Note that if you add this method to the String class, you have to move it into one of your own packages, so that it doesn't get lost when you upgrade to the next version of Dolphin Smalltalk. I have a package called "Extensions" for this purpose. When I install a new version (or start with a clean image) I install this package and Dolphin acts in the way I want again.
>
> For this you first have to create the "Extensions" package in the package browser (see Section 3.4) and then you can drag and drop the method into the package. Select the method in the method list of the CHB and then drop it on the "Extensions" label in the package list. Remember to save the package in the package manager, otherwise the changes aren't written to your package file on disk.

We have to call this method when we set the first name or surname. From what we know of the precedence in Smalltalk, we can combine it in the assignment:

```
Driver>>firstname: aString
    ...
    firstname := aString capitalizeEachWord.
    ...

Driver>>surname: aString
    ...
    surname := aString capitalizeEachWord.
    ...
```

We can use this same method when we set the name in the RacingActor class.

```
RacingActor>>name: aString
     name := aString capitalizeEachWord.
```

Calculations with dates.

The Driver's age As we don't want to store the age of a driver in an instance variable, we have to find a way to calculate the age based on the date of birth. How are we going to approach that? We can of course build a method that takes the current year and subtracts the year part of the dateOfBirth and then fiddle with the situation where today is before the birthday or after the birthday. Alternatively we can have a look in the Date class and see if there is something that we can use. We can quickly find the Date class by using the finder (the binoculars) in the CHB. The finder will find two classes, "DATE" and "Date". If a name is completely in capitals, then it is typically some kind of interface class with the Windows operating system, so for now of no interest to us. Therefore, we concentrate on the other class. Let's see if we can find something that can help us in calculating the age. We want to subtract one date from another, so #subtractDate: is a candidate. However, this returns a number of days. Then we have to start working out how many years that number of days is, taking into account leap years and so on. There must be an easier solution. What about #yearsSince:? The description says that it returns the number of actual years since a date. If we make today the receiver and the date of birth the argument, then we get the age as per today. We can ask the Date class to create an object for today's date by sending the class the message #today. Let's try that in a workspace:

```
Date today yearsSince: (Date fromString: 'Nov 13, 1962')
```

This indeed gives my age. So now we can put that in a method to return the age of a driver:

```
Driver>>age
     "Return the age based on the dateOfBirth"
     dateOfBirth isNil ifTrue: [^nil].
     ^Date today yearsSince: dateOfBirth.
```

Now we can test the model in the workspace (Figure 4.4). Create a variable driver1 in the workspace as a new driver. If you inspect the driver, you will see that it used the initialize method that we created for the RacingActor. Now give the driver a surname and ask for the name. Then add a first name, check the name, change the first name to a new string and check the name again. Then give the driver a birth date and check the age.

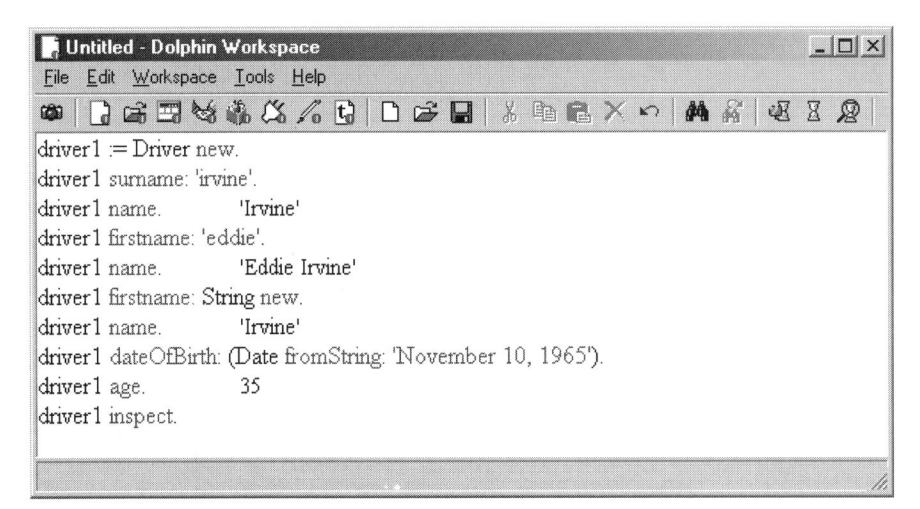

Figure 4.4
Test the Driver model

```
driver1 := Driver new.
driver1 surname: 'irvine'.
driver1 name.           'Irvine'
driver1 firstname: 'eddie'.
driver1 name.           'Eddie Irvine'
driver1 firstname: String new.
driver1 name.           'Irvine'
driver1 dateOfBirth: (Date fromString: 'November 10, 1965').
driver1 age.            35
driver1 inspect.
```

4.1.4 Summary

In this section we've created an abstract class that cannot have instances. This abstract class is the superclass of the Team and Driver classes and contains the variables and methods that these two classes share. To implement the abstract superclass we had to reclassify the Team class.

To automatically capitalize the name, we've done some string manipulation and to calculate the age we've visited the Date class briefly.

4.2 The Driver presenter and view

In this chapter we are going to build both the presenter and the view for the Driver. In subsequent chapters we will extend them with additional functionality. We will make the first view look like Figure 4.5.

4.2.1 The Driver presenter

The next step is to build the presenter for the driver. Just like with the team, we have to consider what type of presenter we are going to use. Well, as the dialog worked fine for the team it is likely to be alright for the driver as well. At least as a start. For now, we leave the gender out; we'll come back to that after we've built the first driver dialog.

How to use presenters that are not directly connected to model aspects.

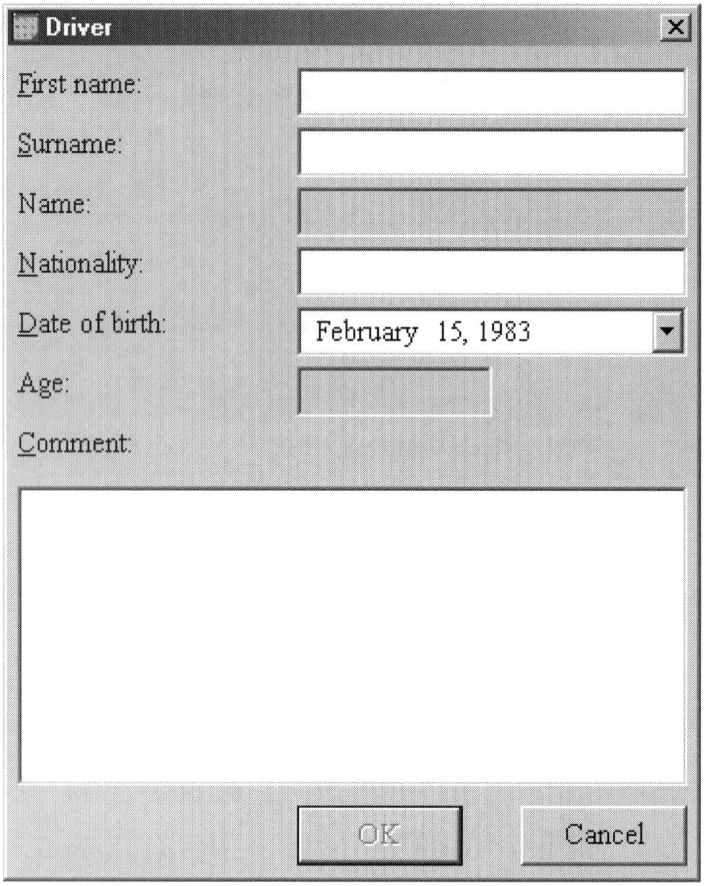

Figure 4.5
The Driver dialog

```
Dialog subclass: #DriverDialogPresenter
    instanceVariableNames: 'firstnamePresenter
    surnamePresenter namePresenter nationalityPresenter
    dateOfBirthPresenter agePresenter commentPresenter'
    classVariableNames: ''
    poolDictionaries: ''
```

We add the minimum number of methods to it, namely #createComponents and #model:.

In the #model: method below we use a temporary variable "aspectBuffer". This is just done so that we don't have to type "self model" all the time and it improves readability. Note also that we don't connect the agePresenter to the model. Remember that we calculate the age, but we do not store it in the model, so there is no age variable. There is, however, an agePresenter, so we have to create it in the #create Components method. The namePresenter looks like any other presenter, even though we intend

THE DRIVER COMPONENT

not to update it directly in the dialog as we build that from the firstname and the surname.

```
DriverDialogPresenter>>model: aDriver
    "Create the link between the model and the presenter
    via a buffer"
    | aspectBuffer |
    super model: aDriver.
    aspectBuffer := self model.
    firstnamePresenter model: (aspectBuffer aspectValue:
        #firstname).
    surnamePresenter model: (aspectBuffer aspectValue:
        #surname).
    namePresenter model: (aspectBuffer aspectValue:
        #name).
    nationalityPresenter model: (aspectBuffer aspectValue:
        #nationality).
    dateOfBirthPresenter model: (aspectBuffer aspectValue:
        #dateOfBirth).
    commentPresenter model: (aspectBuffer aspectValue:
        #comment).

DriverDialogPresenter>>createComponents
    "Create the view components"
    super createComponents.
    firstnamePresenter := self add: TextPresenter new
        name: 'firstname'.
    surnamePresenter := self add: TextPresenter new name:
        'surname'.
    namePresenter := self add: TextPresenter new name:
        'name'.
    nationalityPresenter := self add: TextPresenter new
        name: 'nationality'.
    dateOfBirthPresenter := self add: DatePresenter new
        name: 'dateOfBirth'.
    agePresenter := self add: NumberPresenter new name:
        'age'.
    commentPresenter := self add: TextPresenter new name:
        'comment'.
```

4.2.2 The Driver view

From the DriverDialogPresenter we build a view, like we did for the team. Select the class in the CHB and select the New View in the context menu.

How to make read-only fields and how to use the Date control.

After adding the fields shown in Table 4.1, it should look like Figure 4.5. For the following fields we have to make some additional aspect changes.

Table 4.1

Fields for the DriverDialog-Presenter view

Type	Field	Position	Extent
Static Text	&First name:	5@10	80@25
Text Edit	firstname	150@10	200@25
Static Text	&Surname:	5@40	80@25
Text Edit	Surname	150@40	200@25
Static Text	Name:	5@70	80@25
Text Edit	Name	150@70	200@25
Static Text	&Nationality:	5@100	80@25
Text Edit	nationality	150@100	200@25
Static Text	&Date of birth:	5@130	80@25
Date Presenter (Default view)	dateOfBirth	150@130	200@25
Static Text	Age:	5@160	80@25
Number Presenter (Integer text)	age	150@160	100@25
Static Text	&Comment:	5@190	80@25
Multiline Text Edit	comment	5@220	345@150
PushButton	OK	150@380	85@30
PushButton	Cancel	265@380	85@30

The fields Name and Age both have to have their "isEnabled" aspect set to "false", as we don't want the user to change the data in these fields. The OK button has the "isDefault" aspect set to "true" and the comment multi-line field has the "wantTab" aspect set to "false" (see the Team dialog). The dialog extent is 360@440 and the caption is "Driver".

The control that we use for the dateOfBirth is an interesting one. This field has a whole range of aspects. It has a check box which allows the user to leave the date blank. We want to force the user to enter the date of birth so that we can calculate his or her age, so we remove this check box by setting the "canShowNone" aspect to "false". We can change the date format to almost anything we like. That is done through either the "hasLongDateFormat" aspect or by setting the displayFormat. The "hasLongDateFormat" setting is ignored if the displayFormat is set. Appendix D contains all the formatting possibilities of the Date field.

Some examples of formatting January 5, 2000 are shown in Table 4.2.

Other interesting aspects of this control are shown in Table 4.3.

After setting all the aspects as required, we save the view as "Default view" like we did with the Team view.

Table 4.2

Some examples of formatting January 5, 2000

Formatting string	Formatted date
'M/d/yyyy'	1/5/2000
'MMMd, yyyy'	Jan 5, 2000
'ddd, MMMMd, yyyy'	Wed, January 5, 2000
'dd-MM-yy'	05-01-00

Table 4.3

Other aspects of the Date-Time control

Aspect	Description
hasUpDown	This changes the field from a pull-down field into an up/down arrow field. This is especially useful if the date field is at the bottom of a form, where the drop-down calendar would draw outside the window.
isTimeMode	This changes the control in a control in which time can be entered. As the resource toolbox has a resource with this setting (TimePresenter Default view), it is easier just to use that resource.
maximum minimum	Here you can set a maximum and a minimum date. We could say, for example, that drivers have to be at least 17 years of age. So the maximum can be set to today −17 years. Enter the following in the workspace next to maximum and then save (Ctrl + S): Date today addYears: −17 Note that the expression is calculated and today −17 years is shown. However, Smalltalk remembers the expression that you entered, and every time you open the dialog the calculation will be made with the current date. We could set the minimum date in the same way, but we can just as well enter a hard date, to allow entry of the very first racers. So let's enter and save: Date fromString: 'Jan 1, 1850'
text	You can ignore the contents of this property; see the "value" aspect below.
value	In this property you can enter and save an expression that sets the default value (and updates the "text" aspect). If you want the default date set to today, then enter "Date today" (without the quotes) and save it. In our case it wouldn't make sense to set it to today, as we set a maximum 17 years before today, so today wouldn't be a valid entry.

4.2.3 *Testing the view*

Triggering changes in the model, triggering changes in specific fields in the view, and updating fields based on the triggers.

Let's test the view on a new Driver object, by entering the following in a workspace:

```
DriverDialogPresenter showOn: Driver new.
```

Try to enter a name. You won't be able to access that field. Enter a first name in lowercase. As you would expect, the first letter of each word is converted into uppercase. You would expect the name to be updated now, but it isn't. Why is that? Well, let's see what is actually happening when you enter a first name. When you exit the field, the model is told about it through the #firstname: message, together with the string that you entered. The string is checked for uppercase first letters, and if something had to be changed, then the changes to firstname are returned to the presenter and displayed on the view. Meanwhile, the name instance variable is updated on the model through the #setName message. But we never tell the name presenter that the name has changed. How can we do that? We can take two approaches:

1. we can update the name field after exiting the firstname field or the surname field;
2. we can drive it from the model.

The first approach works locally on the view in which we are changing things, and therefore only updates that specific view. The second approach will not only update the view that we are looking at, but also all other views that are looking at the same object. Both approaches have their use, as we will see below.

For updating the name we are better off using the second approach, as we otherwise have to keep track of changes in both the firstname field and the surname field. By moving it to the model we only have to check changes to the "name" instance variable. This sounds as if it contradicts the picture that we drew in Section 2.3, where we said that the model doesn't know about the presenters. Well, Smalltalk has a very smart way of dealing with this, namely by using dependants. The presenter tells the model that it has an interest in the model and whenever the model changes, it broadcasts to all those objects that are interested in the change the fact that it has changed. The model doesn't know what kind of objects are interested in its change, it just tells them. Those objects can then decide for themselves what they want to do with that knowledge.

The Model-Presenter-View (MPV) paradigm uses this dependency mechanism by automatically making every subpresenter dependent on their model's aspect. Therefore, when we inform the Driver object that its name has changed, it will send a notification to everybody that has an interest in that specific aspect. One of these interested parties is the name presenter on our form, which will then ask the Driver object what the new value is.

To make this work, we have to add the following line to the #setName message in the Driver class:

Driver>>setName
```
    ...
    self trigger: #nameChanged.
```

Now when you leave the firstname field (either by mouse or tab) you will see that the Name field is updated. Enter a surname and you'll see the same. Remove the firstname – no space in front of the surname.

Let's now concentrate on what we can do with the date field that we created. Try to enter a date outside the range. Note the different ways you can enter a date; select the month in the combo and use the up and down keys. Open the combo and select a date. But the age field stays empty, whatever we do! This looks very similar to what happened with the name field above. However, we can't take the same approach here, as we don't have an instance variable for the age, so we can't trigger changes to the age.

How can we solve this? We have to start by capturing the change of date on the view. You can capture anything that happens to a view in a method called #createSchematicWiring. This method is a sort of watchdog for the view. Each line consists of two elements:

1 which action you want to be captured for the specified view, for example exiting the field or clicking in the field;

2 which message you want to send when that action occurs.

In our case we want the age field to be updated when the user leaves the date field.

We could write the calculation of the age in the #createSchematicWiring method as well, but it doesn't really belong there as it would mix up the triggering of the change with the action to be performed based on the trigger. It is better to make the action a separate method and call that method when the change is captured. We will call that method #dateOfBirthChanged.

DriverDialogPresenter>>dateOfBirthChanged
```
    "The date of birth changed, so the age needs to be
    recalculated"
    agePresenter value: self model age.
```

There you can see the link between the agePresenter and the calculation of the age through the model (the instance of the Driver class). Note that we are actually talking to a copy of the model, as we are using the Dialog's aspectBuffer. But as that copy is an instance of the same Driver class, we can still ask it to calculate the age!

The #createSchematicWiring method looks like this (as we inherited this method from our superclass and don't want to lose the definition in our superclass, we have to call the superclass's method as well):

```
DriverDialogPresenter>>createSchematicWiring
    "Create the trigger wiring"
    super createSchematicWiring.
    dateOfBirthPresenter when: #valueChanged send:
        #dateOfBirthChanged to: self.
```

Here we send the message #dateOfBirthChanged to the object itself when the value of the dateOfBirthPresenter changes. When we now open the dialog and change the date of birth, we see that the age is shown for the date. There is just one minor problem remaining. If we open an existing driver which already has a date of birth, the age is not shown. Only after changing the date of birth is the age calculated. This is because #dateOfBirthChanged is only called after such a change. So we have to call this method also when we open the dialog. The easiest way is just to add the following line to the bottom of the #model: method of the DriverDialogPresenter.

```
DriverDialogPresenter>>model: aDriver
    ...
    self dateOfBirthChanged.
```

The #model: method is called when opening the view, so during execution of this method it calls the above line and the age is calculated and shown.

4.2.4 Summary

In the above subsections we've created the DriverDialogPresenter and view, similar to what we did for the team. We've used some additional aspects and investigated the possibilities of the Date presenter. While testing the view we learned how to update fields based on other fields by triggering the changes. This triggering of changes can be done either in the model or in the presenter.

4.3 The driver's gender

Booleans and 1-of-n variables and how to present them.

So far we have left the gender of the driver aside. There are many ways in which we can present this kind of variable. In this chapter we will learn which possibilities there are, what the advantages and disadvantages are, and how to present those different options.

The easiest way is to make the gender a boolean. We would then have to agree that true means male and false means female, or the other way round. There are two problems with this option. First, what if you don't know the gender of the driver? A boolean can only be true or false, so you have to make a choice. You can't set it to "unknown". Another disadvantage is that you have to remember which one of the two choices you made into true, and which one you made into false. Because of this we will make our gender variable into a 1-of-n variable.

Let's first concentrate on the model side and then see the different options for presenting this.

4.3.1 *The 1-of-n variable in the model*

The simplest method to store 1-of-n variables is to store the real value, in our case "Male" or "Female". Now storing a string in a variable isn't really a problem, unless you want to use it frequently for comparison. Each string is an object in its own right, so if you want to do string comparison, you have to do it character by character. You can imagine that that could take some processing. That's why there is an alternative in Smalltalk: the Symbol.

The difference between strings and symbols.

The Symbol class is a subclass of the String class, therefore you can use them in a similar way, but they have one significant difference, which is that they are unique within the system. This means that if you create a symbol #Male (symbols are created by putting a # in front of them), which you assign to the gender variable of one driver, and you create a second driver to which you also assign the symbol #Male, then those two gender variables both point to the same unique object. When you then try to compare those values, the comparison is done by checking whether the variables point to the same object instead of whether the contents of the variables are the same. This is called identity comparison as opposed to equality comparison.

Identity comparison is done by sending the message #== as opposed to #= for equality. We can demonstrate the difference by evaluating the following lines one by one in a workspace. (When you evaluate all the lines in a single go, Dolphin does some optimization which would make the two strings one and the same object. This would defeat the purpose of this demonstration.)

```
"String comparison"
a := 'Male'.
b := 'Male'.
"Display the equality test"
a = b
```

```
"Display the identity test"
a == b
"Symbol comparison"
c := #Male.
d := #Male.
"Display the equality test"
c = d
"Display the identity test"
c == d
```

This shows us that two strings can be equal to each other, but are not one and the same string; they are different objects. Whereas when you do symbol comparison, if they are equal, then they are one and the same object.

Back to our gender variable. Now that we have decided that we want to store a symbol in it, we want to make sure that it can only be set to Male or Female. Therefore we add a check to the setter method:

```
Driver>>gender: aSymbol
    (#(#Male #Female) includes: aSymbol)
        ifFalse: [^self error: 'Not a valid symbol'].
    gender := aSymbol
```

The format of this check might be a bit different from what you would have expected. You might have thought that you want to check the argument, therefore send a message to the argument. Something like: `aSymbol areYouASymbol ifTrue:` and so on. But as that object can be anything, this check can become quite complicated, like "if it is a string, do this", "if it is a symbol, do that", "if it is a number, do something else again". But we know what we want to check the object against, so why not turn it round, and send the unknown object to something that we know. That is what we do here; we create an array with the allowed values, and ask if the unknown parameter is a member of the array. If not, we raise an error, otherwise we just continue processing.

To make sure that a driver always has a gender, we create an instance initialize method:

```
Driver>>initialize
    "Initialize the receiver"
    super initialize.
    self gender: #Male.
```

4.3.2 *Presenting 1-of-n variables*

Now that we know what we store in the "gender" instance variable of Driver instances, we can move on to presenting it.

One-of-n variables can be presented in a number of different ways:

- A drop-down listbox showing the choices. The user can make a selection from these choices and when the form is opened on an existing instance the right value can be shown as the current selection. This type of presentation is typically used if the list to choose from is dynamic or relatively large.
- If the number of choices is limited to four or less, you most often see the radio button group.

As we have a choice between two (male and female), the radio button sounds like the most appropriate. There is one less-used alternative that is worth mentioning here, which is the tab strip presented as buttons. That presenter shows a number of buttons, of which only one can be or even has to be pressed.

4.3.3 *Radio buttons*

Before we look into how to implement the radio buttons in our Driver model, presenter, and view, we are first going to play around a bit with radio buttons on a test form so that we know how these buttons work.

The working of radio buttons.

Testing the radio button behavior   Open the view composer from the Tools menu (not from a presenter class). Create a new shell view (File – New Shell View), drag two radio buttons (BooleanPresenter.Radio Button) onto the form and press F5 to test it. As you can see (Figure 4.6), when you press one of them, the other switches off.

This demonstrates that the radio buttons know about each other. This is not controlled by Dolphin Smalltalk, but by the Win32 controls.

If you need multiple groups of radio buttons, you need a way to separate them, otherwise setting one of the radio buttons in one group would impact the setting of the radio buttons in another group. Normally, you see that separation done with group boxes around the radio buttons. They

Figure 4.6

Radio button test

Figure 4.7
Radio button groups

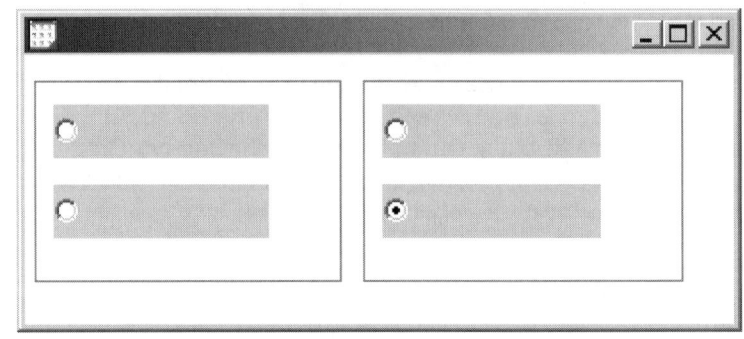

are not only used to separate the groups, they can also be used as shortcuts. Let's see what we can do with those group boxes.

Start a new form and drag two group boxes (GroupBox.Static group box) onto the form. Drag two radio buttons into both those group boxes and test again (Figure 4.7).

To our surprise, all four radio buttons still act as a single group. So the so-called group boxes are of no help; at least, not for grouping. As you can see in the view hierarchy, all the items are on the same level, so there is no distinction. What we want is to separate the two groups. We can do that by putting them on different shells within the same form.

Start a new form and drag two CompositePresenter.Default views onto your test form. These are shown as container views in the view hierarchy. Make sure that you do not drop the second container in the first one. You can recognize that when the sizing corners of the first container change color. If you drop the second in the first, then the second becomes a child of the first, but we want them both to be children of the main view. Now drag a group box and two radio buttons onto each container view. Test the view: now you can have two buttons switched on, as long as they are in different containers.

Now give the frames and buttons a caption; set the Text aspect of one frame to "&Color" and its buttons to "&Red" and "&Blue", and set the Text aspect of the other frame to "&Shape", with the radio buttons to "Circle" and "Square" (Figure 4.8).

Test the frame and try to use the tab and the shortcuts. They don't work! The radio buttons have their aspect "isTabStop" set to true, so that can't be it. Have a look at the container views. Set their "isGroupStop" to true. Now it works – at least partly. You can get to the Red and Blue via the shortcut and as soon as one of the group is selected, you can get to that group via the group shortcut and via the tab. That is one of the reasons why you should always initialize the underlying variable in the model, so that one of the group is set when you open the window.

A simple layout manager If you are using containers in the way described above, then you typically don't want the burden of having to

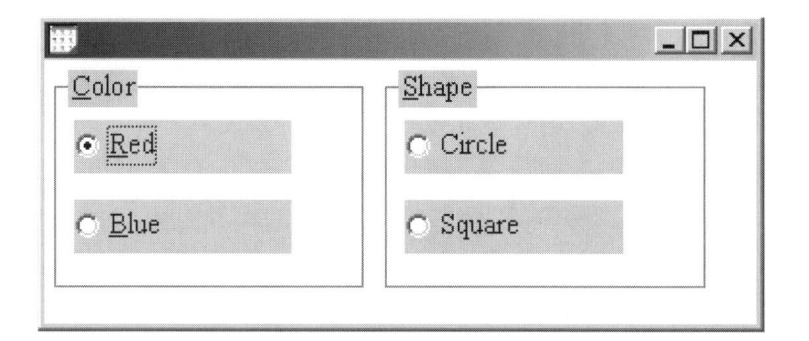

Figure 4.8
Radio button shortcuts

resize all the individual parts separately, especially resizing the group box when you resize the container. We can use a layout manager to do the work for us here. The layout managers have a wider use than we are describing here, but we'll come back to that in later sections (see Section 9.1.3).

To use a layout manager, select the container and double-click on the layoutManager aspect. This opens a dialog box with the different layout managers that can be used on the selected container (Figure 4.9). As we just want the group box to be "glued" against the borders of the container, the BorderLayout manager is the most appropriate here.

When you select the manager and close the dialog, you will see that the aspect is extended with a level below it. Depending on the type of layout manager, you can set a number of aspects. In the case of the BorderLayout manager, you can set the horizontal and vertical gap. That is, the gap between the border of the container and the views contained within it. In our case we want the group box right on the borders, so we leave the gaps set to 0.

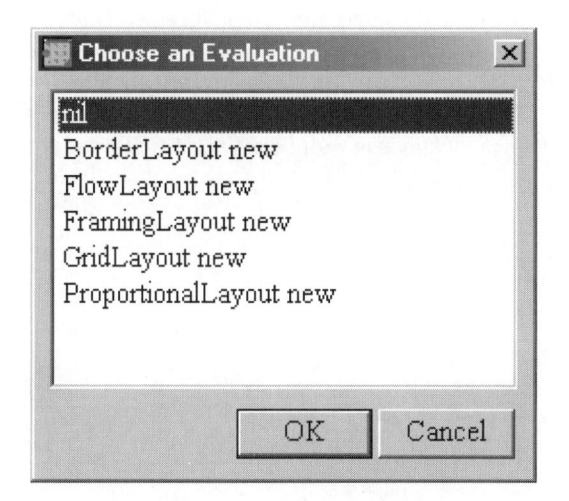

Figure 4.9
Layout manager dialog

Figure 4.10

Arrangement aspect for BorderLayout manager

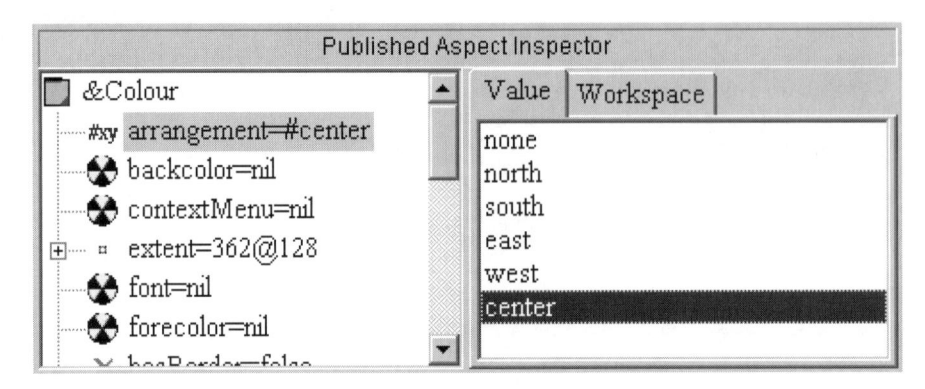

Now select the group box. You will notice that the list of aspects is extended with the "arrangement" aspect (Figure 4.10).

If you select that aspect you will see the list of allowed values, the possible arrangements within this type of layout manager. Using one of the compass directions will glue the view to that border of the container, and center tries to glue it to all the borders, size of the view permitting. This is exactly what we want here, therefore we set the aspect to center. You can see that the group box changes size to fit exactly in the container. If you now try to change the extent of the group box, you won't be able to, as it is controlled by the layout manager. Now select the container and change the size. You'll see that the size of the group box automatically changes as well.

We don't have to change the arrangement aspect of the radio buttons, as we don't want to glue them to any border. Even worse, if you use the layout manager on one of the radio buttons, it will try to rearrange the group box as well.

Radio buttons on the Driver dialog As you can see in the resource toolbox, the radio button is a boolean presenter. This means that it can only show a true/false value of its variable. Therefore we have to create methods that allow them to talk boolean with the model. We can do that by creating methods which answer "true" or "false" to a message like #isMale and #isFemale. In the same way we can set the gender; if the Driver instance receives the message #isMale: true, then the gender variable should be set to #Male.

```
Driver>>isFemale
    "Return true if gender is female, otherwise return
    false"
    ^gender == #Female

Driver>>isMale
    "Return true if gender is male, otherwise return
    false"
    ^gender == #Male
```

```
Driver>>isFemale: aBoolean
    "Set gender to female if boolean is true"
    aBoolean ifTrue: [self gender: #Female]

Driver>>isMale: aBoolean
    "Set gender to male if boolean is true"
    aBoolean ifTrue: [self gender: #Male]
```

Now that we have these getters and setters, we can let the presenter just think that we have a separate isMale variable and a separate isFemale variable, each of which has its own boolean presenter. The class definition should now look like this:

```
Dialog subclass: #DriverDialogPresenter
    instanceVariableNames: 'firstnamePresenter
    surnamePresenter namePresenter nationalityPresenter
    dateOfBirthPresenter agePresenter malePresenter
    femalePresenter commentPresenter'
    classVariableNames: ''
    poolDictionaries: ''
```

In the #model: method we link these presenters to the quasi variables:

```
DriverDialogPresenter>>model: aDriver
    "Create the link between the model and the presenter
    via a buffer"
    ...
    malePresenter model: (aspectBuffer aspectValue:
        #isMale).
    femalePresenter model: (aspectBuffer aspectValue:
        #isFemale).
```

The #createComponents method has to be extended for the new presenters:

```
DriverDialogPresenter>>createComponents
    ...
    malePresenter := self add: BooleanPresenter new name:
        'male'.
    femalePresenter := self add: BooleanPresenter new
        name: 'female'.
```

We can now add this to the view. Select the DriverDialogPresenter class and select Edit view from the context manager to open the view composer with the Driver dialog that we've built so far. We are going to modify it so that it will look like Figure 4.11.

First make the form a bit bigger, so that we have room to move our fields around (`self extent: 600@600`). Now select all the fields below

Figure 4.11
Radio buttons on the Driver dialog

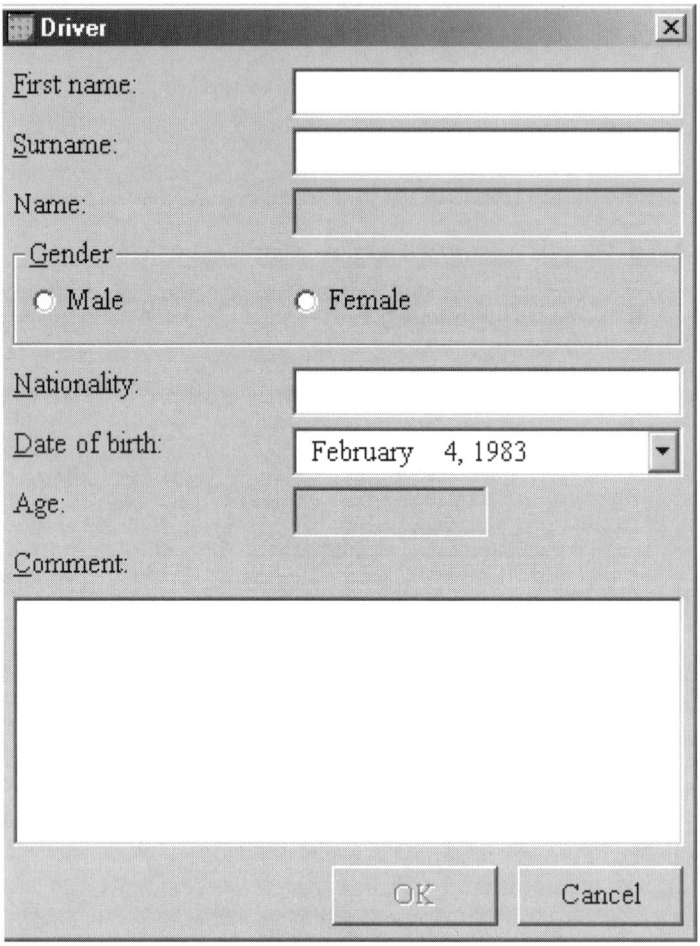

name and move them down so that we have a gap of about 100 pixels between the name and the origin.

> Note that you can move all the fields in one go by selecting them while holding down the Ctrl button, then pick up the last selected field and drag it to the new location.

Drag a container (CompositePresenter.Default view) from the toolbox onto the free space at the right of the dialog. Drag a group box (GroupBox.Static group box) and two radio buttons (BooleanPresenter. Radio button) onto the container. Make sure that they are really dragged onto the container. You can check this through the view hierarchy, where they should show up within the container. If not, you can move them

Table 4.4

Aspects of the Driver dialog fields

Aspect	Container	Group box	Male	Female
Name			Male	female
Text		&Gender	Male	Female
Position	5@95		10@20	145@20
Extent	345@55		85@25	85@25
isGroupStop	true	false	false	false
isTabStop	false	false	true	true

around in the view container by selecting it in the view hierarchy and dragging it in the container. Now change the layoutManager aspect of the container to be a BorderLayout. Change the arrangement aspect of the group box to "center". See Table 4.4 for the other aspects of these fields. Also make sure that the sequence of fields is as shown in the table (first the group box and then the radio buttons).

Move the fields below the group box back so that the origin label has position 5@160, and change the tab sequence so that the container is in between the name text field and the origin label. Finally, change the size of the form to 360@470.

Now test it on one of your temporary variables in your workspace. Create a new driver. As you will see, the gender is male by default. Change it into female, OK the dialog and inspect the variable. It should show the value #Female.

```
driver2 := Driver new.
DriverDialogPresenter showOn: driver2.
driver2 inspect.
```

In the next section we will investigate some alternatives to the radio buttons.

4.3.4 *List presenters*

In the introduction to this section we mentioned a number of alternative presenters to select the gender. We came up with radio buttons as the number of possible genders is limited. If we have a large number of possible answers to select from, we usually present the user with a list of choices, either via a drop-down box or via a list in which the user can make his or her selection. One of the benefits of list presenters is that you can dynamically create or modify the list while the view is open. Doing something like that with radio buttons (other than enabling/disabling them) would quite likely look confusing to the user.

As we are talking about a list presenter for the gender, we have to have a list presenter variable available in our presenter class. But in our model

How to use list presenters, the sequence of events when showing a view, and how to make use of that.

class we have the gender variable storing a symbol. So we can't link these two directly. The solution to this is to create a list presenter on a local list, and communicate the selection in the list to the model, as in Figure 4.12. The genderListPresenter shows the items from the ListModel. When the user selects one of the items from the ListModel, the gender instance variable in the Driver instance is updated with that symbol.

We start by creating the instance variable for the list presenter by adding genderListPresenter to the instance variables of the class definition.

```
Dialog subclass: #DriverDialogPresenter
     instanceVariableNames: 'firstnamePresenter
     surnamePresenter namePresenter nationalityPresenter
     dateOfBirthPresenter agePresenter genderListPresenter
     malePresenter femalePresenter commentPresenter'
     classVariableNames: ''
     poolDictionaries: ''
```

The method #createComponents has to be extended for the new presenter:

DriverDialogPresenter>>createComponents
```
     ...
     genderListPresenter := self add: ListPresenter new
          name: 'genderList'.
```

As we are using symbols as the values in the gender variable, we can use these same symbols to show in the list. We create the list in the #model: method as an array of symbols. If we had to translate our application into other languages, we couldn't take this approach as the symbols will literally be the elements in our list, but for now this will do.

DriverDialogPresenter>>model: aDriver
```
     "Create the link between the model and the presenter
     via a buffer"
     ...
     genderListPresenter model: (ListModel on: #(#Male
          #Female)).
```

Figure 4.12
The ListModel supporting the gender presenter

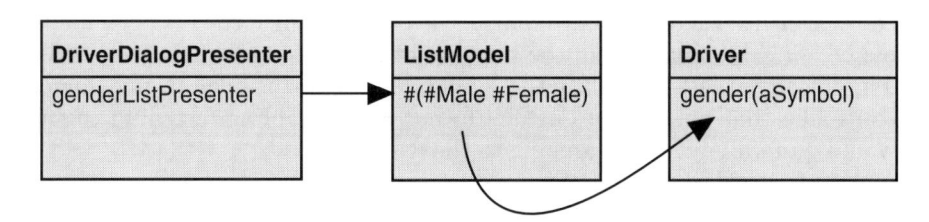

Now we have to create a wiring so that the model is informed when we change the selection. We do that with a line in #createSchematicWiring that triggers the change of selection in the list. This line calls another method which then communicates the change to the model.

```
DriverDialogPresenter>>createSchematicWiring
    "Create the trigger wiring"
    super createSchematicWiring.
    ...
    genderListPresenter when: #selectionChanged
        send: #genderSelectionChanged to: self.

DriverDialogPresenter>>genderSelectionChanged
    "The selection in the gender listbox changed,
    communicate that to the model"
    self model gender: genderListPresenter selection.
```

Here you see that the gender is set to the symbol that we selected in the list. We make convenient use of the fact that Symbol is a subclass of String, as the list can only display strings. This saves us from having to convert the selection into something else.

There is one more thing that we have to do, and that is to show the current gender of the model. If we open a female driver, then we want the "Female" line to be selected. This is similar to #genderSelectionChanged, but the other way round.

```
DriverDialogPresenter>>setGenderListSelection
    "Set the initial gender selected"
    genderListPresenter selection: self model gender.
```

The only problem is, when do we call this method? So far we just added these kinds of messages to the #model: method. But this is not always the right place, as certain things might not yet have been created, which is the case here. You can't set a selection in a list if the list doesn't exist yet. To decide on where we can set it, we will first have a look at the sequence in which Dolphin Smalltalk opens a window. Table 4.5 shows a slightly simplified picture of what is going on.

In this table you can see that if we try to set the selection by calling it in the #model method as we've done so far, we try to do something on a view that doesn't exist yet. Based on this schema it looks like we could use #createSchematicWiring, as that is called after creating the views. That indeed works, but #createSchematicWiring is called whenever something changes, so it is meant for triggers and not for initialization. Both #onViewOpened and #onViewAvailable sound like good candidates, as we have the view available by the time that these are called. Either of these will work, but the latter is really meant to do dynamic changes to aspects of views, not so much for setting initial selections.

Table 4.5

Sequence in which Dolphin Smalltalk opens a window

Method	Description
Presenter class » showOn:	One of the many invocation methods to open a view.
Presenter class » new	Here an instance of the presenter class is created.
Presenter » initialize	Any initialization can be set here.
Presenter » createComponents	This is where the subpresenters are created.
Presenter » model:	Here you connect the model to the subpresenters.
Presenter » createView:	This method creates the view by calling the method Presenter class » #loadViewResource:inContext:.
Presenter » view:	This method lets each subpresenter know which is its subview.
Presenter » onViewAvailable	This allows you to modify aspects of subviews before opening the view. The presenter knows about the view, but the view itself is not yet connected.
Presenter » connectView	Here the view is connected to the presenter and to the model. When the view connects to the model (through the View » #model: method), the View » #onModelChanged method is triggered.
Presenter » onViewOpened	This is a trigger that allows you to insert methods that you want to run immediately before the view opens. It already exists in memory, but it is not yet drawn.
Presenter » createSchematicwiring	This is where you connect the trigger wiring to the view.
View » onViewOpened	This triggers the Presenter » #viewOpened.
Presenter » updateCaption	Set the caption when the view opens.
Presenter » setInitialFocus	Set the cursor when the view opens.
View » show	And finally, this makes the view visible.

Therefore we add an #onViewOpened method to our DriverDialog-Presenter class, overriding the Presenter » onViewOpened method. As we don't want to lose any of the superclass's method, we start by calling the super method:

DriverDialogPresenter>>onViewOpened
```
"Make the model's gender the currently selected one"
super onViewOpened.
self setGenderListSelection.
```

THE DRIVER COMPONENT

Now we can create a view to show the gender through a list presenter. Select the class in the CHB and select "New view" from the context menu. This will open a copy of the existing view that we are going to modify. Delete the container with the radio buttons in it, and replace it with a Static text: "&Gender" and a ListPresenter: Default view. Set the "name" aspect to "genderList", save the view as "Listbox view" and test it with the following line in the workspace, assuming that you still have the driver2 variable available from the previous section (Test view won't give you much, as that doesn't initialize the list):

```
DriverDialogPresenter show: 'Listbox view' on: driver2
```

As you can see, you've just created a fully functional view with a completely different selection method for the gender. It should now look like Figure 4.13.

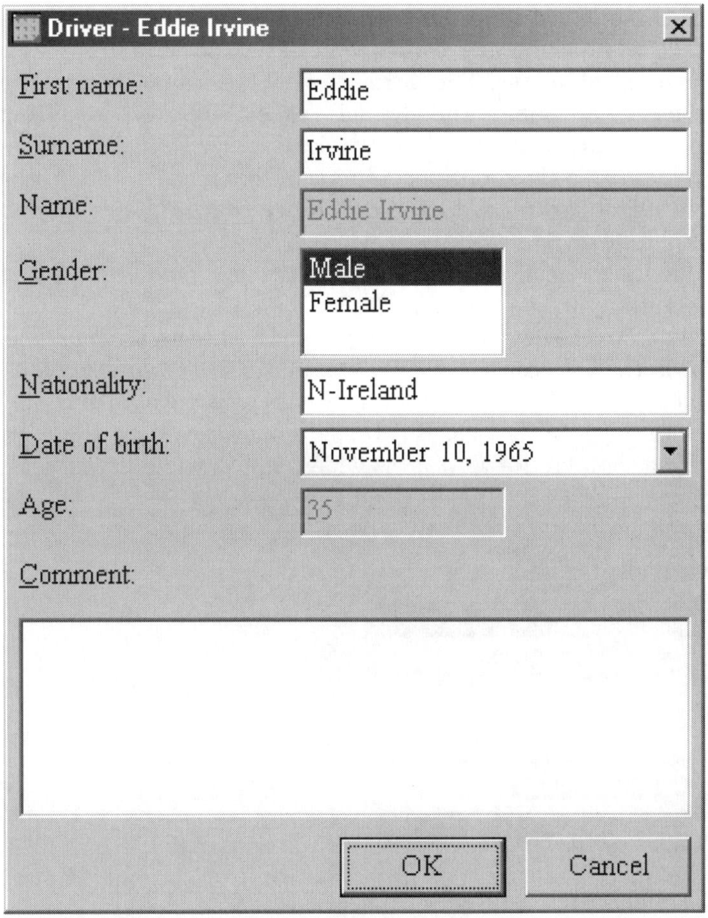

Figure 4.13
The Driver dialog with a list

Create a female driver and check if you can change the gender. Close the dialog with "OK" and reopen on the same driver. It should now open with "Female" selected.

Now let's try some other list views. Go into the view composer, select the list box and select "Mutate view" from the context menu. Here you see a list of views in which you can change the view. Most of them are of no use as they require a different presenter in the #createSchematicWiring method, but if we know the views to which we can mutate, this is quite a handy option. Select ComboBox from the list. Save the view and test it (don't worry about repositioning; we would do that in a finalized view, but we're not yet finished with testing).

As you can see, this simple mutate works quite well (Figure 4.14). There's just one thing that we don't like, and that is that we can enter other values in the list; try, for example, "Neuter". The combo box can be a confusing presenter; it can present items from a list, but return a string instead of the selection index (that is, if you enter text instead of making a selection from the list). As we only look at the selection index, our model will just ignore the entered text. The combo can work in two different ways, as a drop-down allowing new values to be entered or as a drop-down with a predefined list of values. The latter is what we want. To use it in that way, we have to change the "mode" aspect in the view from "dropDown" into "dropDownList". Now it works like we want it to.

The mode aspect has a third option: "simple". This mode works in the same way as the "dropDown", with the difference that it shows the list permanently (Figure 4.15).

The user can make a selection from the list, which is copied into the text box, or enter something in the text box directly.

The last view option that we want to show here is quite an unusual one, but usable in this case. Select the combo box and select "Mutate view". Select TabView in the list. This might sound strange, as you would normally associate complete pages with tabs. But be patient; we will see that this doesn't look too bad. Make the view a bit wider, say as wide as the fields

Figure 4.14
The Gender drop-down presenter

Figure 4.15
The combo box in simple mode

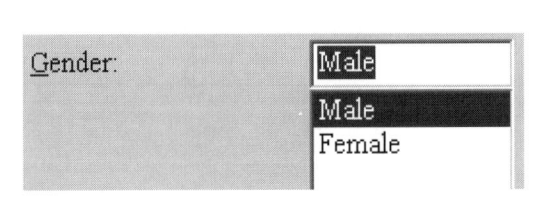

Figure 4.16
The tab buttons

above. Save the view and open it. It looks as you would expect, with two tabs on a strip (Figure 4.16). Still, it works. You would typically use this view when you have a form that shows multiple instances of the same data. Here that is not the case, so we go back to our view composer and change the "hasButtons" aspect to "true" and the "hasClientEdge" aspect to "false". Change the extent into 200@30 for the right look. It makes a difference!

4.3.5 Summary

In this section we have investigated how to deal with 1-of-n variables and how to present them. We've introduced the Symbol class as a kind of String with the benefit of uniqueness. To present the 1-of-n variables we looked into the radio buttons and the different types of ListPresenters. While looking into the radio buttons, we dealt with grouping them using container views and we introduced the LayoutManager to automatically resize the GroupBox with the Container. For the ListPresenters we had to set up some event triggering, like we did in the previous chapter. To set the initial selection we looked into the sequence of events when opening a window.

4.4 Some loose ends

In the following sections we will add some niceties to the Driver dialog. We will start with a default caption that is dynamically set and after that we will add a picture to the Driver.

4.4.1 The caption

Wouldn't it be nice if we could see on the caption whether we are modifying an existing driver or creating a new one? The usual caption for something new is "Application name – New". And when you open an existing object you see "Application name – Object name". That shouldn't be too difficult to build. The most important question is again – when do we set the caption? As we have seen in Section 4.3.4, we have a lot of possibilities. But we have to be sure that we can already send messages to the view, as that is the holder of the caption. So why not set it

How to set the caption dynamically and how to show the current object in the caption.

immediately before the view is opened; #onViewOpened. We could of course write the code in the #onViewOpened method itself, but that makes it a bit harder to find, therefore we make a separate method #setCaption and call that method from #onViewOpened. As Alec Sharp writes in his book *Smalltalk by Example* (Sharp, 1997): "Let a method do only one thing". Therefore, we use #onViewOpened as a caller of other methods, and write the code in the other methods, even if they are only one-liners.

```
DriverDialogPresenter>>setCaption
    "Set the view's caption"
    | text |
    text := namePresenter value isEmpty
        ifTrue: ['New']
        ifFalse: [namePresenter value].
    self caption: 'Driver - ', text.
```

```
DriverDialogPresenter>>onViewOpened
    "Set the caption and the current gender selection"
    super onViewOpened.
    self setGenderListSelection.
    self setCaption.
```

This works nicely for the driver, but what about the team? We don't want to do that same #setCaption method again and again in all our presenters. Therefore we have to place it in a class from where all our presenters can access it. So far we have built two subclasses of the Dialog class, which makes that the main suspect for our #setCaption method. For now that will do; we can always move it up the hierarchy later on if we feel the need. If we had to write the #setCaption method for the TeamDialogPresenter, the only thing that we would have to change is the line where we hard-coded the string "Driver – ", therefore, we have to make that variable. We can do that by adding the following method.

```
DriverDialogPresenter>>captionSubstring
    "Return the class-specific substring for the caption"
    ^'Driver - '
```

The other problem with moving it up the class hierarchy is that it relies on the namePresenter instance variable. We don't want to move that up the hierarchy as well, so we have to change our #setCaption method so that it asks the instance for its name instead of just reading the instance variable. As the namePresenter is just a wrapper around the model's name, we can just as well ask whether the model's name is empty or not. The new #setCaption now looks like this.

```
DriverDialogPresenter>>setCaption
    "Set the view's caption"
    | text |
    text := self model name isEmpty
            ifTrue: ['New']
            ifFalse: [self model name].
    self caption: self captionSubString, text.
```

After testing that everything still works, we can move the method to the Dialog class. You can do that by selecting it in the method list and dropping it onto the class where you want it to be. You still have to delete the original method, otherwise you would override the superclass's definition with exactly the same. Don't forget to change the package for the Dialog ≫ setCaption method to your base extensions package, otherwise it is owned by the Dolphin package.

Now we can add the necessary modifications to the Team class so that it can make use of the same method.

```
TeamDialogPresenter>>onViewOpened
    "Set the caption"
    super onViewOpened.
    self setCaption.
```

```
TeamDialogPresenter>>captionSubstring
    "Return the class-specific substring for the caption"
    ^'Team - '
```

We could have chosen to modify the caption while changing the name (can you see how?) but as we are working with dialogs, we don't really want to do that, as the user can still cancel the changes.

4.4.2 A picture paints a thousand words

Modern user interfaces are able to integrate all kinds of objects and display them, so we should be able to display a picture of the driver. First we have to have those pictures available, of course. With the Web that shouldn't be too big a problem: find a Web site with pictures of race drivers and select the picture of your preference (have a look at the following Web site, for example (thanks to Emma Louise Crawley): http://www.excalvehs.demon.co.uk/eddie.htm). Choose "Save picture as" from the context menu and save it in the directory where you store the FormulaOne package. Now we want that picture to appear in the Driver dialog as shown in Figure 4.17.

How to call the standard Windows file selector, how to link a picture to an object and display it.

Dolphin Smalltalk is able to handle all kinds of pictures, images, and icons. To see what the possibilities are, browse through the Image class and its subclasses.

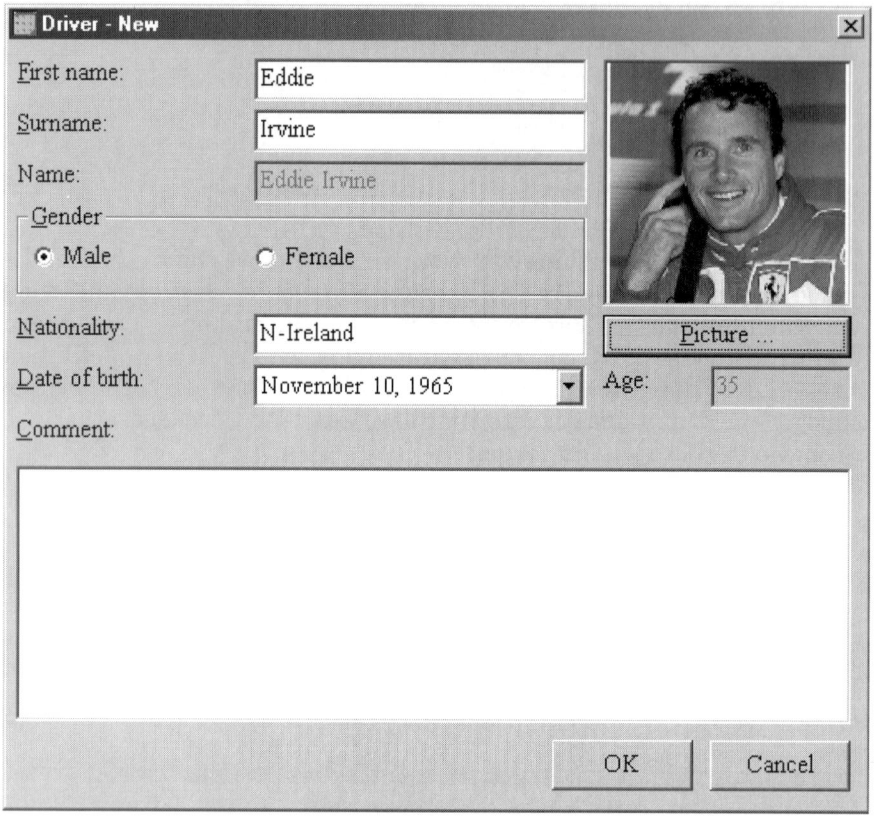

Figure 4.17
Driver dialog with picture

Looking at the comment on the OLEPicture class, that is exactly what we need. We have an OLE picture (GIF, JPG), and we want to link that to our Driver object.

Starting with the model, we have to extend it with a variable to hold the picture. That variable needs to have the standard accessors.

```
RacingActor subclass: #Driver
    instanceVariableNames: 'firstname surname nationality
    dateOfBirth gender picture'
    classVariableNames: ''
    poolDictionaries: ''
```
Driver>>picture
```
    ^picture
```

Driver>>picture: anObject
```
    picture := anObject
```

That's all we have to do in the model. The presenter has to be extended with a presenter for the picture, which means an instance variable, a line in #model: and a line in #createComponents.

```
Dialog subclass: #DriverDialogPresenter
    instanceVariableNames: 'firstnamePresenter
    surnamePresenter namePresenter nationalityPresenter
    dateOfBirthPresenter agePresenter genderListPresenter
    malePresenter femalePresenter commentPresenter
    picturePresenter'
    classVariableNames: ''
    poolDictionaries: ''

DriverDialogPresenter>>createComponents
    "Create the view components"
    ...
    picturePresenter := self add: ImagePresenter new name:
        'picture'.

DriverDialogPresenter>>model: aDriver
    "Create the link between the model and the presenter
    via a buffer"
    ...
    picturePresenter model: (aspectBuffer aspectValue:
        #picture).
    ...
```

Apart from using the ImagePresenter, nothing new so far. Now we have to find a way to select a picture from a file, which we then link to our model variable. One of the easiest ways to do that is to have a button underneath the place for the picture which opens a "file select" window. When the user selects a file of the right type, the class OLEPicture creates a handle to the picture and the image presenter can display it.

```
DriverDialogPresenter>>getPicture
    "Open a file select dialog to select a picture and
    associate it with the appropriate variable"
    | file |
    file := FileOpenDialog new
        fileTypes: #(('Pictures' '*.gif;*.jpg')
        ('Bitmaps' '*.bmp'));
        showModal.
    file notNil ifTrue: [
        picturePresenter value: (OLEPicture fromFile:
            file)
        ].
```

The only thing that remains is to modify the view. We add an ImagePresenter(Basic Image) and a button to the view and modify some aspects according to Table 4.6. First, change the width of the dialog so that we can place a picture next to the name fields.

Table 4.6

Aspects of the Picture field and button

Aspect	ImageView	Button
name	Picture	
command		#getPicture
text		&Picture ...
position	360@10	360@160
extent	150@145	150@25
hasBorder	False	
hasClientEdge	True	
viewMode	ScaleToFit	
backColor	white (255, 255, 255)	

I made the background of the picture white, so that if you have a picture that doesn't exactly fit, it will show a white background. Try the other view modes as well; the #scale option can be quite funny when you have a picture with a different ratio from the frame.

4.4.3 Summary

In the preceding subsections we have seen how we can dynamically create and set the caption of a view, how we can refactor it so that common code can be reused, and we have learned how we can link pictures to our instances and show them in our views. As part of that, we've seen how we can make use of standard file selectors.

The Season component 5

Many aspects in sport are season related. Most teams come with new cars each season. Based on the results of the previous season, the starting numbers on the cars change for the new season, and quite regularly drivers swap teams as well. Therefore we will build the Season component as our next step.

What do we need for a season? Do we need more than a name? Well, I can't remember the scoring definition being changed in Formula One, but if the Federation Internationale de l'Automobile (FIA) decides to change it, it would be for a new season. And as we want the model to be able to cater for future changes, we will make the scoring structure part of the season.

While we build the Season component, we will have a closer look at collections and how we can present them.

5.1 The Season model

The class definition of the Season class is straightforward; we subclass it from the Model class to be able to make use of the MPV framework. We give it two instance variables, one to store the name of the season and one to store the score definition.

Our first dealings with collections, how to set up sort blocks and how to select by index.

```
Model subclass: #Season
      instanceVariableNames: 'name scoreDefinition'
      classVariableNames: ''
      poolDictionaries: ''
```

Via the by-now-familiar menu option we create the standard accessors for the name variable.

Season>>name
```
      ^name
```

Season>>name: anObject
```
      name := anObject
```

The scoreDefinition needs to be treated in a different way, as that is going to be a collection of points. As collections are one of the most used classes in Smalltalk, we will discuss the different types and how to choose between them in a bit more detail first.

5.1.1 *The Collection classes*

The Collection classes are probably the most frequently used of all classes within Smalltalk, and not just because String is a subclass of Collection as well. The main reason is that they are so flexible, you can use them for almost anything. Within different dialects of Smalltalk you will find slight differences between subclasses, but the main classes should all be there and have the same characteristics.

The **Bag** can be compared with a shopping bag, you can throw anything in it you like. You can have duplicates in a bag. In the Dolphin implementation duplicates aren't really stored as two members in the bag; each member has a counter associated with it and if you try to add a duplicate, the counter is incremented. As the members are stored in random order, you can only retrieve the members by walking through the whole bag.

The **Set** is similar to the Bag, with the difference that the Set doesn't allow duplicates. So if you want to remove duplicates from a bag, you just send it the message #asSet. It really is that simple.

If you've done programming before, it is quite likely that you've come across the **Array**. We've used the Array a couple of times already in examples. The Array keeps its members neatly in order, and you can insert members in specific slots. The Array has one big disadvantage: when you want to add a member that requires the Array to grow, the whole Array is copied into a new Array of the bigger size. So if you want to add a couple of thousand members to an Array and you do it one by one, the Array is copied thousands of times. Usage of the Array is very efficient apart from that, so if you know how many members you want to add, then create an Array of the right size (for example, Array new: 1000).

The **OrderedCollection** has (almost) all the advantages of the Array, but not the disadvantage in that the OrderedCollection can grow dynamically. This makes the OrderedCollection one of the most widely used collections. Because it grows dynamically, you cannot have "empty slots". We will see an example of the importance of this later in this book (Section 6.1.2).

The **SortedCollection** is a sorted OrderedCollection. It has most of the advantages of the OrderedCollection, but it adds members in the right sort order. This means that after adding and removing members the whole collection will be resorted, which can be quite inefficient on larger collections. It is therefore often better to maintain the members in an OrderedCollection and sort them when you need it by sending the Ordered-Collection the message #asSortedCollection or #asSortedCollection: with a specific sort block. In Section 8.3 we will discuss sorting more comprehensively.

The **Dictionary** is a special Set with its own protocol, as it stores key-value associations. The keys have to be unique within the dictionary, while the values can occur in multiple key-value associations. Values can be retrieved through the key and keys can be retrieved through values. The

Smalltalk system itself makes widespread use of the dictionary, as all the methods are stored in dictionaries. The method name is the key, the method itself is the value. The Dictionary has some very useful subclasses, see Section 6.1.2 where we discuss the LookupTable and the IdentityDictionary. A special dictionary is the PoolDictionary. This is a dictionary that is associated with one or more classes. The information within that dictionary is accessible to all objects of those classes. Typical use of the PoolDictionary is the definition of constants.

Based on the above description of the main collections we can create a decision table (Figure 5.1), which will help us choose the right collection. Note that the Dictionary is left out of this decision table, as its use is quite different from the other main collections.

Most of the collections have the same protocol; they understand the same messages. In Table 5.1 I've summarized some of the most frequently used messages for the main collections. The first column shows the message, and in the other columns you see what the collection returns. If it is not implemented for that type of collection, I put a × in the cell.

The first group of messages is to retrieve elements. The second group are the so-called discriminators, which check every element to see if they have to do something with them. The third group is the operational group; these messages send a message to every member of the collection.

At the back of the book you will find this table and the decision table printed on a tear-out page, so that you can take it out and always have it to hand.

Try the following examples with DisplayIt. Make sure that the system transcript is visible.

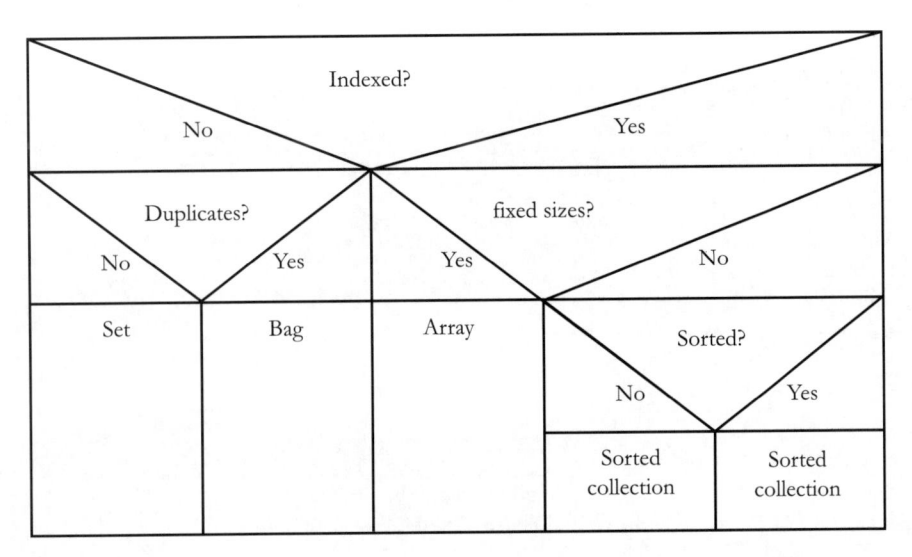

Figure 5.1

Collection decision table

THE DOLPHIN SMALLTALK COMPANION

Table 5.1

The most frequently used messages for the main collections

Message	Set	Bag	Array	OC/SC
#at: index	✗	✗	element	element
#find: element	element	✗	✗	✗
#includes: element	boolean	boolean	boolean	boolean
Discriminators	[each	(each at: 1) # $D]		
#findFirst: discriminator #findLast: discriminator	✗	✗	index	index
#detect: discriminator	element	element	element	element
#select: discriminator #reject: discriminator	new set	new bag	new array	new oc/sc
Operational	[:each	Transcript cr; show: each, 'book']		
#do: operation	itself	itself	itself	itself
#collect: operation	new set	new bag	new array	new oc/sc
#inject: initialValue into: operation	result value	result value	result value	result value

```
array := # ('Smalltalk' 'Dolphin' 'User' 'Interface'
     'Dolphin').
set := array asSet.
bag := array asBag.
oc := array asOrderedCollection.
sc := array asSortedCollection.

array at: 2
oc at: 2
sc at: 2

set find: 'Dolphin'

set includes: 'Dolphin'
bag includes: 'Dolphin'
array includes: 'Dolphin'
oc includes: 'Dolphin'
sc includes: 'Dolphin'

array findFirst: [ :each | (each at: 1) = $D ]
oc findFirst: [ :each | (each at: 1) = $D ]
sc findFirst: [ :each | (each at: 1) = $D ]
```

```
set detect: [ :each | (each at: 1) = $D ]
bag detect: [ :each | (each at: 1) = $D ]
array detect: [ :each | (each at: 1) = $D ]
oc detect: [ :each | (each at: 1) = $D ]
sc detect: [ :each | (each at: 1) = $D ]

set select: [ :each | (each at: 1) = $D ]
bag select: [ :each | (each at: 1) = $D ]
array select: [ :each | (each at: 1) = $D ]
oc select: [ :each | (each at: 1) = $D ]
sc select: [ :each | (each at: 1) = $D ]

array do: [ :each | Transcript cr; show: each, 'book' ]
set do: [ :each | Transcript cr; show: each, 'book' ]
bag do: [ :each | Transcript cr; show: each, 'book' ]
oc do: [ :each | Transcript cr; show: each, 'book' ]
sc do: [ :each | Transcript cr; show: each, 'book' ]

array collect: [ :each | each, 'book' ]
set collect: [ :each | each, 'book' ]
bag collect: [ :each | each, 'book' ]
oc collect: [ :each | each, 'book' ]
sc collect: [ :each | each, 'book' ]

set inject: 'Book on' into: [ :inj :elm | inj, ' ', elm ]
bag inject: 'Book on' into: [ :inj :elm | inj, ' ', elm ]
array inject: 'Book on' into: [ :inj :elm | inj, ' ', elm ]
oc inject: 'Book on' into: [ :inj :elm | inj, ' ', elm ]
sc inject: 'Book on' into: [ :inj :elm | inj, ' ', elm ]
```

Strangely enough you don't see #inject:into: used very often. You have to get used to it, but then you will find it very useful. The example most often used for #inject:into: is creating the total value of a collection of elements. But you can also find the minimum value or the greatest common divisor with it:

```
array := #(6 9 15 12 21).
array inject: (array at: 1) into: [ :init :each | init gcd:
     each ].
```

5.1.2 The score definition

After this discussion about the collections, we can use that knowledge to implement the score definition. We want to be able to get the score for a certain position, so if we ask the score for position 1, we want it to return 10 points, for position 2 we want it to return 6 points, and so on up to position 6, whereafter we won't get any points. Based on our decision table, we follow the route for the indexable collection; give me the result for a certain index. If the index is outside the definition, you won't get any points. And as we know that the first will always get the most points, the second a few less and so on, we can even assume that the points form a sorted collection.

Normally a sorted collection sorts from lowest to highest, so we have to change the sort order. We do that by defining a sort block. A sort block reads two elements from the collection at a time and then compares them in the way you define it. The normal comparison is whether the first element is less than or equal to the second element. You can make the comparison not only on the element itself, but also on anything that the element wants to expose of itself. For example, you can sort the drivers of the previous chapter by age, even though we don't store the age as a variable. It is just a matter of sending the appropriate message to the elements that you want to compare. Such a sort block would look something like:

```
[ :first :second | first age <= second age]
```

The block uses two temporary variables which are defined before the vertical bar. After the vertical bar we use those two variables for the comparison. For our point scoring definition the sort block is simpler as we can compare the elements directly. We define the sort block while creating the sorted collection. We have to be sure that the scoreDefinition is a sorted collection, therefore we make it part of the initialize method.

```
Season>>initialize
    "Initialize the variables"
    super initialize.
    scoreDefinition := SortedCollection sortBlock:
        [ :a :b | a >= b ].
```

When we want to retrieve the whole score list, we need a standard getter.

```
Season>>scoreDefinition
    ^scoreDefinition
```

Adding and removing score definitions is now a matter of using the right methods of the collection, and so is finding out the points for a certain result.

```
Season>>addScoreDefinition: aScoreDefinition
    "Add a line to the score definition"
    ^self scoreDefinition add: aScoreDefinition.

Season>>removeScoreDefinition: aScoreDefinition
    "Remove a line from the score definition"
    ^self scoreDefinition remove: aScoreDefinition.
```

```
Season>>pointsFor: aRaceResult
    "Return the points for a race result"
    ^scoreDefinition at: aRaceResult ifAbsent: [0]
```

That is all that we have to do on the model side. Let's see if it works in the way we expect. Create a new season in a workspace:

```
mySeason := Season new.
mySeason name: '2000'.
mySeason addScoreDefinition: 6.
mySeason addScoreDefinition: 3.
mySeason addScoreDefinition: 10.
mySeason addScoreDefinition: 2.
mySeason addScoreDefinition: 1.
mySeason addScoreDefinition: 4.
```

And now inspect it. You will see that the list is neatly sorted. Ask the season how many points you get when you finish in second place:

```
mySeason pointsFor: 2.
```

5.1.3 Summary

In the above subsections we have investigated the collection classes, seen how to choose between them, and looked at their main protocol. We implemented the SortedCollection in our Season model and learned how to sort using sort blocks.

5.2 The name of an object

How to show the name of an object as part of the standard description.

When we inspect an object, we see the class name as its description (for example, "a Season"). But that doesn't say much, especially if you have a whole list of them. Therefore I virtually always have an instance variable "name" in my model classes. But to display that name as the standard description of an object, we have to add something to the #printOn: method. As we only want to apply this to our own Model subclasses, we add a MyModel class in between the Model class and our application subclasses. We have done something similar before in Section 4.1 for the RacingActor.

```
Model subclass: #MyModel
    instanceVariableNames: ''
    classVariableNames: ''
    poolDictionaries: ''
```

Now move the Season and RacingActor classes so that they become subclasses of the MyModel class. By moving the RacingActor class, we automatically move the subclasses Team and Driver.

```
MyModel subclass: #Season
    instanceVariableNames: 'name scoreDefinition'
    classVariableNames: ''
    poolDictionaries: ''

MyModel subclass: #RacingActor
    instanceVariableNames: 'name comment'
    classVariableNames: ''
    poolDictionaries: ''
```

Here you can see that both subclasses have a "name" instance variable, so we can remove it from the subclasses and add it to the MyModel class. Both subclasses also have the standard accessor methods for it, so we can move those to the MyModel class as well. In the RacingActor class we had an #initialize method where we initialized the name as an empty string. Now that we've moved the name to the MyModel class, we can move the #initialize method to the MyModel class as well.

```
Model subclass: #MyModel
    instanceVariableNames: 'name'
    classVariableNames: ''
    poolDictionaries: ''
```

Now we can add this method to the MyModel class:

```
MyModel>>printOn: aStream
    "Override the standard printOn so that the name of the
    object is shown"
    aStream
        basicPrint: self.
    self name isEmpty ifFalse: [
        aStream nextPut: $(;
        display: self name;
        nextPut: $) ].
```

In this way we don't have to add the #printOn: method to every class (like season, team, and so on) and still see something useful when we inspect an object.

5.3 The Season presenter and view

As we are used to working with dialogs by now, we will create the Season presenter in the same way as we did with the Team and the Driver. We know that we don't have to worry about the name and the caption, that's all straightforward by now.

That leaves us with the list. For the driver's gender we have already done some work with a list. We know how to display a list and we know how to detect which line is selected in the list. But in this case we want to be able to add lines to the list and remove them. For adding a line we need to have a so-called postbox, in which we can enter the points, and then a button to add them to the score definition. Based on a selected line and a "remove" button we can delete lines. To start with we will make the dialog look like Figure 5.2.

How to use the ListPresenter as a presenter for collections and how to maintain entries in a collection. Also how to check input and how to control the focus after an event.

5.3.1 *The SeasonDialogPresenter definition*

As before, we have to create a new subclass of the Dialog class, with the field presenters as instance variables.

```
Dialog subclass: #SeasonDialogPresenter
     instanceVariableNames: 'namePresenter
     scoreListPresenter scoreFieldPresenter'
     classVariableNames: ''
     poolDictionaries: ''
```

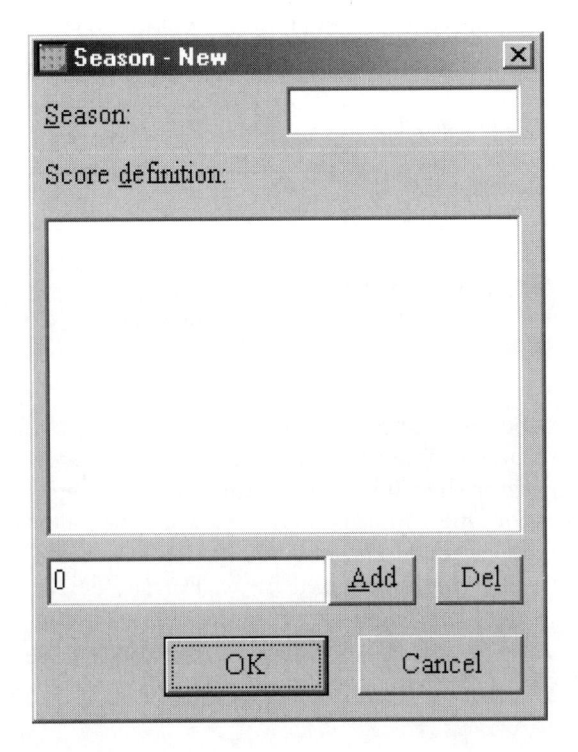

Figure 5.2
The Season dialog

A collection cannot be wrapped in a value model like we have done with the instance variables so far, as collections can contain all kinds of objects. Therefore the list presenter has to communicate directly with the collection.

```
SeasonDialogPresenter>>model: aSeason
    "Create the link between the model and the presenter
    via a buffer"
    | aspectBuffer |
    super model: aSeason.
    aspectBuffer := self model.
    namePresenter model: (aspectBuffer aspectValue:
            #name).
    scoreListPresenter model: (aspectBuffer
            scoreDefinition).

SeasonDialogPresenter>>createComponents
    "Create the view components"
    super createComponents.
    namePresenter := self add: TextPresenter new name:
            "name".
    scoreListPresenter := self add: ListPresenter new
            name: "scoreList".
    scoreFieldPresenter := self add: NumberPresenter new
            name: 'scoreField'.

SeasonDialogPresenter>>onViewOpened
    "Set the caption"
    super onViewOpened.
    self setCaption.

SeasonDialogPresenter>>captionSubstring
    "Return the class specific substring for the caption"
    ^'Season - '
```

In the #addScore and #deleteScore methods we're putting some extra gadgets to make them act a bit better. When we press the add button we want to be sure that a value greater than 0 is added, otherwise it doesn't make sense to add the line. And for "high volume input" we want the focus set back to the postbox after we've added the new entry. We select the default value, so that it can be overridden straight away. For the delete function we don't want to get any errors when we press the delete button while we don't have anything selected, so we check if a score line is selected with the message #selectionOrNil.

```
SeasonDialogPresenter>>addScore
    "Add a score line to the list"
    scoreFieldPresenter value > 0 ifTrue: [
        self model addScoreDefinition:
            scoreFieldPresenter value.
        scoreFieldPresenter value: 0].
    scoreFieldPresenter view selectAll.
    scoreFieldPresenter setFocus.

SeasonDialogPresenter>>deleteScore
    "Remove a score line from the list"
    | line |
    line := scoreListPresenter selectionOrNil.
    line isNil ifFalse: [ self model
            removeScoreDefinition: line ].
```

5.3.2 *The Season view*

As a start we will make a simple Season view which doesn't have anything new in it. Table 5.2 is a table of fields with their appropriate

Aspect	TextPresenter Static text	TextPresenter Static text
Text	&Season:	Score &Definition:
Position	5@10	5@40
Extent	120@25	120@25

Table 5.2
Aspects for the fields on the Season view

Aspect	TextPresenter Default view	ListPresenter Default view	NumberPresenter Integer text
Name	name	scoreList	scoreField
Position	130@5	5@70	5@240
Extent	120@25	245@160	145@25

Aspect	PushButton	PushButton
Command	#addScore	#deleteScore
Text	&Add	De&l
Position	150@240	205@240
Extent	45@25	45@25

aspects. Note that when you create lists it looks a bit silly to show half entries, or to show the scroll bars even if all entries are visible. This can be prevented by making the height of the view a multiple of the height of each individual line. The standard font (Times New Roman 12 pt) requires 20 pixels per line, so making the list 160 pixels allows 8 entries to be shown without any scroll bars. Adding a ninth entry creates a scroll bar and shows either the top entry or the bottom entry in full.

We can now test the view. It looks like it all works as expected. Or does it? Open an existing season and add a silly score line, say 20123. Now cancel the form, and reopen the same season. You will see that the silly score is added, even though we worked with a dialog, and thus with a buffer on the model. Where did it go wrong?

5.3.3 Copy and deepCopy

The difference between #copy and #deepCopy and how to use them in an aspect buffer, and the difference between an elementary object and an object composed of other objects.

We have seen that the link between the model and the presenter is made in the #model: method, and that a Dialog presenter has something in between, namely the aspectBuffer. This aspectBuffer makes a copy of the model and then all the modifications are made on that copy. When you press OK, the changes are copied from the aspectBuffer to the original.

So why does that work for the name, but not for the list? Let's do some testing in a workspace.

```
a := OrderedCollection with: (OrderedCollection with: 1
       with: 2 with: 3) with: 'some text'.
b := a copy.
b inspect.
(a at: 1) add: 4.
a add: 'some more text'.
a inspect.
b inspect.
```

When you inspect b the first time, you will see that it is an exact copy of a, as you would expect. If you then change something in a, you won't see those changes in b. But when you change something in the OrderedCollection held in a, you will see these changes reflected in b as well. This is because the OrderedCollection within a is not really contained, but is pointed at; it is an object in its own right (Figure 5.3). So any changes made to that object are shown, whether you look at that object from within a or from within b.

Now do the same with #deepCopy.

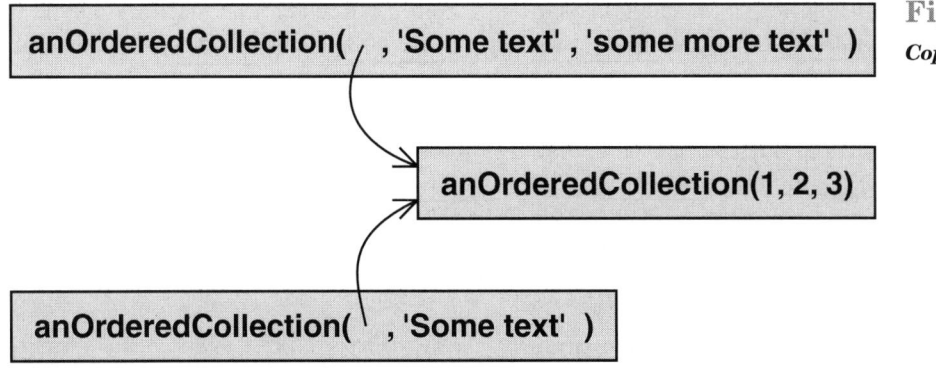

Figure 5.3
Copying collections

```
a := OrderedCollection with: (OrderedCollection with: 1
    with: 2 with: 3) with: 'some text'.
b := a deepCopy.
b inspect.
(a at: 1) add: 4.
a add: 'some more text'.
a inspect.
b inspect.
```

Now you will see that the changes made to the OrderedCollection within a are not shown in b, as b has its own OrderedCollection at the first position.

Going back to our dialog, you will now understand why the changes to the list are communicated directly to the model instead of to the copy in the aspectBuffer. Have a look in the aspectBuffer class; here you can see what is going on when you use the dialog presenters. The #subject: message makes the copy of the model, and #apply puts the values of the individual aspects back in the original model's aspects. And that's exactly where the difficulty lies. You might wonder why the people at Dolphin didn't use #deepCopy in the #subject: message. The reason lies in the fact that you cannot use deepCopy for everything. In some cases you really have to maintain that pointer to the other object as you are not able to make a copy of it. A good example is the picture that we saw in the previous chapter. We can't make a copy of the picture, as we don't know anything about its internals. So for our list we have to come up with a different solution. What we can do is simulate the aspectBuffer situation, by making a local (deep-) copy of the list, making all changes to the local copy, and then writing those changes back to the model. First, we have to have an instance variable to hold the list. Then we need to decide how and especially when we are going to initialize this variable. We possibly need to change our #addScore and #deleteScore messages and finally we need to decide how and when we write the changes back to our main model. The first step is the easiest, just add the variable localScoreList to the class definition.

```
Dialog subclass: #SeasonDialogPresenter
    instanceVariableNames: 'namePresenter localScoreList
    scoreListPresenter scoreFieldPresenter'
    classVariableNames: ''
    poolDictionaries: ''
```

The second step is to decide when we want to make the copy of the original list. Going back to the sequence of events that we saw in the previous chapter, we can't just do it anywhere. For example, we can't do it before the #model: message, as at that point we don't know where to copy the list from. We can't do it after the #model: message either, as we have to connect the scoreListPresenter to this list. So it sounds like the #model: message itself is the best place. To be more precise, we have to copy the list to the local list before we link the presenter to the list, otherwise we link the presenter initially to a variable with nil contents.

```
SeasonDialogPresenter>>model: aSeason
    "Create the link between the model and the presenter
    via a buffer. Copy the scoreDefinition to a local copy
    to handle canceled changes"
    | aspectBuffer |
    super model: aSeason.
    aspectBuffer := self model.
    namePresenter model: (aspectBuffer aspectValue:
        #name).
    localScoreList := ListModel on: (self model
        scoreDefinition deepCopy).
    scoreListPresenter model: localScoreList.
```

Now we have to modify #addScore and #deleteScore so that they communicate with the local list. In our original situation we let the model take care of the deletion. We created #addScoreDefinition: and #removeScoreDefinition: for this. The only thing these messages did was adding to and removing from the collection. Now that we are talking to a list model directly, we have to use the messages that are understood by the ListModel class.

```
SeasonDialogPresenter>>addScore
    "Add the score from the postbox"
    scoreFieldPresenter value > ifTrue: [
        localScoreList add: scoreFieldPresenter value.
        scoreFieldPresenter value: 0].
    scoreFieldPresenter view selectAll.
    scoreFieldPresenter setFocus.

SeasonDialogPresenter>>deleteScore
    "Delete the selected score line"
    | line |
    line := scoreListPresenter selectionOrNil.
    line isNil ifFalse: [
        localScoreList remove: line].
```

We could have written it the first way round in such a way that we wouldn't have had to change it. We can ask the presenter its model. As the model is a ListModel in both cases, we can just say `scoreListPresenter model add:` or `scoreListPresenter model remove:`. Here you can see that most of the time you have many ways to achieve the same thing.

We have seen that when we press OK, the dialog lets the #apply message update the model, so that sounds like the best place to do the same for our list. Now we have several ways to update our original list with the local list:

1 We can compare the elements in the two lists and then add/remove the differences.

2 We can replace all items in the original list with the new ones.

3 We can just remove the original list and put the new list in place.

The first option is a valid option if you're talking big lists, but then we should have chosen another solution for adding and removing; we would have been better off with a separate list containing all the additions and a separate list containing all the deletions.

The second has its own method in one of the superclasses of ListModel: #replaceFrom:to:with:. However, this message only works if the original list and the target list are the same length.

So by the sound of it we have to remove the original list and put the new list in place. The easiest way to do this is by making the collection in the model a ListModel, as the ListModel is better at handling whole collections at a time than sorted collections. We still want the list to be sorted, therefore we make the underlying model of the ListModel a SortedCollection.

```
Season>>initialize
    ...
    scoreDefinition := ListModel on: (SortedCollection
        sortBlock: [ :a :b | a >= b ]).
```

To apply the changes we have to override the #apply method. We'd better not forget the `super apply` as we still want the changes to the name field to be communicated to the model as well.

```
SeasonDialogPresenter>>apply
    "Apply the changes. This method adds to the original
    method that communicates the changes in the local list
    to the model's list"
    super apply.
    self model scoreDefinition removeAll.
    self model scoreDefinition list: localScoreList list.
```

Now try opening the dialog again and see if you can make changes to the list and cancel them.

5.3.4 Summary

In the previous subsections we have learned about sorted collections and how to create sort blocks. We have seen that collections require a bit more work in the presenter; you have to use a postbox or similar technique to add items to the collection and you can't use ValueModels to wrap around the collection. We have learned the difference between #copy and #deepCopy and how to make use of them.

5.4 Multi-column lists

How to build labels for a collection dynamically and how to display them making use of multi-column lists.

The way in which we show the list to the user isn't very helpful yet, as the user still has to count the number of items to find out how many points you get if you finish fifth. What we need here is a label in front of each item, showing the position to which the score applies. Something like Figure 5.4.

This type of list is – not surprisingly – called a multi-column list. We are going to use the multi-column list more extensively later on in this book; here we just give it a start. The simplest way to work with a multi-column list is by thinking of a list of lines that consist of objects where you want to show different information about those objects in each column. For example, you might want to create a list of drivers with their names in the

Position	Points
1st	10
2nd	6
3rd	4
4th	3
5th	2
6th	1

Figure 5.4
Multi-column list

first column and their age in the second. Both the name and the age refer to the same object, it's just different information about the same object that you are showing in each column.

5.4.1 *A virtual list*

In our case that doesn't work though, as we only hold the points in our collection, and not the labels. We can solve that by using a virtual list where we generate the label based on the position of the value that we are showing.

To make this work we need to modify the way we communicate the list to the view. The view needs to think that each item in the list consists of two elements, the position and the score. We can make the view think like that by creating a method that shows the list in the way we want it:

```
SeasonDialogPresenter>>localScoreListWithLabels
    "Return the score list with labels"
    | labels |
    labels := #('st' 'nd' 'rd' 'th').
    ^ListModel on:
        ((1 to: localScoreList size) collect: [ :each |
        | label |
        label := each printString, (labels at: (4 min:
            each)).
        Array with: label with: (localScoreList at:
            each)]).
```

As you can see, we create a label based on the index of the score in the collection. We can do that because we store the collection as a SortedCollection; the highest score always has index 1. Then, depending on the number, we put "st", "nd", "rd" or "th" behind the number, forming 1st, 2nd, 3rd, 4th, 5th and so on. Of course this only works until we reach 20 (21 needs the "st" addition again), but we don't expect the list to be that long. If so, we can always make this routine a bit more complicated (try it for yourself, it's not that difficult).

After running through the whole local score list, we return the "virtual" list which can then be displayed by the view. Remember we did something similar with the age of the driver? There we had a method that calculated the age based on the date of birth. Every time the date of birth changed, we recalculated the age and displayed it in the age field. We will take a similar approach here. We start by modifying the #model: method.

```
SeasonDialogPresenter>>model: aSeason
    ...
    scoreListPresenter model: self
        localScoreListWithLabels.
```

When we add a score, we have to rebuild the whole score list, as we don't know where the added score will be inserted. In the previous situation, the view was directly connected to the local list, so we didn't have to do anything. Now we have to explicitly tell the view. The simplest way of telling the view is just make a new connection to the model. For clarification I include the whole method; you can include the new line anywhere, as long as it is after the line where you have added the new score to the local list.

```
SeasonDialogPresenter>>addScore
    "Add the score from the postbox and recalculate the
    displayed list"
    scoreFieldPresenter value > 0 ifTrue: [
        localScoreList add: scoreFieldPresenter value.
        scoreFieldPresenter value: 0].
    scoreListPresenter model: self
        localScoreListWithLabels.
    scoreFieldPresenter view selectAll.
    scoreFieldPresenter setFocus.
```

When we deleted a line in the previous setup, we could ask the list which object was selected, and then delete that object from the list. In the current setup that won't work, as the object in the list is an object containing a label and a score. But luckily enough we can also ask the index of the selected item. Based on that, we can work out which item we want to delete in the "real" list. And again, after deleting, we have to rebuild our list with labels.

```
SeasonDialogPresenter>>deleteScore
    "Delete the selected score line"
    scoreListPresenter selectionOrNil isNil ifFalse: [
        localScoreList removeAtIndex:
            scoreListPresenter selectionByIndex].
    scoreListPresenter model: self
        localScoreListWithLabels.
```

5.4.2 *The multi-column ListView*

Now we are ready to modify our view. Open the view composer on the existing view (it won't work anymore, so we can just as well modify it). Select the list and mutate it to a ListView (ListPresenter.Enhanced list view). Save the view and open it on a model. It will display something like Figure 5.5.

Not bad for a start, but not exactly what we had in mind. We already see the labels and the values displayed, even though they are displayed in a single column. If we now go back to the view composer, we see that columnsList is an OrderedCollection, holding one ListViewColumn. We want two columns, so we add one with the * icon on the Value tab of the Published Aspect Inspector. Now we have to tell each column what to

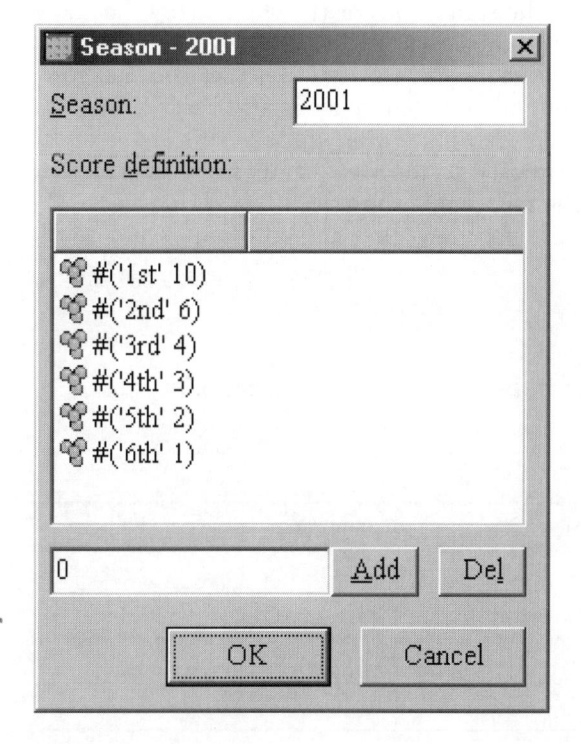

Figure 5.5

Multi-column dialog

display. We do that by setting the getContentsBlock aspect on each column. Like the name suggests, this is a block that is evaluated for each object, therefore it is a block like you would see for evaluating expressions on each object in a collection. In the first column we want to display element 1 of our array, so the getContentsBlock for column 1 is:

```
[ :each | each at: 1 ]
```

For the second column we want to show the integer, so we have to do slightly more:

```
[ :each | (each at: 2) printString ]
```

These columns allow us to do some more formatting than we were able to do with the list box. Note that these capabilities or limitations are straight from the Win32 controls – don't blame Dolphin Smalltalk for it. For the columns we set the aspects shown in Table 5.3.

For the ListView itself we set the aspect "hasGridLines" to true and the aspect "hasSortHeaders" to false. Save the form and open it. It already starts to look good, apart from that strange propellor in the first column. That is the image that is attached to the object that it shows. In our case we are showing an array, so it shows the icon for arrays. If you look in the CHB you will see the same icon for the class Array. For now, we just want to get rid of that icon, so set the "getImageBlock" aspects to nil. When you now open the dialog, you will see that the icon has gone. But if you select the line, you will see that space is still reserved for the icon. We want to get rid of that as well. Unfortunately, this is one of the aspects that is not directly exposed to the view composer, so we have to type it in manually. Select the top item in the tree of ListView aspects, the ListView itself. Clear the workspace next to it and enter and evaluate the following line:

```
self imageManager: nil
```

Now save the view and open it. It should look like Figure 5.6.

Table 5.3

Aspects for the columns of the multi-column view

Aspect	Column 1	Column 2
alignment	#center	#center
getContentsBlock	[:each	each at: 1]	[:each	(each at: 2) printString]
text	Position	Points
width	110	110

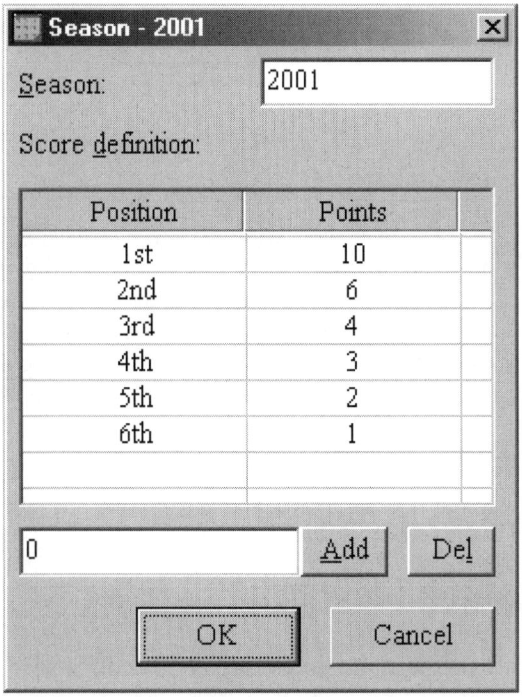

Figure 5.6
Finished Season dialog

5.4.3 Summary

In the above subsections we have created a virtual list of arrays with two elements each, based on a collection. We used that list to do a first exploration of the multi-column view.

6 The RaceCar component

The components that we have built so far were very much independent; they didn't have associations with each other. The race car appears to be different in that sense; it has a driver, it is owned by a team, and it is for a specific season. In this chapter we will learn how we can make those associations and how we can validate them; we don't want a driver to have to drive more than one car at the same time, and a team is not allowed to turn up with more than two cars. We also want to make sure that there are no duplicate starting numbers.

6.1 The RaceCar model

How to make links between objects and different ways of validating and maintaining these links.

Depending on the perspective, we can implement the car in a number of different ways. You could say that a car is owned by the team, therefore the team should have an "ownership" relation (aggregation). This would mean that the car cannot exist outside the scope of a team. From a modeling point of view we could say the same for the relation between the car and the season; you could even argue that this relation is stronger, as the starting number is really controlled by the season. As we don't want to make this choice up front, we will keep the relationship between the car and the associated objects bidirectional (Figure 6.1). Then we can take both perspectives: we can see to which team the car belongs, which cars are owned by a team, which cars are lined up for a season, and for which season a specific car is scheduled.

The link with the driver is of a different order. Of course we want to know which driver drives a car, but this can change during the season as drivers can get injured or contracts get renegotiated. In those cases someone else will take their place. Therefore we will only set up a default driver for the car. When it comes to races we will be able to change the actual driver.

6.1.1 The RaceCar class definition

The class definition shows the relations with the other classes as instance variables. These instance variables must have their accessors, which we will modify later to put more control on them, but as a starting point we can generate them with the "Generate Accessors" menu option.

THE RACECAR COMPONENT

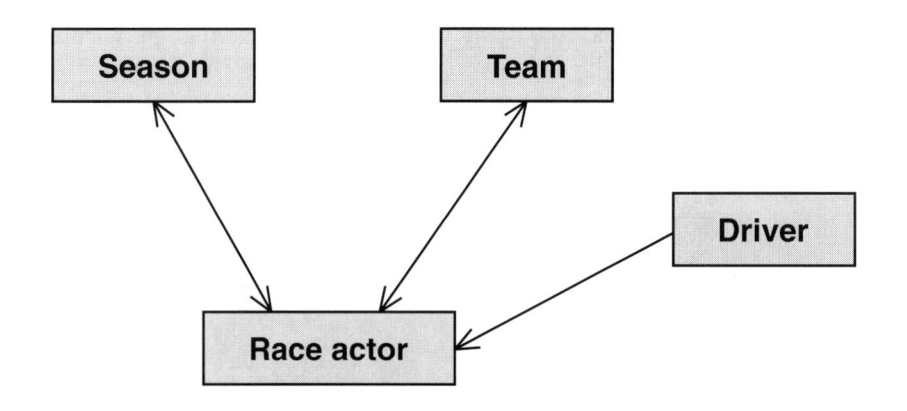

Figure 6.1
The RaceCar relations

```
MyModel subclass: #RaceCar
    instanceVariableNames: 'season team startingNumber
    defaultDriver'
    classVariableNames: ''
    poolDictionaries: ''
```

RaceCar>>season
```
    ^season
```

RaceCar>>season: anObject
```
    season := anObject
```

RaceCar>>team
```
    ^team
```

RaceCar>>team: anObject
```
    team := anObject
```

RaceCar>>startingNumber
```
    ^startingNumber
```

RaceCar>>startingNumber: anObject
```
    startingNumber := anObject
```

RaceCar>>defaultDriver
```
    ^defaultDriver
```

RaceCar>>defaultDriver: anObject
```
    defaultDriver := anObject
```

For showing the objects, we cannot totally rely on the MyModel ≫ #printOn: method that we wrote in Section 5.2, as we don't put anything in the "name" instance variable. However, as we use the message "self name" in the #printOn: method, we can just as well override the #name method to display whatever we want to display from the car. What would we like to show for a car? The team name and the starting number sound like good candidates, but as the starting number is season dependent, we want the season in the name as well.

RaceCar>>name
```
"Return a name made up of the team name and the start-
ing number.
MyModel expects a name, this does the job."
| answer |
answer := String new.
team notNil ifTrue: [answer := team name].
answer := answer, ' #', startingNumber printString.
season notNil ifTrue: [answer := answer, ' season ',
    season name].
^answer
```

As we are relying on the starting number to be numeric, we have to initialize it.

RaceCar>>initialize
```
super initialize.
startingNumber := 0.
```

6.1.2 The starting number

In this section we will make use of some specific behavior of the Array class to check whether a number is used.

Control over the starting numbers has to be from within the season, as they are season dependent. Each season there will be a race car with starting number 5, but within a season there can only be one race car with starting number 5.

This means that we need to maintain the available starting numbers from within the season. Or can we find another way? We already want to maintain a link to the cars from within the season, so can we use that link? We could just walk through all the existing links with cars and see if the starting number that we want to use has already been taken, but there is an easier way. What if we maintain the link from within the season in such a way that we can see straight away which numbers have been taken?

We can do that by making the starting number the index of the link. If the index number has been taken, then that starting number already exists. If the index does not exist, then we can use that starting number and link the car to that index number. This means that we need to maintain the link in an indexed collection.

However, not all indexed collections are able to have "gaps" in their indexes. If you create an empty OrderedCollection with size 20, and you then ask if index 5 has been used, it will tell you that index 5 is out of bounds; you have to use index 1 first. Luckily enough, the Array behaves

THE RACECAR COMPONENT

differently; we can create an array of a certain length, for example 20, which is then filled with the "nil" object in every position. If we then ask if index 5 has been used, it will return the value "nil".

This means that we can test on that value and insert the car if it is free and otherwise return an appropriate message (Figure 6.2).

As we don't know up front how big we need to make the array, we also have to cover the situation where the starting number is higher than the size of the array. In that case we have to resize the array up to the starting number.

Let's test this approach in a workspace (Figure 6.3).

If you run the code from Figure 6.3, the first time round it will insert the string in position 22. The second time round it will return an error stating that it is already in use.

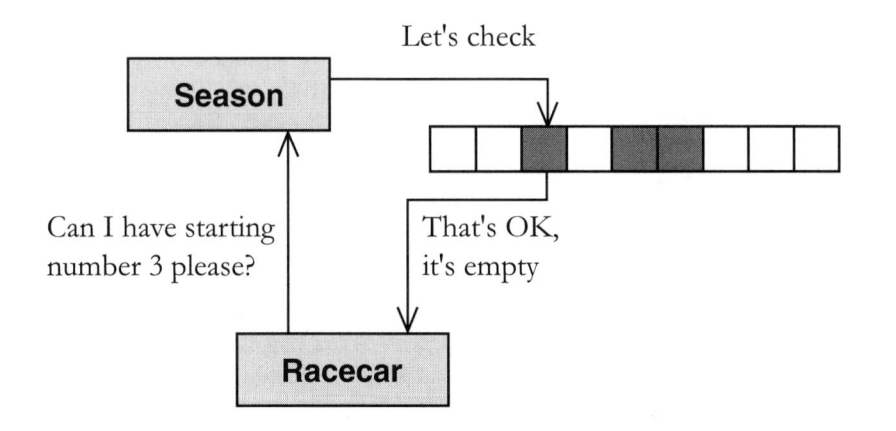

Figure 6.2

Testing the starting number

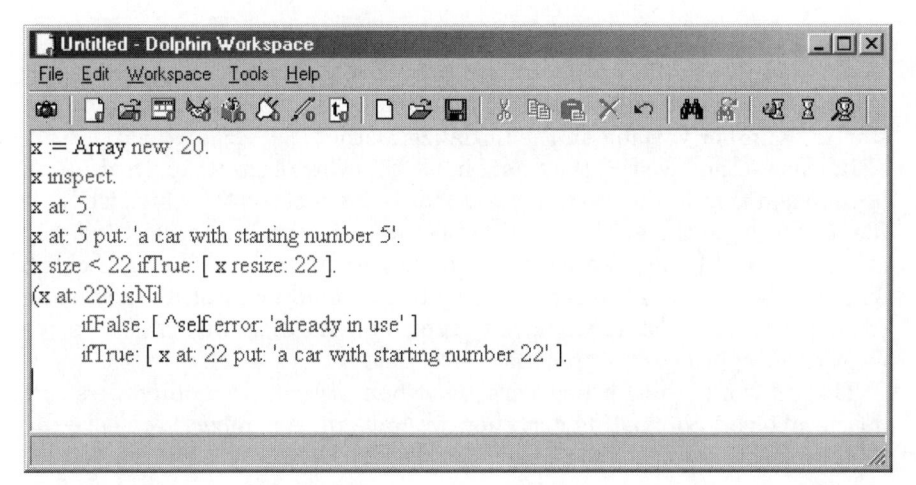

Figure 6.3

The starting number prototype code

```
x := Array new: 20.
x inspect.
x at: 5.
x at: 5 put: 'a car with starting number 5'.
x size < 22 ifTrue: [ x resize: 22 ].
(x at: 22) isNil
    ifFalse: [ ^self error: 'already in use' ]
    ifTrue: [ x at: 22 put: 'a car with starting number 22' ].
```

Now that we know how to approach this, we have to amend our Season class with the array of race cars. As part of the initialization of the season we have to initialize this array as well. As resizing an Array is quite expensive, it is best to initialize it with a "best guess" size. As a Formula One season typically has around 20 cars racing, we will initialize the Array with 20 positions.

```
MyModel subclass: #Season
    instanceVariableNames: 'scoreDefinition raceCars'
    classVariableNames: ''
    poolDictionaries: ''
```

Season>>initialize
```
    ...
    raceCars := Array new: 20.
```

When we want to set the starting number from a RaceCar instance, we first have to make sure that the RaceCar instance already has a season, otherwise we don't know which season to check to see whether we can use that starting number. Then we want to communicate the starting number to the season, so that the season can add the car to the array.

RaceCar>>startingNumber: aStartingNumber
```
    "Set the startingNumber to aStartingNumber. Tell the
    season to update itself with this number"
    self season isNil ifTrue: [ ^self error: 'A starting
        number cannot be allocated before setting the
        season' ].
    self season raceCarsAt: aStartingNumber put: self.
    startingNumber := aStartingNumber
```

We have to make sure that the initialize method doesn't call this method, as during initialization we don't yet have a season. That is why we don't use the #startingNumber: method in initialize, but assign 0 directly to the startingNumber variable in the initialize method.

In this method we call the Season >> raceCarsAt:put: method, so we have to add that to the Season class. This is the method for which we built the prototype in the workspace. We first want to check whether the array is big enough. If not, we resize it to the required size. Then we check whether the "slot" in the array is free. If not, another car is already using this starting number, so we have to report an error. If the slot is free, we want to assign the car to that slot.

This all works fine for new cars, but when we want to modify the starting number on an existing car, then we have to remember to release the original number in the list of used numbers in the season. We can do that by letting the season ask the car what the old number was and then set it to nil before assigning the new number to the car.

```
Season>>raceCarsAt: startingNumber put: raceCar
    "This method adds race cars to the raceCars array in
    the startingNumber slot if that's free and removes
    them from their old slot. It makes the array grow if
    necessary."
    raceCars size < startingNumber ifTrue: [ raceCars
            resize: startingNumber ].
    (raceCars at: startingNumber) isNil ifFalse: [
        ^self error: ('Starting number ', startingNumber
            printString, ' is already in use')].
    raceCars at: startingNumber put: raceCar.
    raceCar startingNumber = 0 ifFalse: [
        raceCars at: raceCar startingNumber put:
          nil ].
```

You can test it by creating a season, a couple of race cars for that season and attaching starting numbers to them. Then inspect the season.

```
season := Season new name: '2001'.
car1 := RaceCar new season: season; startingNumber: 5.
car2 := RaceCar new season: season; startingNumber: 1.
car3 := RaceCar new season: season; startingNumber: 18.
car4 := RaceCar new season: season; startingNumber: 5.
car5 := RaceCar new startingNumber: 7.
car3 startingNumber: 2.
```

The LookupTable and the IdentityDictionary As an alternative to the Array we could have chosen the LookupTable or the IdentityDictionary. A LookupTable is similar to the Dictionary, but in most cases it is more efficient as pointers are used between keys and values instead of associations. (If you make heavy use of the fact that the keys and values form associations, then the Dictionary is more efficient.) The IdentityDictionary is even more efficient for lookups as long as the keys can be compared with identity instead of equality (the difference between #== and #=, which we discussed in Section 4.3.1). In our case, where we use the starting numbers as our keys, we can use the IdentityDictionary here.

With this IdentityDictionary our approach is slightly different from the way we've solved it before. In the case of an Array we rely on the fact that the empty slots have a value of nil. In a dictionary unused "slots" just don't exist. This means that we have to ask whether the key is used. We can use the #includesKey: message for that. If it isn't, then we add the startingNumber as the key and the RaceCar as the value. We don't have to worry about growing the dictionary; that happens automatically.

To implement the IdentityDictionary we have to make the following changes.

Season >> initialize has to change to initialize the raceCars variable to be an IdentityDictionary.

```
Season>>initialize
    ...
    raceCars := IdentityDictionary new.
```

In Season >> raceCarsAt:put: we have to make some more modifications. First of all, we can remove the line that resizes the Array. Then we check if there is already a key for that starting number. If it doesn't exist then we add the race car with that key. If necessary we remove the old key, which automatically removes the old value as well.

```
Season>>raceCarsAt: startingNumber put: raceCar
    "This method adds race cars to the raceCars
    IdentityDictionary in the startingNumber key if that's
    unused and removes the old key."
    (raceCars includesKey: startingNumber)
        ifTrue: [ ^self error: ('Starting number ',
            startingNumber printString, ' is already
            in use')].
    raceCars at: startingNumber put: raceCar.
    raceCar startingNumber = 0 ifFalse:
        [raceCars removeKey: raceCar startingNumber
            ifAbsent: []]
```

In the situation with the Array we could just ask for all the race cars by asking for the Array. With the IdentityDictionary we have to do a bit more, as we only want the values.

```
Season>>raceCars
    ^raceCars values
```

6.1.3 *The Team association*

Using a dictionary for validation.

From the car's perspective the association with the team is just as straightforward as the association with the season. A car can only have a single association with a team; it can't "belong" to two teams at the same time. Therefore we can build that in the same way as we did with the season.

From the team's perspective we want to make sure that a team has only two cars for each season. How can we achieve that? One possibility is just to have a collection of cars in the team, and whenever you want to add a car for a specific season you check all the cars to see whether you already have two cars for that season. That sounds like a lot of work; there must be an easier way. What if we combine the two, and store both the season and the car associated to each other in the team. Then you can easily check whether you already have two cars for a specific season; you would just ask for all the cars for a specific season. If the number of cars retrieved is less than two, you can add the car for that season.

As we saw in the previous subsection, a dictionary combines two objects, and either can be called via the other. One of the objects is called the key, which has to be unique within the dictionary. The other object is called the value, which doesn't necessarily have to be unique. This would make the car the key and the season the value, as the season can occur twice and each car can only exist once in the team's side of the association. But that has the disadvantage that we still have to go through the whole dictionary to find out whether that team already has two cars for a season. There must be an easier way. What if we make the season the key, and as the value we hold either zero, one or two cars? Then we can just ask for the size of the value for a certain season, and if it is less than two, we can add the car. That would look like Figure 6.4.

Let's start with the link from the RaceCar side. Here again we have to check whether we have a season, as the validation between the RaceCar and the Team involves the Season. The next step is to check if this is a change of team or a new car that doesn't yet have a team. Then we add the car to the team, and if everything has gone well, we link the team to the team variable in the car itself.

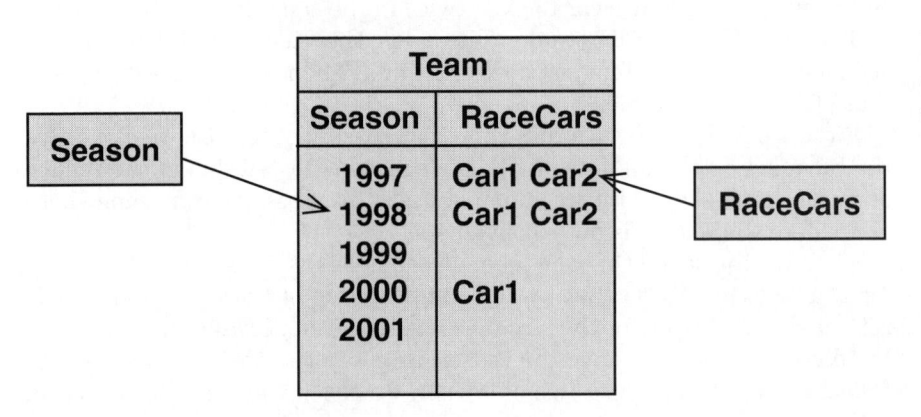

Figure 6.4

The RaceCars dictionary in the Team class

```
RaceCar>>team: aTeam
    "Set the team variable to aTeam, and communicate
    yourself to the team. Remove yourself from the old
    team if there is one"
    self season isNil ifTrue: [ ^self error: 'The team
        cannot be allocated before setting the season'
        ].
    self team isNil ifFalse: [ self team removeRaceCar:
        self ifAbsent: [nil]].
    aTeam addRaceCar: self.
    team := aTeam.
```

This automatically shows which methods we need to create on the team side: #removeRaceCar:ifAbsent: and #addRaceCar:. But first we have to add a variable to the class definition of the Team in which we are going to hold the dictionary. This dictionary has to be initialized when we create the team.

```
RacingActor subclass: #Team
    instanceVariableNames: 'origin foundationYear
    raceCars'
    classVariableNames: ''
    poolDictionaries: ''
```

Team>>initialize

```
    ...
    raceCars := Dictionary new.
```

Each "row" of the dictionary is going to hold the season as the key and the cars as the value. As the value has to be a single object, we have to wrap the cars into a collection. Here we don't really care about the order in which the cars are held, we just want to access them in the easiest way possible. But as we do not allow a car to exist twice in the same row, we use a Set.

The #addRaceCar: has to do quite a lot, therefore we first build it in such a way that every line just does one thing. Then we refactor it to make it as efficient as possible.

First, we need to be sure that there is a season, otherwise we can't give the car a key in the dictionary. We have already tested this in the sender of this message, but in future you might use this message from somewhere else where the season is not so obvious.

Then we check whether the team already has two cars in the dictionary for that season. We do that by checking the size of the collection that is returned as the value for the key aSeason. As we don't want an error when the dictionary doesn't have the season as a key yet, we return an empty collection which returns a size of 0 when we check whether the collection

THE RACECAR COMPONENT

is 2. If the collection already has a size of 2, there are two cars stored against this season, so we report an error.

In the next step we assign the current return value of the season to a temporary variable. If the season doesn't yet exist as a key, we create a new set. We add the car to the set and as the last step we add the set to the dictionary with the season as the key. If the dictionary already contains the season as the key, it will replace the old set (which had one car in it) with the new set with two cars in it.

```
Team>>addRaceCar: aRaceCar
    "Add a race car to the raceCars dictionary, with its
    season as the key. Return an error if there are
    already two race cars for that season"
    | seasonCars season |
    season := aRaceCar season.
    season isNil ifTrue: [ ^self error: 'A race car has to
        be linked to a season' ].
    ((raceCars at: season ifAbsent: [#()]) size = 2)
        ifTrue: [^self error: 'A team cannot have
                more than two race cars for the
                same season'].
    seasonCars := raceCars at: season ifAbsent: [ Set new
        ].
    seasonCars add: aRaceCar.
    raceCars at: season put: seasonCars.
```

When we refactor this method, we take out the temporary variables where possible, as they add overhead to the method. Then we split the test for the size of the set; we first ask whether the season is already a key. If not, we don't have to do the second test. The block after the #and: message is only executed if the first test returns true. If so, we check whether the size of the set is 2 and we report an error if that is the case.

In the last line we combine the creation of the set with writing the whole lot into the dictionary.

```
Team>>addRaceCar: aRaceCar
    "Add a race car to the raceCars dictionary, with its
    season as the key. Return an error if there are
    already two race cars for that season"
    aRaceCar season isNil ifTrue: [ ^self error: 'A race
        car has to be linked to a season' ].
    ((raceCars includesKey: aRaceCar season) and:
        [(raceCars at: aRaceCar season) size = 2])
            ifTrue: [^self error: 'A team cannot have
                more than two race cars for the
                same season'].
```

```
          (raceCars at: aRaceCar season ifAbsentPut: [Set new])
               add: aRaceCar
```

The method #removeRaceCar: is straightforward after this.

```
Team>>removeRaceCar: aRaceCar
     "Remove a race car from the cars dictionary"
     aRaceCar season isNil ifTrue: [ ^self error: 'A race
          car has to be linked to a season' ].
     (raceCars at: aRaceCar season) remove: aRaceCar
          ifAbsent: [nil].
```

To test the link between the teams and the race cars we can use the cars that we created in the previous section, and attach them to teams.

```
season := Season new name: '2001'.
team1 := Team new name: 'Ferrari'.
team2 := Team new name: 'McLaren'.
season := Season new name: '2001'.
car1 := RaceCar new season: season; team: team1.
car2 := RaceCar new season: season; team: team1.
car3 := RaceCar new season: season; team: team1.
car4 := RaceCar new season: season; team: team2.
car5 := RaceCar new team: team2.
car1 team: team2.
```

6.1.4 *The default driver*

In this section we will use the #anySatisfy: method to do the validation.

The default driver in the race car is a uni-directional link between the driver model and the race car model. In our model a driver doesn't really need to know about the link, as only the driver that actually drives during races can score points. On the other hand, a car has to have a default driver which can be modified for individual races. In our model this means that we have to make a reference in our RaceCar class to a Driver instance, but not the other way round. As a driver can only be the default driver for a single car at a particular time, we have to check that a driver is not linked to two cars for a specific season.

In this setup we cannot ask the driver whether he is already a default driver for a car, as we decided to have a uni-directional link, and therefore we have to find another method. But the season knows about all the cars and all the cars know about their default driver, so we can try to follow that route. This would mean that we ask the car's season to return all the cars, and then check that collection of cars to see whether any of them has the current driver as its default driver. Saying it like that almost generates the code:

```
RaceCar>>defaultDriver: aDriver
    "Check if the driver is already the default driver for
    another car. Note that it is a uni-directional
    relationship, therefore we don't inform the driver."
    (self season raceCars anySatisfy:
        [ :each | each defaultDriver == aDriver ])
            ifTrue: [ ^self error: aDriver name, ' is
            already the default driver for another car'
            ].
    defaultDriver := aDriver
```

We use the #anySatisfy: method here, which does what the name suggests; it walks through the collection, and as soon as the condition in the block is met, it returns the value "true". If the end of the collection is reached without meeting the condition, the value "false" is returned.

The reason for testing the driver instance for identity is that we otherwise have to define what equality is in the Driver class. When are two Driver instances one and the same driver? If their names are the same? Or if their names and date of birth and nationality are the same? Therefore, we'd better make sure that every driver has only one instance in our model.

6.1.5 The link with the season

We have seen that for validating the starting number, the team and the default driver, we have to be sure that we have a season. Wouldn't it therefore be simpler if we attach the season to the car when we create the car? In our tests we sort of did that by setting the season straight after creating a new car. We can do this in one go if we create a class method for the RaceCar that does the same.

In this section we will set an instance variable based on a parameter that is provided as part of the instance creation method.

First we want to make sure that the normal #new doesn't work anymore. We can do that with the following class method.

```
RaceCar class>>new
    "Disallow direct creation - use #forSeason: instead"
    ^self shouldNotImplement
```

This tells the sender that #new shouldn't be used. Instead we want them to use #forSeason:.

```
RaceCar class>>forSeason: aSeason
    "Create a new race car for a specific season"
    ^self basicNew initialize; season: aSeason
```

Here we call the #basicNew method, as we just disabled the RaceCar class's #new method. We did not use "super new", as we can't rely on the superclass not redefining the #new method as well. On top of that, if we were to subclass RaceCar in future, then the subclass would call "super new", which would call RaceCar class >> new, which we just made unavailable.

6.1.6 Summary

In the previous subsections we made associations between instances and validated them according to their specific rules. The first validation was based on a number being used, which we initially solved with the index of an array but eventually we used an IdentityDictionary. In the second validation we had to make a test based on two pieces of information, which we solved by making one the key of a dictionary and checking the size of the value. In the third validation, we had to ask another (associated) object for all the instances to see whether the requester was already in use.

As all validations required the object to have an association with another object, we invalidated the normal way of creating such an object and replaced it with a creation method that creates the association at the same time.

6.2 Error handling and the debugger

So far, whenever we wanted to capture an unwanted situation, we just said something like `^self error: 'error text'`. The message #error: raises an exception that, if it is not captured, opens an error dialog with a number of buttons on it. In this section we are going to investigate that error mechanism, which leads us to the debugger. The debugger is an excellent development tool, but our end users should not be exposed to it as they could easily break our application with it. Therefore we will add our own error handling later on in this chapter, making use of the standard Windows message boxes.

6.2.1 Error handling in Dolphin Smalltalk

What happens when an error occurs and how you can enforce it manually.

Now that we have built some software in Smalltalk, we know that everything revolves around sending messages to objects. These objects know to which class they belong, and the classes have a library of methods at their disposal. If everything goes well, the message selector is found in the library of available methods and the method can be executed by the object.

That is if everything goes well, but what if it doesn't? What can go wrong? Well, the receiver might not have an appropriate method for the message that is sent to it. Or the receiver might decide that in its current state, it can't or won't handle the request.

In the first case, the sent message is not understood by the receiver. If that is the case, the receiver responds by saying exactly that. The receiver will send a message to the MessageNotUnderstood class (can you believe that there's a class actually called that?), which will "raise an exception".

The second case is what we have done ourselves in the previous sections. Our receiving object was in a condition based on which it didn't want to respond in a normal way to the message received; instead it wanted to report an error. We sent the message #error: to "self" with a string containing the error message. The message #error: (defined in the class Object) sends a message to the Error class, which raises an exception similar to the above case.

There is a third case which puts you in exactly the same situation, but enforced by yourself, namely by using breakpoints. You can set breakpoints anywhere in any method by sending the message #halt to the object (`self halt.`).

All three cases are handled in the same way: a dialog is shown with the stack of messages that lead to the exception (the stack trace). The only difference between the three cases is the title. As you can see in the title of the dialog shown in Figure 6.5, it was caused by a breakpoint. When an exception dialog shows up, don't overlook the title, as often it contains enough information to solve the problem.

From the exception dialog you have the choice to go into the debugger (see next section), resume the execution of the method that raised the exception if possible, or terminate the execution. In some cases the Terminate key just opens a new exception dialog, and so on. With the Copy button you can copy the stack trace to the clipboard. This is especially

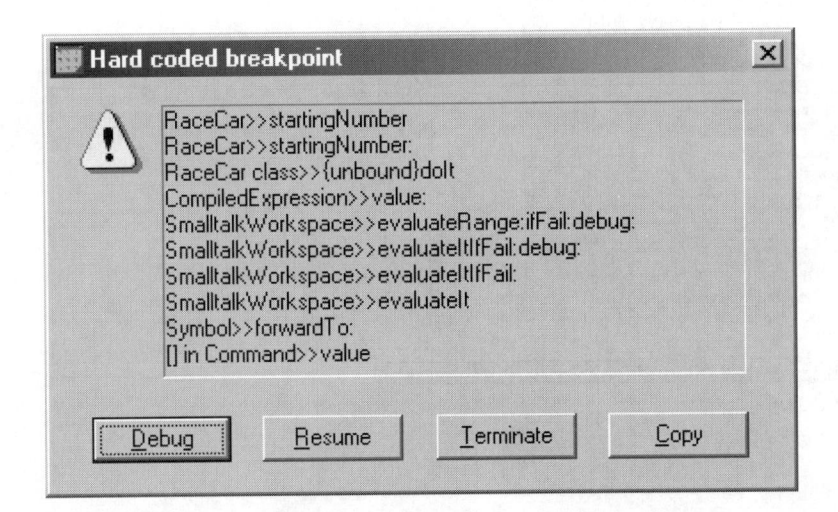

Figure 6.5

Exception dialog

handy if you want to send the trace to the Dolphin newsgroup to report a problem.

6.2.2 *The debugger*

An introduction to the debugger and how we can use it.

The debugger is an extremely helpful tool allowing you to browse through (and modify!) the code that raised the exception. The debugger consists of four panes which are described below (Figure 6.6).

The **stack trace** shows you the most recent methods that were executed before the error occurred. As the whole error messaging system is written in Smalltalk as well, you will find that the first one or two lines most often show you the actual messages that led to opening the debugger. Therefore the problem most often occurs in the third line from above or below that. When you select a line in the stack trace, the other three panes are updated.

The **parameters list** shows you the object to which the message is sent, all the instance variables of the object, the parameters that are sent with the message, and the temporary variables of the method. Selecting one of the lines in the parameters list updates the **parameter value** pane. This pane shows the value of the currently selected parameter. But as it is

Figure 6.6
The debugger

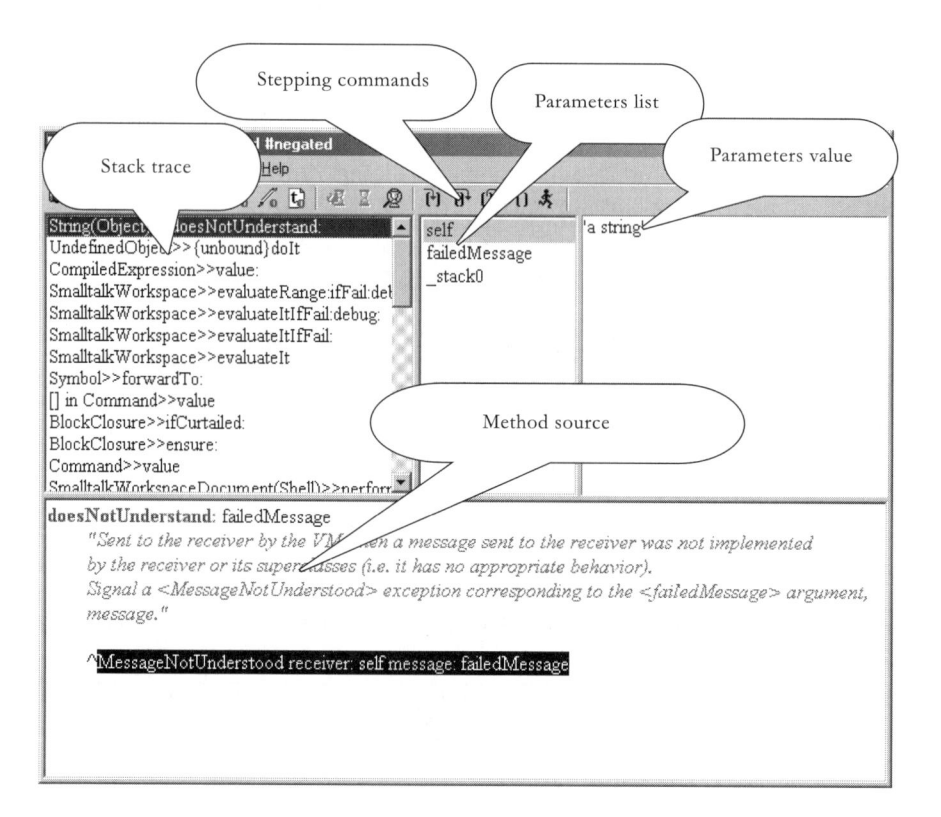

a text pane attached to the receiving object, you can send messages to the object through this pane. We will experiment with this later in the book.

The **method source** pane shows the source of the method as it was sent to the receiver. This is exactly the same as what you can see in the CHB. Therefore you can modify the code here, save it, and resend it to the object. When you then go back to the CHB and look at the method, you will see the source as modified in the debugger. Some Smalltalkers build half their applications in the debugger.

In the toolbar you will find the stepping commands with which you can step through the processing in the following ways:

- The Step-into command executes each successive message one by one in full detail. This means that it takes you right through all the different classes involved in the execution of the method.

- The Step-over command executes each successive message within the current method without going into the receiver's classes. This means that it just steps through the messages of the current method.

- The Step-out command executes the whole currently selected method in one go.

- The Run-to-Cursor command executes the currently selected method up to the last message where the current method replies.

- The Go command closes the debugger and continues normal execution.

When you use the stepping commands, keep an eye on the parameters and parameter value frame. You can see the instance variables of the object that you are working on being updated while stepping through the messages.

6.2.3 *Debugger playground*

Let's see how we can work with the debugger. Let's set a breakpoint in one of the methods that we created in the previous section and see what happens.

```
RaceCar>>startingNumber: aStartingNumber
    "Set the startingNumber to aStartingNumber. Tell the
    season to update itself with this number"
self halt.
    (aStartingNumber = 0) ifTrue: [startingNumber := 0.
        ^nil].
    self season isNil ifTrue:
        [ ^self error: 'A starting number cannot be
        allocated before setting the season' ].
    (self season raceCarsAt: aStartingNumber put: self)
        isNil ifTrue: [^nil].
    startingNumber := aStartingNumber
```

We could have put the breakpoint anywhere in the method, but we've put it right at the start, so that we can walk though the whole method. Now evaluate the following in a workspace:

```
season := Season new name: '2001'.
car := RaceCar forSeason: season.
car startingNumber: 3
```

When you evaluate it the exception dialog shows up as expected, with, in the title, the message that it was caused by a hard-coded breakpoint. Press the Debug button. The debugger opens with the same information as the dialog in the stack trace and in the caption (Figure 6.7).

You can already see some interesting stuff on this screen. If you select, for example, the "season" instance variable in the parameters pane, you see that the parameter value pane is updated. Double-clicking on the instance variable opens an inspector on it.

The parameters pane also contains a parameter called aStartingNumber. This is the argument that we sent with the #startingNumber: message. The _stackX parameters are internal parameters for the process. They are used to maintain the state.

Now press the Step-into button. This takes you to the "self season" expression on the line underneath the "self halt" line, as that is the next

Figure 6.7

A debugger on the #startingNumber: method

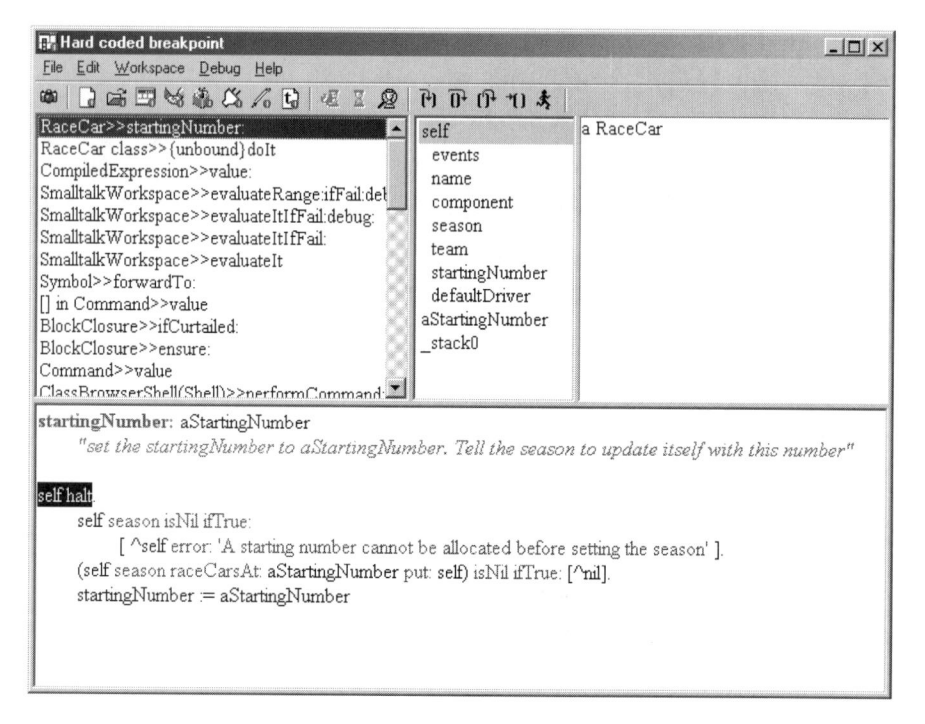

expression in the evaluation order. As you can see, the _stack1 parameter is added.

When you do the next Step-into, the result of the previous message is stored in this parameter, which is the receiver of the #isNil message. As that evaluates to false, the next expression is again "self season", followed by the message #raceCarsAt:put:. Here it starts to become interesting, as the next step takes us to the Season class which is the receiver of the message #raceCarsAt:put:.

Doing another Step-into takes you to the IdentityDictionary >> includesKey: message. To skip all the Collection messages, we use the Step-out key which brings us to the next expression in Season >> raceCarsAt:put:.

To avoid going back into the Collection expressions, we just execute the next expression as a whole with the Step-over command. Now we want to go to the end of this method, so we select the Run-to-Cursor button.

After doing the next step it looks as if there is nothing selected. That is right, as the whole method has been executed. If there is something to return other than the object itself, you can inspect it in the Parameters pane.

The next step brings you back into the original method, with the result of the expression in one of the _stack parameters.

If you want to walk through the whole process again without having to click those buttons, you can select the Animate function in the Debug menu. A more useful menu option is the Restart option, which takes you back to the breakpoint.

6.2.4 *Another way of writing Smalltalk*

So far we have been writing our methods in the CHB whenever we thought of them. We analyzed what we needed to validate the starting number and created the necessary supporting methods in the Season class. In our case this wasn't too difficult, as we are building an application with relatively low complexity.

Using the debugger as your main coding tool.

When the system becomes more complex, you run the risk of overlooking the creation of these supporting methods. But is that a real risk? You could turn it round and just build your method without the supporting methods. Then when you test it, the debugger will of course come up with MessageNotUnderstood exceptions. However, those messages come up at exactly the right position; they tell you exactly which message is missing in which class. The debugger even shows you which information you have available with that message. The ideal place to build your missing method! And as the text area in the debugger is exactly the same as the text area in the CHB, you can do exactly the same.

To stick with the #startingNumber: example, we would just build it in the RaceCar class like we did before, but instead of moving on to the

Season class and building the supporting method (#raceCarsAt:put:), we would start testing the method. This would open the debugger, saying that Season doesn't understand #raceCarsAt:put:. That would be the point where we would add that method in the debugger. After adding it, we would restart the test. As we only had a single supporting method, it would run (assuming that we coded it bug free). But if the supporting method relied on another supporting method, then that method wouldn't exist either, so the debugger would come up again, and so on.

The testing tool SUnit, mentioned earlier, which automates the testing, is an invaluable tool for working in this way. Write a method, run the automated test, open the debugger, write the next missing method, run the automated test, and so on. One of the leading writers on this method of programming is Kent Beck. See Appendix A.

6.2.5 *Our own error handling mechanism*

Understanding the exception handling mechanism and using standard Windows message boxes.

Going back to the application that we are building, we raised exceptions when our validation failed. So far we have used the standard exception dialog, but for an end user this is not appropriate. An end user should just receive a message stating what's wrong and an action button so that it can be corrected. The standard Microsoft Windows message boxes do just that.

We can call these message boxes through the MessageBox class. The MessageBox comes in a number of flavors. You can define which icon to show, which buttons are on the message box, which one of those buttons is the default, the caption of the message box, and of course the message text. You can try them all out in a workspace. The standard ones can be called as class methods. When you want to do something more advanced, you have to create one with the right widgets and then open it. Below are some examples that you can try in a workspace. Don't just evaluate each line but display the result (Ctrl + D); then you see what kind of return value they give. You can use that return value to perform the right action based on the selected button:

```
MessageBox confirm: 'Do you really want to do this?'.
MessageBox confirm: 'Do you really want to do this?'
      caption: 'Delete action'.
MessageBox warning: 'I am going to delete this'
MessageBox notify: 'I am going to delete this'
MessageBox errorMsg: 'I am going to delete this'
MessageBox new prompt; text: 'Do you really want to do
      this?'; yesNoCancel; defaultButton: 3; beep; open
```

In our case we want to tell the user that we are missing some information and therefore we can't execute the action that the user wants. The MessageBox class >> errorMsg: looks promising; it comes up with an error message dialog, which the user can only close with the OK button, after which the user is back where he or she started. Let's use that as a starting point for our standard error handling and test it on the starting number:

```
RaceCar>>startingNumber: aStartingNumber
    ...
    self season isNil ifTrue: [ ^MessageBox errorMsg: 'A
    starting number cannot be allocated before setting the
    season' ].
    ...
```

To create a race car that doesn't belong to a season, we have to explicitly set the season to nil, as we can only create cars for a season.

```
    s1 := Season new.
    testCar := RaceCar forSeason: s1.
    testCar season: nil.
    testCar startingNumber: 4.
```

For the season test this works fine, as we jump out of the method before we do any updates. In the cases where we want to update a bidirectional relationship, or where we need to ask another object to perform the validation, like in our case the other side of the relationship, this schema is a bit too simple. Sticking to the example of the starting number, but now with a valid season, the following would happen if we tried to set a starting number that was already used:

1 In RaceCar ≫ startingNumber: we first check whether we have a season. We have one so we continue.

2 On the next line we give control to the race car's season, to set this car at the starting number.

3 In Season ≫ raceCarsAt:put: we check whether the requested slot is free. If not, we want to open the error message box.

4 The user takes notification of that and closes the box.

5 After closing the message box, control is returned to the RaceCar method from the point where we went to the season.

This means that the starting number on the race car gets updated, even though we got the error message in the Season method!

How can we prevent this? We could invent some complicated scheme with variables which get set when an error occurs and if that variable is set then we do not update the model. This would mean that we have to maintain those variables from all the different sides of the relationships. In our current model that would be manageable, but you can imagine how complicated this would get in more sophisticated models. Luckily enough, there is a mechanism in Smalltalk where we can check whether an error occurs and, if so, we jump out of the method. This mechanism makes use of the BlockClosure >> on:do: message. For example:

```
[ a test ] on: Error do: [ :each | ^MessageBox errorMsg:
    'The test raised an error']
```

If the result of the BlockClosure meets the first argument in the message (if it does raise an error), then the block in the second argument is executed. In that second argument we get the chance to jump out of the method before executing any other update methods.

Now we have to make sure that wherever we want to do an update, we use this mechanism.

```
RaceCar>>startingNumber: aStartingNumber
    "Set the startingNumber to aStartingNumber. Tell the
    season to update itself with this number"
    self season isNil ifTrue:
        [ ^self error: 'A starting number cannot be
        allocated before setting the season' ].
    [self season raceCarsAt: aStartingNumber put: self]
        on: Error do: [ :each | ^MessageBox errorMsg:
                        each messageText].
    startingNumber := aStartingNumber

Season>>raceCarsAt: startingNumber put: raceCar
    "This method adds race cars to the raceCars dictionary
    with the startingNumber as the key if that's free. If
    not, an error is reported. If the raceCar has an old
    startingNumber it's removed from the old slot."
    (raceCars includesKey: startingNumber) ifTrue: [
        ^self error: ('Starting number ', startingNumber
        printString, ' is already in use')].
    raceCars at: startingNumber put: raceCar.
    raceCar startingNumber = 0 ifFalse: [
        raceCars removeKey: raceCar startingNumber
        ifAbsent: []].
    ^raceCar

RaceCar>>team: aTeam
    "Set the team variable to aTeam, and communicate your-
    self to the team. Remove yourself from the old team if
    there is one"
    self season isNil ifTrue:
        [ ^self error: 'The team cannot be allocated
            before setting the season' ].
```

```
        aTeam isNil ifFalse: [
            [aTeam addRaceCar: self] on: Error do:
                [ :each | ^MessageBox errorMsg: each
                    messageText]].
        self team isNil ifFalse: [
            [self team removeRaceCar: self] on: Error do:
                [ :each | ^MessageBox errorMsg: each
messageText]].
        team := aTeam
```

Team>>addRaceCar: aRaceCar
```
    "Add a race car to the raceCars dictionary, with its
    season as the key. Return an error if there are
    already two race cars for that season"
    aRaceCar season isNil ifTrue:
        [ ^self error: 'A race car has to be of a
            season' ].
    ((raceCars includesKey: aRaceCar season) and:
    [(raceCars at: aRaceCar season) size = 2])
        ifTrue: [^self error: 'A team cannot have more
        than two race cars for the same season'].
    (raceCars at: aRaceCar season ifAbsentPut:
        [Set new]) add: aRaceCar.
```

Team>>removeRaceCar: aRaceCar
```
    "Remove a race car from the cars dictionary"
    aRaceCar season isNil ifTrue:
        [ ^self error: 'A race car has to be of a
            season' ].
    (raceCars at: aRaceCar season) remove: aRaceCar
        ifAbsent: []
```

RaceCar>>defaultDriver: aDriver
```
    "Check if the driver is already the default driver for
    another car. Note that it is a uni-directional rela-
    tionship, therefore we don't inform the driver."
    (self season raceCars anySatisfy:
        [ :each | each defaultDriver == aDriver ])
            ifTrue:
                [ ^MessageBox errorMsg: aDriver name, ' is
                already the default driver for another
                car' ].
    defaultDriver := aDriver
```

6.2.6 Summary

In the above subsections we investigated error handling in Smalltalk and introduced the debugger. We captured the error handling for our own application so that we can use it as the error messaging vehicle for the end user. As part of that, we had a look at the standard Windows message boxes and how to use them from within Dolphin Smalltalk.

6.3 The RaceCar presenter and view

So far we have used the dialog for the windows that we built. We liked it because we could enter something, and if we weren't happy with it, we could just cancel the entry. We saw that all this was done by creating a copy of the original object, making all the modifications to the copy and, if we liked it, replacing the original object with the copy. Otherwise we just threw away the copy.

In the case of the race car this becomes a bit difficult with all the testing that we want to do. If we make a copy of the race car with starting number 1, our error handling will tell us that we already have a race car with starting number 1. The same goes for the team: if we already have two cars for a team in a specific season, and we make a copy, the team will complain that it can't have an additional car.

We could try to find ways around this by modifying the way in which the dialog copies the data, but that would become unnecessarily complicated. It would be better just to create a window that does not work with copies of the original objects.

Like we said in Section 3.2, if we don't want any specific behavior, we just use the standard Shell as the basis. We can always add specific behavior ourselves. We are going to make it look like Figure 6.8.

6.3.1 *The lists of teams and drivers*

How to use global variables.

Before we start building the presenter, we first have to consider how we can fill the drop-down lists with the teams and drivers.

Figure 6.8
The RaceCar view

So far we have created teams, drivers, and seasons in the workspace and associated them with workspace variables like "team1" and so on. Whenever we closed the workspace, these variables were deleted and the garbage collector would remove those teams, drivers, and seasons that were not associated with anything. Now we want the teams and drivers to live a bit longer, otherwise we can't show them in our lists. In Chapter 9 we will bring all the objects together under one umbrella, but for now we have to resort to a temporary solution.

Our temporary solution is to create persistent variables which hold collections of our teams and drivers. These persistent variables are called global variables, and they are held in a dictionary in the image. Whenever you save your image, this dictionary is saved with it, so the next time you start Smalltalk, the dictionary still exists with all the global variables.

You can create a global variable in the same way as you create workspace variables, with the difference that global variables have to start with a capital letter.

```
AllTeams := OrderedCollection new.
```

When you execute that, the system warns you that you are about to create a global variable (Figure 6.9). Choosing "yes" will create the global variable. Choosing "no" assumes that you want the variable to be a normal workspace variable, albeit that it starts with a capital letter; choosing "cancel" will stop the execution. In our case we do want to create the global variable.

Now that we have the global variable, we can add teams to it by executing the following line a number of times:

```
AllTeams add: Team new.
```

This will create "empty" Team objects, so we want to give them their name and other information. Well, we made a nice dialog for them, so let's use that.

```
AllTeams do: [ :each | TeamDialogPresenter showOn: each ].
```

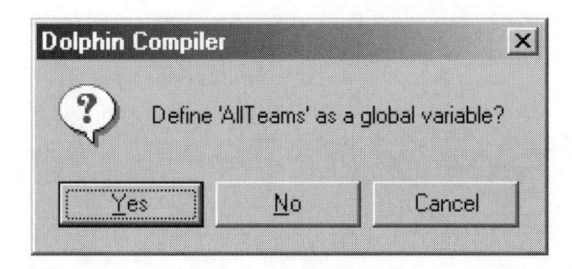

Figure 6.9

Global variable warning message

This will go through all the Team instances in the global variable and present them one by one in the dialog. Now inspect the AllTeams variable; you will see a neat list of the teams that you created.

For the drivers we will do exactly the same; we will call this global variable AllDrivers.

As the global variables are persistent, you have to delete them explicitly. The dictionary of persistent objects can be accessed through the variable name "Smalltalk", therefore, removing the AllTeams global variable can be done by executing the following line:

```
Smalltalk removeKey: 'AllTeams'
```

A lazy and poor alternative to the above solution is to use the message #allInstances. This message can be sent to classes. The disadvantage is that it collects all the existing instances, so if you have a temporary copy of an instance (for example through the aspectBuffer), the message #allInstances will show you both objects up to the point where the copy is collected by the garbage collector.

6.3.2 *The RaceCarView as subclass of the Shell class*

In this section we will build a Shell that acts similar to a Dialog without using the aspectBuffer.

For the RaceCar we create a RaceCarView presenter class as a subclass of the Shell class with instance variables for every instance variable from the RaceCar model class.

```
Shell subclass: #RaceCarView
    instanceVariableNames: 'seasonPresenter teamPresenter
    startingNumberPresenter defaultDriverPresenter'
    classVariableNames: ''
    poolDictionaries: ''
```

The #createComponents method is similar to the ones we built before. As we want the user to be able to select a team and a driver from a drop-down box, we make those presenters instances of ListPresenter.

```
RaceCarView>>createComponents
    "Create the view components"
    super createComponents.
    seasonPresenter := self add: TextPresenter new name:
        'season'.
    teamPresenter := self add: ListPresenter new name:
        'team'.
    startingNumberPresenter := self add: NumberPresenter
        new name: 'startingNumber'.
    defaultDriverPresenter := self add: ListPresenter new
        name: 'defaultDriver'.
```

In the #model: method we have to read all our teams and drivers into ListModels, which we link to the drop-down presenters.

As we like them to be sorted, we send the result #asSortedCollection: with the required sort block. For the driver we want to sort first on surname and then on first name, therefore we make a new string out of surname and then firstname before sorting it.

```
RaceCarView>>model: aRaceCar
    "Create the link between the model and the presenter"
    super model: aRaceCar.
    seasonPresenter model: (self model season name).
    startingNumberPresenter model: (self model
            startingNumber).
    teamPresenter model: (ListModel on: (self allTeams)).
    defaultDriverPresenter model: (ListModel on: (self
            allDrivers)).

RaceCarView>>allTeams
    "Collect all teams"
    ^AllTeams asSortedCollection: [ :a :b | a name <= b
            name ]

RaceCarView>>allDrivers
    "Collect all drivers"
    ^AllDrivers asSortedCollection: [ :a :b |
        (a surname, a firstname) <= (b surname, b
                firstname) ]
```

For the caption we want to make use of the #setCaption method, but there are two problems. First of all, we defined the #setCaption method in the Dialog class, and we're now in a subclass of the Shell class, so we don't inherit that method. Well, we can just move the #setCaption method up the hierarchy. The other problem is that the RaceCar doesn't really have a name, and in the #setCaption method we rely on the name being available. Therefore we add a #name method to the RaceCar class in Section 6.1.1 that returns what we want to display as the name.

```
RaceCarView>>captionSubstring
    "Return the class-specific substring for the caption"
    ^'Race Car - '
```

When we open the view on an existing car, we want the team and driver that are currently attached to the car to be shown as the current selection.

```
RaceCarView>>onViewOpened
    "Set the caption and initial selection"
    super onViewOpened.
    self showTeamSelection.
    self showDefaultDriverSelection.
    self setCaption.

RaceCarView>>showTeamSelection
    "Show the team selected"
    | team |
    team := self model team.
    team isNil ifFalse: [ teamPresenter selection: team ]

RaceCarView>>showDefaultDriverSelection
    "Show the initial default driver selected"
    | driver |
    driver := self model defaultDriver.
    driver isNil ifFalse: [ defaultDriverPresenter
        selection: driver ]
```

We haven't made a connection between the team presenter and the team variable in the model, so if we change the selection in the presenter, we still have to tell the model about the change. We capture the changes in the view with #createSchematicWiring, like we've seen before.

For the list we can choose to monitor a change by a number of events. You can see all the events that can be monitored by evaluating and displaying the following expression:

```
ListView publishedEventsOfInstances.
```

Here you see many events that we are not interested in (yet), but some look promising. The most generic one is #changed, but that is called when the model has changed, which is the list of instances. Not what we want to capture here. The event #actionPerformed is very generic as well; it is called when some action has been performed that affects the presenter. This can be something like a selection by the mouse, keyboard input, and so on.

More specific events are #selectionChanged and #focusLost. The first is called when the selection action has finished, and the second is called when the cursor moves to another field or button. Either of these will do for now; in the next section we will see that certain conditions will force us to use one or the other.

```
RaceCarView>>createSchematicWiring
    "Create the trigger wiring"
    super createSchematicWiring.
```

```
teamPresenter when: #selectionChanged send:
    #teamSelectionChanged to: self.
defaultDriverPresenter when: #selectionChanged send:
    #defaultDriverSelectionChanged to: self.
```

RaceCarView>>teamSelectionChanged
    "The selected team changed, communicate that to the model"
    `self model team: teamPresenter selection.`

RaceCarView>>defaultDriverSelectionChanged
    "The selected default driver changed, communicate that to the model"
    `self model defaultDriver: defaultDriverPresenter selection.`

6.3.3 Building the view for the race cars

Now we can build a view for this presenter. As it's not a dialog like we built before, we will build some dialog-like behavior ourselves.

When you create a new view, it won't have the standard gray background color like we saw with dialogs. We have to set it ourselves in the aspect backColor. When you double-click on the aspect, it will open a color chooser where you can select the preferred color.

By setting both the hasMinimized and hasMaximized aspects to false, the buttons are removed from the frame. We also have to change the frame (aspect hasThickFrame = false), otherwise the view can be resized, which you can't do for dialogs. The last aspect that we have to change on the Shell is the usePreferredExtent, which has to be set to false, otherwise the Shell will open on the default preferredExtent, which is different from how you size the view yourself.

For the fields we use the settings listed in Table 6.1

For the team and driver lists we have to define a block in which we tell the list what to display about the team or the driver. We saw something similar in the multi-column list on the Season dialog. If we had left the getTextBlock set to nil, then we would have seen something like "aDriver(Michael Schumacher)". Thanks to our modified #printOn: method we can at least see which driver we are talking about.

In the Dialog presenters we got the OK and Cancel buttons without having to do anything for it. In a Shell presenter we have to build that functionality ourselves. When we press Cancel in a dialog, the changes are not applied to the model that we are viewing. With OK the changes are applied. Here we can do the opposite; if we press OK, we just close the view and if we press Cancel, we revert back to the original values. To store the old values we create additional instance variables in the RaceCarView.

Table 6.1

Aspects for the fields of the race car view

Component	Aspects
TextPresenter.Default view	name: season enabled: false
NumberPresenter.Integer text	name: startingNumber
Listpresenter.Drop-down list	name: team getTextBlock: [:each | each name]
Listpresenter.Drop-down list	name: defaultDriver getTextBlock: [:each | each name]
PushButton.OK button	command: #ok
PushButton.Cancel button	command: #cancel

When opening the view we copy the original values in those variables and when we press the Cancel button, we copy them back.

```
Shell subclass: #RaceCarView
      instanceVariableNames: 'seasonPresenter teamPresenter
      startingNumberPresenter defaultDriverPresenter
      origTeam origStartingNumber origDefaultDriver'
      classVariableNames: ''
      poolDictionaries: ''
```

RaceCarView>>onViewOpened
```
      ...
      self copyOriginalValues.
```

RaceCarView>>copyOriginalValues
```
      "Copy the original values so that we can cancel the
      changes"
      origStartingNumber := startingNumberPresenter value.
      origTeam := teamPresenter selectionOrNil.
      origDefaultDriver := defaultDriverPresenter
            selectionOrNil.
```

RaceCarView>>ok
```
      self view close
```

RaceCarView>>cancel
```
      self resetValues.
      self view close
```

RaceCarView>>resetValues
```
      "Cancel the changes"
      self model startingNumber: origStartingNumber.
      self model team: origTeam.
      self model defaultDriver: origDefaultDriver.
```

When you now try to open the view on an existing race car, you might be surprised by the error messages that you receive. You will see the error messages that we built ourselves earlier in this chapter. This sounds strange, as you don't have two cars with Michael Schumacher as the default driver and we're not working with a copy of the model like we did with dialogs.

So, what causes the error messages? Well, we've told the view to do something when the selection changes, namely try to set the selected value onto the model. We have a race car with Michael Schumacher as the driver, and when we try to "change" that, we ask the season if he's already a default driver, which he is, namely in the car that we're trying to change!

As this problem only occurs when we open a view on an existing race car, we can add a check to these "change" methods to see whether the presenter value is the same as the model value. If so, we don't have to worry because then it is the original setting.

RaceCarView>>teamSelectionChanged
```
    "The selected team changed, communicate that to the
    model"
    self model team: teamPresenter selection.
    teamPresenter selectionOrNil == self model team
        ifFalse: [
        self showTeamSelection.
        teamPresenter setFocus.
        ].
```

RaceCarView>>defaultDriverSelectionChanged
```
    "The selected default driver changed, communicate that
    to the model"
    self model defaultDriver: defaultDriverPresenter
        selection.
    DefaultDriverPresenter selectionOrNil == self model
        defaultDriver ifFalse: [
            self showDefaultDriverSelection.
            defaultDriverPresenter setFocus.
            ].
```

Now that we have it working properly, we can also check whether the starting number is already in use, and react accordingly.

RaceCarView>>createSchematicWiring
```
    ...
    startingNumberPresenter when: #focusLost send:
        #checkStartingNumber to: self.
    ...
```

```
RaceCarView>>checkStartingNumber
    "Check if starting number is OK. If not, reset focus"
    self model startingNumber: startingNumberPresenter
        value.
    startingNumberPresenter value = self model
        startingNumber
        ifFalse: [
            startingNumberPresenter value: (self model
                startingNumber).
            startingNumberPresenter view selectAll;
                setFocus.
        ].
    self setCaption.
```

6.3.4 Summary

In this section we have built a view that simulates the dialog functionality without the disadvantages of it by letting the presenter remember the original settings. We introduced global variables to hold the created teams and drivers so that we could fill the lists. By triggering the selection change events, we saw the validation error messages pop up when opening existing race cars. We managed our way round this problem by using a flag that enables the triggering.

The Circuit component

Before we can put all the components together in a race, we have to build one more component, namely the race circuit. We could make the race circuit similar to the team, with just a name and a location. But that wouldn't be much fun, so we'll add some complication to it. First we will add the length of the circuit, with an option to swap between miles and kilometers. And secondly we will add the current lap record, with a link to the driver who drove this lap record. To add the lap record, we have to extend the Time class and we have to build our own specific Time view.

We will end up with a view that looks like Figure 7.1.

Figure 7.1
The Circuit dialog

7.1 The basic Circuit model

The basic model is similar to what we've built before, therefore you can find the listing for it below.

```
MyModel subclass: #Circuit
    instanceVariableNames: 'location length lapRecord
    lapRecordDriver comment'
    classVariableNames: ''
    poolDictionaries: ''
```

Generate the standard accessors for all the instance variables. We will modify the ones that need modifying as we go.

7.1.1 The length of the circuit

Working with different measurement units.

For the length of the circuit, you would typically choose to record the length either in miles or kilometers. If required, you could then convert the presented value into the other unit. This is the simplest way, but not much fun. Therefore we are going to build it in such a way that you store the length in the unit in which you enter it. (This is typically the way in which you would build a multi-currency system. You would want to record the original currency value so that you don't lose the exact value in conversion errors.) This method ensures that what you've entered is actually stored, so that you don't lose precision in the conversion. However, you still might want to know the length in the other unit, so we build a function to convert between the two.

The kilometers and miles are two different units of measurement, therefore you could say that they are both subclasses of a common superclass, say length. The length itself is abstract, as it doesn't have a unit. But it does contain the length. The subclasses add their measurement unit to it. In this way we can give both units the same protocol; you can ask the Kilometer object to return itself as miles or as kilometers, and if you have a Mile object you can ask it the same question. In the abstract Length class we define the instance variable that holds the length and we define the way to create such a Length object. The length variable requires the standard accessors.

```
Object subclass: #Length
    instanceVariableNames: 'length'
    classVariableNames: ''
    poolDictionaries: ''
```

Length class>>length: aLength
    ^self basicNew length: aLength

```
Length subclass: #Kilometer
      instanceVariableNames: ''
      classVariableNames: ''
      poolDictionaries: ''
```

Kilometer>>asKilometers
```
      ^self length
```

```
Length subclass: #Mile
      instanceVariableNames: ''
      classVariableNames: ''
      poolDictionaries: ''
```

Mile>>asMiles
```
      ^self length
```

For the conversion we could just enter the conversion constant in both the Kilometer >> asMiles and the Mile >> asKilometers methods. But that would mean that if you find a more precise number, you would have to change it in both classes. Therefore, it would be better if we could just hold the constant in a place where both the Kilometer instances and the Mile instances could make use of it. The most obvious place is of course their joint superclass. As we want this to be available to all instances, we make it a class method.

Length class>>mileToKilometerConversionConstant
```
      ^1.609344
```

Now we can use this in our two conversion methods; in one case we divide the length by the constant, in the other we multiply. But wouldn't it be clearer if we used the same system of conversion, say multiply by the factor? We can do that by adding another class method in the Length class that does the division. Then both the conversion methods look virtually the same.

Length class>>kilometerToMileConversionConstant
```
      ^1/self mileToKilometerConversionConstant
```

Mile>>asKilometers
```
      ^self length*self class
           mileToKilometerConversionConstant
```

Kilometer>>asMiles
```
      ^self length*self class
           kilometerToMileConversionConstant
```

Now we can store either a Mile object or a Kilometer object in the length variable in the Circuit, and that object itself knows whether it is Miles or

Kilometers. If you want to know the length in the other unit, then the object itself knows whether to convert or not.

`Circuit>>lengthInKM`
```
    "Return the length of the circuit in kilometers"
    ^length asKilometers
```

`Circuit>>lengthInMile`
```
    "Return the length of the circuit in miles"
    ^length asMiles
```

As we are relying on the length to be either a Kilometer object or a Mile object, we'd better set it to either when we create a new instance:

`Circuit>>initialize`
```
    "Initialize the receiver"
    super initialize.
    self length: (Mile length: 0).
```

To set the length we can use different methods for the different length types.

`Circuit>>lengthInKM: aLength`
```
    "Set the length of the circuit in kilometers"
    self length: (Kilometer length: aLength).
```

`Circuit>>lengthInMile: aLength`
```
    "Set the length of the circuit in miles"
    self length: (Mile length: aLength).
```

With the following method we can display which type of length is used for the circuit.

`Circuit>>lengthType`
```
    ^length class
```

Now you can test the Circuit model in a workspace:

```
circuit := Circuit new.
circuit name: 'Silverstone'.
circuit location: 'United Kingdom'.
circuit lengthInMile: 3.194.
circuit inspect
circuit lengthInMile
circuit lengthInKM
circuit lengthType
```

7.1.2 *The lap record*

The lap record puts us in an interesting situation. We cannot use the standard Time presenters, as they show us either the 12-hour clock or the 24-hour clock. Even worse, they don't show us the milliseconds, even though the milliseconds make the difference between winning and losing in F1 racing.

Extending the Time class to allow setting and retrieving milliseconds.

What to do? We can't just use numbers, as they don't distinguish between hours, minutes, seconds, and milliseconds, unless we make them separate fields. We could just store and display the lap time as normal text, but then we can't do calculations with it and we can't control what the user is entering. It looks like the basic classes are failing on us. Well, not really, because we can extend the base classes so that they give us what we need.

The most obvious starting point is Time, as that already allows for calculations. Go into the CHB and have a look at the Time class. You will see that it already uses milliseconds as the basis for a Time instance; milliseconds is the instance variable of an instance of Time, and from there hours, minutes, and seconds are calculated. So now it is only a matter of finding a way to create a Time instance with milliseconds and to display it with those milliseconds. But before we do that we will first do some experimenting with the standard Time methods.

Most often Time instances are created from a Stream, like:

```
Time readFrom: (ReadStream on: '14:30').
```

Have a look in the CHB at this #readFrom: method in the Time class (Figure 7.2). It is of course a class method, as it creates a new Time instance.

In this case we create a time with 14 hours and 30 minutes. The 14 hours are converted to milliseconds, the 30 minutes are converted to milliseconds, and they are added together. Whenever we want to display the instance, the whole calculation is converted back to hours and minutes.

We are lucky that this is the way in which time is kept, because now we only have to add the number of milliseconds. There is one snag, however. In the above string we only had hours and minutes. We can add seconds to the string (try "14:30:16" for example), but it expects the stream to start with hours, and you can leave the seconds out.

In our case we want to do exactly the opposite; we always want to record the milliseconds and we can leave the hours and minutes out if we don't need them. We also might want to use different separators. The Time class works with the Windows Regional settings, typically a colon between the hours, minutes, and seconds. However, for recording lap times, quite often the minutes and seconds are separated by a ' (single quote) and the seconds and milliseconds are separated by a " (double quote). You also see just spaces in between the minutes, seconds, and milliseconds. So basically

Figure 7.2

Time class >> readFrom: method

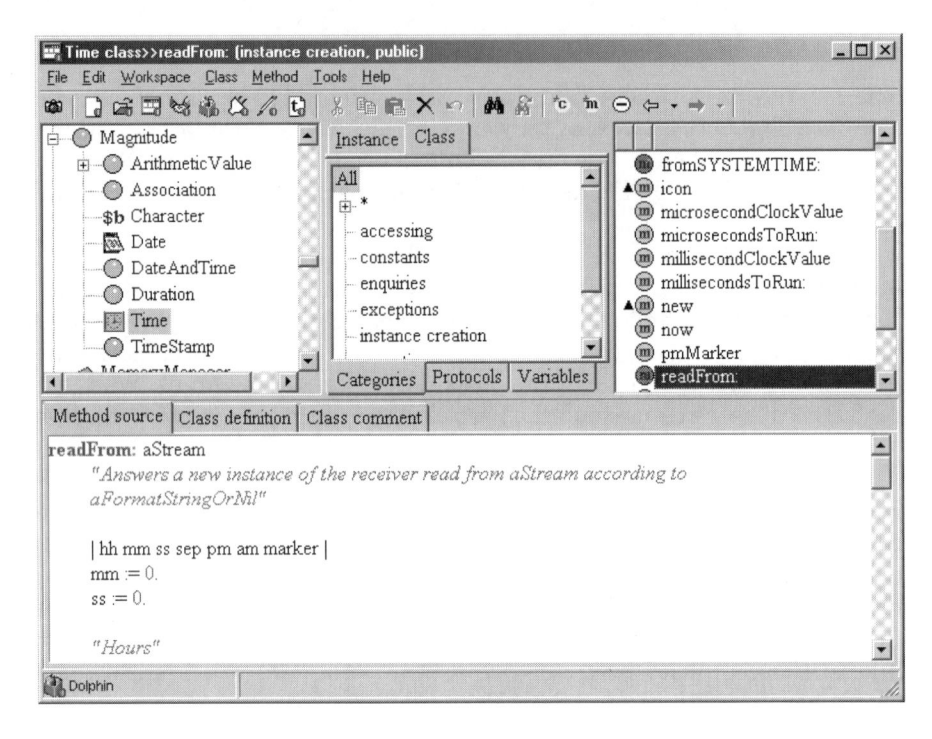

we can't rely on any specific character that separates the time elements. We do, however, know that each block of numbers represents something that we want. Then it is just a matter of counting the number of numeric blocks to know which are the milliseconds, which are the seconds, and so on.

The method below is a modified copy of the #readFrom: class method. You can create a copy by selecting the method and then just changing the method name in the method source. Remember that Smalltalk doesn't follow arithmetic precedence. The last line is a demonstration of the Smalltalk method send precedence, ignoring arithmetic precedence.

In our method we will allow for five blocks of numbers, so that you can also record sporting events that have elapsed times of more than a day, like round the world sailing. If there are more than five blocks of numbers, an error is raised. The method walks through the argument, aStream. It checks whether the next character is a digit. If so, we use the Integer class >> readFrom: method to read the whole number which we add to our collection. After going through the stream we check how many numbers we have in the collection. If there are fewer than five, we have to add zeros at the start, as we assume in the last line that we always have five numbers.

```
Time class>>readWithMillisecondsFrom: aStream
    "Answer a new instance of the receiver read from the
    argument, aStream.
    There is no expected format; any non-numeric character
    between days, hours, minutes, seconds, and
    milliseconds is allowed.
    It assumes always to have milliseconds, and from there
    it works backwards.
    An error is raised if there are more than 5 blocks of
    numbers"
    | coll |
    coll := OrderedCollection new.
    [aStream atEnd] whileFalse: [
         aStream peek isDigit ifTrue: [coll add: (Integer
              readFrom: aStream)].
         aStream atEnd ifFalse: [aStream next]
         ].
    (coll size > 5) ifTrue: [self error: 'Not a valid
         time'].
    [coll size < 5] whileTrue: [coll addFirst: 0].

    ^self fromMilliseconds:
         (coll at: 1) * 24  "days"
       +(coll at: 2) * 60  "hours"
       +(coll at: 3) * 60  "minutes"
       +(coll at: 4) * 1000 * "seconds"
       +(coll at: 5) "milliseconds"
```

Now that we are able to create a time suitable for sports, we also want to be able to get the information out. We can already ask an object of this type to show the number of hours, minutes, seconds, and milliseconds. But we can't ask the number of days yet. Therefore we add the following (instance) method, which is just a modified copy of the #hours method:

```
Time>>days
    "Answer the number of days represented by the
    receiver"
    ^(milliseconds // ##(24*60*60*1000))
```

This method uses two expressions that we haven't seen before, `//` and `##`. The `//` can be found in the ArithmeticValue class; it is a method to divide and truncate the result. The `##` is an internal Dolphin Smalltalk optimization. When you accept this method, the expression inside the `##` is actually calculated instead of stored as is. This means that the calculation doesn't have to be done every time you use this method. The alternative would have been to work out the multiplication ourselves and store that in our method, but that number (86 400 000) isn't as self-explanatory as the multiplication.

And finally we want a way to display the whole Time instance according to our own format. Therefore we need to create our own #printOn: message in the Time class. As we don't want to override the existing one, we call our method #printWithMillisecondsOn:. To use it in a workspace we add a #printWithMilliseconds as well, which uses the #printWithMillisecondsOn: method.

```
Time>>printWithMillisecondsOn: aStream
    "Print the time with milliseconds. Ignore days, hours,
    and minutes if they are zero.
    Used to show sport results"
    (self days = 0) ifFalse: [
        aStream nextPutAll: self days printString.
        aStream nextPut: $d.
            ].
    ((self days = 0) and: [ self hours = 0 ]) ifFalse: [
        aStream nextPutAll: self hours printString.
        aStream nextPut: $:.
        (self minutes < 10) ifTrue: [ aStream nextPut:
            $0 ].
            ].
    ((self days = 0) and: [ (self hours = 0) and:
        [ self minutes= 0 ]]) ifFalse: [
            aStream nextPutAll: self minutes
                printString.
            aStream nextPut: $:.
            (self seconds < 10) ifTrue: [aStream
                nextPut: $0].
                ].
    aStream nextPutAll: self seconds printString.
    aStream nextPut: $..
    (self milliseconds < 100) ifTrue: [ aStream nextPut:
        $0 ].
    (self milliseconds < 10) ifTrue: [ aStream nextPut: $0
        ].
    aStream nextPutAll: self milliseconds printString.
    ^aStream
```

In the first block we test whether we have days. If so, we print them and we print a separator, in this case the character d. In the next block we test whether we should print hours. We have to print hours when they are not 0 or when we have days. If we print hours and the number of minutes is less than 10, then we want a leading 0 on the minutes. In the seconds block we do the same. We always want to print the seconds, even if they are 0, therefore we don't do a test here. Finally we test whether the milliseconds require leading zeros.

```
Time>>printWithMilliseconds
      "Print the time with milliseconds. Ignore days, hours,
      and minutes if they are zero.
      Used to show sport results"
      | aStream |
      aStream := WriteStream on: String new.
      self printWithMillisecondsOn: aStream.
      ^aStream contents
```

Let's see if it all works as expected. Try the following lines in a workspace with Ctrl + E:

```
time1 := Time readWithMillisecondsFrom: (ReadStream on:
      '1:29:125').
time1 printWithMilliseconds
time2 := Time readWithMillisecondsFrom: (ReadStream on:
      '1:05:29:125').
time2 printWithMilliseconds
time3 := Time readWithMillisecondsFrom: (ReadStream on:
      '16 14 31 49 625').
time3 printWithMilliseconds
time4 := Time readWithMillisecondsFrom: (ReadStream on:
      '16d14h31m49s625').
time4 printWithMilliseconds
time5 := time3 addTime: time4.
time5 printWithMilliseconds
time6 := Time readWithMillisecondsFrom: (ReadStream on:
      '25 16 14 31 49 625').
```

Now we can test this for the Circuit instance that we created in Section 7.1.

```
circuit lapRecord: (Time readWithMillisecondsFrom:
      (ReadStream on: '1:24.475').
circuit lapRecord printWithMilliseconds.
```

That's step one. The next step is to integrate this new way of recording and displaying time in the views.

7.1.3 Summary

In these subsections we have seen two ways of storing values with their units. We can decide always to store the value in a predefined unit and then convert the value whenever asked. This means that the value has to be converted to the predefined unit, which might cause conversion differences. The alternative is to store the unit with the value, exactly as entered. As this unit is basically the same as a class, we made an abstract class with two subclasses for the specific units. These two classes share their protocol, so that the user of those classes doesn't need to know whether the instance needs to be converted. The instances themselves are capable of showing themselves in either unit.

The other subject that we've covered in these subsections is an extension to the Time class so that we can record milliseconds and if necessary days. We had to build a method to create a Time instance and methods to retrieve the additional information in the Time instance.

7.2 The Circuit presenter and view

Now that we have cracked the circuit length and the lap time, we can concentrate on building the circuit presenter and view. We are going to build the Circuit view as a dialog view, like we've done before. Therefore, we have to subclass the Dialog presenter class for the Circuit presenter class. Like we said at the beginning of this chapter, we want the dialog to look like Figure 7.3.

On the view we find the following elements:

- a text presenter for the name;
- a text presenter for the location;
- a number presenter for the length;
- a group of buttons to decide whether the length is in miles or kilometers;
- a time presenter to show the current lap record;
- a drop-down list from which we can select the driver who drove the lap record;
- a multi-line text box for comment about the circuit.

The text presenters aren't very exciting anymore, they are just like the ones we've done in the previous components. Therefore we won't pay much attention to them.

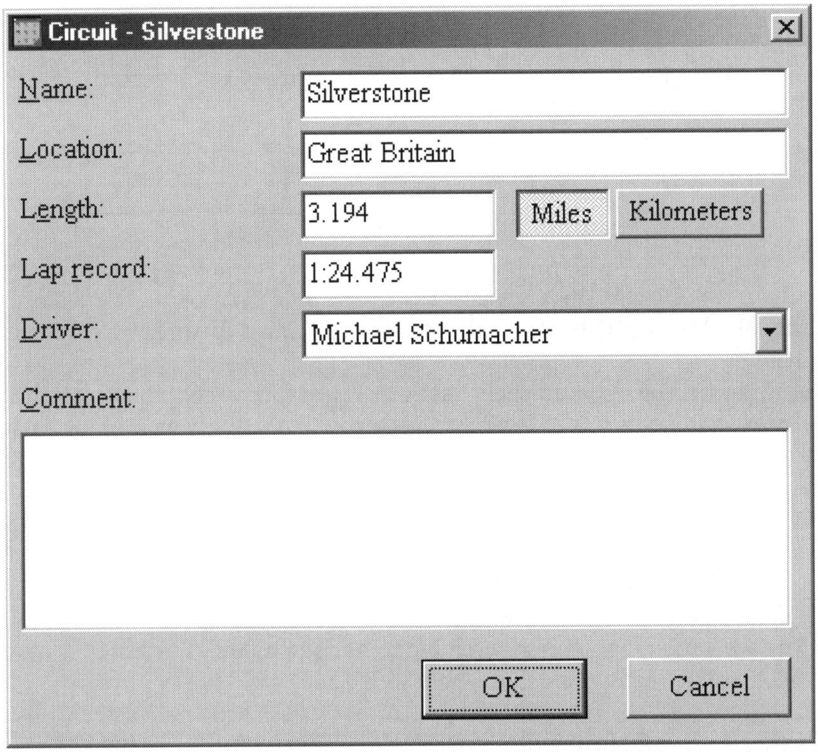

THE CIRCUIT COMPONENT

Figure 7.3
The Circuit dialog

We start by creating a presenter class, holding the presenter variables:

```
Dialog subclass: #CircuitDialogPresenter
    instanceVariableNames: 'namePresenter
    locationPresenter lengthPresenter lengthTypePresenter
    lapRecordPresenter lapRecordDriverPresenter
    commentPresenter'
    classVariableNames: ''
    poolDictionaries: ''
```

And the #createComponents method:

```
CircuitDialogPresenter>>createComponents
    "Create the view components"
    super createComponents.
    namePresenter := self add: TextPresenter new name:
        'name'.
    locationPresenter := self add: TextPresenter new name:
        'location'.
    lengthPresenter := self add: NumberPresenter new name:
        'length'.
```

```
lengthTypePresenter := self add: ListPresenter new
        name: 'mileOrKM'.
lapRecordPresenter := self add: TimePresenter new
        name: 'lapRecord'.
lapRecordDriverPresenter := self add: ListPresenter
        new name: 'lapRecordDriver'.
commentPresenter := self add: TextPresenter new name:
        'comment'.
```

This allows us to build the view according to Table 7.1.

Some of the controls have additional settings different from the default.

The mileOrKM view has the "hasButtons" aspect set to true, so that the tabs appear as buttons. We have seen this before, when we looked at the ways in which we could display the gender setting of the driver (see Section 4.3.4).

As we have done before, we change the "wantTab" aspect in the multi-line text box for the comment to false, and we change the "isDefault" aspect in the OK button to true. And that is all as far as the view is concerned.

Before we can test the view, we have to add a #model: method.

Table 7.1

Fields of the circuit view

Type	Field	Position	Extent
TextPresenter.Static text	&Name:	5@10	80@25
TextPresenter.Default view	name	150@10	250@25
TextPresenter.Static text	&Location:	5@40	80@25
TextPresenter.Default view	location	150@40	250@25
TextPresenter.Static text	&Length:	5@70	80@25
NumberPresenter.Default view	length	150@70	100@25
ListPresenter.Tab view	mileOrKM	260@70	140@30
TextPresenter.Static text	Lap &record:	5@100	80@25
TimePresenter.Text view	lapRecord	150@100	100@25
TextPresenter.Static text	&Driver:	5@130	80@25
ListPresenter.Drop down list	lapRecordDriver	150@130	250@27
TextPresenter.Static text	&Comment:	5@160	80@25
TextPresenter.Multiline text	comment	5@190	395@100
PushButton.OK button	OK	210@300	85@30
PushButton.Cancel button	Cancel	315@300	85@30

THE CIRCUIT COMPONENT

```
CircuitDialogPresenter>>model: aCircuit
    "Create the link between the model and the presenter
    via a buffer"
    | aspectBuffer |
    super model: aCircuit.
    aspectBuffer := self model.
    namePresenter model: (aspectBuffer aspectValue:
        #name).
    locationPresenter model: (aspectBuffer aspectValue:
        #location).
    lapRecordPresenter model: (aspectBuffer aspectValue:
        #lapRecord).
    commentPresenter model: (aspectBuffer aspectValue:
        #comment).
```

For the caption we need the #captionSubstring method and we need to call the #setCaption method in our #onViewOpened method.

```
CircuitDialogPresenter>>captionSubstring
    "Return the class specific substring for the caption"
    ^'Circuit - '
```

```
CircuitDialogPresenter>>onViewOpened
    "Set the caption"
    super onViewOpened.
    self setCaption.
```

The next task is to fill the combo box with the available drivers, and if you open a circuit where a driver is already set, then that driver should be shown. For now we take the same approach as in the previous chapter.

```
CircuitDialogPresenter>>allDrivers
    "Build a sorted list of drivers to choose from"
    ^AllDrivers asSortedCollection: [ :a :b |
        (a surname, a firstname) <= (b surname, b
        firstname)]
```

This method has to be connected to the lapRecordDriverPresenter in the #model: method:

```
CircuitDialogPresenter>>model: aCircuit
    "Create the link between the model and the presenter
    via a buffer"
    ...
    lapRecordDriverPresenter model: (ListModel on: (self
        allDrivers)).
```

We have to communicate the current lapRecordDriver from the Circuit to the listPresenter, so that we see it when we open the dialog. We call this method while we open the view:

CircuitDialogPresenter>>onViewOpened
```
...
    lapRecordDriverPresenter selection: (self model
        lapRecordDriver) ifAbsent: [nil].
```

Now when we open a circuit with an existing lap record driver, it is shown as the current one. What remains is updating the model when we change the selection. As the listPresenter is not directly connected to the Circuit model, we have to do something ourselves. But we only want to update the driver if OK is pressed, not if Cancel is pressed. In the Season presenter we did something similar with the scorelist (see Section 5.3.3). We updated the value in the model through the #apply method. Here we will do the same.

CircuitDialogPresenter>>apply
```
    "Communicate the changes"
    super apply.
    self updateLapRecordDriver.
```

The #updateLapRecordDriver just reads the current selection from the listPresenter and updates the model. Note that the model in a dialog is an aspectBuffer, holding a subject and a subjectCopy. As we want to update the subject, we have to specify that explicitly.

CircuitDialogPresenter>>updateLapRecordDriver
```
    "Update the lap record driver on the model"
    self model subject lapRecordDriver:
        lapRecordDriverPresenter selectionOrNil.
```

The dialog should now work apart from the length and the lap record. For those we have to do a bit extra.

7.2.1 *The milliseconds TypeConverter*

We will create a type converter that converts text to a time with milliseconds and the other way round.

Before we start building our own milliseconds view, let's have a look how the current Time field works. In the list of resources you can see that there are two resources linked to the TimePresenter, the Default view and the Text view. The Default view is based on the Microsoft DateTimePicker control and the second one is based on an Edit control. We have used the DateTimePicker control before, namely to set the date of birth for the driver (see Section 4.2.2). When you use this control for a Time, you are presented with up and down arrows with which you can modify the time. The time segments (hours, minutes, and seconds) are hard-coded in the control, therefore this control cannot be used to show the milliseconds. This means that we have to focus on the Edit control.

The Edit control is basically a field that allows any text to be entered. However, it can be extended with a converter, where the entered text is converted into whatever you want. It works the other way round as well when the field has to display data. That sounds like what we need. We already have a method to convert a Stream into a Time object with milliseconds, and we have a method to display a Time object with milliseconds. Now we only have to find out how this conversion takes place.

If you open a TimePresenter.Text view, you will see in the list of aspects that it has a TimeToText type converter. This is a class like any other class, so we can have a look in the CHB to see what it does. The most important methods are #leftToRight: and #rightToLeft:, which do the conversion. For the rest there are methods that are related to formatting, which use the Microsoft formatting string (again, see Section 4.2.2). We don't want to use all that, so we are better off creating a new class at the same level as the TimeToText class instead of using a subclass.

```
AbstractToTextConverter subclass: #MillisecondsTimeToText
    instanceVariableNames: ''
    classVariableNames: ''
    poolDictionaries: ''
```

(Following Smalltalk naming conventions, you would call the #MillisecondsTimesToText class the MillisecondsTimeToText<u>Converter</u> class; however, this convention was not followed for the other converters in Dolphin, therefore I choose to follow the naming conventions in Dolphin.)

This class requires its own #leftToRight: and #rightToLeft: methods and that's it. The method #leftToRight: converts the Time object to a string, which we have already done in Time >> #printWithMilliseconds. Therefore we can just call that method:

```
MillisecondsTimeToText>>leftToRight: aTime
    "Private - Answers the result of converting aTime with
    milliseconds to a String"
    ^aTime printWithMilliseconds
```

The method #rightToLeft: converts the entered string into a Time instance, for which we wrote the Time class >> readWithMillisecondsFrom:. That method expects a stream, so we have to convert the string into a stream:

```
MillisecondsTimeToText>>rightToLeft: aString
    "Private - Answers the result of converting aString to
    a Time with milliseconds"
    ^Time readWithMillisecondsFrom: (ReadStream on:
        aString)
```

We have to make sure that the system does not try to make a conversion when there is nothing to convert. This is done by setting the rightExceptionalValue. You can see how it all works in TypeConverter >> convertFromRightToLeft: and TypeConverter >> convertFromLeftToRight:. The #initialize method is just a copy of the #initialize method of the TimeToText class:

```
MillisecondsTimeToText>>initialize
    "Private - Initialize the receiver"
    rightExceptionalValue := String empty
```

The last thing we have to do before we can use this is to create a resource with this type converter. As we want it to be similar to the TimePresenter.Text view, we can just as well copy and modify that. Therefore double-click on the TimePresenter.Text view in the resource list. This opens a view composer with the resource. Evaluate the following in the workspace of the view composer, which sets the type converter to the one we've just created.

```
self typeconverter: MillisecondsTimeToText new
```

Save it as MillisecondsText view. Now it is ready for use.

Remember to move the Time methods, MillisecondsTimeToText class, and the MillisecondsText resource to your own extension package.

To use it in our Circuit dialog we can replace the current lap-record field with the one that we just created. But that would mean that we have to delete the current field, add the new field, set all the aspects again and sort out the tab order. There should be a better way, and there is. We can just change the typeConverter aspect of the field to our MillisecondsTimeToText converter. However, if you double-click on the type converter, you don't see the MillisecondsTimeToText converter. Why doesn't it appear there? This list is built up through a ClassCategory. You can find it by looking at the TextEdit class method #applicableTypeConverter Categories. Here you see that it looks for classes with a ClassCategory called "MVP-Type Converters-Text". This means that we have to add our MillisecondsTimeToText class to the list of classes held in that ClassCategory. We do that with the Class menu option Category. Select the above-mentioned category and when you now double-click on the type converter in a TextEdit box, the MillisecondsTimeToText converter will appear as well. Select our converter, save the view, and test it. You should now be able to see the milliseconds and edit them.

This shows how relatively simple it is to add your own controls to Dolphin Smalltalk.

In some cases we want to convert the displayed value, other times we want to store the displayed value.

7.2.2 *The length of the circuit*

The way in which we set up the length in our model gives us the opportunity to store the length in either miles or kilometers, and independent of that, display it in either miles or kilometers. It will automatically convert the stored value if necessary without changing it, so that we don't lose any precision after a number of conversions. The downside of this approach is that we cannot link the length presenter straight to the length variable in our model. We also have to keep track of the difference between just displaying a converted value and actually changing the value. The first can be caused by the user wanting to see the length of the track in the other measurement type, whereas with the second we have to update the model with the new value.

Let's start by making a local copy of the model's length variable, which we copy back to the model when we apply the changes.

```
Dialog subclass: #CircuitDialogPresenter
     instanceVariableNames: 'namePresenter
     locationPresenter lengthPresenter lengthTypePresenter
     localLength
     lapRecordPresenter lapRecordDriverPresenter
     commentPresenter'
     classVariableNames: ''
     poolDictionaries: ''
```

CircuitDialogPresenter>>model: aCircuit
```
    ...
    localLength := aspectBuffer length copy.
```

The next step is to show the locally stored length and length type. Here we have to split the information into the actual length and the length type, which is its class. The length type then needs to be mapped to the buttons on the dialog.

CircuitDialogPresenter>>showLength
```
    lengthPresenter value: (localLength length).
    lengthTypePresenter selectionByIndex: (#(Mile
        Kilometer)
            identityIndexOf: localLength class name)
```

CircuitDialogPresenter>>onViewOpened
```
    ...
    self showLength.
```

Before we can use the lengthTypePresenter, we first have to fill the list with values. We can just set these values in the model. Add the following line to the #model: method:

CircuitDialogPresenter>>model: aCircuit
```
    ...
    lengthTypePresenter model: (ListModel on #(#Miles
    #Kilometers)).
```

If you now test it on a circuit in which you have set a length and a length type, you should be able to see the length with the correct button pressed for the length type. Pressing the other button or changing the length won't do anything yet though. To let the buttons work, we want to send either #asMiles or #asKilometers to the Length instance, depending on which button is pressed. The value that is returned needs to be displayed in the length presenter.

As we only want a single method that can do the job for both miles and kilometers, we have to translate the selection into either of the methods that we want to call. We can do that by using symbols, and then "perform" the selected symbol on the model. Here you see another use of the symbol, as a means of communicating a method name within messages. (The #perform: group of messages is very powerful, but there are downsides to it. First of all, they do not perform as well as direct message sends, as they take an indirect route. The other downside, which is a more serious one, is that this indirect way of sending messages makes it harder to trace which methods are used. As debugging and refactoring tools heavily rely on the traceability of method use, the #perform: group of messages is normally avoided.)

```
CircuitDialogPresenter>>convertLength
    "Show the length in the requested length type"
    | symbol |
    lengthPresenter value notNil ifTrue: [
        symbol := (#(#asMiles #asKilometers) at:
            lengthTypePresenter selectionByIndex).
        lengthPresenter value: (localLength perform:
            symbol)]
```

Suppose we have the Kilometer button pressed and this method is called. In that case lengthTypePresenter selectionByIndex will return 2. Therefore the symbol variable is set to the second symbol in the array, #asKilometers. In the last line the lengthPresenter value is set to whatever the Length instance returns from #asKilometers. So now we only have to make sure that this method is called whenever the user changes the selected button. As we have seen before, we do that in createSchematicWiring:

```
CircuitDialogPresenter>>createSchematicWiring
    "Create the trigger wiring"
    super createSchematicWiring.
    lengthTypePresenter when: #selectionChanged send:
        #convertLength to: self.
```

If you now open a circuit with a length, it will convert the length whenever you change between Kilometers and Miles.

For changing the length we can take a similar approach to what we have done with the lap record driver. We enter something in the field, and update the model when we #apply the changes. That sounds simple enough, but in this case there is a complication.

First of all, if we display a Mile instance, and then convert it to kilometers, we change the displayed value, which means that we would normally write that back to the model. That's not what we want. We can avoid that by using a flag that is set whenever the user really changes the length by typing something in the lengthPresenter field. We extend the model with a variable called lengthChanged that can hold the flag, and set the flag to false when opening the view. When it comes to updating the local length, we first check whether the user really entered something or whether the value was changed because of conversion.

```
Dialog subclass: #CircuitDialogPresenter
      instanceVariableNames: 'namePresenter
      locationPresenter lengthPresenter lengthTypePresenter
      localLength lengthChanged lapRecordPresenter
      lapRecordDriverPresenter commentPresenter'
      classVariableNames: ''
      poolDictionaries: ''
```

CircuitDialogPresenter>>model: aCircuit
      ...
      lengthChanged := false.

CircuitDialogPresenter>>updateLocalLength
      "Check if the length has changed and update the local
      length if required"
      lengthChanged ifTrue: [
           lengthTypePresenter selectionByIndex = 1 ifTrue:
                [localLength :=
                     Mile length: lengthPresenter value].
           lengthTypePresenter selectionByIndex = 2 ifTrue:
                [localLength :=
                     Kilometer length: lengthPresenter value].
           lengthChanged := false.
           ].

Now we have to find appropriate triggers to set the lengthChanged variable and to update the local length. We can see those triggers by asking the field's class its publishedEventsOfInstances. Remember that even though we present a number, we are using a TextEdit field to show it. The next line returns a set of all the symbols that are triggered by the field.

      TextEdit publishedEventsOfInstances

The NumberPresenter adds the trigger #valueChanged to this list. For the #updateLocalLength method the #valueChanged trigger is appropriate, as long as we make sure that the lengthChanged variable is set at the right time, as that is not only triggered when the user enters a new value, but also when the length is shown in the other length type. The trigger to use for setting the lengthChanged variable is #keyTyped:, as that is triggered when the user presses any character while in the field.

```
CircuitDialogPresenter>>createSchematicWiring
    ...
    lengthPresenter when: #keyTyped: send:
    #setLengthChangedFlag to: self.
    lengthPresenter when: #valueChanged send:
    #updateLocalLength to: self.

CircuitDialogPresenter>>setLengthChangedFlag
    lengthChanged := true
```

When we press OK on the dialog, we want to apply the changes, which means that we update the length variable in the model with the local length variable.

```
CircuitDialogPresenter>>apply
    ...
    self updateLength.

CircuitDialogPresenter>>updateLength
    "Update the model with the local length instance"
    self model subject length: localLength.
```

7.2.3 Summary

In the above subsections we have built a new view resource which enables us to enter and display Time objects with days, hours, minutes, seconds, and milliseconds. To support this we had to build a type converter between text and time with milliseconds. After we integrated that into our dialog, we linked the unit buttons to the conversion routines in our Length subclasses, so that the user can do on-the-fly conversions. We added event triggering and flags to the presenter so that the length is only updated after the user enters a new value.

8 The Race component

Now that we have all the components for a race, we can start thinking about the race itself. In this chapter we will first consider what constitutes a race and from there we will implement it. We will make two screens, one to create the race and one to enter and maintain the results of a race. That maintenance screen will look like Figure 8.1.

8.1 The Race model

How to create, hold and access complex objects, the advantages and disadvantages of lazy initialization, and the use of temporary variables within blocks.

As the race is quite a complex object, we start by discussing what it actually is. First of all, a race is held at a certain location on a certain date within a season. This already gives us a starting point from which we can explore a race further. The season plays a central role in our overall model, therefore it needs easy access to the race. This means that we have to make that relationship bidirectional. The relationship between the race and the circuit is slightly different, as you would normally not require access to the races from within a race circuit. If needed, we can always find a less direct way to collect that information.

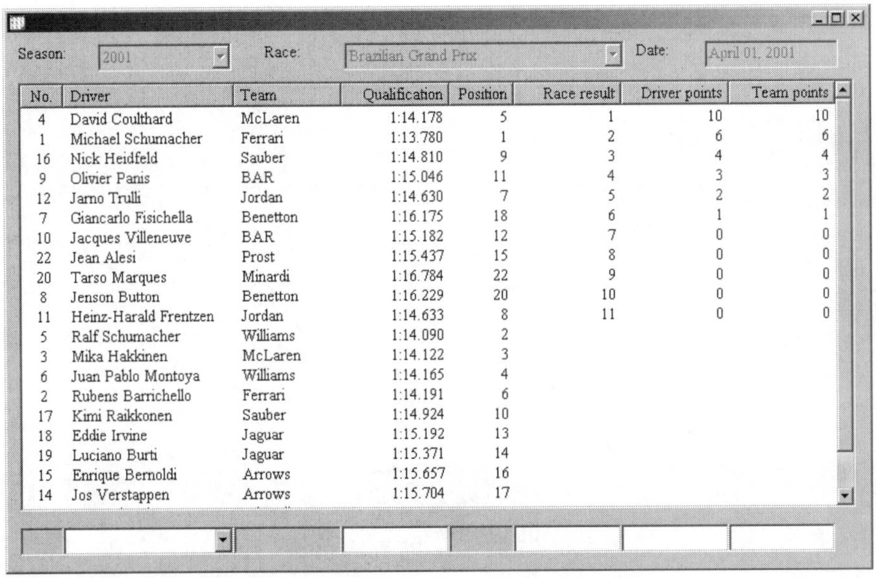

No.	Driver	Team	Qualification	Position	Race result	Driver points	Team points
4	David Coulthard	McLaren	1:14.178	5	1	10	10
1	Michael Schumacher	Ferrari	1:13.780	1	2	6	6
16	Nick Heidfeld	Sauber	1:14.810	9	3	4	4
9	Olivier Panis	BAR	1:15.046	11	4	3	3
12	Jarno Trulli	Jordan	1:14.630	7	5	2	2
7	Giancarlo Fisichella	Benetton	1:16.175	18	6	1	1
10	Jacques Villeneuve	BAR	1:15.182	12	7	0	0
22	Jean Alesi	Prost	1:15.437	15	8	0	0
20	Tarso Marques	Minardi	1:16.784	22	9	0	0
8	Jenson Button	Benetton	1:16.229	20	10	0	0
11	Heinz-Harald Frentzen	Jordan	1:14.633	8	11	0	0
5	Ralf Schumacher	Williams	1:14.090	2			
3	Mika Hakkinen	McLaren	1:14.122	3			
6	Juan Pablo Montoya	Williams	1:14.165	4			
2	Rubens Barrichello	Ferrari	1:14.191	6			
17	Kimi Raikkonen	Sauber	1:14.924	10			
18	Eddie Irvine	Jaguar	1:15.192	13			
19	Luciano Burti	Jaguar	1:15.371	14			
15	Enrique Bernoldi	Arrows	1:15.657	16			
14	Jos Verstappen	Arrows	1:15.704	17			

Figure 8.1
The race maintenance window

Based on this summary we can draw the class diagram shown in Figure 8.2.

The race cars require a bit more consideration. From the discussions in the RaceCar chapter (Chapter 6), we already know that we need to do something special for the driver. In the RaceCar class we gave the cars a default driver, as we acknowledged that the actual driver in a specific race can be different from the driver that we originally associated with a car.

Together (the driver and the car) these objects hopefully create a starting position in the race through the qualification rounds. If their qualification time is more than 107 percent of the fastest, then they don't get a starting position. If they do manage to stay within the 107 percent, then they get a starting position, sorted based on the qualification time, the fastest first. During the race they create a result, which might provide points for the team and the driver as per our points definition in the Season object.

Be aware that the team and the driver both qualify for points, because the FIA, the ruling organization, can decide to disqualify a team and/or a driver, thus depriving them of their points. Even though this is rare, we do have to cater for the situation where the team gets points and the driver doesn't, or the other way round.

Taking all this into consideration, it looks like we can't resolve this from within the race model, we have to do something different. Well, why not make a separate class for this complicated "thing", and just tie it all together in that class. Within a race we can hold all these complex objects so that we hold all information regarding a race within the race itself.

Based on the description above, this complex object needs to hold the following:

- a race car
- a driver

Figure 8.2
The Race model

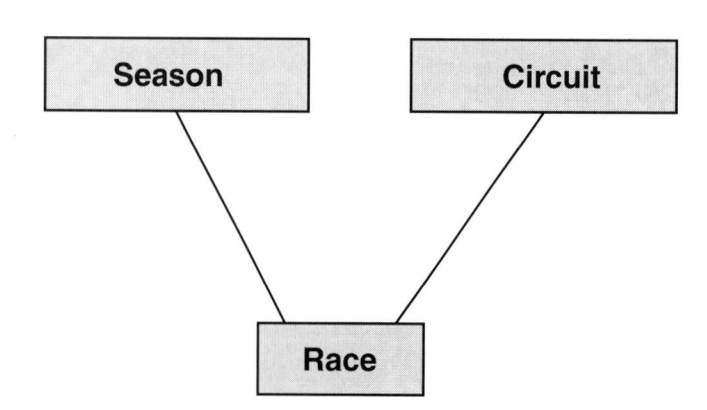

- a qualification result
- a race result
- team points gained
- driver points gained.

We might want to maintain additional information like fastest lap and racing distance, but we can easily extend the class definition to cater for that.

In Smalltalk development you will see this kind of situation very regularly. You come to a point where you can't see how to capture all that information in a single object. Virtually always the way out is just to make it a separate class of a "complex object", which can then be held in a collection held by the holder. Let's call our "complex object" a Starter, as it tries to gain a starting position in the race (Figure 8.3).

Concluding this little design discussion, we need to create two classes, with the following definitions:

```
MyModel subclass: #Race
     instanceVariableNames: 'season circuit date starters'
     classVariableNames: ''
     poolDictionaries: ''
```

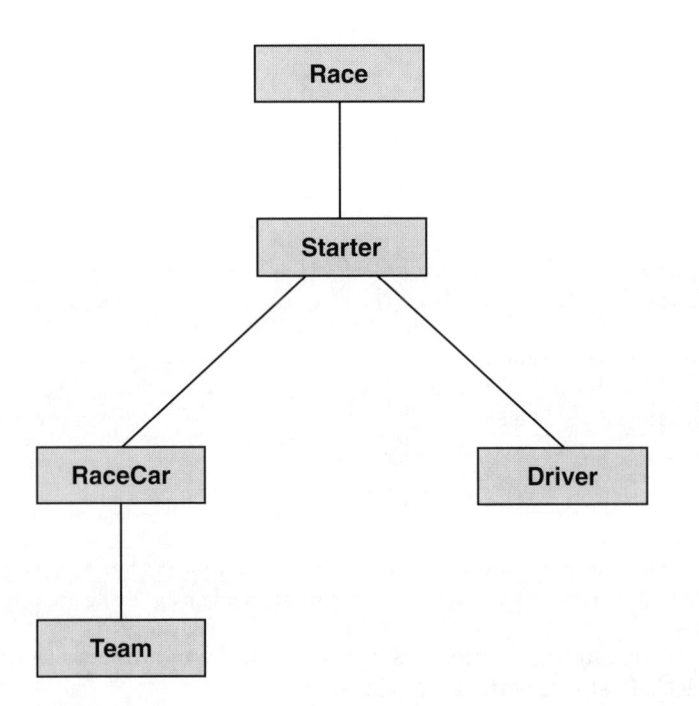

Figure 8.3
The Starter model

```
MyModel subclass: #Starter
    instanceVariableNames: 'race raceCar driver
    qualificationResult startingPosition raceResult
    driverPoints teamPoints'
    classVariableNames: ''
    poolDictionaries: ''
```

Generate the standard accessors for the variables; we'll modify them where needed. As we want to be able to see the starting number of the race car, we add the following methods.

Starter>>startingNumber
```
^self raceCar startingNumber
```

Starter>>name
```
^self startingNumber printString
```

We have to modify the Season class to hold the races, similar to what we did for the RaceCar. Here we will make use of the error mechanism that we discussed in Section 6.2. For now, we initialize the races variable on the season as an OrderedCollection.

```
MyModel subclass: #Season
    instanceVariableNames: 'scoreDefinition raceCars
    races'
    classVariableNames: ''
    poolDictionaries: ''
```

Season>>initialize
```
    ...
    races := OrderedCollection new.
```

Season>>races
```
    "Return the races in their date order"
    ^races asSortedCollection: [ :a :b | a date < b date ]
```

Season>>addRace: aRace
```
    "Add a race"
    races add: aRace.
```

Season>>removeRace: aRace
```
    "Remove a race. Report an error if the race can't be
    found"
    races remove: aRace ifAbsent: [^MessageBox errorMsg:
        'This race doesn''t exist in this season'].
```

Apart from the standard accessors, we won't add any methods to the race for now; let's first concentrate on the starters.

A starter always belongs to a race, therefore we use the same technique that we used before to guarantee that we have an association between the race and the starter.

Starter class>>new
    `"Disallow direct creation - use #forRace: instead"`
    `^self shouldNotImplement`

Starter class>>forRace: aRace
    `"Create a new starter for a specific race"`
    `^super new race: aRace`

The starters are held in a collection in the race. We have to initialize this collection before we can use it. So far we have used the #initialize method to initialize instance variables. There is, however, another way to handle this situation, which is called "lazy initialization". This approach takes the view that you shouldn't initialize an instance variable until the moment that you need it. Especially if the initialization is quite costly (in terms of either performance or memory consumption) and the instance variable is not always used, this approach has its value.

In our case you could argue that creating the collection is quite costly; however, we always need it as a race without starters can hardly be called a race. But to demonstrate the principle we will implement the "lazy initialization" nevertheless. The main thing to remember about lazy initialization is that you don't want to end up getting error messages because you are sending collection-type messages to a non-initialized variable. This can be avoided by always using the accessor and modifying the accessor so that it always returns the required type. So you just move the initialization of the variable to the accessor.

Race>>starters
    `"return the starters. If not yet initialized,`
    `initialize the variable"`
    `starters isNil ifTrue: [ starters := OrderedCollection`
        `new ].`
    `^starters`

Race>>addStarter: aStarter
    `"Add a starter. Make sure that a race car doesn't`
    `exist twice"`
    `self starters isEmpty ifFalse: [`
        `self starters anySatisfy: [ :each |`
            `each raceCar == aStarter raceCar ]`
                `ifTrue: [ ^MessageBox errorMsg: 'This race`
                `car already exists for this race' ]].`
    `starters add: aStarter.`

```
Race>>removeStarter: aStarter
    "Remove a starter. Report an error if the starter
    can't be found"
    self starters remove: aStarter ifAbsent: [^MessageBox
        errorMsg:
        'This starter doesn''t exist in this race'].
```

We can assume that all race cars in a season want to qualify for a race, therefore we can build a method that takes all RaceCars for a season and generates Starter objects for them. Here we use the defaultDriver to set the drivers, and allow them to be changed for this specific race.

```
Race>>generateStarters
    "Generate the starters based on the race cars for the
    season"
    self starters addAll:
        ( self season raceCars collect:
            [ :each | | aStarter |
            aStarter := Starter forRace: self.
            aStarter raceCar: each;
                driver: each defaultDriver ])
```

> Note that we use a temporary variable within a block. Not all versions of Smalltalk support this option. In that case you have to declare the temporary variable at the start of the method and then assign it from within the method. The advantages of declaring it within the block are performance and allocation of resources, but within these relatively small objects you will hardly notice the difference.

8.2 The Race presenter and view

In this chapter we will build two different views, one to create the race and one to maintain the race results.

When we create a new race, we select a season and a circuit, give it a name and then generate the starters. For the creation of a race we will make use of a dialog like we built before.

Once we've created the race, we want to see the list of starters. In the list we want to be able to modify the qualifying results and the race results. Based on the race results the points can be shown, which on rare occasions have to be modified. We could make the screen look like Figure 8.4.

THE RACE COMPONENT

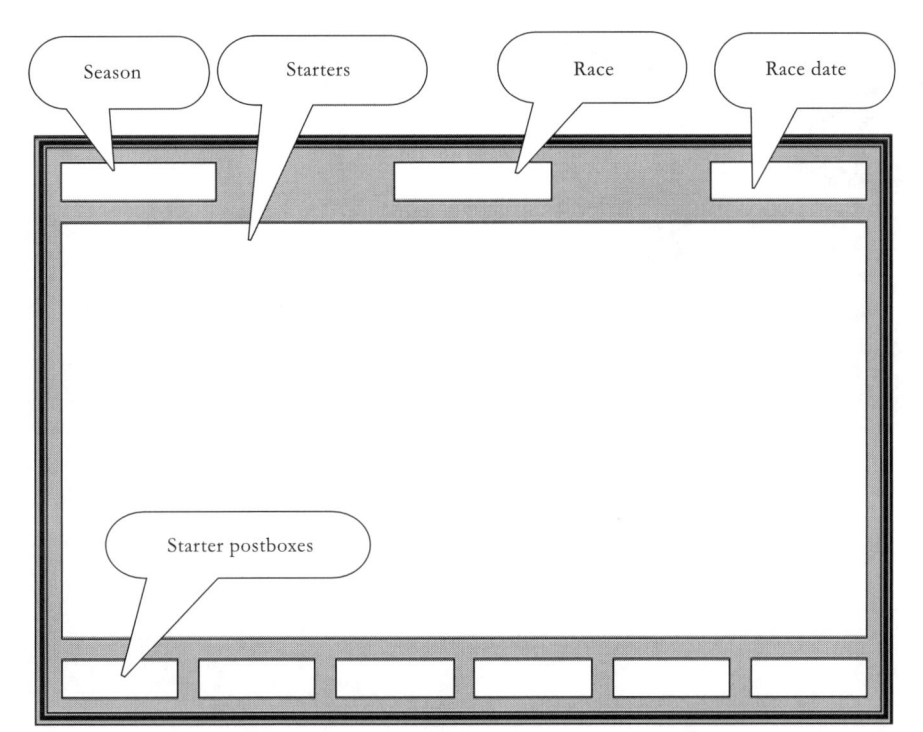

Figure 8.4
A drawing of the race maintenance screen

[Figure 8.4: A drawing of the race maintenance screen with labeled fields: Season, Starters, Race, Race date, and Starter postboxes]

Let's start with the dialog so that we can create races. After that we can create the main view.

8.2.1 The Race dialog

The Race dialog doesn't have many secrets for us anymore. We will make it look like Figure 8.5.

The circuit and the season are made part of the aspect buffer by creating "dummy" variables and value presenters for them like we did before, so that we don't have to worry about canceling the changes. To fill the lists of seasons and circuits we have to create global variables, like we did in Section 6.3.1.

Generating objects as a result of the creation of another object.

```
Dialog subclass: #RaceDialog
    instanceVariableNames: 'namePresenter seasonsPresenter
    currentSeason circuitsPresenter currentCircuit
    datePresenter'
    classVariableNames: ''
    poolDictionaries: ''
```

Figure 8.5
The Race dialog

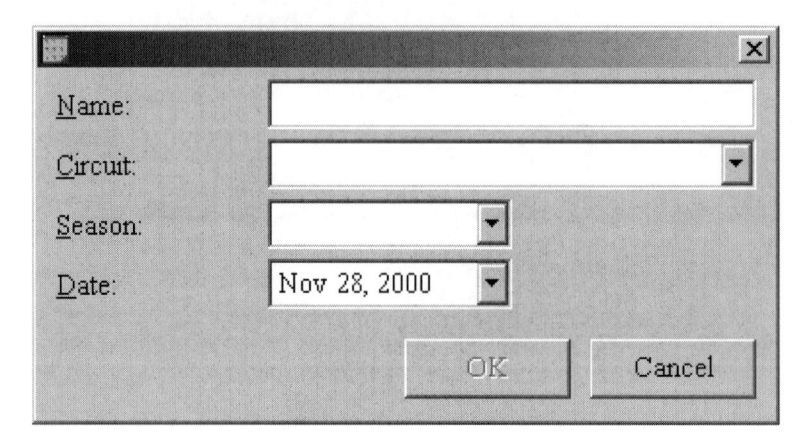

```
RaceDialog>>createComponents
    "Create the view components"
    super createComponents.
    namePresenter := self add: TextPresenter new name:
        'name'.
    seasonsPresenter := self add: ListPresenter new name:
        'seasons'.
    currentSeason := self add: ValuePresenter new name:
        'currentSeason'.
    circuitsPresenter := self add: ListPresenter new name:
        'circuits'.
    currentCircuit := self add: ValuePresenter new name:
        'currentCircuit'.
    datePresenter := self add: DatePresenter new name:
        'date'.


RaceDialog>>model: aRace
    "Create the link between the model and the presenter
    via a buffer"
    super model: aRace.
    namePresenter model: (self model aspectValue: #name).
    seasonsPresenter model: (ListModel on: (self
        allSeasons)).
    currentSeason model: (self model aspectValue:
        #season).
    circuitsPresenter model: (ListModel on: (self
        allCircuits)).
    currentCircuit model: (self model aspectValue:
        #circuit).
    datePresenter model: (self model aspectValue: #date).
```

RaceDialog>>allSeasons
> *"Collect all seasons"*
> ^AllSeasons asSortedCollection: [:a :b | a name < b
>   name]

RaceDialog>>allCircuits
> *"Collect all circuits"*
> ^AllCircuits asSortedCollection: [:a :b | a name < b
>   name]

RaceDialog>>onViewOpened
> *"Set the caption and the initial values. If the season
> is already set, disallow changes"*
> super onViewOpened.
> self setCaption.
> seasonsPresenter selectionOrNil: currentSeason value.
> circuitsPresenter selectionOrNil: currentCircuit
>   value.
> currentSeason value isNil
>   ifTrue: [seasonsPresenter view enable]
>   ifFalse: [seasonsPresenter view disable].

RaceDialog>>captionSubstring
> *"Return the class specific substring for the caption"*
> ^'Race - '

RaceDialog>>createSchematicWiring
> *"Create the trigger wiring"*
> super createSchematicWiring.
> seasonsPresenter when: #selectionChanged send:
> #seasonSelectionChanged to: self.
> circuitsPresenter when: #selectionChanged send:
> #circuitSelectionChanged to: self.

RaceDialog>>circuitSelectionChanged
> *"Communicate the change of selection"*
> currentCircuit value: circuitsPresenter
>   selectionOrNil.

RaceDialog>>seasonSelectionChanged
> *"Communicate the change of selection"*
> currentSeason value: seasonsPresenter selectionOrNil.

In the #apply method we want to generate the starters and, as we are working with a dialog, we need to make sure that the copy that was made in the aspect buffer doesn't stay around in the list of races in the season. We have to do the same when we close the dialog without applying the changes.

```
RaceDialog>>apply
    "Apply the changes and generate the starters"
    super apply.
    self removeCopyFromSeason.
    self model subject generateStarters.
RaceDialog>>cancel
    "Close the receiver without applying the changes back
    to the original model"
    self removeCopyFromSeason.
    super cancel.

RaceDialog>>removeCopyFromSeason
    "Check if the aspectBuffer's copy is added to the
    season. If so, remove manually"
    (self model season isNil) ifFalse: [
        (self model season races includes: (self model
                value))
                    ifTrue: [ self model season removeRace:
                        self model value ]]
```

For the circuit and the season presenters we have to change the "getTextBlock" aspect to `[ :each | each name ]` to show the name of the circuit and the season. The date can default to today by changing the "value" aspect to `Date today`. See Section 4.2 for the formatting of the date.

8.2.2 The main Race view

Updating lists based on selections in other fields.

In the main race view we want to select a race and then we want to see a list of all the starters. We will use the same technique as we did in the previous chapter where we first had to select something before we could fill the list. Here we will extend that.

We will want the end result to look like Figure 8.6.

As this is not a dialog and we also don't want it to be a document shell, we will make the presenter a subclass of Shell. Based on the picture we can see which variables we want. There are two additional variables which hold the currently selected race and the currently selected starter. These are just for convenience.

```
Shell subclass: #RaceShell
    instanceVariableNames: 'seasonsPresenter
    racesPresenter currentRace datePresenter
    startersPresenter currentStarter
    startingNumberPresenter driversPresenter teamPresenter
    qualificationResultPresenter startingPositionPresenter
    raceResultPresenter driverPointsPresenter
    teamPointsPresenter'
    classVariableNames: ''
    poolDictionaries: ''
```

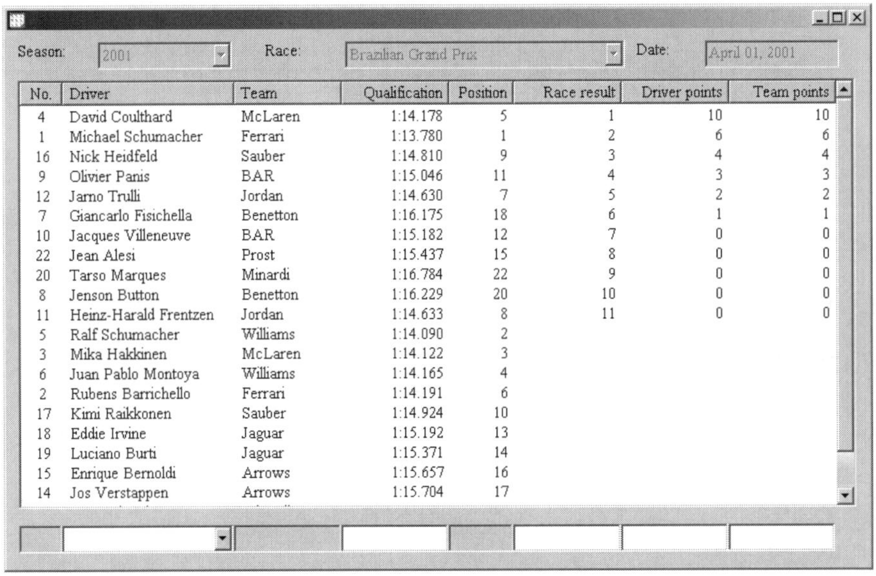

THE RACE COMPONENT

Figure 8.6
Race view

No.	Driver	Team	Qualification	Position	Race result	Driver points	Team points
4	David Coulthard	McLaren	1:14.178	5	1	10	10
1	Michael Schumacher	Ferrari	1:13.780	1	2	6	6
16	Nick Heidfeld	Sauber	1:14.810	9	3	4	4
9	Olivier Panis	BAR	1:15.046	11	4	3	3
12	Jarno Trulli	Jordan	1:14.630	7	5	2	2
7	Giancarlo Fisichella	Benetton	1:16.175	18	6	1	1
10	Jacques Villeneuve	BAR	1:15.182	12	7	0	0
22	Jean Alesi	Prost	1:15.437	15	8	0	0
20	Tarso Marques	Minardi	1:16.784	22	9	0	0
8	Jenson Button	Benetton	1:16.229	20	10	0	0
11	Heinz-Harald Frentzen	Jordan	1:14.633	8	11	0	0
5	Ralf Schumacher	Williams	1:14.090	2			
3	Mika Hakkinen	McLaren	1:14.122	3			
6	Juan Pablo Montoya	Williams	1:14.165	4			
2	Rubens Barrichello	Ferrari	1:14.191	6			
17	Kimi Raikkonen	Sauber	1:14.924	10			
18	Eddie Irvine	Jaguar	1:15.192	13			
19	Luciano Burti	Jaguar	1:15.371	14			
15	Enrique Bernoldi	Arrows	1:15.657	16			
14	Jos Verstappen	Arrows	1:15.704	17			

The next step is to create the components for the view and create the link to the model. In this case the model of most of the presenters depends on the selection elsewhere, so we can only make the link between those presenters and their model after we have made a selection. Therefore the #model: method only links the seasonsPresenter to all instances of the Season class that we have in our AllSeasons global variable and the driversPresenter to all instances of the Driver class that we have in our AllDrivers global variable.

```
RaceShell>>createComponents
    super createComponents.
    seasonsPresenter := self add: ListPresenter new name:
        'seasons'.
    racesPresenter := self add: ListPresenter new name:
        'races'.
    datePresenter := self add: DatePresenter new name:
        'date'.
    startersPresenter := self add: ListPresenter new name:
        'starters'.
    startingNumberPresenter := self add: NumberPresenter
        new name: 'startingNumber'.
    driversPresenter := self add: ListPresenter new name:
        'drivers'.
    teamPresenter := self add: TextPresenter new name:
        'team'.
```

```smalltalk
        qualificationResultPresenter := self add:
            TimePresenter new name: 'qualificationResult'.
        startingPositionPresenter := self add: NumberPresenter
            new name: 'startingPosition'.
        raceResultPresenter := self add: NumberPresenter new
            name: 'raceResult'.
        driverPointsPresenter := self add: NumberPresenter new
            name: 'driverPoints'.
        teamPointsPresenter := self add: NumberPresenter new
            name: 'teamPoints'.
```

RaceShell>>model: aModel
```smalltalk
        super model: aModel.
        seasonsPresenter model: (ListModel on: (self
            allSeasons)).
        driversPresenter model: (ListModel on: (self
            allDrivers)).
```

RaceShell>>allSeasons
```smalltalk
        "Collect all season objects in the system"
        ^AllSeasons asSortedCollection: [ :a :b | a name < b
            name ]
```

RaceShell>>allDrivers
```smalltalk
        "Collect all Driver objects that are available in the
        system"
        ^AllDrivers asSortedCollection: [ :a :b | a name < b
            name ]
```

When a user opens the screen, the first step is to select a season, which will update the list of races.

RaceShell>>seasonSelectionChanged
```smalltalk
        "The selected season has changed, rebuild the race
        list"
        racesPresenter resetSelection.
        self allRaces.
```

RaceShell>>allRaces
```smalltalk
        "Collect all races for the currently selected season
        and connect the drop-down list to this collection"
        | currentSeason racesList |
        currentSeason := seasonsPresenter selectionOrNil.
        currentSeason isNil
```

THE RACE COMPONENT

```
            ifTrue: [racesList :# OrderedCollection new]
            ifFalse: [racesList :# currentSeason races
                asSortedCollection: [ :a :b | a date < b
                    date ]].
    racesPresenter model: (ListModel on: racesList).
```

To trigger the change of selection, we have to add it to the #create SchematicWiring method.

RaceShell>>createSchematicWiring
```
    "Create the trigger wiring"
    super createSchematicWiring.
    seasonsPresenter when: #selectionChanged send:
    #seasonSelectionChanged to: self.
```

Once we have a season, we can select a race. When a race is selected, a similar chain of actions is performed, with the difference that the whole list of starters is shown.

RaceShell>>createSchematicWiring
```
    ...
    racesPresenter when: #selectionChanged send:
    #raceSelectionChanged to: self.
```

RaceShell>>raceSelectionChanged
```
    "The selected race has changed. Show the date and
    starters for this race"
    self resetCurrentStarter.
    currentRace := racesPresenter selectionOrNil.
    self showDate.
    self showStarters.
```

Ignore the first line for now, we will come back to that later.

RaceShell>>showDate
```
    "Link the date presenter to the #date aspect of the
    current race"
    currentRace isNil ifTrue: [ ^datePresenter model: nil
        ].
    datePresenter model: currentRace date.
```

RaceShell>>showStarters
```
    "Show the starters for the current race"
    currentRace isNil ifTrue: [ ^startersPresenter model:
        nil ].
    startersPresenter model: (ListModel on:
        (currentRace starters)).
```

For the view we use the field definitions shown in Table 8.1.

Note that we use normal text presenters for displaying the starting number and the starting position. We don't need the extra input control and conversion from text to integer that the number presenter gives, as these fields are disabled. For this same reason we could have used a normal text view for the disabled date view, but if you have a look in the typeConverter aspect, you will see that it has a sub-aspect "format", where you can set the display format. If you use the normal text view, it will default to the long format.

The most interesting column is the qualification, where we use the #printWithMilliseconds method that we built earlier. We have to capture the situation where the time is nil explicitly here, as we haven't defined #printWithMilliseconds for the UndefinedObject. In the other columns the standard #displayOn: is used, which returns an empty string for an UndefinedObject.

8.2.3 Entering the results

Updating fields based on entering information in other fields.

Now that we can show the starters, we want to be able to select one and enter the qualifying results and the race results. The first step is to enable

Table 8.1

Field definitions for the Race view

Name	Type	Additional settings
seasons	ListPresenter.Drop down list	getTextBlock: [:each | each name]
races	ListPresenter.Drop down list	getTextBlock: [:each | each name]
date	DatePresenter.Text view	isEnabled: false
starters	ListPresenter.Enhanced list view	See Table 8.2
startingNumber	TextPresenter.Default view	isEnabled: false
Drivers	ListPresenter.Drop down list	getTextBlock: [:each | each name]
Team	TextPresenter.Default view	isEnabled: false
qualificationResult	TimePresenter.MillisecondsText view	
startingPosition	TextPresenter.Default view	isEnabled: false
RaceResult	NumberPresenter.Integer text	
driverPoints	NumberPresenter.Integer text	
TeamPoints	NumberPresenter.Integer text	

selection of one in the list which copies it into the edit boxes. We will make this functionality available by double-clicking on a line in the list.

```
RaceShell>>createSchematicWiring
    ...
    startersPresenter when: #leftButtonDoubleClicked:
        send:#setCurrentStarter to: self.


RaceShell>>setCurrentStarter
    "A starter has been selected, set the current starter
    and link the presenters to it"
    currentStarter := startersPresenter selectionOrNil.
    currentStarter notNil ifTrue: [
        startingNumberPresenter model: (self
            currentStarter aspectValue:
            #startingNumber).
        driversPresenter selectionOrNil: (self
            currentStarter driver).
        teamPresenter model: (self currentStarter
            aspectValue: #teamName).
```

Table 8.2

Aspects of the fields on the Race view

Column	Aspects
No.	self imageManager: nil. alignment: #center getContentsBlock: [:each | each startingNumber]
Driver	getContentsBlock: [:each | each driver] getTextBlock: [:each | each name]
Team	getContentsBlock: [:each | each team] getTextBlock: [:each | each name]
Qualification	alignment: #right getContentsBlock: [:each | each qualificationResult] getTextBlock: [:each | each isNil ifTrue: [''] ifFalse: [each printWithMilliseconds]]
Position	alignment: #right getContentsBlock: [:each | each startingPosition]
Race result	alignment: #right getContentsBlock: [:each | each raceResult]
Driver points	alignment: #right getContentsBlock: [:each | each driverPoints]
Team points	alignment: #right getContentsBlock: [:each | each teamPoints]

```
    qualificationResultPresenter model: (self
        currentStarter aspectValue:
        #qualificationResult).
    startingPositionPresenter model: (self
        currentStarter aspectValue:
        #startingPosition).
    raceResultPresenter model: (self currentStarter
        aspectValue: #raceResult).
    driverPointsPresenter model: (self currentStarter
        aspectValue: #driverPoints).
    teamPointsPresenter model: (self currentStarter
        aspectValue: #teamPoints).
    self setCurrentStarterFocus ].
```

To make it easier for the user, we set the focus based on the status of the current starter. We assume that when there is no qualification result, the user will want to set it. If there is already a qualification result, we assume that the user wants to set the race result.

RaceShell>>setCurrentStarterFocus
```
    "Set the focus based on the assumption that the user
    will want to enter the qualification if that is still
    nil. Otherwise set the focus to the race result
    presenter"
    startersPresenter resetSelection.
    qualificationResultPresenter value isNil ifTrue: [
        ^qualificationResultPresenter setFocus ].
    raceResultPresenter view selectAll.
    raceResultPresenter setFocus
```

The opposite method to #setCurrentStarter is #resetCurrentStarter, which sets the model of all those currentStarter presenters to nil. We call this method whenever we want the fields to be cleared, which is when either the season or the race changes.

RaceShell>>resetCurrentStarter
```
    "Set the model of the currentStarter presenters to
    nil, so that all the currentStarter presenters are
    blanked"
    currentStarter := nil.
    startingNumberPresenter model: nil.
    driversPresenter resetSelection.
    teamPresenter model: nil.
    qualificationResultPresenter model: nil.
    startingPositionPresenter model: nil.
    raceResultPresenter model: nil.
    driverPointsPresenter model: nil.
    teamPointsPresenter model: nil.
```

THE RACE COMPONENT

When the user changes the driver in the current starter, we want to check that that driver doesn't drive another car in the same race. As the individual starters don't know of each other, we have to ask the race whether this driver is free. You might tend to ask the race for all the drivers from within the starter object, and then try to find the driver in that collection, but this would make the driver have to do all the work. It is far more logical just to ask the race for a boolean; true if the driver is free, false if (s)he already drives.

```
Starter>>driver: aDriver
    "Set the driver. Check that (s)he is not driving
    another car in the same race"
    (self race driverIsFree: aDriver) ifFalse:
        [^MessageBox errorMsg: (aDriver name, ' is
            already driving another car in this
            race') ].
    driver := aDriver

Race>>driverIsFree: aDriver
    "Check that the driver is not yet driving another car.
    Answer a boolean"
    ^(starters anySatisfy: [ :each | each driver ==
        aDriver ]) not
```

Now that we have the check in place, we can set the driver from within our view. We trigger the change with #selectionChanged. However, this has the problem that it is also triggered when a new currentStarter is set. Therefore it is also triggered when the original driver is set, which is of course already allocated to a car, namely the current one. Therefore we have to cater for that situation by checking whether the current selection is the same as the driver for the current starter. For error situations we make use of what we learned about error handling in Section 6.2, so that we can reset the current selection to the current driver.

```
RaceShell>>createSchematicWiring
    ...
    driversPresenter when: #selectionChanged send:
        #setDriver to: self.

RaceShell>>setDriver
    "Change the driver if no error occurs. Otherwise reset
    to original"
    currentStarter isNil ifTrue: [ ^nil ].
    (currentStarter driver == driversPresenter
        selectionOrNil)
            ifFalse: [currentStarter driver:
```

```
                driversPresenter selectionOrNil] on:
                    Error do: [
                    driversPresenter selectionOrNil:
                        currentStarter driver]]].
```

If the user enters a qualification result, we can work out what the starting position is. To do that we have to compare the qualification results of all the starters. Again, the most logical place to do the work is in the Race, as that holds all the starters. If a starter doesn't have a qualification result yet or if the time doesn't fall within 107 percent of the fastest, then we don't set the starting position. We have to check the starting position every time a car has set a new time, as it might occur that somebody set a time which was originally within the 107 percent, but with a new fastest time, falls outside it. In that case the position has to be set back to nil.

We have to cater for the situation where we don't have a starting time yet, so there we take an extreme number, in this case an hour; as the qualification only lasts an hour, the worst time can never be more than an hour.

RaceShell>>createSchematicWiring
```
    ...
    qualificationResultPresenter when: #focusLost send:
        #setStartingPosition to: self.
```

RaceShell>>setStartingPosition
```
    "Set the starting position for all the cars that have
    a qualification result"
    currentRace setStartingPosition.
    self showStarters.
```

Race>>setStartingPosition
```
    "Sort all the cars that have a qualification result.
    Based on the sort order, set the starting position if
    within 107%"
    | qualified minTime maxTime |
    qualified := (starters select: [ :each | each
        qualificationResult notNil ])
        asSortedCollection: [:a :b|
            a qualificationResult <= b
            qualificationResult].
    minTime := qualified inject: (Time fromSeconds: 3600)
        into:
        [ :a :b | a min: b qualificationResult ].
    maxTime := Time fromMilliseconds:
        (minTime asMilliseconds * 1.07).
```

```
qualified do: [ :each |
    (each qualificationResult <= maxTime)
        ifTrue: [ each startingPosition:
            (qualified identityIndexOf: each) ]
        ifFalse: [ each startingPosition: nil ]].
```

When the race result is entered, we can automatically set the points for the team and the driver, based on the table that we created in our Season model.

<RaceShell>>createSchematicWiring
```
    ...
    raceResultPresenter when: #focusLost send: #setPoints
        to: self.
```

RaceShell>>setPoints
```
    "Set the points for the driver and the team based on
    their race result. The points come from the season's
    points table"
    | points |
    points := seasonsPresenter selection pointsFor:
    raceResultPresenter value.
    driverPointsPresenter value: points.
    teamPointsPresenter value: points.
    self showStarters.
```

Season>>pointsFor: aRaceResult
```
    "Return the points for a race result"
    aRaceResult isNil ifTrue: [^nil].
    ^scoreDefinition at: aRaceResult ifAbsent: [^0]
```

With these listings you can see how readable Smalltalk code is. Just follow the flow and you hardly need comment or other descriptive text.

8.3 Sorting the starters

Sorting the starters can become quite complicated, therefore we want to avoid putting the sort definition in the sort block. But we don't need a sort block if the starters know how to compare themselves. Based on the comparison result, the SortedCollection can take care of the sorting. Like, for example, numbers, they know how to be compared, so you don't have to specify a sort block. Let's see how that works:

Multiple levels of sorting avoiding procedural code through refactoring.

```
#(3 7 5 2) asSortedCollection
```

This gives the result as expected, so what's going on here? Have a look at the methods in the SortedCollection class. You'll see that whenever something is changed in the sorted collection, a #reSort is performed. This #reSort calls the most important method in the sorted collection, #sortFrom:to:. This method walks through the elements of the collection, compares each of them and decides whether the first element should be in front of the next element. This decision is made based on the result of the element comparison. So if we walk through the numbers in the above example, we compare the first and second elements by sending 3 the message `#<=7`. If that returns true, the sorted collection leaves the 3 in front of the 7. Then the message `#<=5` is sent and finally the message `#<=2`. This last one returns false, so the 2 is put in front of the 3. Now the process starts all over again, until all elements are in the right order. (In theory this is the way sorting works, but you can imagine that it would take forever to sort a big collection in this recursive way. Therefore all kinds of sorting algorithms have been developed that take shortcuts, still ensuring the right sort result.)

So whenever we want elements in a sorted order without us having to specify a sort block, we have to make sure that the elements can compare themselves with the `#<=` message (note that this might change in the future, as the ANSI specification for Smalltalk suggests moving to `#<`). Therefore, if objects understand `#<=`, and answer true or false to that, then we don't have to specify a sort block. So if we need to make a complicated sort, we can just implement a `#<=` in the class of the objects, like in the situation with the starters. Alternatively, we can add methods to the class that compare two objects like `#<=`, but name them differently; we can then call them from within the sort block. The latter approach has the advantage that you can sort differently for different purposes: just change the method in the sort block. We will start with a fixed sort block and from there build a more flexible way of dealing with it.

What kind of sort would we like for the starters? Here we have to consider that some sorting information might not yet be available when we want to sort. If the race has been held, we want the starters to be sorted by finish result. If the race has not yet been held but the qualification results are known, then we want to sort by that information. And finally, if there is no race information available yet, we just want to sort by starting number. Based on this, our method would look as follows:

```
Starter>><= anotherStarter
    "Compare self to another starter. If aspect is nil for
    both, compare according to next aspect"
    "First check race result"
    (self raceResult notNil and:
        [anotherStarter raceResult notNil])ifTrue:
            [^(self raceResult <= anotherStarter
                raceResult)].
```

```
(self raceResult notNil and: [anotherStarter
    raceResult isNil])
        ifTrue: [^true].
(self raceResult isNil and: [anotherStarter raceResult
    notNil])
        ifTrue: [^false].
"then check starting position"
(self startingPosition notNil and: [anotherStarter
    startingPosition notNil]) ifTrue:
        [^(self startingPosition <= anotherStarter
            startingPosition)].
(self startingPosition notNil and: [anotherStarter
    startingPosition isNil]) ifTrue: [^true].
(self startingPosition isNil and: [anotherStarter
    startingPosition notNil]) ifTrue: [^false].
"then check starting number"
(self startingNumber notNil and: [anotherStarter
    startingNumber notNil]) ifTrue:
        [^(self startingNumber <= anotherStarter
            startingNumber)].
(self startingNumber notNil and: [anotherStarter
    startingNumber isNil]) ifTrue: [^true].
(self startingNumber isNil and: [anotherStarter
    startingNumber notNil]) ifTrue: [^false].
"if all else fails"
^false
```

This method does the job, but it is very procedural; if this, then that; if that, then something else, and so on. So how can we make this less procedural? We can start by delegating. This means that we create other methods that we call from within this method. The other methods do the work, and this method controls it.

```
Starter>><= anotherStarter
    "Compare self to another starter. If aspect is nil
    for both, compare according to next aspect"
    | result |
    result := self compareRaceResult: anotherStarter.
    result isNil ifTrue: [result := self
        compareStartingPosition: anotherStarter].
    result isNil ifTrue: [result := self
        compareStartingNumber: anotherStarter].
    result isNil ifTrue: [result := false].
    ^result
```

```
Starter>>compareRaceResult: anotherStarter
    "Compare the race result between self and
    anotherStarter"
    (self raceResult notNil and: [anotherStarter
        raceResult notNil]) ifTrue:
        [^(self raceResult <= anotherStarter
            raceResult)].
    (self raceResult notNil and: [anotherStarter
        raceResult isNil])
        ifTrue: [^true].
    (self raceResult isNil and: [anotherStarter raceResult
        notNil])
        ifTrue: [^false].
    ^nil

Starter>>compareStartingPosition: anotherStarter
    "Compare the starting position between self and
    anotherStarter"
    (self startingPosition notNil and: [anotherStarter
        startingPosition notNil]) ifTrue:
        [^(self startingPosition <= anotherStarter
            startingPosition)].
    (self startingPosition notNil and: [anotherStarter
        startingPosition isNil]) ifTrue: [^true].
    (self startingPosition isNil and: [anotherStarter
        startingPosition notNil]) ifTrue: [^false].
    ^nil

Starter>>compareStartingNumber: anotherStarter
    "Compare the starting number between self and
    anotherStarter"
    (self startingNumber notNil and: [anotherStarter
        startingNumber notNil]) ifTrue:
        [^(self startingNumber <= anotherStarter
            startingNumber)].
    (self startingNumber notNil and: [anotherStarter
        startingNumber isNil]) ifTrue: [^true].
    (self startingNumber isNil and: [anotherStarter
        startingNumber notNil]) ifTrue: [^false].
    ^nil
```

This already looks a lot better, but you can see that apart from the aspect, we do the same thing in those three methods. That means that we can replace the methods with a single one which requires an additional parameter, namely the aspect.

```
Starter>>compare: anotherStarter forAspect: anAspect
    "Compare self and anotherStarter for anAspect"
    | mine his |
    mine := self perform: anAspect.
    his := anotherStarter perform: anAspect.
    (mine notNil and: [his notNil]) ifTrue:
        [^(mine <= his)].
    (mine isNil and: [his notNil]) ifTrue: [^false].
    (mine notNil and: [his isNil]) ifTrue: [^true].
    ^nil

Starter>><= anotherStarter
    "Compare self to another starter. If aspect is nil for
    both, compare according to next aspect"
    | result |
    result := self compare: anotherStarter forAspect:
            #raceResult.
    result isNil ifTrue: [result := self compare:
            anotherStarter forAspect: #startingPosition].
    result isNil ifTrue: [result := self compare:
            anotherStarter forAspect: #startingNumber].
    result isNil ifTrue: [result := false].
    ^result
```

Now that we've made the code more readable, we can see that we can simplify the #compare:forAspect: even further.

```
Starter>>compare: anotherStarter forAspect: anAspect
    "Compare self and anotherStarter for anAspect"
    | mine his |
    mine := self perform: anAspect.
    his := anotherStarter perform: anAspect.
    (mine isNil and: [his isNil]) ifTrue: [^nil].
    mine isNil ifTrue: [^false].
    his isNil ifTrue: [^true].
    ^(mine <= his)
```

This process of simplifying code is called refactoring. It is especially suited for Smalltalk and allows you to make your code simpler, more readable and therefore more easily maintainable. Within the Smalltalk community there are a number of packages that help you with this process (see Appendix A).

With the above code we can ask for any collection of starters to be sorted by just sending it the message #asSortedCollection. As we said at the beginning of this section, the only problem with this approach is that we always sort according to the sequence of aspects as defined in the method

`#<=`. Is there a way to make that flexible as well? We can do it by sending an array of the aspects as part of the parameters for the sorting. Something like: `aStarter compare: anotherStarter forAspects: #(#raceResult #startingPosition #startingNumber)`.

Have a look at the following method. This method calls itself if necessary with the first aspect dropped, until it doesn't have any more aspects to process.

```
Starter>>compare: anotherStarter forAspects: arrayOfAspects
    "This method compares self with another starter
    according to the array of aspects"
    arrayOfAspects do: [ :each | | answer |
        answer := self compare: anotherStarter
                forAspect: each.
        answer isNil ifFalse: [^answer]
        ].
```

With this method in place we can use it in our #showStarters method in the RaceShell in the following way:

```
RaceShell>>showStarters
    "Show the starters for the current race, sorted by
    race result, qualification result or starting number,
    depending on availability"
    currentRace isNil ifTrue: [ ^startersPresenter model:
        nil ].
    startersPresenter model: (ListModel on: (currentRace
        starters asSortedCollection: [ :a :b | a
            compare: b forAspects: #(#raceResult
            #qualificationResult #startingNumber)] )).
```

Now whenever you enter results for the starters, the list will automatically be sorted according to the sequence of aspects.

8.4 Summary

In this chapter we have built a view in which we brought together all the hard work of the previous chapters, and more. We learned that when objects become too complicated, we typically can split them into finer-grain objects. One object then becomes the holder of the other objects. When you create the holder, you would typically automatically generate the other objects.

The view that we built displays information that depends on the selection in other fields on the same display. The display contains a postbox in which the information in the main list can be manipulated. Based on the information entered, other information in the list is updated as well.

And finally we concentrated on sorting complex objects. We created a sorting routine that accepts a sequence of parameters, which allows sorting within sorting.

9   Bringing the components together

So far we have been building components that make up what we need for our Formula One application, but we haven't done anything yet to glue it all together. We still have to open all the forms from a workspace, and when we close the workspace we lose all the objects that we created. In this chapter we are going to build a form from which we can open the dialogs that we've built so far, either on existing objects or on new objects.

At the moment the fashion is to have an application form with a tree list on the left-hand side, showing the object types (classes), and when one of those types is selected, the right-hand side shows a list of objects of that type. When the user selects one of those objects he or she can do something with it, open it, modify it, or delete it. When the user selects the type, he or she can create a new object of that type. This approach is called the Object-Action model. You first select an object, and then tell the object what you want to do with it. This as opposed to the Action-Object model, where you select an action, typically from a menu. This action opens a form, and then you select the object that you want to work on.

Well, as the Object-Action approach is the current fashion and as it quite fits in with object-oriented thinking, let's go for that approach. We will start simple, but at the end of the chapter we will have built an application screen that looks like Figure 9.1.

9.1 The basic racing application model

9.1.1 *The model*

How to maintain different types of objects in a generic way.

As usual, we first focus on the model. Like we said above, the application model holds all other objects together, so the application model has a relationship with all the other components that we have built so far.

As we don't want the application model to have too much knowledge about what it is holding, we have to find a way to delegate that knowledge; make the application model a holder of objects that know about the components. So the application model would hold an object that knows all about the Driver objects, how to create them, how to present them, and which drivers are actually there. The same goes for all the other components.

The objects that hold the components have a lot in common, so you might tend to think that we could create a single class that has instances

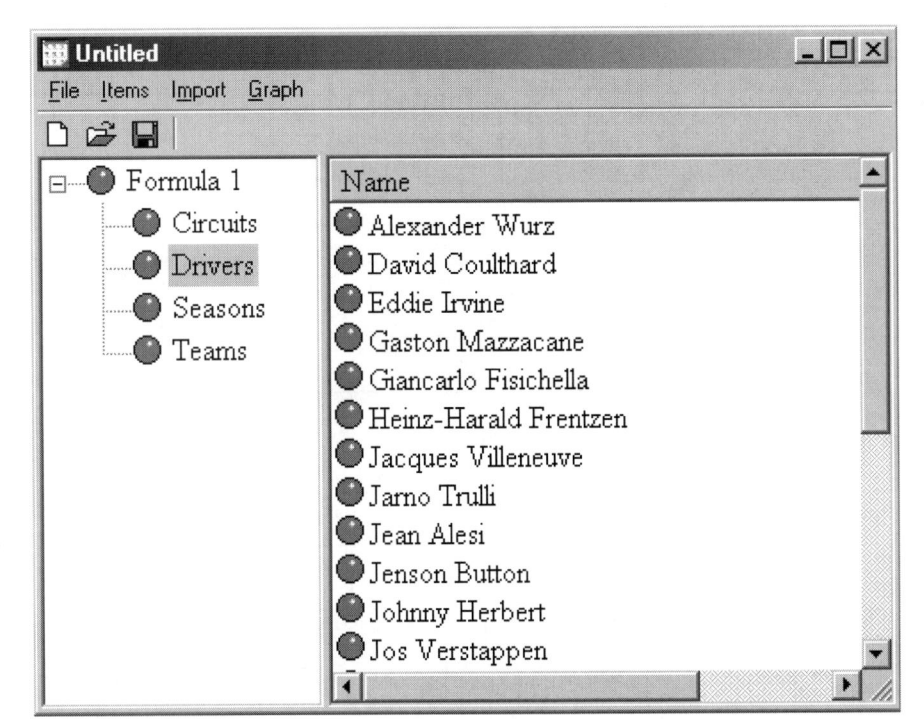

BRINGING THE COMPONENTS TOGETHER

Figure 9.1
The finished race application view

for the individual components. In an application like this, where almost all the components are treated in a similar way, that would be the simplest solution that would work. However, as we will see in Section 9.3, one of the components needs to be treated in a different way, which causes the need for extra checking like "if it is this component, do this, otherwise do that" in many places. The alternative is to build the common knowledge of the components in an abstract class and subclass that abstract class for each of the components. These subclasses can then hold the specific knowledge. The class diagram for this model looks as shown in Figure 9.2.

We start with the class definition of the RaceApplication. For now, its only responsibility is to hold the RaceApplicationComponents. Therefore, a RaceApplication has an instance variable which is a collection holding all the RaceApplicationComponents. When we create a new RaceApplication, we have to initialize the collection. Like we have done before, we add the standard methods for adding and removing RaceApplicationComponents to and from the collection, and we add the getter for the collection. For now, that will do.

```
MyModel subclass: #RaceApplication
    instanceVariableNames: 'raceAppComponents'
    classVariableNames: ''
    poolDictionaries: ''
```

Figure 9.2

The race application class model

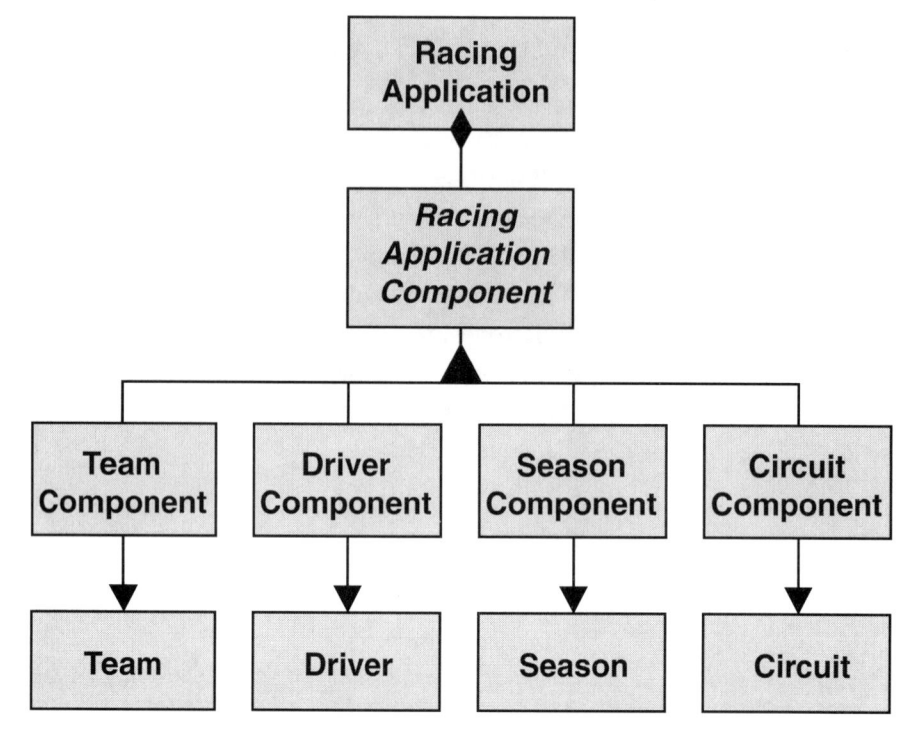

[Diagram: Racing Application (composition) → Racing Application Component, which is the superclass of Team Component, Driver Component, Season Component, and Circuit Component. Each of these references Team, Driver, Season, and Circuit respectively.]

```
RaceApplication>>initialize
    "Initialize a new race application"
    super initialize.
    raceAppComponents := OrderedCollection new.

RaceApplication>>raceAppComponents
    "Return the list of race application components"
    ^raceAppComponents

RaceApplication>>addRaceAppComponent: aRaceAppComponent
    "Add a race application component"
    self raceAppComponents add: aRaceAppComponent

RaceApplication>>removeRaceAppComponent: aRaceAppComponent
    "Remove a race application component"
    self raceAppComponents remove: aRaceAppComponent
        ifAbsent: [nil]
```

Like we discussed at the beginning of this section, the RaceAppComponent class holds the shared knowledge of the components. Do we yet know what that is? One of the things we know is that each of the components will hold a list with the items of their specific type. Therefore we can move that into

BRINGING THE COMPONENTS TOGETHER

the shared abstract class. We also know that we want the component to have a name which will be shown on the left-hand side of the screen so that we can select it. Well, as we already inherit the "name" variable from the MyModel class, we don't have to do anything there.

We will initialize the "items" variable as a ListModel on an OrderedCollection. The reason for this is that the ListModel automatically tells all the dependants (which are the screens in our case) when something has changed in the list. When the dependants receive that message, they will take the appropriate action so that they display the changed list immediately.

We will add a method for removing but not for adding. We will leave that to the subclasses, as it is specific to each component. To get hold of the whole collection we will add a getter method.

```
MyModel subclass: #RaceAppComponent
    instanceVariableNames: 'items'
    classVariableNames: ''
    poolDictionaries: ''
```

RaceAppComponent>>initialize
```
    "Initialize a new race application component"
    super initialize.
    items := ListModel on: OrderedCollection new.
```

RaceAppComponent>>items
```
    "Return the list of items"
    ^items
```

RaceAppComponent>>removeItem: anItem
```
    "Remove an item"
    self items remove: anItem
        ifAbsent: [nil]
```

The next step is to build specific classes for each component. These classes need to be able to create new items of their specific type and present them with the right form. They also need to know how to open an existing item in the right form so that the user can change the information of an item. As we said before, the components are also responsible for knowing the name that is going to be displayed on the screen. We will make the name plural as you would typically have multiple items in each component. Let's start with the very first component that we built at the beginning of the book, the Team.

```
RaceAppComponent subclass: #TeamComponent
    instanceVariableNames: ''
    classVariableNames: ''
    poolDictionaries: ''
```

```
TeamComponent>>name
    "Return the name of the component"
    ^'Teams'

TeamComponent>>addItem
    "Create a new item of this type and show it in the
    appropriate form"
    | item |
    item := Team new.
    (TeamDialogPresenter showOn: item) when: #viewClosed
    send: #checkItem: to: self with: item.
```

We only want to add the item if it has a name. As this check is the same for all the components, we can put it in the RaceAppComponent class.

```
RaceAppComponent>>checkItem: anItem
    "Check if the item has a name. If that is the case,
    add the item to the list"
    anItem name isEmpty ifFalse: [ self items add: anItem
        ].

TeamComponent>>openItem: anItem
    "Show the item in the appropriate form"
    TeamDialogPresenter showOn: anItem.
```

Let's see if this works. Open a workspace and create a TeamComponent. Create some TeamComponent items, cancel some of them in the dialog and check that the right ones are added and the canceled ones are not added. Open some of the items and try to modify them and cancel some of the modifications.

```
tc := TeamComponent new.
tc addItem.
tc items inspect
tc openItem: (tc items at: 2).
tc items inspect
```

Now we can do the same for the other components.

```
RaceAppComponent subclass: #DriverComponent
    instanceVariableNames: ''
    classVariableNames: ''
    poolDictionaries: ''

DriverComponent>>name
    "Return the name of the component"
    ^'Drivers'
```

BRINGING THE COMPONENTS TOGETHER

```
DriverComponent>>addItem
    "Create a new item of this type and show it in the
    appropriate form. If not canceled, add the item to the
    collection of items"
    | item |
    item := Driver new.
    (DriverDialogPresenter showOn: item) when: #viewClosed
        send: #checkItem: to: self with: item.

DriverComponent>>openItem: anItem
    "Show the item in the appropriate form"
    DriverDialogPresenter showOn: anItem.

RaceAppComponent subclass: #SeasonComponent
    instanceVariableNames: ''
    classVariableNames: ''
    poolDictionaries: ''

SeasonComponent>>name
    "Return the name of the component"
    ^'Seasons'

SeasonComponent>>addItem
    "Create a new item of this type and show it in the
    appropriate form. If not canceled, add the item to the
    collection of items"
    | item |
    item := Season new.
    (SeasonDialogPresenter showOn: item) when: #viewClosed
        send: #checkItem: to: self with: item.

SeasonComponent>>openItem: anItem
    "Show the item in the appropriate form"
    SeasonDialogPresenter showOn: anItem.

RaceAppComponent subclass: #CircuitComponent
    instanceVariableNames: ''
    classVariableNames: ''
    poolDictionaries: ''

CircuitComponent>>name
    "Return the name of the component"
    ^'Circuits'

CircuitComponent>>addItem
    "Create a new item of this type and show it in the
    appropriate form. If not canceled, add the item to the
    collection of items"
    | item |
```

```
item := Circuit new.
(CircuitDialogPresenter showOn: item) when:
    #viewClosed send: #checkItem: to: self with:
    item.
```

CircuitComponent>>openItem: anItem
```
"Show the item in the appropriate form"
CircuitDialogPresenter showOn: anItem.
```

9.1.2 *The race application presenter*

To start with, we will make the presenter a subclass of the Shell class. As this has nothing new, here is the listing.

```
Shell subclass: #RaceApplicationShell
    instanceVariableNames: 'componentsPresenter
    itemsPresenter'
    classVariableNames: ''
    poolDictionaries: ''
```

RaceApplicationShell>>createComponents
```
"Create the view components"
super createComponents.
componentsPresenter := self add: ListPresenter new
        name: 'componentsList'.
itemsPresenter := self add: ListPresenter new name:
        'itemsList'.
```

RaceApplicationShell>>model: aRaceApplication
```
"Create the link between the model and the presenter"
super model: aRaceApplication.
componentsPresenter model: (ListModel on:
        (aRaceApplication raceAppComponents)).
```

RaceApplicationShell>>createSchematicWiring
```
"Create the trigger wiring"
super createSchematicWiring.
componentsPresenter when: #selectionChanged send:
        #showItemsList to: self.
```

RaceApplicationShell>>showItemsList
```
"Show the itemslist for the currently selected
component"
componentsPresenter selectionOrNil isNil ifFalse: [
        itemsPresenter model:
                componentsPresenter selection items]
```

So far, no new issues here. We use a similar approach for the items list to what we did in Race view. This gives us enough to set us going with the view. Thereafter we will add functionality to maintain the items in their own dialog and functionality to delete items.

9.1.3 *The application framework view*

Before creating the view, we are first going to consider what we want to have. We want to have a list on the left-hand side of the form for the components and a list for the objects on the right-hand side of the form. In some cases that right-hand list will be fairly wide, in other cases it probably won't. The left-hand list will initially not be very wide, just a list of the object types (Team, Driver, Circuit, and Season), but once we extend it to a tree view, we might need to make the list wider depending on how deep we are in the tree. Therefore this form needs a splitter bar between the columns, so that the user can decide how wide the columns are relative to each other.

Using a splitter bar and proportional layout managers.

In Dolphin, a splitter bar is implemented by making use of layout managers – a logical choice if you think about it. You have a container that you want to split in two, but you don't know the proportions. So you just say that depending on where the splitter bar is, fill up the space that is available for the individual parts. Layout managers are designed to do just that.

As we saw in Section 4.3.3 when we used the layout manager for the group box with radio buttons, the layout managers are attached to shells. Therefore we have to create a shell that fills up the whole form, and then create two shells that hold the actual lists. A splitter bar separates the two containers of the lists (Figure 9.3). At first it might feel like a lot of shells, but with the above explanation you'll understand the background to it.

We start by creating a new view on the RaceApplicationShell. Drop a CompositePresenter.Default view on the form. This is going to be the container for the two containers that hold the lists and the splitter bar.

We want this first container to fill up the whole form, so we have to give the form a layout manager and then give this container an arrangement so that it fills the form independent of the resizing of the form. We can use a number of layout managers, but the one we used before, the BorderLayout, is the easiest one to fill a whole container. Remember, the form itself is the container in this case.

Select the ShellView (the form) in the view hierarchy and set the layout manager aspect to BorderLayout. Now select the container in the hierarchy and set the arrangement aspect to #center. You'll see that the container is stretched to the borders of the form. Just what we want (for now). When we resize the form, the container resizes with it. This container will contain the other containers and the splitter bar.

Make sure that the container is the currently selected item in the hierarchy, and drop two new containers (CompositePresenter.Default

Figure 9.3

The Shell hierarchy

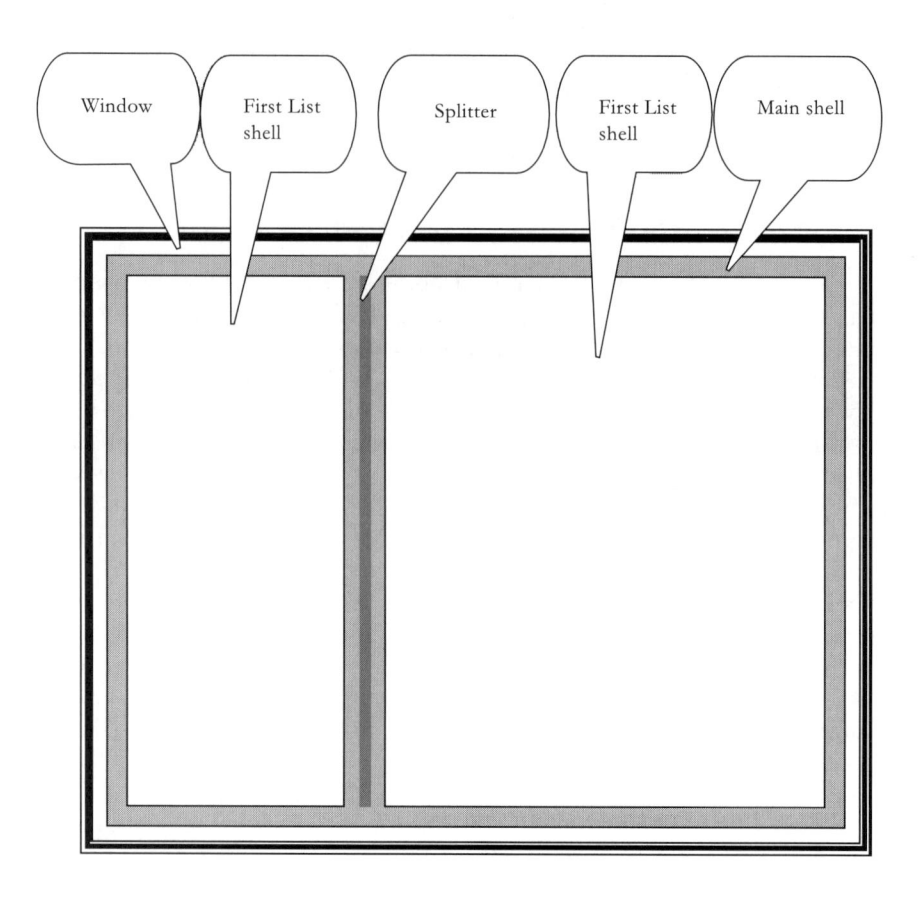

Window | First List shell | Splitter | First List shell | Main shell

view) and a splitter bar on it. Make sure that these three items are "children" of the container we just created on the form. You can check that in the view hierarchy. If necessary you can change it by selecting the item that you want to change and dropping it in the container in which it should go.

Now select the splitter and move it in between the two containers in the hierarchy (Figure 9.4). You can do that with the Bring Forward/Bring Backwards arrows or with the Modify – View Arrange menu commands.

The next step is to set the layout manager on the main container. We want the two lists split proportionally, which can be done with the proportional layout manager. Note that this only gives us our initial split; the user can change it in any way he or she wants by moving the splitter bar. Select the main container (the child of the form) and set the layoutManager aspect to ProportionalLayout. Now we can decide what kind of split we want to make between the two containers, something like a $\frac{1}{3}$–$\frac{2}{3}$ split sounds reasonable. We don't have to account for the splitter bar, as we don't want the width of that to change when we change the size of the main window.

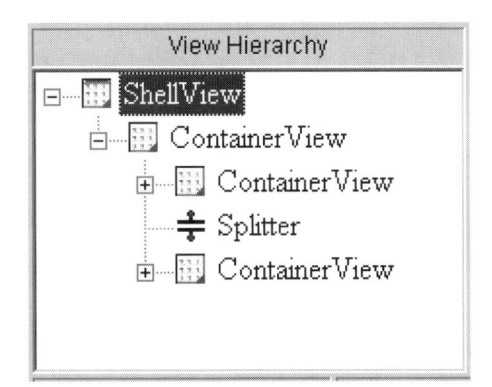

Figure 9.4

The view hierarchy with splitter bar

Select the first child container of that main container, and give it a proportion of 1. Do the same with the other container but give it a proportion of 2. We could have given them proportions of $(\frac{1}{3})$ and $(\frac{2}{3})$, but that would have had the same effect. The layout manager just calculates the total of the proportions and gives each their share of that total. Test the form with the F5 button. Try to move the splitter bar; it should work as you would expect.

So how do we make horizontal splitter bars? For that we have to ask ourselves who is actually controlling the splitting of the views. Not the splitter bar – that is just a line that can be grabbed by the mouse. No, it is the container with the proportional layout manager that controls the splitting. So that's where you should look for horizontal or vertical splitting. If you look at the layoutManager aspect of the main container, you will see that there is a sub-aspect called isVertical. Setting that to True changes the view so that it has a horizontal splitter bar. This sounds contradicting, having the isVertical setting as true gives us a horizontal splitter bar. However, the isVertical aspect controls the proportions, like $\frac{1}{3}$ and $\frac{2}{3}$. These proportions are the vertical proportions when the aspect is set to true, resulting in a horizontal splitter bar.

Now let's continue with our Framework view. Set the proportional layout manager to horizontal (isVertical = false) and drag a normal listbox (ListPresenter – Default view) on the left-hand container and an enhanced list view on the right-hand container. Set the layoutManager of both containers to BorderLayout and set the arrangement aspect for both lists to #center. Now it is just a matter of connecting the lists to the names that we've given in the presenter and setting up a column to show the name in the multi-column list. We won't bother putting more columns in, we can do that later. Set the name aspect of the first list to "componentsList" and the getTextBlock aspect to:

```
[ :each | each name ]
```

Set the name aspect of the second list to "itemsList". Open the first column of the columnsList and set the title to "Name" and the getContentsBlock to:

```
[ :each | each name ]
```

It might sound strange to use getTextBlock in the first list and getContentsBlock in the second, even though we have a getTextBlock in each column of the enhanced list as well. The reason is that the enhanced list supports sorting on each individual column. If you sort a list of numbers from 1 to 20, you expect the 10 after the 9 and so on. But if you sort a string containing "11", it will be sorted after "1" and before "2". The getContentsBlock will get you the integers which allow you to sort, and in the getTextBlock you define how you want to show them. We will see the use of that when we come to the scores of the drivers and teams. But for now, we are ready to test our form. Save the form with the name "First view" and open it on a RaceApplication variable in the workspace.

```
teams := TeamComponent new.
teams addItem.
drivers := DriverComponent new.
drivers addItem.
circuits := CircuitComponent new.
circuits addItem.
seasons := SeasonComponent new.
seasons addItem.
raceApp := RaceApplication new.
raceApp addRaceAppComponent: teams.
raceApp addRaceAppComponent: drivers.
raceApp addRaceAppComponent: circuits.
raceApp addRaceAppComponent: seasons.
RaceApplicationPresenter show: 'First view' on:
    raceApp.
```

It should look something like Figure 9.5.

When you select one of the components in the left-hand column, the right-hand column shows the items that you added to the appropriate component.

9.1.4 Summary

In the above subsections we have explored how we can put all the components together in a single application view. We have seen that we can use the different presenters that we built for the different components

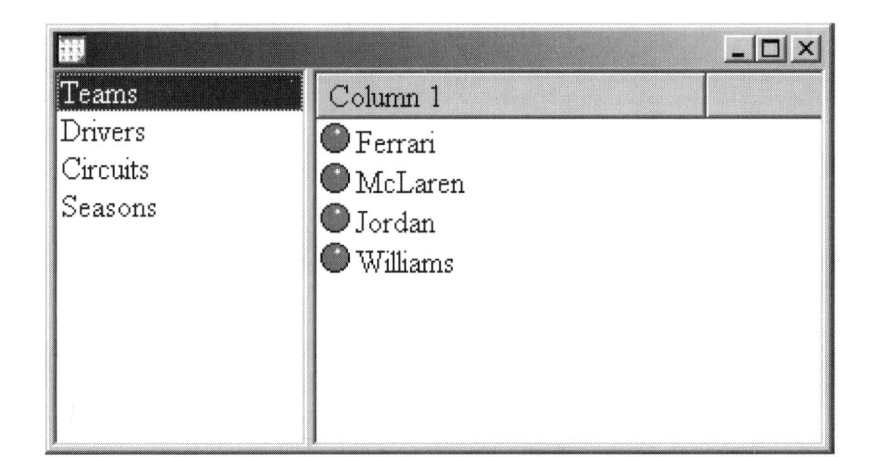

Figure 9.5
The basic RaceApplication form

depending on selection of the component in the view. We have also explored the layout manager and how to create a splitter bar.

9.2 Maintaining items

So far we have created items in the workspace and added them manually to the appropriate application component. For a user, of course, that is no good; he or she wants to maintain (create, modify, and delete) items right there in the framework. So far the interaction that we built has been specific buttons and in a couple of cases a double-click action. There we saw that the interaction consists of two distinct parts; we have an action method, like #addItem, and we have a user interface way of calling that action. In this section we will explore other ways of allowing the user to call these commands: context menus, menu bars, and toolbars. We will also learn how to enable and disable these actions dynamically.

9.2.1 *The maintenance methods*

For the maintenance of items we want to use the dialogs that we specifically built for that purpose. Here we can see the term "polymorphism" at work. It doesn't matter which of the components is selected, they all understand #addItem and #openItem:, but they all react differently to it, as they open a different dialog. This means that we can just select a component, and then send it the message #addItem. The component should then know what to do.

```
RaceApplicationShell>>addItem
     "Create a new item of the selected component"
     componentsPresenter selectionOrNil isNil ifFalse: [
         componentsPresenter selection addItem ]
```

When we want to open or delete an item, we must of course have a selected item. We can then send the message to the component with the item as the argument.

```
RaceApplicationShell>>openItem
    "Open the selected item in its own maintenance form"
    itemsPresenter selectionOrNil isNil ifFalse: [
        componentsPresenter selection openItem:
            itemsPresenter selection ]
```

For deletion we want to give the user a warning before we actually delete the item. We can use the standard Microsoft message boxes for that (see Section 6.2). In our case the standard MessageBox class >> confirm: message is just what we want. Based on the result, true (when the user selects yes) or false (when the user selects no), we can either delete the selected item or not do anything at all. To give the user some clue as to which item he or she is going to delete, we create a text string with the class name and the item name:

```
RaceApplicationShell>>deleteItem
    "Delete the selected item from the list"
    | text sel |
    itemsPresenter selectionOrNil isNil ifFalse: [
        sel := itemsPresenter selection.
        text := 'Are you sure that you want to delete ',
            sel class printString asLowercase, ' ',
            sel name, '?'.
        (MessageBox confirm: text) ifTrue: [
            componentsPresenter selection removeItem:
                sel ]]
```

9.2.2 *Context menus and menu bars*

How to use one and the same action method on different menus.

Now that we have created all the messages, we can link them to menu options in our view. We will start by creating context menus in the lists. Context menus are linked to specific views, so when the user has the mouse in a specific view and clicks the right mouse button, the context menu for that view is opened. Therefore, to create context menus, you have to select the view to which you want to link the context menu and then create it as part of the view.

When you select the itemsList in the view composer, you will find that it has an aspect "contextMenu". When you double-click on it, it brings up the menu composer (Figure 9.6).

Add three commands and a separator line after the second command. You can add these through the "New" menu option. You don't have to add

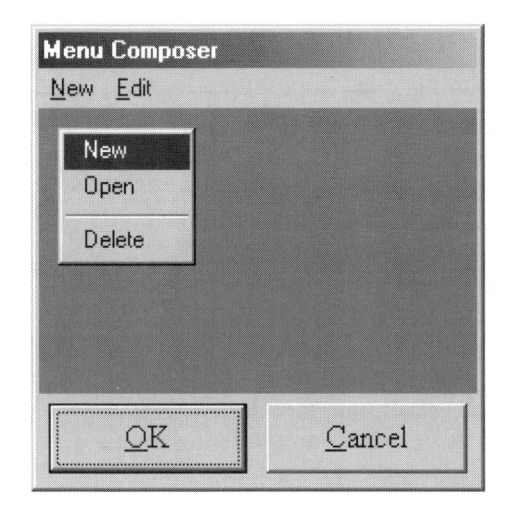

Figure 9.6
The menu composer

a menu, as that would create a cascaded menu from the context menu. Now when you select one of the lines, you can set the properties for that menu item either through the "Edit" menu or through the context menu. (You can also define the menu complete with its aspects in the view composer, similar to how a multi-column list is defined.) Set them for this menu as shown in Table 9.1.

Add a context menu to the first list as well, but with the New menu option only.

Menu bars are created in the same way, albeit that they are linked to the main form. As we are using the layoutManagers to sort out the proportions, we don't have to worry about how it all fits; the menu bar just moves the containers down a bit.

Select the form in the view composer and double-click on the menuBar aspect. Call the menu item &Items and add the new, open, separator, and delete items as you did before in the context menu for the items list. For clarity you'd best name the menu items "New Item", "Open Item", and "Delete Item" so that they won't be confused with the File menu options that we will add later.

Here you see the advantage of splitting the user interaction part and the action method. We only have one method #addItem, but it is called from three different menus.

Item text	Command
New	#addItem
Open	#openItem
Delete	#deleteItem

Table 9.1
Menu properties

9.2.3 *Enabling and disabling commands*

How to enable/disable menu commands, the #queryCommand: method.

We want to make sure that the open and delete menu items are only available when there is a selected item, and we only want the new menu item to be available when there is a selected type. For this Dolphin Smalltalk takes a slightly different approach compared to other languages. In Dolphin Smalltalk you enable or disable the command itself. Then all menus and buttons referring to that command are automatically enabled or disabled. This has the advantage that you only have to do it once, which in our case en/disables both the menu item in the context menus and the menu item in the menu bar.

Enabling and disabling is done through the #queryCommand: message. Whenever you open a menu, #queryCommand: is called for every menu item. Depending on the definition in #queryCommand, the menu items are enabled or disabled.

As there is only one #queryCommand: in the presenter which handles the enablement for all commands, we first have to test that we are talking about the right command. For example:

```
(aCommandQuery command == #addItem) ifTrue: [ test to enable
    or disable ]
```

This checks whether the command of the menu item is #addItem. If so, the test for enablement/disablement is executed.

For new items we want to be sure that there is a selection in the types list, so our queryCommand would look like this:

```
(aCommandQuery command == #addItem) ifTrue: [
    typesPresenter selectionOrNil notNil
        ifTrue: [aCommandQuery beEnabled]
        ifFalse: [aCommandQuery beDisabled]
    ].
```

There is nothing wrong with this. However, if you have many commands that you want to test in this way, the queryCommand will become quite big and unreadable. Therefore quite often you will see a more compressed way. The statements are juggled around a bit, making it a bit less obvious what is going on.

```
(aCommandQuery command == #addItem) ifTrue: [
    aCommandQuery isEnabled: (typesPresenter
        selectionOrNil notNil)].
```

Smalltalk evaluates whether typesPresenter selectionOrNil returns nil or not, and then aCommandQuery is enabled or not.

For the edit and delete items we want to do the same test, so we can combine them in a single validation:

```
(#(openItem deleteItem) includes: aCommandQuery command)
    ifTrue: [ aCommandQuery isEnabled: (itemsPresenter
    selectionOrNil notNil) ]
```

The queryCommand: message now looks like this:

```
RaceApplicationShell>>queryCommand: aCommandQuery
    "Add enabling/disabling for the new/open/delete
    commands"
    super queryCommand: aCommandQuery.
    (aCommandQuery command == #addItem) ifTrue: [
        aCommandQuery isEnabled: (componentsPresenter
            selectionOrNil notNil)].
    (#(openItem deleteItem) includes: aCommandQuery
        command) ifTrue: [ aCommandQuery isEnabled:
        (itemsPresenter
            selectionOrNil notNil)].
```

9.2.4 Toolbars

Most modern applications use toolbars as shortcuts for the menus. These toolbars show icons that should clearly represent the functionality that is called when the button is pressed. As those icons are relatively small, so-called tooltips have been invented. These are short pieces of text that show up when you have the mouse pointer on the icon (without clicking it). Toolbars typically have separators that divide groups of buttons. As a rule of thumb, you would use a separator between buttons that come from different menu options.

How to create a toolbar and use the available toolbar buttons.

Dolphin Smalltalk comes with a number of pre-set toolbars, which you can just drag onto your form and use "out of the box", like for example the File Toolbar, containing the standard New, Open, and Save buttons. Alternatively you can build your own toolbar.

As opposed to the menu which pushes itself onto our form, we have to make room for the toolbar ourselves. Again we will let the layout manager do the work for us. We used the BorderLayout as our layout manager, and gave the main container an arrangement of #center, which meant that it uses all the space available for it. So when we push a toolbar in between the top and the main container, the main container will just use up whatever is left after adding the toolbar. We just have to make sure that the toolbar is pushed to the top and has a fixed height. Pushing the toolbar to the top can be achieved by giving it the arrangement #north.

Let's see how that works. Select a blank Toolbar from the Resource toolbox and drop it on the main form. This might sound a bit awkward, as the main container occupies the whole form. However, you can also drop resources on the title bar of the form or just drop them in the view hierarchy. This will place the resource fairly randomly, but that's no problem as we are going to let the layout manager take care of the positioning. Now select the toolbar and set its "arrangement" aspect to #north. This should move the toolbar to the top and push the main form down just so that the toolbar fits.

Select the "items" aspect of the Toolbar and select New (or press the * button on the inspector next to the aspect list). This opens a dialog where you have to choose whether you want a normal button, a system button, or a separator (Figure 9.7).

The difference between normal buttons and system buttons is that the system buttons are Microsoft buttons, whereas for the normal buttons you can either make a selection from the Dolphin Smalltalk buttons or create your own.

For the #newItem and #openItem commands we will use Dolphin buttons, and for the #deleteItem command we will use a system button. Therefore create two standard buttons and a system button and then a separator.

When you open the items aspect tree, you see the individual buttons and separators. Select the first button and open it so that you see its aspects. These aspects are described in Table 9.2.

As you can see, when you add a system button it automatically selects a button with index 8.

When you create a standard button, it automatically selects the button with index 35 from the Dolphin bitmaps. The Dolphin development

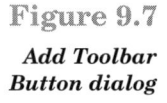

Figure 9.7

Add Toolbar Button dialog

Table 9.2 *Button aspects*

Aspect	Description
bitmap	Here you can point to either an external bitmap or a bitmap that is loaded as part of the system. A bitmap can contain multiple icons. They are indexed based on the size as defined in the toolbar (property bitmapSize x).
bitmapIndex	Here you can specify which of the icons in the bitmap should be displayed. Note that the first index is index 0. If the bitmap only contains a single icon, that is identified with index 0.
checked	Here you can set the button to be pressed when opening the view.
command	This is the method that is called when the button is pressed. If the method doesn't exist, the button is disabled.
enabled	Here the button can be disabled when opening the form.
isCheckStyle	This allows the button to become a toggle. Note that this is hardly used, as "checked" can be set programmatically.
isDropdownStyle	This adds a drop-down arrow next to the button.
isGroupStyle	This allows a number of CheckStyle buttons to act as a group.
text	This is the tooltip text.

environment (version 3) comes with 43 icons in the "Tools.bmp" bitmap (Figure 9.8). You can see them by evaluating:

```
ImagePresenter showOn: (Bitmap fromId: 'Tools.bmp')
```

You have to adjust the form to show them in the right aspect.

Now you can select one of the icons for the addItem button, for example index 36, and one for the openItem button, for example index 12.

For the ToolbarSystemButton we can choose from any of the buttons shown in Table 9.3.

Choosing the button with index 5 makes our view looks like Figure 9.9.

In addition to the Dolphin buttons and the standard Microsoft buttons we can also use the Microsoft View and History buttons. We have to do a bit more for those though. If we would like to use the VIEW_NEWFOLDER icon for our "newItem" command, we have to evaluate the following in the workspace of that button:

```
self class newFolder
```

Figure 9.8 *The standard Dolphin toolbar buttons*

Table 9.3

Standard Microsoft buttons

Bitmap	Index	Index value	Description
✂	0	STD_CUT	Cut operation
📋	1	STD_COPY	Copy operation
📋	2	STD_PASTE	Paste operation
↶	3	STD_UNDO	Undo operation
↷	4	STD_REDOW	Redo operation
✕	5	STD_DELETE	Delete operation
📄	6	STD_FILENEW	New file operation
📂	7	STD_FILEOPEN	Open file operation
💾	8	STD_FILESAVE	Save file operation
🔍	9	STD_PRINTPRE	Print preview operation
📋	10	STD_PROPERTIES	Properties operation
❓	11	STD_HELP	Help operation
🔍	12	STD_FIND	Find operation
🔍	13	STD_REPLACE	Replace operation
🖨	14	STD_PRINT	Print operation

Figure 9.9

The application view with toolbar

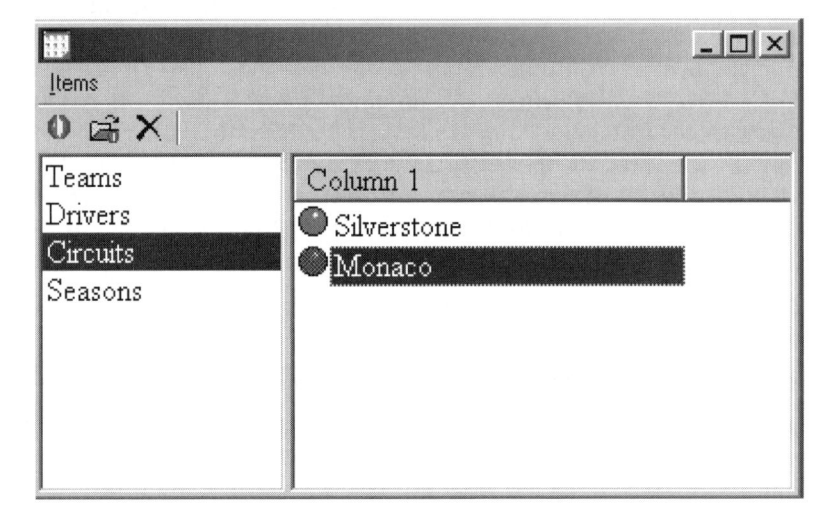

This calls the class method #newFolder from the ToolbarButton class. Have a look at this method. Here you can see that it creates a button from the IDB_VIEW_SMALL_COLOR group. As it is a (Microsoft) system button, it automatically changes the class to a ToolbarSystemButton. But the difference with the standard system button is that you can now select an index from the View buttons (Table 9.4). In the same way you can choose from the History buttons. The bitmapIndex aspect only accepts integers, but if you prefer the Microsoft values, then you can evaluate in the workspace:

```
self index: VIEW_NEWFOLDER
```

In Table 9.5 HIST_BACK and HIST_FORWARD have the aspect "dropdownStyle" set to true. You can set this aspect to true on any button. A good example where that is used is the Views button in Windows Explorer.

If you intend to use a certain button of a certain category on a regular basis, you can add your own class method calling the right button (remember to change the package for that method):

Table 9.4

Microsoft View buttons

Bitmap	Index	Index value	Description
	0	VIEW_LARGEICONS	Large icon view
	1	VIEW_SMALLICONS	Small icon view
	2	VIEW_LIST	List view
	3	VIEW_DETAILS	Details view
	4	VIEW_SORTNAME	Sort by name
	5	VIEW_SORTSIZE	Sort by size
	6	VIEW_SORTDATE	Sort by date
	7	VIEW_SORTTYPE	Sort by type
	8	VIEW_PARENTFOLDER	Go to parent folder
	9	VIEW_NETCONNECT	Connect network drive
	10	VIEW_NETDISCONNECT	Disconnect network drive
	11	VIEW_NEWFOLDER	New folder

Table 9.5
Microsoft History buttons

Bitmap	Index	Index value	Description
⇦ ▾	0	HIST_BACK	Move back
⇨ ▾	1	HIST_FORWARD	Move forward
📁	2	HIST_FAVORITES	Open favorites folder
📁+	3	HIST_ADDTOFAVORITES	Add to favorites
📄	4	HIST_VIEWTREE	View tree

```
ToolbarButton class>>netConnect
    "Answer a sub-instance of the receiver for the
    #netConnect command"
    ^self viewImage: VIEW_NETCONNECT command: #netConnect
    description: 'Connect'
```

Large toolbar buttons Some Microsoft applications use large toolbuttons, for example Internet Explorer. If you want, you can use large icons in your toolbar. These large toolbar buttons typically have the tooltip text underneath the button. You can switch this on by setting the "hasLabels" aspect of the Toolbar to "true". To support the text, the buttons become quite a bit larger. The large icons themselves are 24@24 pixels, and the size of the buttons is 52@45. This width is required to show the tooltip text. The text is shown in Arial 8 pt. The height of the toolbar is 48 pixels for the large buttons. Before we can use the large buttons, we have to add some class methods to the ToolbarButton class (again, don't forget to change the package where the methods are stored). If we look at the #fileOpen method, we see that it calls the #standardImage:command: description:method. This method defines which bitmap is used, and which of the icons in that bitmap is used. As we want to use a different bitmap, namely the bitmap with the large icons, we have to create methods that call those large images. The easiest way is just to copy the original methods and put "Large" in the name (just open the method, append the method name with Large, modify the method, and save it):

```
ToolbarButton class>>fileOpenLarge
    "Answer a sub-instance of the receiver for the
    #fileOpen command"
    ^self standardImageLarge: STD_FILEOPEN command:
        #fileOpen description: 'Open'
```

```
ToolbarButton class>>standardImageLarge: bitmapIndex
    command: aCommand description: aString
    "Private - Answer a new instance of the receiver using
    a Standard system toolbar bitmap
    identified by bitmapName and issuing aCommand"
    ^self systemButtonClass
        bitmap: IDB_STD_LARGE_COLOR
        index: bitmapIndex
        commandDescription: (CommandDescription command:
            aCommand description: aString)
```

You can do the same for the View buttons, but as the IDB_HIST_LARGE_COLOR bitmap isn't included in the wrapped image (as yet), you can't use these.

Using your own bitmaps It is quite likely that you want to use bitmaps other than the ones provided by Microsoft and Object Arts. In that case you have to create your own (or get them from elsewhere). You can basically use any painting program that can generate bitmap files to create the bitmaps, but some are of course more convenient than others. One of Ian Bartholomew's Dolphin goodies (see Appendix A) is a bitmap editor, very convenient for this task.

You can create an individual bitmap file for every bitmap (button) that you need, but you can also follow the approach that is used for the Dolphin and Microsoft bitmaps. In that case you create a "stream" of bitmaps in a single file, and then based on the size you call the individual bitmaps through an index number (starting with zero).

When you have created your bitmap, you have to select it by double-clicking on the bitmap aspect of the toolbar button. This opens a file-open dialog, where you can select your file. Then set the bitmapIndex aspect to the right number and your bitmap is shown. If it only shows half the bitmap, or a different one, then it is likely that the sizes of the bitmaps in the file do not correspond with the bitmapSize aspect of the toolbar.

> Note that when you use your own bitmaps, you make a reference to an external file from within your application. This means that the path to that file has to be stored within your application as well. When you create the reference, Dolphin will try to make that path relative to the image that you are working from, but if that is impossible, then the whole path starting from the drive will be stored. This can cause problems when you deploy the application to other computers. Therefore the preferred way to use your own bitmaps (or other external resources) is to store them either in the same directory as the image or in a subdirectory from the image directory.

9.2.5 *Summary*

In this section we have explored commands, how to create menus and toolbars for them and how to enable and disable them. Dolphin doesn't enable/disable the menu items and buttons themselves, but enables and disables the commands instead. This is done through the #queryCommand: message.

9.3 Integrating the season-dependent components

So far we have only included the "independent" components in our racing application: drivers, teams, circuits, and seasons. The other components are less straightforward, as they depend on the season. We could of course just add them in the same way as we did with the other components, but then the items list for the races would show all races for all seasons.

Alternatively, we could add a drop-down list to the view where we could select the season like we did in the race view, but that wouldn't fit in with our Object-Action approach. Another solution is to present the components in a tree and add the individual seasons to the tree as branches of the season. Underneath the individual seasons we could then add the season-dependent items. That would make the tree look like Figure 9.10.

This approach also allows us to maintain different branches of motor racing in a single application. We can, for example, have a branch for Formula One, with all the different components underneath, and a separate branch for Indycar racing, using the same components, but independent from Formula One.

9.3.1 *The tree model*

How we can build and maintain trees and the difference between standard trees and virtual trees.

Trees can be built in two ways in Dolphin Smalltalk: you can either create a tree and connect the objects to the branches of the tree, or use a so-called virtual tree. The first option has the advantage that the underlying model doesn't need to know that you are presenting it in the form of a tree. The disadvantage is that you have to maintain the tree yourself whenever you change something in the underlying model. This means that when you add something to the underlying model that affects the tree, you have to remember to add it to the tree as well. In the virtual tree you build the knowledge of the tree in the underlying model. Therefore, if you add something to the model, the tree is automatically updated.

BRINGING THE COMPONENTS TOGETHER

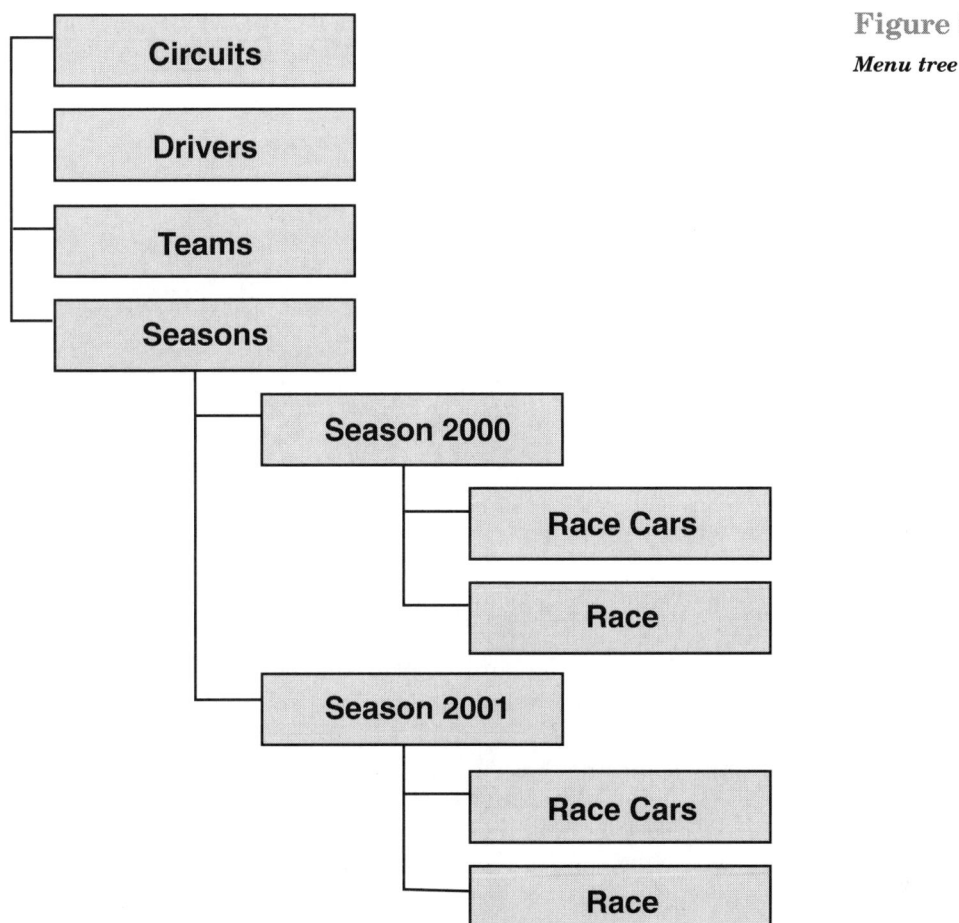

Figure 9.10
Menu tree

[Tree diagram showing: Circuits, Drivers, Teams, Seasons as top-level nodes. Seasons has children Season 2000 and Season 2001. Season 2000 has children Race Cars and Race. Season 2001 has children Race Cars and Race.]

In our case we can easily build the knowledge of the tree in the RaceAppComponent and subclasses, therefore the virtual tree is the right choice. However, as the normal tree is easier to understand, we will first build a standard tree in our Application model, and once we have it working we will convert it to a virtual tree.

The basic TreeModel   A tree is all about parents and children. We start by creating a root, which is the parent of all children. We can have multiple roots, for example one root called Formula One and one root called Indycar. These roots have children, which have the root as their parent (sounds obvious, doesn't it?). Those children can have their own children, and so on. This is exactly how the tree works. Have a look at class TreeModel. The most important public method is #add:asChildOf:. If you add an object to the TreeModel with parent nil, then the TreeModel

How to build a simple tree.

interprets that as a root. Let's build a shell in which we can demonstrate the working of the tree. Create the TreeDemo as subclass of Shell:

```
Shell subclass: #TreeDemo
     instanceVariableNames: ''
     classVariableNames: ''
     poolDictionaries: ''
```

Add the minimum number of methods:

TreeDemo>>createComponents
```
     super createComponents.
     self add: TreePresenter new name: 'tree'.
```

TreeDemo>>model: aTree
```
     super model: aTree.
     (self presenterNamed: 'tree') model: aTree.
```

Build a view for this model; just drop a TreePresenter.Default view on the shell and set the name property to "tree". To expand the tree presenter over the shell, we use the BorderLayout manager like before. Now add the following test data in a workspace:

```
xx := TreeModel new
     add: #Top asChildOf: nil;
     add: #First asChildOf: #Top;
     add: #Second asChildOf: #First;
     add: #Another asChildOf: #First;
     add: #AndAgain asChildOf: #First;
     add: #Next asChildOf: #Top;
     add: #Last asChildOf: nil;
     yourself.
```

We need the #yourself message as we concatenated everything. Without the #yourself message the symbol #Last would be the last return value of the concatenated messages and thus would be the assignment to the xx variable.

Now we can show the tree in the shell view that we just created:

```
TreeDemo showOn: xx
```

After showing all levels the result should look like Figure 9.11.

We can apply the same to our application. The RaceApplication requires an instance variable to store the tree. As the tree holds all the components, we don't need the raceAppComponents instance variable anymore. When you remove it you have to modify the methods that refer to it. You can also

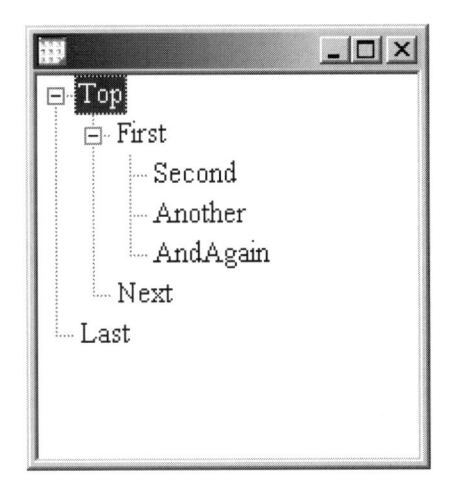

Figure 9.11
Tree demo

leave it in place so that your framework view with list continues to work. The new tree variable requires the standard accessors.

```
MyModel subclass: #RaceApplication
      instanceVariableNames: 'tree'
      classVariableNames: ''
      poolDictionaries: ''
```

RaceApplication>>tree
```
      ^tree
```

RaceApplication>>tree: anObject
```
      tree := anObject
```

To create a root, we have to create a new subclass to our RaceAppComponent which we will not enable to have items. How can we make sure that it doesn't have items? We can of course add the #addItem method with the message #shouldNotImplement, but then we still can't disable the menu option. What about adding a method #canHaveItems, which returns true for the normal components, and false for the root components. Then we can add a check in the #queryCommand: and enable the #addItem for those that return true to this.

RaceAppComponent>>canHaveItems
```
      ^true
```

```
RaceAppComponent subclass: #RootComponent
      instanceVariableNames: ''
      classVariableNames: ''
      poolDictionaries: ''
```

```
RootComponent>>addItem
    ^self shouldNotImplement

RootComponent>>canHaveItems
    ^false

RaceApplicationShell>>queryCommand: aCommandQuery
    ...
    (aCommandQuery command == #addItem) ifTrue: [
        aCommandQuery isEnabled: (componentsPresenter
            selectionOrNil notNil and:
                [componentsPresenter selectionOrNil
                    canHaveItems])].
    ...
```

Now we can create some components and a RaceApplication instance.

```
f1teams := TeamComponent new.
f1drivers := DriverComponent new.
f1 := DummyComponent new name: 'Formula One'.
indyteams := TeamComponent new.
indydrivers := DriverComponent new.
indy := DummyComponent new name: 'Indycar'.
raceApp := RaceApplication new.
raceApp addRaceAppComponent: f1teams.
raceApp addRaceAppComponent: f1drivers.
raceApp addRaceAppComponent: f1.
raceApp addRaceAppComponent: indyteams.
raceApp addRaceAppComponent: indydrivers.
raceApp addRaceAppComponent: indy.
```

The next step is to create the tree structure just like we did for our tree demo:

```
raceApp tree: (TreeModel new
    add: f1 asChildOf: nil;
    add: f1teams asChildOf: f1;
    add: f1drivers asChildOf: f1;
    add: indy asChildOf: nil;
    add: indyteams asChildOf: indy;
    add: indydrivers asChildOf: indy;
    yourself)
```

We have to make slightly more modifications to the presenter, as we have to replace the ListPresenter with a TreePresenter.

```
RaceApplicationShell>>createComponents
    ...
    componentsPresenter := self add: TreePresenter new
    name: 'componentsList'.
    ...

RaceApplicationShell>>model: aRaceApplication
    ...
    typesPresenter model: (aRaceApplication tree).
```

In the view we have to modify the typesList from a ListView into a TreeView. We can use the Mutate view command here. There are a number of other aspects to mention here. With the hasLinesAtRoot setting you can show a line in front of the root, and if you have multiple root objects, then these are connected. The hasButtons aspect puts a + in front of an expandable node if it is not expanded. The + changes to a − when the node is expanded. Note that this button is only shown at the root if you also set the hasLinesAtRoot. The final aspect setting that we discuss before we have a look at our view is the viewMode. This aspect allows you to show an icon in front of the node. By default this is the icon connected to the class of the node object that you show.

After these modifications our view now looks like Figure 9.12.

Note that all the other functionality still works. With the modification to the #queryCommand: you can also see that when selecting a root component the "add item" commands are all disabled.

The virtual tree – parent-child relationships To convert this static tree into a virtual tree we have to modify the application components, so that each application component knows who its parent is and

How to maintain bidirectional relationships from either side.

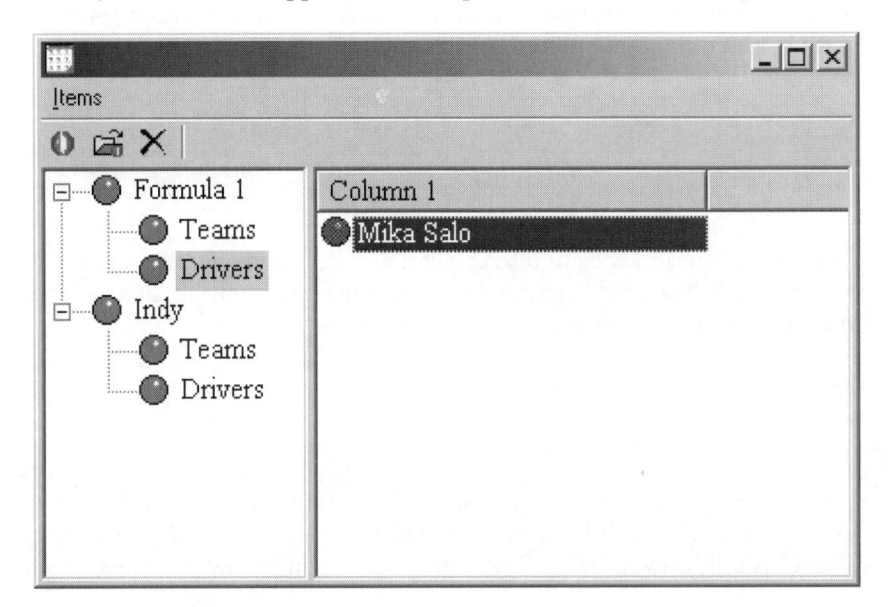

Figure 9.12

Tree view

who its children are. When we have that working, we can just walk through all the application components and build the tree nodes based on that information.

First we have to add the parent and children instance variables to the RaceAppComponent class.

```
MyModel subclass: #RaceAppComponent
    instanceVariableNames: 'items parent children'
    classVariableNames: ''
    poolDictionaries: ''
```

As we want the children variable to contain a list, we have to initialize it. We also have to create getters for the new variables.

```
RaceAppComponent>>initialize
    ...
    children := ListModel on: OrderedCollection new.

RaceAppComponent>>parent
    ^parent

RaceAppComponent>>children
    ^children
```

We want to be sure that when an application component is set as the parent of another application component, the other application component is added to the list of children of the first. The same applies the other way round; if an application component is added to the list of children of another application component, then we want to be sure that the parent of the first is updated. Therefore, these methods should somehow refer to each other. Let's have a look how we can organize this from the viewpoint of the parent:

```
RaceAppComponent>>addChild: aChild
    children add: aChild.
    aChild parent: self.
```

In the first line we add the child to the list, and in the second line we make sure that the object itself becomes the parent of that child. Taking the viewpoint of the child, we would code it like this:

```
RaceAppComponent>>parent: aParent
    parent := aParent.
    aParent addChild: self.
```

Here we set the parent variable in the first line, and in the second line we make sure that this child object is added to the list of children of the parent. This might look OK at first sight, but if you follow it through you will see that this is a loop that runs forever, so we need to find a way to jump out of that loop. We can do that by testing whether the child is already in the list of children, and whether the parent of the child is already stored in the child's parent variable. The simplest option is just to test everything from the method that is called, so when you send the message #addChild:, you first check whether that child is already in the list, if not, add it. Then you check whether the parent of that child is already set to itself, if not, you set it. You could do the same for the #parent: method, so if the parent of the receiver is already set to the parameter, you do nothing, otherwise you set it, and if the child is already in the list, you don't set it, otherwise you do. This would look like:

```
RaceAppComponent>>addChild: aChild
    (children includes: aChild) ifFalse: [ children add:
        aChild ].
    (aChild parent == self) ifFalse: [ aChild parent: self
        ].

RaceAppComponent>>parent: aParent
    (parent == aParent) ifFalse: [ parent := aParent ].
    (aParent children includes: self) ifFalse: [ aParent
        addChild: self ].
```

This isn't very elegant as we test everything twice. It would be better if we left the testing to the right object; the parent object should only test itself and the child object should only test itself as well. The parent should only ask the child to set its parent if the parent added the child, and the child should only ask the parent to add the child if the child's parent has changed.

```
RaceAppComponent>>addChild: aChild
    (children includes: aChild) ifFalse: [
        children add: aChild.
        aChild parent: self ].

RaceAppComponent>>parent: aParent
    (parent == aParent) ifFalse: [
        parent := aParent.
        aParent addChild: self ].
```

Now what if a child already had a parent? In that case the child should be removed from the old parent's children list. But if we allow a child to be removed, then we have to consider again that we can initiate it both from the parent and from the child. To start with the child, we can just extend the #parent: method. If the parent was nil, then we don't have to do anything, otherwise we have to do a #removeChild: on the old parent.

```
RaceAppComponent>>parent: aParent
    | oldParent |
    (self parent == aParent) ifFalse: [
        oldParent := self parent.
        parent := aParent.
        oldParent isNil ifFalse: [oldParent removeChild:
            self].
        aParent isNil ifFalse: [aParent addChild: self].
    ].
```

We added a check on the new parent, as we might want to make a child an orphan, which means that the parent is nil. If we then try to add the orphan with #addChild:, we will get an error message as nil won't understand the message #addChild:.

For the old parent we need the #removeChild: method. This again needs to check whether it has to communicate with the child to be orphaned. As we cannot leave the testing to the child in this case, we have to do the test within the #removeChild: method itself. (Can you see why we can't leave it to the child itself?)

```
RaceAppComponent>>removeChild: aChild
    children remove: aChild ifAbsent: [nil].
    (aChild parent == self) ifTrue: [aChild parent: nil].
```

You can check whether you have covered every situation by doing some tests. Inspect the parent and child variables after each message.

```
p1 := RootComponent new name: 'parent 1'.
p2 := RootComponent new name: 'parent 2'.

c1 := TeamComponent new name: 'child 1'.
c2 := TeamComponent new name: 'child 2'.

p1 addChild: c1.
c2 parent: p2.
p1 addChild: c2.
c1 parent: p2.
c2 parent: nil.
p2 removeChild: c1.
```

Now that we can put each application component in the right place in the hierarchy, we can focus on the virtual tree again.

Where to maintain the virtual tree.

The virtual tree in the racing application The virtual tree relies on the fact that every item in the tree knows its position in the hierarchy. Because of this it is in principle enough for the virtual tree to know about the roots. From there it can work out the hierarchy itself by asking all the roots their children, and those children for their children and so on. However, it is both simpler and better to add every application component to this virtual tree. It is simpler because it means that every application component is treated in the same way. It is better because when a change occurs, the virtual tree doesn't have to rebuild itself completely, it just has to rebuild that part of the tree. This is especially apparent when you have an application where children can change parent and where you allow drag and drop operations within the tree.

The virtual tree can be held either in the model or in the presenter. When holding it in the presenter, each view has its own virtual tree. The disadvantage of that is that when an application component is added or when the parent of an application component is changed, the individual virtual trees have to be informed of that change, which does not happen automatically. Therefore it is better to have the actual virtual tree contained within the RaceApplication.

```
MyModel subclass: #RaceApplication
    instanceVariableNames: 'raceAppComponents tree
    virtualTree'
    classVariableNames: ''
    poolDictionaries: ''
```

We initialize the virtualTree as a VirtualTreeModel.

RaceApplication>>initialize
```
    ...
    virtualTree := VirtualTreeModel new.
```

RaceApplication>>virtualTree
```
    ^virtualTree
```

For adding, moving, and removing framework types in the tree, we have to create the following methods in the Framework class.

RaceApplication>>addRaceAppComponent: aRaceAppComponent
    parent: aParent
```
    "Add a racing application component"
    self raceAppComponents add: aRaceAppComponent.
    aRaceAppComponent parent: aParent.
    virtualTree add: aRaceAppComponent asChildOf: aParent.
```

RaceApplication>>moveRaceAppComponent: aRaceAppComponent
    parent: aParent
```
    "Move a racing application component to a parent"
    aRaceAppComponent parent: aParent.
    virtualTree move: aRaceAppComponent asChildOf:
        aParent.
```

```
RaceApplication>>removeRaceAppComponent: aRaceAppComponent
    "Remove a racing application component"
    aRaceAppComponent isNil ifFalse: [
        aRaceAppComponent children do: [ :each | self
            removeRaceAppComponent: each ].
    self raceAppComponents remove: aRaceAppComponent
        ifAbsent: [^nil].
    virtualTree remove: aRaceAppComponent].
```

To make use of this virtual tree in our view, we have to modify the #model: method so that the tree list connects to the virtualTree instead of the tree that we built before. Modify the #model: method in the RaceApplicationShell class as follows:

```
RaceApplicationShell>>model: aRaceApplication
    ...
    componentsPresenter model: aRaceApplication
        virtualTree.
```

Now we can test our virtual tree. We have to reinitialize our RaceApplication instance, as that doesn't know about the virtual tree yet. We also have to reinitialize the component instances, as we added the parent and children variables to that class. Then we can add the nodes to the virtual tree and tell them who their parent is.

```
f1teams := TeamComponent new.
f1drivers := DriverComponent new.
f1 := RootComponent new name: 'Formula One'.
indyteams := TeamComponent new.
indydrivers := DriverComponent new.
indy := RootComponent new name: 'Indycar'.
raceApp := RaceApplication new.
raceApp addRaceAppComponent: f1 parent: nil.
raceApp addRaceAppComponent: f1teams parent: f1.
raceApp addRaceAppComponent: f1drivers parent: f1.
raceApp addRaceAppComponent: indy parent: nil.
raceApp addRaceAppComponent: indyteams parent: indy.
raceApp addRaceAppComponent: indydrivers parent: indy.
```

As we didn't change anything in the view, it looks exactly the same as with the standard tree (Figure 9.13).

The difference from the normal tree shows when we add the seasons and the circuits to the tree.

```
f1seasons := SeasonComponent new.
f1circuits := CircuitComponent new.
raceApp addRaceAppComponent: f1seasons parent: f1.
raceApp addRaceAppComponent: f1circuits parent: f1.
```

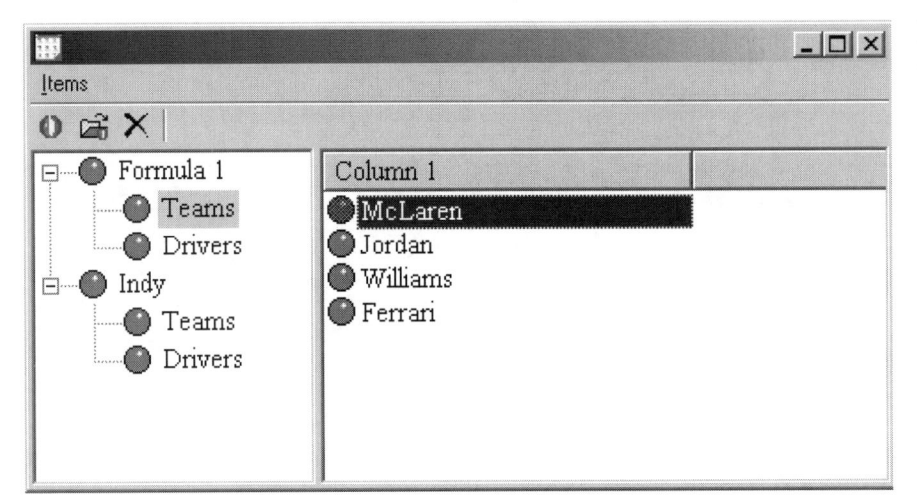

Figure 9.13
Virtual tree

You will see that the tree is dynamically updated.

Setting up a default tree   When we open a new model, we need to have the basic race application components already there, as they form the interface to the individual components. We can build that by creating a #setup method in the RaceApplication that is called when a new RaceApplication is created. Therefore we call the #setup message from the #initialize method.

How to initialize a tree when opening a new model.

```
RaceApplication>>initialize
    ...
    self setup.

RaceApplication>>setup
    "Set up the initial race application components tree"
    | root |
    root := RootComponent new name: 'Formula 1'.
    self addRaceAppComponent: root parent: nil.
    self addRaceAppComponent: TeamComponent new parent:
        root.
    self addRaceAppComponent: DriverComponent new parent:
        root.
    self addRaceAppComponent: CircuitComponent new parent:
        root.
    self addRaceAppComponent: SeasonComponent new parent:
        root.
```

When you now open the view on a new RaceApplication it will look like Figure 9.14.

Figure 9.14
New RaceApplication

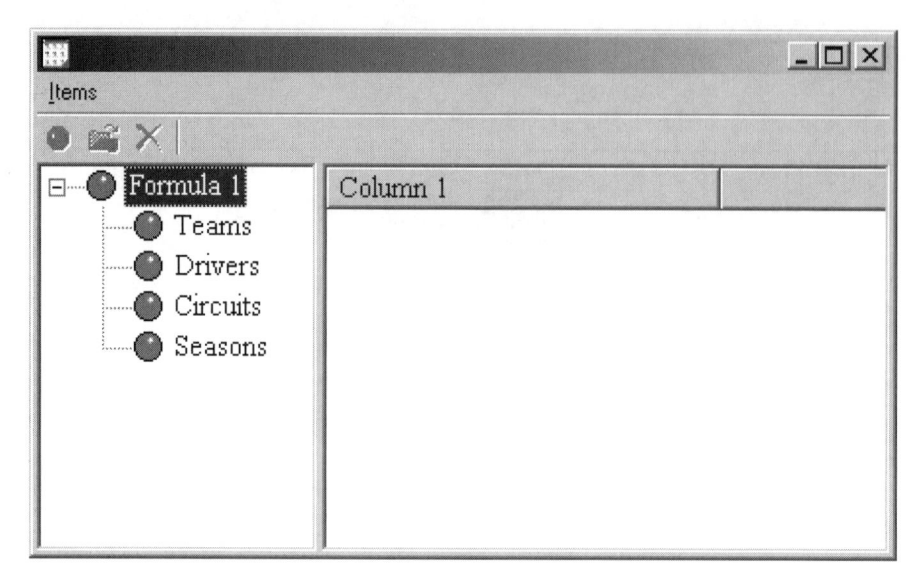

Summary

In the above subsections we have explored the tree models. We have learned the difference between hard-coded tree models and virtual tree models; in the hard-coded model the knowledge of the tree hierarchy lives in the tree itself whereas in case of the virtual tree it lives in the underlying objects. Each of the underlying objects has a parent and a collection of children. If the parent is nil, the object is a root. Because the parent-child relationship has to be maintained from both the parent and the child, we have learned how to ensure that these relationships stay in sync. We have also learned how to get the tree sorted at every level. And finally we have learned how to set up a tree as part of the creation of a new model object.

9.3.2 Add branches for the Race and RaceCar

How to dynamically add branches to a tree.

As the Races and RaceCars are dependent on specific seasons, they should be on a branch below individual seasons. This means that individual seasons themselves need to be branches as well, with the race cars and the races underneath them. Therefore, whenever we add a season, we have to add a branch to the tree for the season itself and underneath that two more branches, one for the races and one for the race cars. As we know from the previous section, to add branches we need to be able to talk to the tree itself. As the tree is owned by the hosting application, the RaceApplication instance, we need to be able to send the hosting application messages from the branch. So far we haven't needed this, therefore we haven't got that facility yet. But as we create the branches from within the RaceApplication instance, we can easily add it at creation time. We only have to add an instance variable to the RaceAppComponent class and set that instance variable when we create an instance.

```
MyModel subclass: #RaceAppComponent
      instanceVariableNames: 'items parent children host'
      classVariableNames: ''
      poolDictionaries: ''
```

The "host" instance variable needs the standard accessors. As we want to be sure that it is set at creation time, we add a class method that creates the component and sets the host variable.

```
RaceAppComponent class>>forHost: aHost
      "Create a new instance and set the 'host' variable"
      ^(self basicNew initialize) host: aHost
```

Now we can create a branch from within a branch. But what kind of branch should we create? We can't make it a SeasonComponent instance, as that type allows creation of new seasons. It is more like the RootComponent that we created earlier. But as we want it to hold the Season instance itself, we will create a specific class for it.

```
RaceAppComponent subclass: #SeasonInstanceComponent
      instanceVariableNames: 'instance'
      classVariableNames: ''
      poolDictionaries: ''
```

```
SeasonInstanceComponent>>addItem
      ^self shouldNotImplement
```

```
SeasonInstanceComponent>>canHaveItems
      ^false
```

```
SeasonInstanceComponent>>instance
      ^instance
```

```
SeasonInstanceComponent>>instance: aSeason
      instance := aSeason
```

```
SeasonInstanceComponent>>name
      ^self instance name
```

For the Race and the RaceCar we also have to create Application Component classes so that we can use them in a similar way to the other components. For opening a race we built a different view from the one that we use when creating a race. Because we are using different messages for opening and creation, we can just use the right view on either action.

```
RaceAppComponent subclass: #RaceComponent
    instanceVariableNames: ''
    classVariableNames: ''
    poolDictionaries: ''
```

RaceComponent>>addItem
```
"Create a new item of this type and show it in the
appropriate form.
If not canceled, add the item to the collection of
items"
| item |
item := Race forSeason: self parent instance.
(RaceDialog showOn: item) when: #viewClosed send:
#checkItem: to: self with: item.
```

RaceComponent>>openItem: anItem
```
"Show the item in the appropriate form"
RaceShell showOn: anItem.
```

RaceComponent>>name
```
"Return the name of the component"
^'Races'
```

For the RaceCar we do the same.

```
RaceAppComponent subclass: #RaceCarComponent
    instanceVariableNames: ''
    classVariableNames: ''
    poolDictionaries: ''
```

RaceCarComponent>>addItem
```
"Create a new item of this type and show it in the
appropriate form.
If not canceled, add the item to the collection of
items"
| item |
item := RaceCar forSeason: self parent instance.
(RaceCarView showOn: item) when: #viewClosed send:
    #checkItem: to: self with: item.
```

RaceCarComponent>>checkItem: anItem
```
"Check if the item has a starting number different
from zero. If that is the case, add the item to the
list of items"
item name isEmpty ifFalse: [ self items add: anItem ].
```

```
RaceCarComponent>>openItem: anItem
    "Show the item in the appropriate form"
    RaceCarView showOn: anItem.


RaceCarComponent>>name
    "Return the name of the component"
    ^'Race cars'
```

As we maintain a bidirectional link between the season and the race cars and races, we now have to make sure that when we delete a race or racecar, we remove it from the appropriate list in the season as well. Otherwise our checks might still fail even though we can't see the race car with, for example, starting number 12.

```
RaceComponent>>removeItem: anItem
    "Remove the item from the itemslist and do the
    necessary cleanup"
    super removeItem: anItem.
    anItem remove.


RaceCarComponent>>removeItem: anItem
    "Remove the item from the itemslist and do the
    necessary cleanup"
    super removeItem: anItem.
    anItem remove.
```

These methods rely on a #remove method in their domain model classes. These domain model classes have a far better knowledge of which links are maintained, therefore that is the right place to break those links. The #beFinalizable method gives the garbage collector a hand by flagging the object so that it can be removed on the next sweep. Otherwise the garbage collector would set that flag on the first sweep and remove the object at the second sweep.

```
Race>>remove
    "Break the bidirectional links with this object"
    self season removeRace: self.
    self beFinalizable.


RaceCar>>remove
    "Break the bidirectional links with this object"
    self season removeRaceCar: self.
    self team notNil ifTrue: [ self team removeRaceCar:
        self ].
    self beFinalizable.
```

Now we have to override the RaceAppComponent >> checkItem: for the SeasonComponent so that it automatically creates an extra branch for the season instance itself and sub-branches for the races and race cars. As we allow seasons to be deleted, we have to make sure that when deleting a season, these extra branches get deleted as well.

```
SeasonComponent>>addItem
    "If the name is not blank, add the item to the
    collection of items and create the sub-branches"
    | itemBranch |
    anItem name isEmpty ifFalse: [ self items add: anItem.
        itemBranch := (SeasonInstanceComponent forHost:
            self host) instance: anItem.
        self host addRaceAppComponent: itemBranch
            parent: self.
        self host addRaceAppComponent: (RaceCarComponent
            forHost: self host) parent: itemBranch.
        self host addRaceAppComponent: (RaceComponent
            forHost: self host) parent: itemBranch.
        ].
```

```
SeasonComponent>>removeItem: anItem
    "Remove an item and remove the sub-branches"
    | itemBranch |
    itemBranch := self children detect: [ :each | each
    instance == anItem ] ifNone: [nil].
    itemBranch notNil ifTrue: [
        itemBranch removeChildren.
        self children remove: itemBranch.
        self host removeRaceAppComponent: itemBranch].
    super removeItem: anItem.
```

```
SeasonInstanceComponent>> removeChildren
    "Remove the child branches"
    self children do: [ :each |
        each items do: [ :item |
            each removeItem: item ].
        self removeChild: each.
        self host removeRaceAppComponent: each]
```

Let's see if all this actually works. Open the RaceApplicationShell on a new RaceApplication and add some seasons. As soon as you create a new season you will see that the Seasons branch gets a child branch and this child branch appears to have children as well (Figure 9.15).

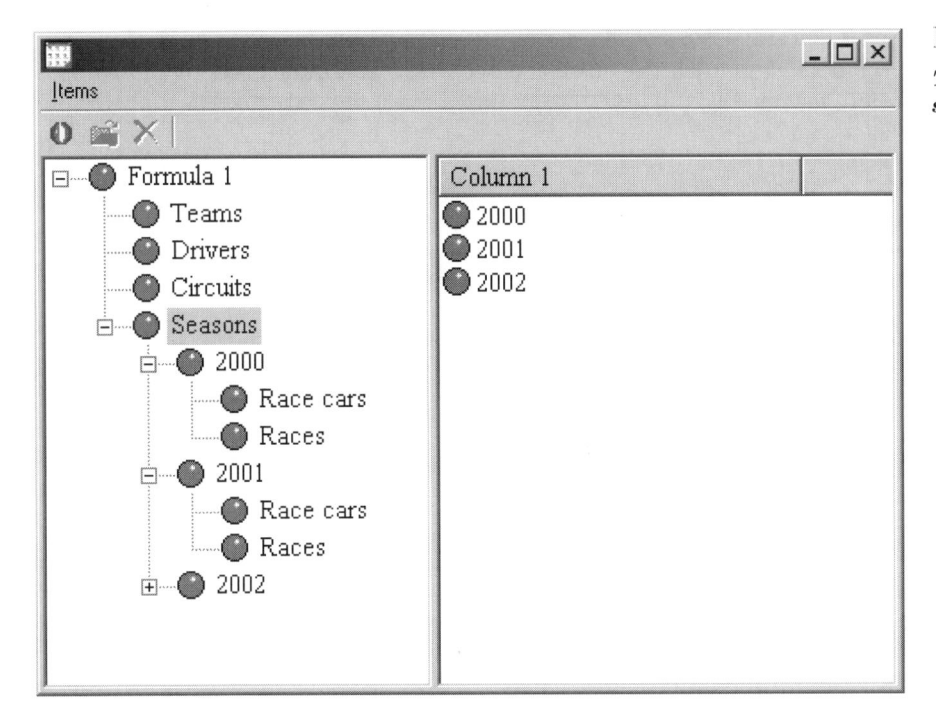

Figure 9.15
The Seasons' sub-branches

9.4 Tidying up the race application components

9.4.1 *Global variables revisited*

There is one remaining problem. When you try to create a race, it will complain that it can't find the season. How is that possible? Well, when we created that view, we didn't have our application environment yet, therefore we introduced some global variables that held instances of the different components. These instances are not the same as the instances that we create in our application environment. So when opening the race dialog, it tries to set the selection of the season drop-down to the season for which we are creating the race, but that doesn't exist in the global variable.

As the global variable solution was only a temporary one, now is the time to change those methods that refer to the global variables so that they look at the application environment instead.

The problem with this is that the individual items do not know who creates them. Therefore we have to introduce a variable that stores which ApplicationComponent instance asked for the creation. With this solution you can, for example, have multiple TeamComponents in a single application and still distinguish them from each other. As we built all our domain classes as subclasses of MyModel, we can add the instance variable to the MyModel class with the standard accessors and only set it in those cases where we need it.

```
Model subclass: #MyModel
    instanceVariableNames: 'name component'
    classVariableNames: ''
    poolDictionaries: ''
```

CircuitComponent>>addItem

```
    ...
    item := Circuit new component: self.
    ...
```

RaceCarComponent>>addItem

```
    ...
    item := (RaceCar forSeason: self parent instance)
        component: self.
    ...
```

RaceComponent>>addItem

```
    ...
    item := (Race forSeason: self parent instance)
        component: self.
    ...
```

Now we can ask the component to walk through the tree until it finds the component that holds all the items. But there is an easier way. The root can just look at its children and find the items of a certain component. If we then enable every component to ask for the root, we have a generic solution that works for all.

RaceAppComponent>>root

```
    "Find the root for this component"
    (self parent isKindOf: RootComponent)
        ifTrue: [ ^self parent ]
        ifFalse: [ ^self parent root ].
```

RootComponent>>allCircuits

```
    "Return all circuit objects"
    ^(self children detect: [ :each | each isKindOf:
        CircuitComponent ]) items
```

RootComponent>>allDrivers

```
    "Return all driver objects"
    ^(self children detect: [ :each | each isKindOf:
        DriverComponent ]) items
```

```
RootComponent>>allSeasons
    "Return all season objects"
    ^(self children detect: [ :each | each isKindOf:
        SeasonComponent ]) items

RootComponent>>allTeams
    "Return all team objects"
    ^(self children detect: [ :each | each isKindOf:
        TeamComponent ]) items
```

Now we have to let the presenters know how to get to these "all*" methods. We could make it a whole string of methods, like "self model component root allDrivers", but that doesn't read very well and it makes all the classes that are visited by this line dependent on each other. Better would be if the presenter could just ask the model to return all drivers. Then the model can sort out how it retrieves them. Now how can we find all methods like allDrivers, allTeams, and so on? The easiest way is to select, for example, the #allDrivers method, and then from the Method menu (or the method context menu) select Browse – Definitions. This shows a list of all the methods referred to in this method, with the selected method itself in bold (Figure 9.16).

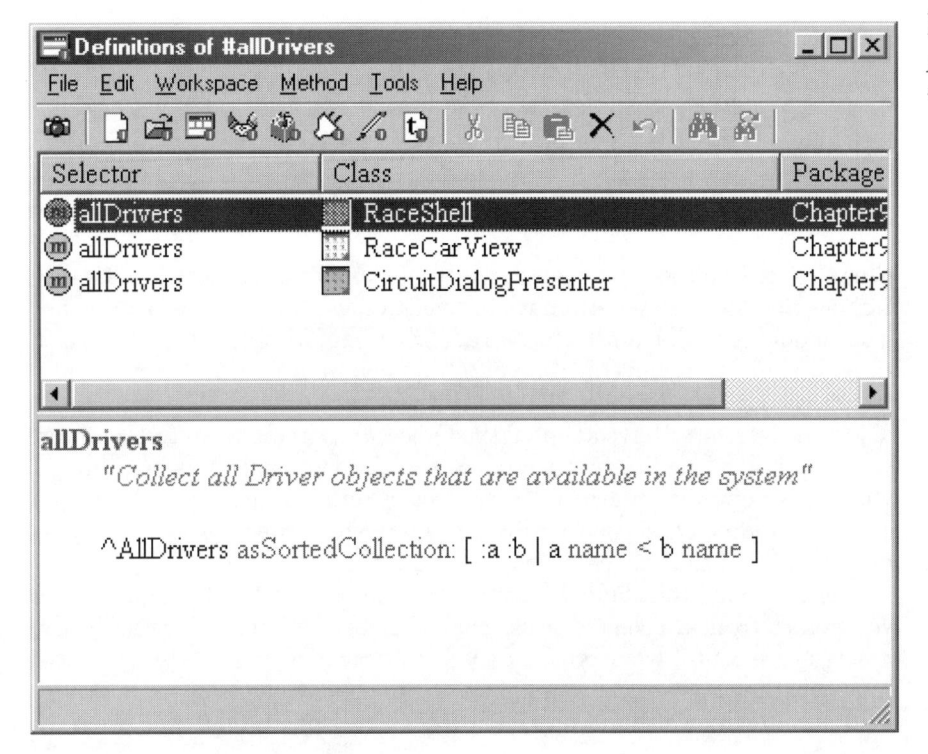

Figure 9.16
Definitions of #allDrivers

The good thing about this screen is that you can immediately start modifying the methods, so just select each of the presenters and replace the reference to the global variable in "self model allDrivers". Do the same for the other global variables.

Now we have to make the "all*" methods available to the different domain models from where they are called. But as they are all the same for the different domain models, we can just as well add them to the MyModel class, then we can share it.

```
MyModel>>allCircuits
    "Return all Circuit objects"
    self component notNil ifTrue: [ ^self component root
        allCircuits ]

MyModel>>allDrivers
    "Return all Driver objects"
    self component notNil ifTrue: [ ^self component root
        allDrivers ]

MyModel>>allSeasons
    "Return all Season objects"
    self component notNil ifTrue: [ ^self component root
        allSeasons ]

MyModel>>allTeams
    "Return all Team objects"
    self component notNil ifTrue: [ ^self component root
        allTeams ]
```

9.4.2 Opening a race for the results

How to pre-select and disable drop-down lists based on available information.

When we select a race and open it, we are just opening the RaceShell. Once the RaceShell is open we still have to select a season and a race. That is not good enough. We have selected a race so it should open with that race. When we built that view (Section 8.2.2) we had in mind that we would just open it without a specific model and then make the selection – the Action-Object model. As we have adopted the Object-Action model in this chapter, we are going to modify the way in which the view opens, depending on whether we open it on a race. If we open it on a race, then we want the season drop-down and the race drop-down to show the appropriate values and be disabled so that the user can't change it.

When we open the shell, we send it the message #showOn: aModel. As we open it from a selected race, this aModel argument is actually the selected race. But if we open the RaceShell from somewhere else, we don't know whether it is a race; we might want to open it on the root, and there is no reason why we shouldn't. Therefore, if we open it on a race, we have to check whether the argument is a race. We can do that by sending the message #isKindOf: to the argument. If the argument is a kind of race, then we set the season and the race and disable them. We do that when opening the view.

```
RaceShell>>onViewOpened
    "Check whether the model is a race. If that is the
    case, open that specific race"
    super onViewOpened.
    (self model isKindOf: Race) ifTrue: [
        currentRace := self model.
        (self presenterNamed: 'seasons')
            selection: currentRace season; view
                disable.
        (self presenterNamed: 'races')
            selection: currentRace; view disable.
        self showDate.
        self showStarters.
        ].
```

Now the view looks like Figure 9.17 when you open it.

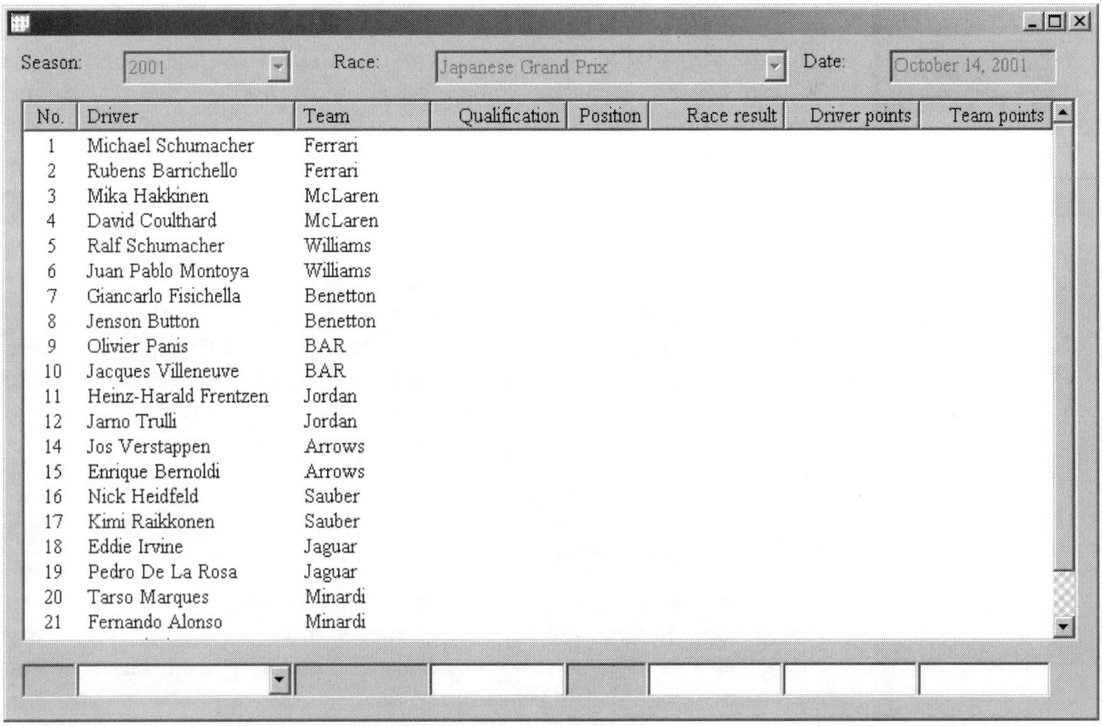

Figure 9.17 *Race shell with pre-selected season and race*

10 The results

In this chapter we are going to explore how we can display the results. The first step is to consider what to do with the points that we allocated to the drivers and the teams as a result of their performance in the races. After that, we are going to show those results in a convenient way, and at the end of this chapter we will build our own user-definable graph view.

10.1 The results for the season

Considerations regarding maintaining a balance.

The holy grail for Formula One is of course to become world champion of a season, both for the team and for the driver. That's the whole reason why we collect the points. But the way we've modeled the application, we can't see how many points each team or driver has gathered so far. Of course we can collect the information, as we store the points for every starter against the race. Here we come to an interesting design decision. Our intuition probably says that we want to store the total points of a driver and the total points of the team against the driver or team. However, the problem with every balance is that it can get out of balance. A balance is supposed to be the sum of the details, so they should be equal. This means that if the details change, then the balance has to change as well. This doesn't sound like a big problem, as we can just add the new detail to the balance. But what if an existing detail changes; say after a week the FIA decides that a button on the winner's car was illegal, and because of that the points are taken off the winner and the second to seventh drivers get the points. Then we can't just add the new points to the balance, we have to subtract the old points first. This can be done of course, but if we realize how many numbers we have to add up, then we can just as well build the balances dynamically whenever we need them, thereby avoiding the complexity.

10.1.1 Collecting the results

How to collect the results.

To build the balance per driver or per team dynamically, we have to ask every race in the season how many points are scored by every individual team or driver. If we rewrite this sentence a bit, then we see that we want to look at the races in a season, so the season is the starting point.

Within the season, we want to investigate all races, which means an operation on the races collection. For each race, we want to check the result of every driver or team, which is another operation, in this case on every starter of a race. The final question is, what do we want as the return object of this operation? We want a convenient combination of each driver or team and their total points, so that we can easily report on them. When we say a combination of two things, it sounds very much like an association, especially if one of the two is unique. A collection of associations is typically kept in a dictionary, therefore we will use that as our resulting object.

The following method does the job for drivers. For teams we do exactly the same.

```
Season>>allDriversAndPoints
    "Collect all drivers with the total of their points.
    Return them in a dictionary"
    | dict |
    dict := Dictionary new.
    races do: [ :race |
        race starters do: [ :each | | points |
            points := each driverPointsOrZero.
            dict at: each driver put: ((dict at: each
                driver ifAbsent: [0]) + points)
        ]].
    ^dict
```

We add a handy little method to Starter, which returns either the driver points or, if the driver didn't finish, zero. In this way we are still able to distinguish between having a result (albeit zero) and having no result at all, but this method saves us from having to check for nil whenever we want to do calculations on the points.

```
Starter>>driverPointsOrZero
    "Private - Answer the value of the receiver's
    'driverPoints' instance variable. If nil, answer zero"
    driverPoints isNil ifTrue: [ ^0 ].
    ^driverPoints
```

It goes without saying that we wrote the same method for team points.

10.1.2 *A presenter for the results*

The method of retrieving points that we used in the previous section fits nicely into our race application structure; when we have a season selected, we can show all the drivers and all the teams with their points, neatly

How to create a presenter that can be used within another presenter.

sorted. As we want to display this as part of the main race application shell, we are going to build a composite presenter that we can dynamically present within the application shell.

```
CompositePresenter subclass: #SeasonResultPresenter
    instanceVariableNames: 'driverTablePresenter
    teamTablePresenter'
    classVariableNames: ''
    poolDictionaries: ''
```

The two instance variables represent the two tables that we want to show, so they have to be connected to the model's methods that return those tables. As we want the tables sorted with the highest numbers first, we have to provide sort blocks. Before we can sort the dictionary, we have to convert it into a collection that understands the #asSortedCollection: method. The #associations method does that; it converts a directory into an OrderedCollection of associations.

```
SeasonResultPresenter>>model: aModel
    super model: aModel.
    driverTablePresenter model: (ListModel on: (self model
        allDriversAndPoints associations
            asSortedCollection:
                [ :d1 :d2 | d1 value >= d2 value ])).
    teamTablePresenter model: (ListModel on: (self model
        allTeamsAndPoints associations
            asSortedCollection:
                [ :t1 :t2 | t1 value >= t2 value ])).
```

We present them in lists, therefore we have to create the lists in the view.

```
SeasonResultPresenter>>createComponents
    super createComponents.
    driverTablePresenter := self add: ListPresenter new
        name: 'driverTable'.
    teamTablePresenter := self add: ListPresenter new
        name: 'teamTable'.
```

Based on this we can create the container view that will show the two lists. As we want a splitter between the two lists, we start by putting two containers and the splitter on the view. We give the top view a layout manager of ProportionalLayout. Each of the subcontainers can have a proportion of 1 and the splitter has a proportion of 0. Each subcontainer holds a multi-column list with two columns. As that is the only component

THE RESULTS

Driver	Points	Team	Points
Michael Schumacher	84	Ferrari	118
David Coulthard	47	McLaren	66
Rubens Barrichello	34	Williams	46
Ralf Schumacher	31	Sauber	19
Mika Hakkinen	19	Jordan	15
Juan Pablo Montoya	15	BAR	12
Nick Heidfeld	10	Jaguar	5
Kimi Raikkonen	9	Prost	3
Jarno Trulli	9	Arrows	1
Jacques Villeneuve	7	Benetton	1
Heinz-Harald Frentzen	6	Minardi	0
Olivier Panis	5		
Eddie Irvine	4		
Jean Alesi	3		
Pedro De La Rosa	1		
Jos Verstappen	1		
Giancarlo Fisichella	1		
Fernando Alonso	0		
Ricardo Zonta	0		
Jenson Button	0		
Gaston Mazzacane	0		
Tarso Marques	0		
Luciano Burti	0		
Enrique Bernoldi	0		

Figure 10.1
The ResultPresenter for both the drivers and the teams

held by the subcontainer, we can set the layout manager for those subcontainers to BorderLayout. Setting the #arrangement aspects of the lists to #center will neatly stretch the list across the whole container (Figure 10.1).

In this case the model for each list is a ListModel with Associations, therefore we can't just use the #getContentsBlock and #getTextBlock in the way we are used to doing it. The association doesn't know about teams, drivers, names, and points, it only knows #key and #value. Therefore we have to set the #getContentsBlock for the first column to [:each | each key] and for the second column to [:each | each value]. We want to show the name of the team and driver, therefore we set the #getTextBlock for the first columns to [:each | each name]. As the lists are already sorted by points, we set the "hasSortHeaders" aspect to false.

10.1.3 *Showing the results in the application shell*

When we select a node in the component tree, we normally show the list of instances for that node. However, when we select a season node, we can't

How to change subviews dynamically – the use of the Wizard card container.

do that as the season itself is an instance. As we don't want to waste that space and we can show something valuable, why not show the results tables that we created in the previous sections. To do this, we first have to find out whether we have a season selected. Therefore, instead of just saying #showItemsList when the selection in the tree changes, we have to say something like #showItemsOrResults. In that method we check whether the selected node needs to show items or the results tables. We can do that with the message #canHaveItems, as that returns true for those components where you want to show the items list, and false for those that can't. We can do the same for the results tables: send a message like #canHaveResults, which only returns true for a SeasonInstanceComponent.

```
RaceApplicationShell>>showItemsOrResults
    "Check which list should be shown and which should be
    hidden"
    | sel |
    sel := componentsPresenter selectionOrNil.
    sel isNil ifTrue: [ ^nil ].
    sel canHaveItems
        ifTrue: [ self showItemsList ]
        ifFalse: [ self hideItemsList ].
    sel canHaveResults
        ifTrue: [ self showResults ]
        ifFalse: [ self hideResults ].


RaceAppComponent>>canHaveResults
    "Returns false for all classes except the season's
    instance component"
    ^false


SeasonInstanceComponent>>canHaveResults
    "This class can show the result tables for the
    instance, therefore return true"
    ^true
```

Now we only have to find out how we can switch between showing the standard list and showing the results tables. Each view understands the messages #show and #hide, so we could do something with that. Depending on the selection, show the results presenter and hide the items list presenter or the other way round. If we put them both in a container, then we should be able to fill the container with the right presenter at the right time. We have to start by adding the variable to the RaceApplicationShell definition and adding the createComponent line.

```
Shell subclass: #RaceApplicationShell
    instanceVariableNames: 'componentsPresenter
    itemsPresenter resultsPresenter'
    classVariableNames: ''
    poolDictionaries: ''

RaceApplicationShell>>createComponents
    ...
    resultsPresenter := self add: SeasonResultPresenter
        new name: 'results'.
```

The next step is to add the SeasonResultPresenter.Default view resource to the container. When you do that, you will notice that you can't have two resources both having the #arrangement aspect set to #center, even though we would like to do that here, as we only make one visible at a time. This shows that the BorderLayout manager is not really suited for this kind of show/hide. We could of course change the arrangement dynamically to #center whenever we want to display one or the other, but there is a more appropriate way. The CardContainer is built to do this kind of show/hide work. Normally the CardContainer will show a tab bar where you can select which card to show, but in our case we want it to be modified based on the selected node. We can use the Wizard card container for that. The typical use for a Wizard card container is to build a "wizard" like we will do in Section 11.2.2, but we can also use it for the purpose we require here.

The modifications to our RaceApplication view are:

- Drop a CompositePresenter.Wizard card container onto the topmost ContainerView (the one that holds the splitter bar and the other two Container views).

- Drag the itemsList out of the current container view and drop it onto the Wizard card container. Delete the by-now-empty container.

- Drop a SeasonResultPresenter.Default view onto the Wizard card container and set the #name aspect to results.

- Set the #arrangement aspect of the Wizard card container to 2 (like we had in the previous container).

The Wizard card container has an automatic BorderLayout manager; it assumes that you will want the view to fill up the whole card, which is what we want in this case.

Now we have to add the #hideItemsList, #hideResults, and #showResults methods and modify the #showItemsList method to make it visible again after being hidden.

RaceApplicationShell>>showItemsList
```
"Show the itemslist for the currently selected
component"
itemsPresenter view show.
itemsPresenter model: componentsPresenter selection
    items
```

RaceApplicationShell>>showResults
```
"Show the results for the currently selected
component"
resultsPresenter view show.
resultsPresenter model: componentsPresenter selection
    instance
```

RaceApplicationShell>>hideItemsList
```
"Hide the itemslist as the selected component doesn't
have items"
itemsPresenter view hide.
```

RaceApplicationShell>>hideResults
```
"Hide the results presenter as the selected component
doesn't have results"
resultsPresenter view hide.
```

When selecting a season, the right-hand view now shows the results (Figure 10.2).

10.1.4 *Dynamic resizing of multi-column lists*

Exploring the ListView columns.

When we resize the main form, the containers within are neatly resized following the arrangement settings for the layout managers. However, the columns in the lists don't follow this layout scheme, which either makes the lists show empty columns, or makes part of the information disappear. The columns do have an #autoResize aspect, but that divides the available space equally between the number of columns available, which in our case is no good as the name column always needs more room than the points column. Time for some investigation.

We know that we can set the individual column width in the view composer, but as the view composer is built in Smalltalk, we should be able to do the same dynamically. Let's first investigate how those columns are constructed. We know that we present our lists though instances of ListPresenter, as we add instances of ListPresenters when we send #createComponents. If we have a look at the ListPresenter class, then we see in the comment that it displays ListModels through ListViews. So let's have a look at ListViews. Here we see some familiar messages, namely the aspects that we can see when we are in the view composer. We can see,

THE RESULTS

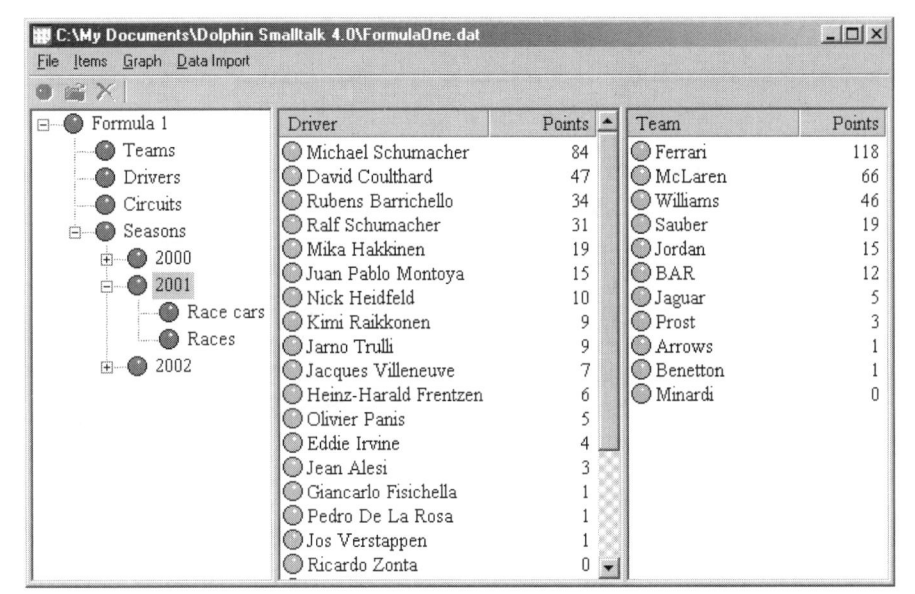

Figure 10.2
The ResultPresenter integrated in the application shell

for example, that when we add a column (method #addColumn), a ListViewColumn instance is created and added to the columns collection. So this means that there is a collection that holds the columns and the columns themselves are instances of the ListViewColumn class.

Further investigation shows us that the columns collection doesn't hold all the collections; the first column is held in a separate instance variable, primaryColumn. This is important to know, as the second visible column is actually the column at the first index of the columns collection. As this might be confusing for Smalltalkers who like simplicity, this construction is hidden for us if we use #columnsAtIndex:. With this method we can just pick up the first column with the number 1, and so on.

In our case we are dealing with two columns; we want the first column to be of a reasonable size, and have the remainder for the second column, making sure that when the list is of a reasonable width, we optimize the width for each column. The easiest way to do this is to set the first column to the preferred width and let the second width be managed by #autoResizeColumns. This will not only manage the remaining space, but also caters for the situation where a scroll bar is added to the list, which takes up space as well. We can take, for example, two-thirds of the total available space for the first column, and leave the rest for the autoResize. To use the really available space, taking into account a possible scroll bar, we can ask the view its #clientWidth. Our resizing method for the drivers list now looks as follows.

```
SeasonResultPresenter>>resizeDriverTable
    | availableWidth |
    availableWidth := driverTablePresenter view
        clientWidth.
    (driverTablePresenter view columnAtIndex: 1) width:
        (availableWidth * 2 / 3) truncated.
```

We can build the same for the team list. We want to call these whenever we do a resize action. These are captured in the #onPositionChanged: event, which is triggered by the #positionChanged: trigger in the presenter. So if we add the following #createSchematicWiring, we will see that the columns automatically adjust for size changes, even if you change the size of each individual column when using the splitter bar.

```
SeasonResultPresenter>>createSchematicWiring
    super createSchematicWiring.
    driverTablePresenter when: #positionChanged: send:
        #resizeDriverTable to: self.
    teamTablePresenter when: #positionChanged: send:
        #resizeTeamTable to: self.
```

By setting the "isAutoResize" aspect for the Points columns to true in the view composer, they will fill up the remainder of the space. If you set this aspect in the SeasonResultPresenter view you might be surprised when you open a race application view – it seems as if this aspect hasn't been updated. This is because the race application view contains an instance of the old definition of the SeasonResultPresenter view. Therefore you have to remove that instance by deleting that container in the race view and adding a new one that you name the same.

10.1.5 Summary

In the above subsections we have considered how to collect the total results for the teams and drivers and how to present them. We came to the conclusion that it is not always necessary to maintain a balance, especially when the volumes of data are low. For the presentation we looked into a way to make a presenter that can be "plugged into" another presenter. And finally we looked into the dynamic resizing of columns in a multi-column list.

10.2 A graph of the results

Wouldn't it be nice if we were able to show the cumulative results of the drivers in a line graph, so that we could see how the scores developed throughout the season? We've got all the information, so it's just a matter of extracting it in the right way and then presenting it in a graph.

But when we look through the list of available resources in the view composer, we don't see anything that can be used as the basis for our graph. Well, as the existing views are built in Smalltalk, we should also be able to add our own view, specific for graphs. However, before we can build that view we first have to decide what kind of information we want to send to the view and in which format.

10.2.1 *A short information requirement analysis*

We would like to have a graph showing a number of drivers or teams. We could give each driver or team a different color so that we can identify them. We want to use the x-axis as our time axis and the y-axis for the total points.

Modeling the graph information.

Based on this short information analysis we have the following elements:

- a collection of colors, representing the selected drivers or teams;
- each color holds a collection of associations between dates and points for the individual driver or team.

Because a collection doesn't care what kinds of objects it is holding, we can have a dictionary holding other dictionaries. The main dictionary holds the colors as keys and the other dictionaries as values. The other dictionaries hold the dates as keys and the points as values. For our graph we can just walk through the main dictionary, set the color based on the key, and draw the line based on the associations held within that color's dictionary.

We want to let the user choose his or her own color for each team or driver, therefore the main dictionary can only be built based on the settings on the screen. In the previous section we have already concluded that the easiest way to collect the race information is via the season. Therefore, we will create a method in the Season class that returns a dictionary of the results for the specified driver or team. The method for the team is slightly more complicated, as a team can have two starters scoring points for a single race.

```
Season>>allResultsForDriver: aDriver
    "Return the results for the specified driver as a dic-
    tionary with the date as key"
    | oc sc result |
    result := Dictionary new.
    oc := OrderedCollection new.
    races do: [ :race | race starters do:
        [ :starter | (starter driver == aDriver) ifTrue:
            [oc add: starter ]]].
```

```
    sc := oc asSortedCollection: [ :a :b |
        a race date <= b race date ].
    sc do: [ :each | result at: each race date
        put: each driverPointsOrZero ].
    ^result
```

Season>>allResultsForTeam: aTeam
"Return the results for the specified team as a dictionary with the date as key"
```
    | oc sc result |
    result := Dictionary new.
    oc := OrderedCollection new.
    races do: [ :race | race starters do:
        [ :starter | (starter team == aTeam) ifTrue: [
            oc add: starter ]]].
    sc := oc asSortedCollection: [ :a :b |
        a race date <= b race date ].
    sc do: [ :each | result at: each race date put:
        ((result at: each race date ifAbsent: [0]) +
            each teamPointsOrZero) ].
    ^result
```

10.2.2 *The LineGraph view*

Drawing lines on a view and creating your own view resource.

Now that we know what kind of data we will use for the graph, we can start thinking about how to build a graph view. We basically want something that draws lines on a view from a specified point to another point. If we take a look at one of the example applications that came with Dolphin, Scribble, then we see that Scribble is also drawing lines from one point to another, albeit that Scribble uses a different type of input. Nevertheless, a good starting point for our investigation.

Have a look how a ScribbleView manages to draw lines. When a ScribbleView is used, it is connected to a ListModel, which contains the points from where the lines are drawn. This is similar to the dictionary that we have, even though we have to make a translation from the scored points to the coordinates. We'll come back to that in a minute. The other two methods in ScribbleView, #onItem:addedAtIndex: and #onPaintRequired:, are two methods that actually draw something on the screen. The first one is used when an additional line needs to be drawn on an existing drawing, something that we don't really need, as we won't make our graph update dynamically. The second one, #onPaintRequired:, is the most interesting one, as this method is called every time the screen needs to be redrawn. Whenever you move a screen, resize a screen, or bring a screen into view, this method is responsible for showing the information.

This method creates a canvas within the current view. A canvas is a Windows-specific drawing board, on which you can draw lines and some basic shapes like rectangles and circles. Canvas is a subclass of Object, which links Smalltalk speak to operating system specific speak. Therefore, the way Canvas is implemented is specific for Dolphin, as this ties in with the Windows operating system. You can create a canvas on the whole hierarchy of views that you can see: the screen itself, the windows on the screen, or the views within these windows. With this knowledge, you can, for example, draw directly on the screen that you are working with:

```
(DesktopView current canvas) lineTo: 500@500
```

This will draw a line right across your screen, starting from the top left corner. That is not exactly what we want to do in our graph, but we can use this to draw our lines within our graph view.

When we draw the graph, we want every line to start from the same point, the origin of the graph. The origin is typically somewhere at the bottom left of the graph, especially as we don't have to deal with negative points. We don't want the origin right at the bottom, but something like 5 percent of the width of the view to the right, and 5 percent of the height up from the bottom. As this origin is used for all the lines that we are going to draw, we can just as well store it in an instance variable.

Let's start by creating the new class with the instance variables origin and canvas. We will need more instance variables, but we will add those as we go along.

```
View subclass: #LineGraphView
    instanceVariableNames: 'canvas origin'
    classVariableNames: ''
    poolDictionaries: ''
```

The origin variable is set with the following method. This method will be called whenever we want the view to be painted.

LineGraphView>>setOrigin
```
    origin := Point new.
    origin x: (self width/20) rounded.
    origin y: (self height - (self height/20) rounded).
```

A graph has to have axes, which we will draw up to 5 percent of the width and height of the view.

LineGraphView>>drawAxes
```
    | xEnd yEnd |
    xEnd := self width - ((self width/20) rounded).
    yEnd := (self height/20) rounded.
    canvas pen: (Pen withStyle: 0 width: 3 color: Color
        black).
    canvas moveTo: origin.
    canvas lineTo: xEnd @ (origin y).
    canvas moveTo: origin.
    canvas lineTo: (origin x) @ yEnd.
```

As we want the lines a bit thicker than the standard 1-pixel line that is automatically used by #lineTo:, we have to define explicitly the pen to be used on the canvas. In the Pen class you will find a number of ways to create a pen, but if you want to set the width then the #withStyle:width:color: is the most convenient method. The style can be set to a number of different variables. Here we can use either the Win32 constants or the associated variable numbers (Table 10.1).

For the color we use one of the predefined Color class methods. This is the simplest way to set a color; in the next section we will see how we can use the whole range of colors, including custom colors.

When we draw the graph itself, we want to make optimal use of the space; we don't want the graph to draw in only a small corner of the screen, neither do we want it to run off the screen. Therefore we have to figure out what the scale is for both the horizontal steps and the vertical steps.

In our case the horizontal steps are defined by the number of dates for which we have race results. We can find them by going through all the dictionaries and collecting the dates (the keys). We can't assume that it would be sufficient just to go through a single dictionary, as some drivers might not have raced every race. The Set is ideal for this kind of collection, as it disallows duplicates. This Set serves multiple purposes; first of all it defines the horizontal step for each line, by telling us how many steps there are, so that we can make every step a proportion of the width of the graph. The second purpose is to collect the data sequentially from the result dictionaries when we are drawing the graph. For this purpose we have to sort the set of dates. As we reuse the set in this way, we have to make an instance variable for it. We also want to save the horizontal step (the distance) in an instance variable.

```
View subclass: #LineGraphView
    instanceVariableNames: 'canvas origin xSteps xStep'
    classVariableNames: ''
    poolDictionaries: ''
```

Table 10.1
Pen styles

Number	Value	Meaning
0	PS_SOLID	The pen is solid
1	PS_DASH	The pen is dashed
2	PS_DOT	The pen is dotted
3	PS_DASHDOT	The pen has alternating dashes and dots
4	PS_DASHDOTDOT	The pen has dashes and double dots
5	PS_NULL	The pen is invisible

LineGraphView>>setXSteps

```
"Find the x-steps and set the x-step"
xSteps := Set new.
model do: [ :each |
     each keys do: [ :x | xSteps add: x ]
     ].
xSteps := xSteps asSortedCollection.
xStep := ((self width * 5/6) / (xSteps size)) rounded.
```

For the vertical steps we have to do something similar; we have to find the maximum value and based on that define the step value. The maximum value is the highest of the total points of each of the result dictionaries. So we first have to sum all the points in a dictionary and then compare it with the other sums. Based on the maximum value we can then define the yStep, which we store in an instance variable. As we have to walk through all the dictionaries again, we best combine this with the setXSteps method, so that we only have to go through the dictionaries once.

```
View subclass: #LineGraphView
     instanceVariableNames: 'canvas origin xSteps xStep
     yStep'
     classVariableNames: ''
     poolDictionaries: ''
```

LineGraphView>>setSteps

```
"Find the x-steps and set the x-step and y-step"
| maxY |
xSteps := Set new.
model do: [ :each | | temp |
     each keys do: [ :x | xSteps add : x ].
     temp := nil.
     each values do: [ :y |
          temp isNil ifTrue: [ temp := y ]
               ifFalse: [temp := temp + y ]].
     maxY isNil ifTrue: [ maxY := temp ].
     maxY := temp max: maxY.
     ].
xSteps := xSteps asSortedCollection.
xStep := ((self width * 5/6) / (xSteps size)) rounded.
yStep := ((self height * 5/6) / maxY) rounded.
```

Now that we have the steps, we can set markers on the axes for the steps. I chose to draw horizontal lines for every 10 y-steps (which is 10 points), but you are free to set different markers of course. I've added it to the #drawAxes method, which means of course that we have to draw the axes after we've calculated the steps.

LineGraphView>>drawAxes
```
...
    canvas pen: (Pen withStyle: 0 width: 1 color: Color
        black).
    0 to: (origin y - yEnd) by: (10 * yStep) do: [ :each |
        canvas moveTo: (origin x)@(origin y - each).
        canvas lineTo: xEnd@(origin y - each)].
```

The graph lines are drawn based on the result dictionaries, with the key of the main dictionary as the color. To prevent gaps in the graph, we are better off walking through the xSteps collection, and checking the result dictionary if there are points. If not, we draw a horizontal line to that xStep, otherwise we draw a line with the points times the yStep to the xStep position.

LineGraphView>>drawGraphFor: anAssoc
```
    | currentPoint |
    canvas moveTo: origin.
    currentPoint := origin copy.
    canvas pen: (Pen withStyle: 0 width: 3 color: anAssoc
        key).
    xSteps do: [ :step |
        currentPoint x: currentPoint x + xStep.
        currentPoint y: currentPoint y -
            ((anAssoc value at: step ifAbsent: [ 0 ])
                * yStep).
        canvas lineTo: currentPoint ].
```

The last step is to bring all these methods together in the #onPaintRequired: method.

LineGraphView>>onPaintRequired: aPaintEvent
```
    (model isNil or: [model size = 0]) ifTrue: [^self].
    canvas := aPaintEvent canvas.
    self setSteps.
    self setOrigin.
    self drawAxes.
    model associationsDo: [ :each | self drawGraphFor:
        each ].
```

We can't just use this view as it is; we first have to create a presenter that can present this view. The presenter itself doesn't do anything, it is only there so that other presenters can use it as a resource.

```
Presenter subclass: #GraphPresenter
    instanceVariableNames: ''
    classVariableNames: ''
    poolDictionaries: ''
```

The presenter doesn't know anything about the view yet, so we have to add the view to the presenter. At the same time we want to add it to the resource list, so that we can use it in other views. We can do that by executing the following line. For convenience I always put such a line in the class comment.

```
GraphPresenter addView: LineGraphView asResource: 'Default view'
```

To test it we have to build a directory with some colors and result directories.

```
line1 := Dictionary new.
line1 at: 1 put: 6; at: 2 put: 3; at: 3 put: 1; at: 4 put:
    10; at: 5 put: 6.
line2 := Dictionary new.
line2 at: 1 put: 10; at: 2 put: 6; at: 4 put: 4; at: 5 put:
    10.
line3 := Dictionary new.
line3 at: 1 put: 4; at: 2 put: 4; at: 3 put: 6; at: 5 put:
    4.
line4 := Dictionary new.
line4 at: 2 put: 10; at: 3 put: 10; at: 4 put: 6.

dict := Dictionary new.
dict at: Color blue put: line1.
dict at: Color red put: line2.
dict at: Color green put: line3.
dict at: Color yellow put: line4.
```

If everything is well, then evaluating the line:

```
GraphPresenter showOn: dict
```

should give you a picture like Figure 10.3.

As we didn't add any redraw functionality on resize actions, the graph won't automatically adjust when you resize it. However, when you drag another window over it, and then make the graph window visible again, it will automatically redraw itself according to the scale that is set at that point. We can add the automatic redraw functionality for resizing to the presenter with the following two methods.

GraphPresenter>>createSchematicWiring
```
    super createSchematicWiring.
    self when: #positionChanged: send: #updateView to:
        self.
```

GraphPresenter>>updateView
```
    self view invalidate
```

Figure 10.3

The Graph view

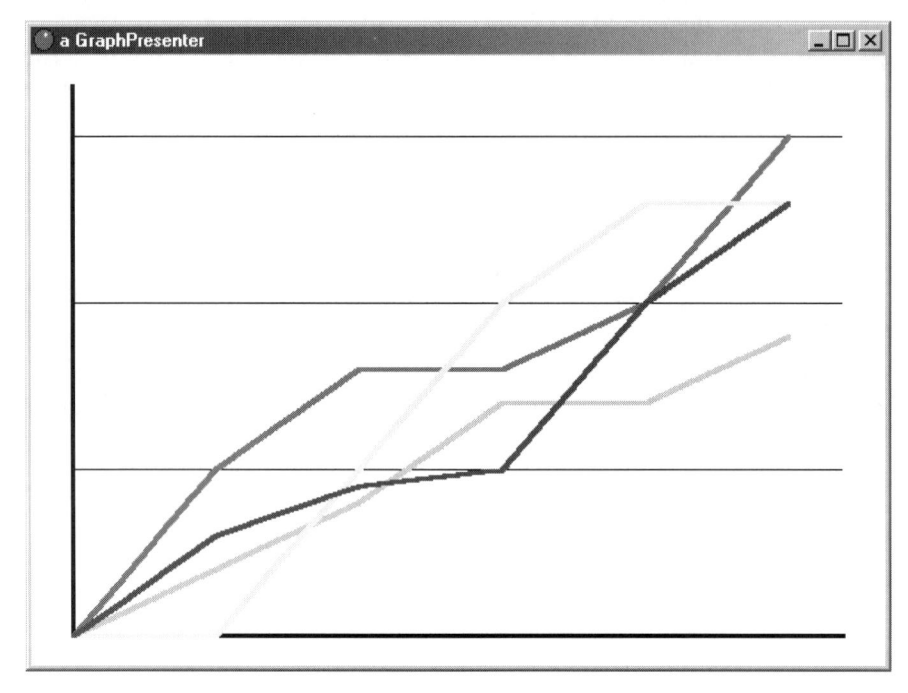

When you now reopen the presenter and resize the window, you will see that it dynamically redraws the graph. You can extend this Graph class to include labels and scales for the axes.

10.2.3 *A user-definable graph*

Using the graph view built in the previous section.

The next step is to create a presenter in which the user can choose colors and link them to drivers or teams, and based on that the graph can be displayed. Here we have to limit ourselves to a maximum number of drivers or teams to be displayed; at some point the graph will become too cluttered if you try to put too many lines on it. We'll set the maximum to 8.

We want it to look like Figure 10.4.

The Team/Driver switch sets a variable to either the symbol #team or the symbol #driver. Based on that, the drop-down list is filled with either the teams or the drivers. The user can select from the drop-down list and then set the color for that selection. The Color button brings up the standard Color dialog where the user can either select one of the predefined colors or create his or her own color. This color is then used as the background for the list of selected items. It is also used as the key in the result dictionary. By selecting the radio button in front of one of the names, the color for that item can be changed. Having the radio button in front of the drop-down selected list means that new items can be added instead of changing the color of an existing one.

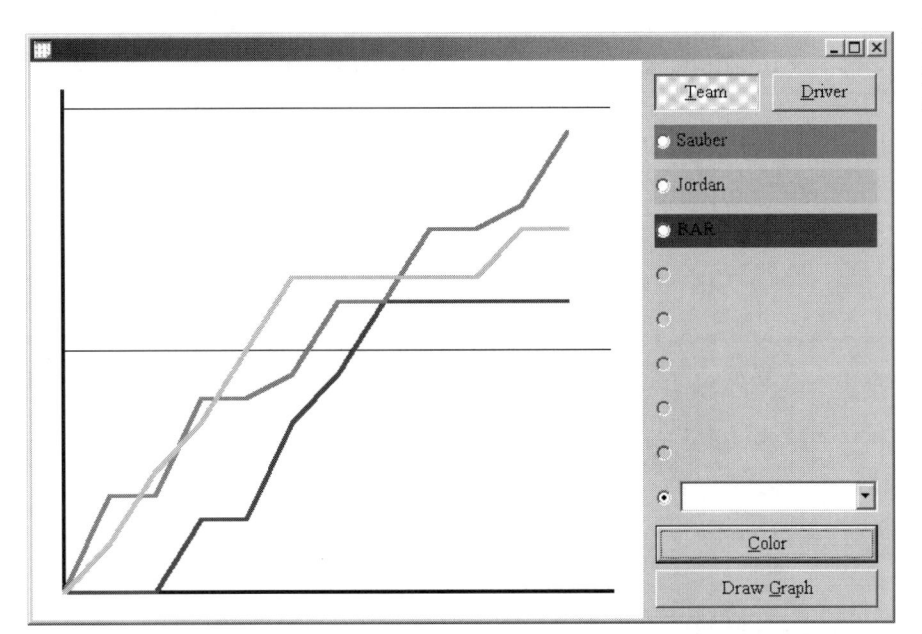

Figure 10.4
The finished user-definable graph

To save us from having to define many instance variables, we will refer to the presenters by name. As we have to check the state of the presenters with the selected lines a number of times, we will create a collection of the names of those presenters.

The dictionary on which we draw our graph is built while setting the parameters, therefore we will store that locally as well.

```
Shell subclass: #SeasonGraphShell
    instanceVariableNames: 'mode graphDict allLines
    season'
    classVariableNames: ''
    poolDictionaries: ''
```

SeasonGraphShell>>createComponents
```
    super createComponents.
    self add: BooleanPresenter new name: 'team'.
    self add: BooleanPresenter new name: 'driver'.
    allLines := #('first' 'second' 'third' 'fourth'
    'fifth' 'sixth' 'seventh' 'eighth').
    allLines do: [ :each | self add: BooleanPresenter new
            name: each ].
    self add: BooleanPresenter new name: 'listButton'.
    self add: ListPresenter new name: 'list'.
    self add: GraphPresenter new name: 'graph'.
```

The mode is set by the team and driver presenters. These have their own getter and setter in addition to the mode getter and setter.

SeasonGraphShell>>driverMode
```
^(mode == #driver)
```

SeasonGraphShell>>driverMode: aBoolean
```
aBoolean ifTrue: [self mode: #driver].
```

SeasonGraphShell>>teamMode
```
^(mode == #team)
```

SeasonGraphShell>>teamMode: aBoolean
```
aBoolean ifTrue: [self mode: #team]
```

SeasonGraphShell>>mode
```
^mode
```

SeasonGraphShell>>mode: aMode
```
mode := aMode.
self clearView.
(self presenterNamed: 'team') model: (self aspectValue: #teamMode).
(self presenterNamed: 'driver') model: (self aspectValue: #driverMode).
```

When setting the mode, we want to reset the whole view. This means that we reset all the radio buttons, set their backcolor to nil, their value to false, their text to an empty string, and disable them. We also reset the selection in the drop-down list and rebuild it for the other mode.

SeasonGraphShell>>clearView
```
graphDict := Dictionary new.
allLines do: [ :each |
    (self presenterNamed: each) view backcolor: nil.
    (self presenterNamed: each) view value: false.
    (self presenterNamed: each) view disable.
    (self presenterNamed: each) view text: '' ].
(self presenterNamed: 'list') resetSelection.
(self presenterNamed: 'listButton') view value: true.
self createList.
```

The list creation is similar to what we've done before, with the difference that we make it dependent on the mode.

SeasonGraphShell>>createList

```
    self mode == #team ifTrue: [
        (self presenterNamed: 'list') model: (ListModel
            on: self model allTeams)].
    self mode == #driver ifTrue: [
        (self presenterNamed: 'list') model: (ListModel
            on: self model allDrivers)].
```

The most complicated method in this class is the #setColor method. After a color is selected we check whether this color is already in use and if so we report the error to the user. The next step is to detect whether we are trying to add an item to the list or change the color of an existing one. When we add one to the list, we have to find the first free space. Once we've found the free space, we set the text and the backcolor and we enable it so that we can change the backcolor of that item. Then we ask the model for the result and add that to the result dictionary with the color as the key.

When we modify an element, we need to detect the old color, as that is the key in the dictionary. Once found, we have to change the key in the directory into the new color and change the backcolor of the element. If you look in the Directory class, you will see that the #changeKey: to: method is a private method. As it is good practice not to use private methods, we just add the new color with a copy of the dictionary and remove the old key.

SeasonGraphShell>>setColor

```
    | selectedLine oldColor newColor |
    newColor := ColorDialog showModal.
    newColor notNil ifTrue: [ (graphDict includesKey:
        newColor) ifTrue:
            [ ^self model error: 'This color is
            already in use']].
    ((self presenterNamed: 'listButton') view value)
    ifTrue: [    "We are adding an item"
        selectedLine := allLines
            detect: [ :each | (self presenterNamed:
                each) view backcolor isNil ]
            ifNone: [nil].
        selectedLine isNil ifTrue: [^self model error:
            'You can''t have more than 8 lines'].
        (self presenterNamed: 'list') selectionOrNil
    isNil
        ifTrue: [^nil]
        ifFalse: [ (self presenterNamed: selectedLine)
            view
```

```
                        backcolor: newColor.
                    (self presenterNamed: selectedLine) view
                            enable.
                    (self presenterNamed: selectedLine) view
                            text:
                        ((self presenterNamed: 'list')
                            selection name).
                    graphDict at: newColor put: self
                            retrieveResults.
                    (self presenterNamed: 'list')
                            resetSelection]]
        ifFalse: [   "we're changing one of the existing"
            selectedLine := allLines
                detect: [ :each | (self presenterNamed:
                    each) view value == true ]
                ifNone: [^nil].
            oldColor := (self presenterNamed: selectedLine)
                    view backcolor.
            graphDict at: newColor put: ((graphDict at:
                    oldColor) copy).
            graphDict removeKey: oldColor.
            (self presenterNamed: selectedLine) view back-
                    color: newColor.
            (self presenterNamed: selectedLine) view value:
                    false.
            (self presenterNamed: 'listButton') view value:
                    true].
        self drawGraph.
```

As this method is too complex for our liking, we are going to break it up into pieces.

We can replace the selection and checking of the color with a one-liner, called #selectColor.

SeasonGraphShell>>selectColor
```
        | color |
        color := ColorDialog showModal.
        color notNil ifTrue: [ (graphDict includesKey: color)
            ifTrue:
                [ ^self model error: 'This color is
                already in use']].
        ^color
```

The next step is to find a free line if we try to add a line.

```
SeasonGraphShell>>findFreeLine
    ^allLines detect: [ :each | (self presenterNamed:
        each) view backcolor isNil ]
            ifNone: [self model error: 'You can''t have more
                than 8 lines'].
```

Then we add the line to the view and add the key-value pair to the dictionary.

```
SeasonGraphShell>>addLine: aLine withColor: aColor
    (self presenterNamed: aLine) view backcolor: aColor.
    (self presenterNamed: aLine) view enable.
    (self presenterNamed: aLine) view text:
        ((self presenterNamed: 'list') selection name).
    graphDict at: aColor put: self retrieveResults.
```

If we modify the color of an existing line, we can capture that in the method #modifyColorFor: into:

```
SeasonGraphShell>>modifyColorFor: aLine into: aColor
    | oldColor |
    oldColor := (self presenterNamed: aLine) view
        backcolor.
    graphDict at: aColor put: ((graphDict at: oldColor)
        copy).
    graphDict removeKey: oldColor.
    (self presenterNamed: aLine) view backcolor: aColor.
    (self presenterNamed: aLine) view value: false.
    (self presenterNamed: 'listButton') view value: true.
```

The resulting #setColor now looks like this.

```
SeasonGraphShell>>setColor
    | selectedLine newColor |
    newColor := self selectColor.
    newColor isNil ifTrue: [ ^nil].
    ((self presenterNamed: 'listButton') view value)
    ifTrue: [    "We are adding an item"
        selectedLine := self findFreeLine.
        selectedLine isNil ifTrue: [^nil].
        (self presenterNamed: 'list') selectionOrNil
            isNil ifTrue: [^nil]
```

```
                    ifFalse: [
                        self addLine: selectedLine withColor:
                            newColor.
                        (self presenterNamed: 'list')
                            resetSelection]]
            ifFalse: [  "we're changing one of the existing"
                selectedLine := allLines
                    detect: [ :each | (self presenterNamed:
                        each) view value == true ]
                    ifNone: [^nil].
                self modifyColorFor: selectedLine into:
                    newColor].
    self drawGraph.
```

When we add a new element to the list, we call the method #retrieveResults. This method checks whether we are in team mode or in driver mode and then finds the results.

```
SeasonGraphShell>>retrieveResults
    | results |
    self mode == #team ifTrue: [
        results := self model instance
            allResultsForTeam:
                ((self presenterNamed: 'list')
                    selection)].
    self mode == #driver ifTrue: [
        results := self model instance
            allResultsForDriver:
                ((self presenterNamed: 'list')
                    selection)].
    ^results
```

Once we've set or changed the color, we (re-)draw the graph with the #drawGraph method. This method sets the model of the graph to the dictionary and invalidates the view. The View ≫ invalidate method tells the view to redraw itself based on the current data.

```
SeasonGraphShell>>drawGraph
    (graphDict size > 0)
        ifTrue: [(self presenterNamed: 'graph') model:
            graphDict]
        ifFalse: [(self presenterNamed: 'graph') model:
            nil].
    (self presenterNamed: 'graph') view invalidate.
```

The last thing we have to do is to set some initial variables. We want the list button to be the currently selected one and we want the mode to have an initial value. As we are using the outside interface method to set the mode, we automatically build the list for the drop-down. We had to use #onViewOpened here because we had to be sure that the presenter was already initialized. Had we used #model: to set the mode, it would have failed, as when #model: is called, you're not able to talk to the presenter instance, so you can't set an instance variable of the presenter yet.

```
SeasonGraphShell>>onViewOpened
     super onViewOpened.
     (self presenterNamed: 'listButton') view value: true.
     self teamMode: true.
```

As we've defined the redraw functionality when resizing in the graph presenter (see GraphPresenter ≫ createSchematicWiring), we don't have to worry about that, it's automatically working in this view as well.

For the view we start with setting the layout manager to a border layout, so that the graph can automatically fill the maximum space next to the labels and buttons. These labels and buttons are put together in a view container with the #arrangement aspect set to #east. To make the graph fill the remaining space the #arrangement aspect is set to #center. As we are making use of boolean presenters for both the mode and the list of selected elements, we need to make sure that they don't interfere. Therefore we put them in separate containers as well. The hierarchy of the view components is as shown in Table 10.2.

To be able to use it from within the application shell, we have to add this as a menu option. As we made it season dependent, we should only have it available when we have a current season.

```
RaceApplicationShell>>showGraph
     "Show the line graph window"
     SeasonGraphShell showOn: componentsPresenter selection

RaceApplicationShell>>queryCommand: aCommandQuery
     ...
     (aCommandQuery command == #showGraph) ifTrue: [
          aCommandQuery isEnabled: (self seasonSelected)].

RaceApplicationShell>>seasonSelected
     "Is a season selected?"
     ^componentsPresenter selectionOrNil isKindOf:
          SeasonInstanceComponent
```

To fill the list with either the drivers or the teams, we make use of the MyModel ≫ allTeams and MyModel ≫ allDrivers methods. We can only do that if the model knows to which component it belongs. As the Season instance is itself a component, the model has to return itself as a way to find the path up the tree.

```
SeasonInstanceComponent>>component
     ^self
```

Table 10.2

Hierarchy of the SeasonGraphShell components

Component	Aspects
GraphPresenter.Default view	name: graph
	arrangement: #center
CompositePresenter.Default view	arrangement: #east
CompositePresenter.Default view	
BooleanPresenter.Push to Toggle	name: team
	text: "&Team"
BooleanPresenter.Push to Toggle	name: driver
	text: "&Driver"
CompositePresenter.Default view	
BooleanPresenter.Radio button	name: first – eighth
	isEnabled: false
BooleanPresenter.Radio button	name: listButton
	isEnabled: true
	value: true
ListPresenter.Drop down list	name: list
	getTextBlock: [:each | each name]
PushButton.Push button	Command: #setColor
	text: "&Color"
PushButton.Push button	Command: #drawGraph
	text: "Draw &Graph"

10.2.4 Summary

In this section we have built our own view resource, making use of the Canvas class to draw line graphs, and we implemented that view resource in a user-definable graph, where the user can choose a color and link that color to a result set.

Saving and importing the race data   11

So far we have built an application that is able to work with all kinds of objects; you can create objects, modify them, delete them, add information to them and display the information in various ways. What is missing in the application is a way to save the data and to retrieve the data. In addition it would be nice to be able to import the data from an external source. As both concepts are very much related, we will cover them in a single chapter.

11.1 Saving object data

In Dolphin Smalltalk there are a number of ways in which you can externally store your objects.

Relational databases Object Arts have an ODBC (Open DataBase Connectivity) package available for Dolphin with which you can access relational databases that allow ODBC access. The ODBC package provides an interface to the database so that you can open the database and access the tables. You can even create the database and tables through ODBC. However, as ODBC consists of a number of layers, it tends to add quite some overhead to the database access and with some databases the ODBC drivers are very sensitive to versioning (especially Oracle).

Most databases allow interfacing through native calls. This is by far the most reliable and fastest way to access the database, but it requires you to build the interface yourself. In some cases the database provider has an ActiveX control with which the native calls can be accessed. With the ActiveX support in the commercial versions of Dolphin Smalltalk you can use this interface. With the latest versions of Microsoft SQLServer this even allows you to build and access multi-dimensional OLAP data cubes.

Object databases Object databases are a lot more convenient to interface with, as you don't need to convert the objects into relational tables. One of the object databases, Omnibase, has a very tight integration with Dolphin. The use of it feels very much like the rest of Dolphin.

Text files Within Dolphin you can convert your objects to text and then write them to files. To be able to read the text back and interpret it, the text needs to have some kind of structure, for example to distinguish the instance variables of the objects. In Section 11.2 we will learn what we mean by structured text and how we can read such structured text.

Binary files   Dolphin comes with a file interface that allows you to file out objects and read them in as objects. This interface is called STB, Smalltalk Binary filing. In the CHB you can find many classes with the STB prefix. The three most important classes are the STBFiler, STBInFiler, and STBOutFiler. The STBFiler is the superclass of STBInFiler and STBOutFiler. The STBOutFiler is used to file out binary data and the STBInFiler is used to read binary data back into the image. These classes are extensively used by Dolphin itself as well; whenever you save a workspace, it is saved using the STBFiler. When you save the Image or when you save packages in the Package Manager, you also use the STBFiler.

For our application we will enable the user to save and retrieve the data through the STBFiler, as that takes care of structuring the data in such a way that we can retrieve it again.

11.1.1 *Modifications to the presenter and the view*

The easiest way to use the STBFiler is to make the main presenter a subclass of the DocumentShell. The DocumentShell provides all the methods for creating new files in which the model can be saved. It also provides methods for opening existing model files and saving modified files.

As we made our RaceApplicationShell a subclass of the Shell class, we have to reclassify it to become a subclass of the DocumentShell. We know that this is just a matter of drag and drop; pick up the class and drop it on the DocumentShell class.

To add the File menu, we go into the menu composer within the view composer. We want it to be the first menu on the menu bar, but in the menu composer it appears impossible to insert the menu in front of the Items menu that we created before. Don't worry, we will do that after we've created the menu. Create a new menu called &File, and add the items shown in Table 11.1 with their commands.

Once you've finished in the menu composer, close it and select the top shell in the view composer. Have a look in the list of aspects; there you will find an aspect "menuBar with sub-aspect "items". When you select the aspect "items", you see the list of menus in the right-hand list (Figure 11.1). Select the File menu and move it right to the top with the arrows.

For the New command we have to create a method which creates a new model and connects that to our view. As we want to do the same when we open the view, we will start by adding a class method and then use that

Table 11.1
File menu properties

Item	Command
&New	#fileNew
&Open	#fileOpen
Separator	
&Save	#fileSave
Sa&ve as	#fileSaveAs
Separator	
E&xit	#exit

class method in our fileNew method. The class method #defaultModel is automatically called when you open a presenter without specifying the model. So far we have ignored that as we always specified the model, but for the framework the #defaultModel is quite appropriate.

`RaceApplicationShell class>>defaultModel`
```
^RaceApplication new
```

We can use this method in our #fileNew method, thereby refreshing the screen.

`RaceApplicationShell>>fileNew`
```
    self model: (self class defaultModel).
    self view invalidate.
```

There is one problem though. When you have items in the right-hand list, and you select the "new" option, that list is not refreshed. This is because we create that list when selecting an item in the tree. As soon as you select any item in the tree, the right-hand list gets refreshed and the old list is

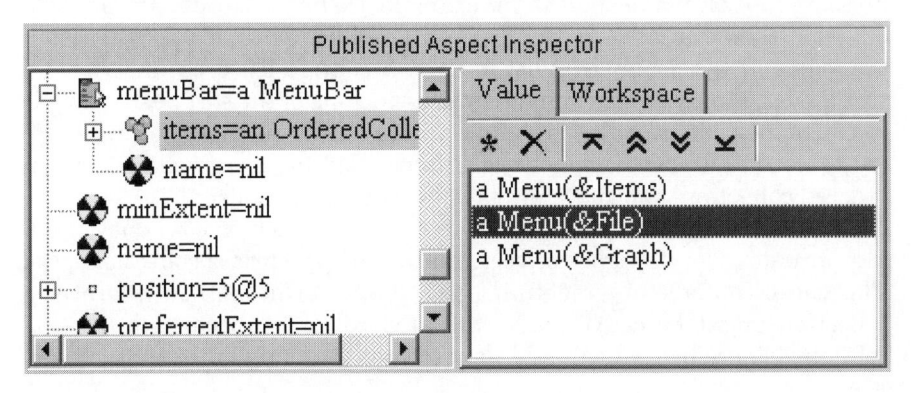

Figure 11.1

The menuBar Aspects

removed. The easiest way to enforce this is by just selecting the first item in the tree.

```
RaceApplicationShell>>fileNew
    self model: (self class defaultModel).
    self view invalidate.
    componentsPresenter selection: (componentsPresenter
        model roots first).
```

When we save the data we want to make sure that it is saved with a recognizable extension. We will give our files the extension .dat for data files. Here again we benefit from inheriting from the DocumentShell class; we only have to add the following two class methods and the #fileOpen, #fileSave, and #fileSaveAs methods automatically make use of it.

```
RaceApplicationShell class>>defaultFileExtension
    "Answer a default extension that will be used for
    files saved from the receiver"
    ^'dat'
```

```
RaceApplicationShell class>>fileTypes
    "Answer an Array of file types that can be associated
    with this class of document"
    ^Array
        with: #('Data Files (*.dat)' '*.dat')
        with: FileDialog allFilesType
```

11.1.2 Modifications to the models

How to override #stbSaveOn: in the model classes to avoid incompatibilities.

One thing to bear in mind with the STBFiler is that it files out the objects with their definition. This means that if a collection is sorted, it is filed out as a sorted collection. However, when filing in the model, the original definition is used. This can lead to conflicts if the original model had the collection defined as an ordered collection and you sort a multi-column list by pressing the column header. If, for example, we have an ordered collection of teams, then that list is normally shown in the order in which we created the teams. If we display that list in a multi-column list presenter, we can sort the list by any of the columns by pressing one of the sort headers. This converts the ordered collection into a sorted collection. However, when we try to read that list back in, the original definition says that it is an ordered collection, and therefore fails to read back the list.

The easiest way to avoid this conflict is to make sure that whenever you file out data, everything is converted into the appropriate collection type. This can be enforced by redefining the #stbSaveOn: method wherever a collection might be converted to a sorted collection because of sorting columns. Therefore we will add an #stbSaveOn: method to those model classes that contain collections. In our case that is only the case for the "items" instance variable in the RaceAppComponent class, as we present those items in the list in the main view and allow the user to sort them.

```
RaceAppComponent>>stbSaveOn: anSTBOutFiler
    "Restore list model to OrderedCollections"
    self items list: self items list asOrderedCollection.
    super stbSaveOn: anSTBOutFiler.
```

Here you again see the advantage of our application environment. As we approach all the different components in the same way in our application, we only have to modify this in a single class and all the underlying components follow.

11.1.3 *Save data on exit*

A typical application that saves to a file will ask you when you exit the application whether you want to save the changes that you have made. Within the DocumentShell this is already halfway implemented, therefore we will add some behavior to our RaceApplicationShell so that we will be asked whether we want to save the changes.

This behavior is implemented through the "isModified" accessors. Have a look at the #fileSave method in the DocumentShell class, for example. There you see that as part of the save function, this flag is set to false. In the #fileRevert method, you can see that #isModified is checked; if it is true, a dialog will pop up asking whether the changes should be saved. However, if we look in the class definition, we don't see an "isModified" variable; the getter always returns "false" and the setter doesn't do anything. This is done so that you can implement this behavior in different ways. For example, the SmalltalkWorkspaceDocument implements this functionality through the view; the view maintains the state of the text it is holding and knows when it is modified.

In our case we will keep it simple; when we open the view, we set the flag to false, and whenever we add, open, or delete an item then we set the flag to true. We will see that when we want to close the view or create a new model after having set the flag, it will automatically come up with the dialog. We start by adding the isModified flag to the instance variables and generating the accessors for it.

```
DocumentShell subclass: #RaceApplicationShell
    instanceVariableNames: 'componentsPresenter
    itemsPresenter resultsPresenter isModified'
    classVariableNames: ''
    poolDictionaries: ''
```

```
RaceApplicationShell>>isModified
    ^isModified
```

Figure 11.2

The Save Changes dialog

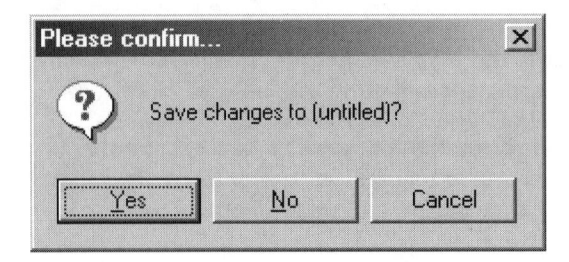

```
RaceApplicationShell>>isModified: aBoolean
    isModified := aBoolean
```

The next step is to set it to false when we open the view.

```
RaceApplicationShell>>onViewOpened
    super onViewOpened.
    self isModified: false
```

And then set the flag whenever we create a new item, open an item, or delete an item.

```
RaceApplicationShell>>addItem
    ...
    self isModified: true
```

```
RaceApplicationShell>>openItem
    ...
    self isModified: true
```

```
RaceApplicationShell>>deleteItem
    ...
            (MessageBox confirm: text) ifTrue: [
                componentsPresenter selection removeItem:
                    sel.
                self isModified: true. ]]
```

When you now open a new model, add for example a team and then try to close it, you will see the dialog shown in Figure 11.2.

For the #fileNew method we want to make use of this standard dialog as well, so we have to make the creation of the new document dependent on the outcome of this dialog. We can do that by using the Document Shell ≫ promptToSaveChanges: method where we store the result of the dialog in a value holder.

```
RaceApplicationShell>>fileNew
      (self promptToSaveChanges: (ValueHolder with: true))
ifTrue: [
            self model: (self class defaultModel).
```

```
self view invalidate.
componentsPresenter selection:
        (componentsPresenter model roots first)].
```

11.1.4 Summary

In this section we investigated external storage of our model data, and implemented the document storage system that comes with Dolphin Smalltalk. To be able to retrieve the data, we had to make sure that collections are written to the file in the same way as they are read from the file, therefore we converted the necessary collections into Ordered Collections before filing out. And finally we have seen how we can implement standard behavior that warns the user if changes have been made and not saved.

11.2 Importing comma-separated data

So far we have built impressive user interfaces in which we can set up a race season, maintain teams, drivers, and so on. However, when we start using this application, we don't want to have to enter all teams and drivers one by one, as the user interface isn't really built for bulk input. Therefore we have to find a better way to get all this base data in. In this section we will see how we can build mass-upload components to have the system do the work for us.

A regularly used format for exchanging data between systems is CSV, which stands for Comma Separated Values. The idea behind this is that each line is a "record" consisting of a specified number of fields, which are separated by the comma character. In some cases the tab character is chosen but the principles are the same. The big advantage of CSV files is that the user can enter the data in his or her favorite spreadsheet, save the data in a CSV file and upload it into the required application. The disadvantage of CSV files is that the sequence of the fields is fixed; you can't have one line with the name in the first field and the next line with the name in the second field. It also is not allowed to skip fields; if you want to skip a field, you still have to add a comma for the empty field. As this format is so strict, it is fairly easy to build an upload application for it.

For the teams this file could look like this, for example:

```
BAR,United Kingdom,1999
Ferrari,Italy,1929
Jordan,United Kingdom,1980
McLaren,United Kingdom,1963
Sauber,Switzerland,1993
Williams,United Kingdom,1969
```

In the next couple of subsections we will build a component that can import these kinds of files, both for the teams and for the drivers.

11.2.1 *A generic import class*

Working with streams, building a generic CSV import class and specific subclasses for the imported types and the use of Class Instance Variables.

When a file is opened from within Dolphin, the information can be read as a stream of characters. The Stream class and subclasses provide a rich protocol for walking through the stream and reading the individual characters.

Working with streams quite often feels very much like procedural programming, as you have to walk through the stream and react to the characters that you read from the stream. As it tends to be so procedural, we can use traditional design techniques to build a prototype. From there we can refactor it to more object-oriented code. We will build our prototype in a workspace before creating a class for it.

We will start with a routine that reads the stream and breaks it up into records. These records are broken up into fields based on the comma separator. The result is an ordered collection of records. Each of these records consists of an ordered collection of fields.

```
records := OrderedCollection new.
[ aStream atEnd ] whileFalse: [
    fields := OrderedCollection new.
    line := ReadStream on: aStream nextLine.
    field := WriteStream on: String new.
    [ line atEnd ] whileFalse: [
        (line peek = $,)
            ifFalse: [ field nextPut: line next]
            ifTrue: [ fields addLast: field contents.
                field := WriteStream on: String new.
                line next]].
    fields addLast: field contents.
    records addLast: fields].
```

This piece of code works for every CSV file; however, what do we do with these ordered collections of ordered collections? We want to create new objects from the records, with the fields mapped to the instance variables of the objects.

For teams we would build it like this.

```
records do: [ :each |
    team := Team new.
    team name: (each at: 1);
        origin: (each at: 2);
        foundationYear: (Number fromString: (each at: 3))].
```

As the fields in the records are all strings, we have to convert the field containing the foundation year into a number.

The problem with the above approach is that we can only use it for teams and the fields have to be in the specified sequence.

Let's take it one step at a time and first try to make the fields more flexible. From the above example you can see that it is not enough just to specify the field order, we also have to convert some data into objects of different classes. We can do that by associating each field with the data type. When we then put these associations in the right order for the CSV file, we can read any CSV file.

Assuming that we have the field definition stored in a collection called "fields", the above code would look like this.

```
fields := OrderedCollection new.
fields at: 1 put: (Association key: #name: value: String).
fields at: 2 put: (Association key: #origin: value: String).
fields at: 3 put: (Association key: #foundationYear: value: Number).

records do: [ :each |
    team := Team new.
    1 to: 3 do: [ :index |
        team perform: (fields at: index) key
            with: ((fields at: index) value
                fromString: (each at: index))]].
```

If the first field in the record contained the string "Ferrari", this would evaluate like:

```
team perform: #name: with: (String fromString: 'Ferrari').
```

The `String fromString: 'aString'` isn't really necessary, but it forms part of the generic solution and it doesn't do any harm.

With this approach we can just put the associations in the right order for the specific CSV file. We can even map to files that miss certain fields; say, for instance, the file doesn't contain the origin, we just map the name and the foundation year.

If we want to make this work for Drivers, then we do virtually the same. Our "fields" variable contains different associations of course, as the driver requires different fields. The other difference is that we create a Driver instance for each CSV record instead of a Team instance. So if we separate out those differences, we have a generic solution with two specializations, which we will implement as subclasses. In future you might want to use this same approach, which means that you just have to add your own subclass.

The parent class can be a subclass of Object, as we don't make it part of the MPV framework. This parent class handles all the generic code. The subclasses are responsible for the type-specific data.

The collection of fields puts us in an interesting situation. On one hand we want it to have the same name for all subclasses, as we want to talk to the collection with generic code. On the other hand, this is what specializes the subclasses; the contents of this collection are different for each subclass. On top of that, individual instances of the subclasses don't need to have their own copy of these associations; you only have to define it once for each subclass. Based on this last requirement, one would typically use a class variable; however, class variables are shared between a class and its subclasses, and cannot be overwritten.

The class instance variable was introduced for this kind of situation. This is a class variable that has its own contents for the superclass and all its subclasses. Just what we are looking for: all subclasses share the name but have a different context. Class instance variables start with a lowercase letter, and can be set by selecting the class tab for the class methods and then the class tab for the class definition.

```
Object subclass: #CSVImport
    instanceVariableNames: 'stream records mappings'
    classVariableNames: ''
    poolDictionaries: ''

CSVImport class instanceVariableNames: 'availableFields'
```

When we create a new CSVImport object, we want to create it on a stream, coming from a file, therefore we create a class method #on:.

```
CSVImport class>>on: aStream
    ^(self new initialize) stream: aStream
```

This requires the setter method for the stream variable (this is an instance method).

```
CSVImport>>stream: aStream
    stream := aStream
```

We need the mappings variable so that we can put the available fields in the right order for the CSV file that we are importing. The initialization method is required to make the mappings variable an ordered collection. With #addMapping: and #removeMapping: we access the mappings variable.

```
CSVImport>>initialize
    super initialize.
    mappings := OrderedCollection new.
```

CSVImport>>addMapping: assoc
```
    mappings addLast: assoc.
    ^mappings
```

CSVImport>>removeMapping: assoc
```
    mappings remove: assoc ifAbsent: [nil].
    ^mappings
```

For setting the mapping we want to be able to access the class instance variable from within the instance. We can do that by asking the instance for its class and then the class for the specified variable. To make it a bit easier, we create an instance method and a class method which does that for us.

CSVImport>>availableFields
```
    ^self class availableFields
```

CSVImport class>>availableFields
```
    ^availableFields
```

Now we can create the methods for which we built the prototypes earlier on.

CSVImport>>splitIntoRecords
```
    "This method reads a stream, creates a record for each
    line, and splits each line up into fields based on the
    ',' character. The records are stored in an ordered
    collection and each record is stored as an ordered
    collection of fields"
    | fields field line |
    records := OrderedCollection new.
    stream position: 0.
    [ stream atEnd ] whileFalse: [
        fields := OrderedCollection new.
        line := ReadStream on: stream nextLine.
        field := WriteStream on: String new.
        [ line atEnd ] whileFalse: [
            (line peek = $,)
                ifFalse: [ field nextPut: line
                    next]
                ifTrue: [ fields addLast: field
                    contents.
                    field := WriteStream on: String
                        new.
                    line next]].
        fields addLast: field contents.
        records addLast: fields].
```

CSVImport>>createResult
```
"Read the records, create a new object of class #mode,
and set the instance variables to the mapped fields in
the record. Return the collection of new objects"
| result |
result := OrderedCollection new.
records do: [ :each | | obj |
    obj := self mode new.
    1 to: mappings size do: [ :index |
        obj perform: (mappings at: index) key
            with: ((mappings at: index) value
                fromString:
                    (each at: index))].
        result addLast: obj ].
^result
```

In #createResult we rely on the #mode method to return the type of object that we want to create. We will specify that in our subclasses. To prevent users from trying to use the superclass, we add a method #mode in here as well, stating that this is a subclass responsibility.

CSVImport>>mode
```
^self subclassResponsibility
```

Now we can create the import classes for the driver and the team. These classes hardly contain any methods; they use everything from the parent except the #mode method and the contents of the availableFields class variable.

```
CSVImport subclass: #CSVImportTeam
    instanceVariableNames: ''
    classVariableNames: ''
    poolDictionaries: ''

CSVImport subclass: #CSVImportDriver
    instanceVariableNames: ''
    classVariableNames: ''
    poolDictionaries: ''
```

CSVImportTeam>>mode
```
^Team
```

CSVImportDriver>>mode
```
^Driver
```

We set the availableFields variable with a class initialize method. This method is automatically run if you file in the class or if you load a package.

Now that we add the class manually, we have to run the initialization method manually.

CSVImportTeam class>>initialize
```
    availableFields := OrderedCollection new.
    availableFields add: (Association key: #name: value:
        String).
    availableFields add: (Association key: #origin: value:
        String).
    availableFields add: (Association key:
        #foundationYear: value: Number).
```

CSVImportDriver class>>initialize
```
    availableFields := OrderedCollection new.
    availableFields add: (Association key: #firstname:
        value: String).
    availableFields add: (Association key: #surname:
        value: String).
    availableFields add: (Association key: #nationality:
        value: String).
    availableFields add: (Association key: #dateOfBirth:
        value: Date).
    availableFields add: (Association key: #gender: value:
        Symbol).
```

Now evaluate in a workspace:

```
CSVImportTeam initialize.
CSVImportDriver initialize.
```

To test what we've built, you can create a CSV file with a spreadsheet or in a text editor. Alternatively, you can pick up the CSV files for teams and drivers from the enclosed CD. Note that the Driver.CSV file has the date of births in US date format. If the date format on your PC is set up for European date format then you have to convert these dates to European format before loading them. You can do this by opening the CSV file in a spreadsheet and changing the date formatting.

The test code could look like this:

```
file := FileStream read: 'teams.csv'.
import := CSVImportTeam on: file.
file close.
```

```
import addMapping: (import instVars at: 1).
import addMapping: (import instVars at: 2).
import addMapping: (import instVars at: 3).
import splitIntoRecords
import createResult
```

If this all worked as expected, it is time to build a more user-friendly way to use this import function. Instead of making a single big user interface for this, we will build a wizard which consists of multiple screens.

11.2.2 *The data import wizard*

In this section we will build a wizard user interface.

A wizard is a set of screens that are presented to the user in a specified order. Each screen is a step in a process. This is ideal for our purpose, as we want the user to go through multiple steps as well for importing data. These steps are as follows:

- Do we want to import Drivers or Teams?
- Which file contains the data?
- How do we map the fields in the data to the instance variables?
- The last step is the actual importing.

The easiest way to think of a wizard is as a screen with tabs where you don't have free access to the tabs. Instead, if you are on tab 1, you can only get to tab 2. From tab 2 you can only go back to tab 1 or forward to tab 3, and so on. In case of a wizard this is typically controlled by buttons; previous (or back) and next.

In our case we can combine the first two; we will create a group of radio buttons where the user can select between a Driver import or a Team import and we will have a field where the user can enter the file name or find a file with the button next to it. Typically wizards show some textual explanation and for a change I've chosen to use some different fonts and colors (Figure 11.3).

Once the user is happy with it he or she can go to the next page where we will show a sample of the file split into records and fields. Below that sample we will show two lists, the first list containing all the instance variables of the Driver or Team. The second list can be filled by the user by selecting list entries from the first and copying them to the second. As the order is of vital importance, we will add buttons to move items in order. When the user is finished with that, an Import button will create the objects and add the items to the framework (Figure 11.4).

As the wizards are just like tabs on a normal form, we have to create our import wizard in a normal shell. The shell requires instance variables for the main presenters and one to store the current mode.

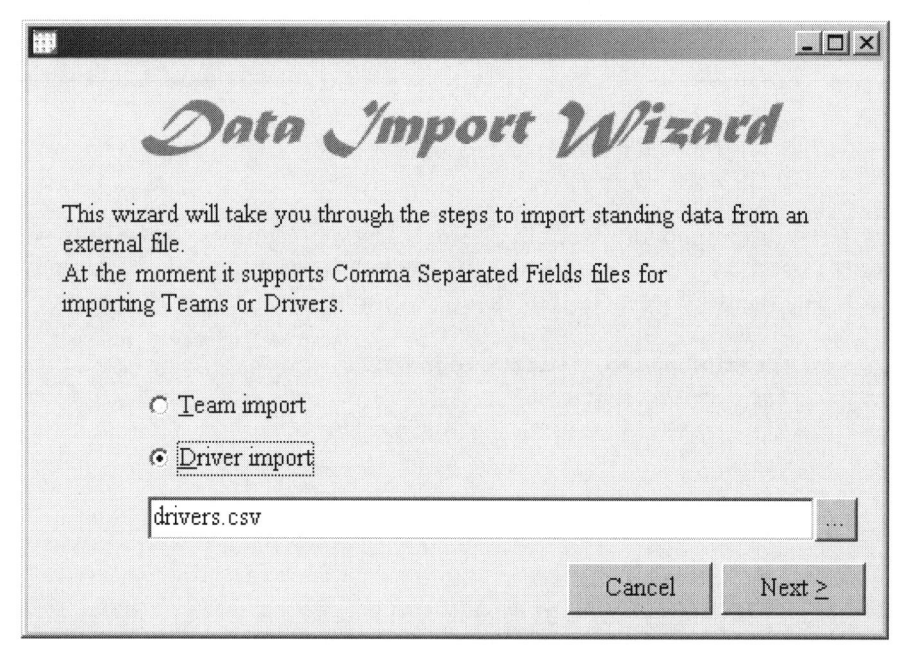

Figure 11.3
Data import wizard – page 1

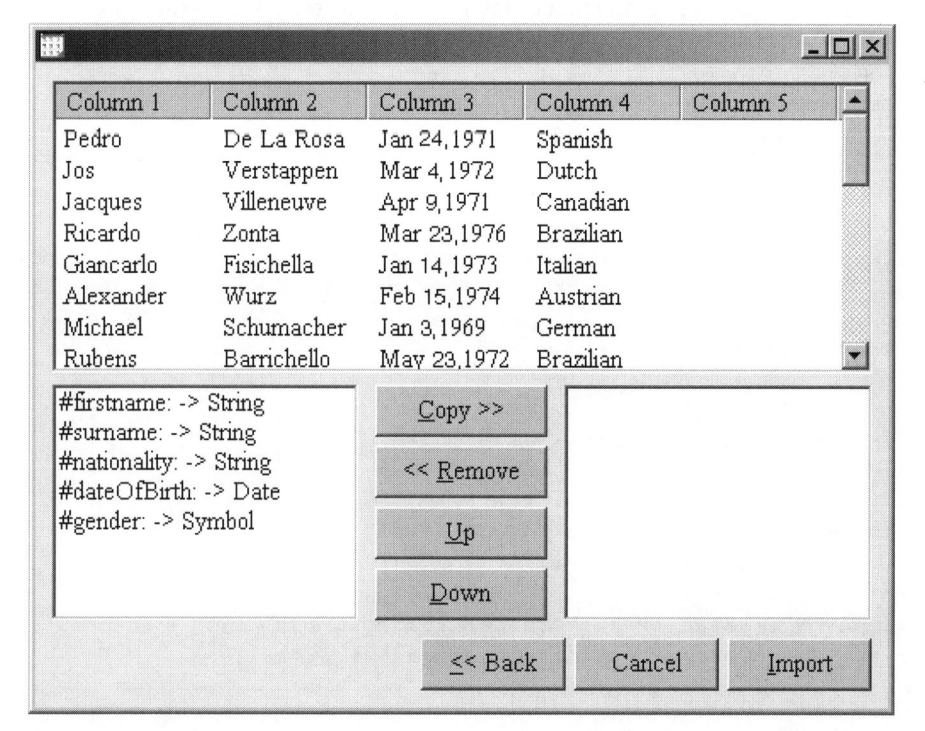

Figure 11.4
Data import wizard – page 2

```
Shell subclass: #ImportWizardShell
    instanceVariableNames: 'mode filePresenter
    modePresenter samplePresenter varsPresenter
    fieldsPresenter'
    classVariableNames: ''
    poolDictionaries: ''
```

In #createComponents we add the necessary presenters. Note that we didn't use instance variables for the boolean presenters, as we already store the result of those in the "mode" variable.

ImportWizardShell>>createComponents
```
    super createComponents.
    filePresenter := self add: TextPresenter new name:
        'filename'.
    self add: BooleanPresenter new name: 'driver'.
    self add: BooleanPresenter new name: 'team'.
    samplePresenter := self add: ListPresenter new name:
        'sample'.
    varsPresenter := self add: ListPresenter new name:
        'variables'.
    fieldsPresenter := self add: ListPresenter new name:
    'csvFields'.
```

The #onViewOpened method creates the connection between the boolean presenters and the "mode" variable.

ImportWizardShell>>onViewOpened
```
    super onViewOpened.
    self teamMode: true.
    (self presenterNamed: 'team') model:
        (self aspectValue: #teamMode).
    (self presenterNamed: 'driver') model:
        (self aspectValue: #driverMode).
```

ImportWizardShell>>mode
```
    ^mode
```

ImportWizardShell>>mode: aSymbol
```
    mode := aSymbol.
```

ImportWizardShell>>driverMode
```
    ^(mode == #driver)
```

ImportWizardShell>>driverMode: aBoolean
```
    aBoolean ifTrue: [self mode: #driver].
```

```
ImportWizardShell>>teamMode
    ^(mode == #team)

ImportWizardShell>>teamMode: aBoolean
    aBoolean ifTrue: [self mode: #team].
```

The user can either enter something in the file presenter or use the button next to the file presenter. When pressing the button we want to open a normal file finder, with the file type pre-set to files with the extension .csv. As this is a standard Windows dialog, this functionality works the same as with other Windows applications. The format for setting the extensions is a bit unusual. It expects an array of definitions. These definitions themselves are arrays as well; the first element is the description and the second element is the filter. When a file is set we want to set the information on the next page of the wizard: the sample list and the list of available fields for the type.

```
ImportWizardShell>>fileChooser
    "Open a standard file-open dialog filtered for CSV
    files. Set the file presenter to the result and
    trigger the change"
    filePresenter model: (FileOpenDialog new
        fileTypes: #(('CSV files (*.csv)' '*.csv')
            ('All Files' '*.*')); showModal).
    filePresenter trigger: #valueChanged

ImportWizardShell>>createSchematicWiring
    super createSchematicWiring.
    filePresenter when: #valueChanged send: #createRecords
        to: self.
```

In the #createRecords method we read the file and call the proper CSVImport subclass to split the file into records and fields. Now that we know which CSVImport subclass to use, we can set the model, which connects the three lists on the second page of the wizard to their model's instance variables. We set the model for the sample presenter after we've created the records, so that we don't have to refresh the list.

```
ImportWizardShell>>createRecords
    "Read the selected CSV file and create the records out
    of it based on the mode setting"
    | file mdl |
    filePresenter value isEmpty ifTrue: [^nil].
    file := FileStream read: (filePresenter value).
    mdl := (self modeClass) on: file.
    self model: mdl.
```

```
        file close.
        self model splitIntoRecords.
        samplePresenter model: (ListModel on: self model
            records).
```

ImportWizardShell>>modeClass
```
    "Return the right CSVImport class for the current mode
    setting"
    (mode == #team) ifTrue: [ ^CSVImportTeam ].
    (mode == #driver) ifTrue: [ ^CSVImportDriver ].
    ^nil
```

ImportWizardShell>>model: aModel
```
        super model: aModel.
        varsPresenter model: (ListModel on: aModel
            availableFields).
        fieldsPresenter model: (ListModel on: aModel mappings).
```

On the first page we have a Cancel button and a Next button. For the Cancel button we have to add a #cancel command, which just closes the view. The Next button on the first page and the Back button on the second page can make use of methods that are defined in the layout manager that we use here – the CardLayout. This layout manager manages the fact that we can only see a single page (card) at a time, and maintains the order of the pages. In the class you can also find methods to jump straight to the first card, the last card, or a specific card.

The buttons in between the two lists on the second page let us copy elements from the first list into the second list, remove items in the second list, and change the order in the second list. Note that when we add an element from the first list to the second list while an element in the second list is selected, we insert the element before the selected element. Otherwise we add the element at the end.

ImportWizardShell>>cancel
```
        self view close.
```

ImportWizardShell>>copyField
```
        | idx |
        idx := fieldsPresenter selectionByIndexIfNone:
            [ fieldsPresenter model size + 1 ].
        (varsPresenter selectionOrNil) isNil ifFalse:
            [ fieldsPresenter model
                add: (varsPresenter selection copy)
                beforeIndex: idx ].
```

ImportWizardShell>>removeField
```
        fieldsPresenter model remove: fieldsPresenter
            selectionOrNil ifAbsent: [nil]
```

ImportWizardShell>>fieldUp

```
"Move the selected field up in the order. Check
whether it is already on top"
| elm oldIdx |
elm := fieldsPresenter selectionOrNil.
elm isNil ifTrue: [^nil].
oldIdx := fieldsPresenter selectionByIndex.
(oldIdx = 1) ifTrue: [ ^nil ].
fieldsPresenter model removeAtIndex: oldIdx.
fieldsPresenter model add: elm afterIndex:
    (oldIdx 0 2).
fieldsPresenter selection: elm.
```

ImportWizardShell>>fieldDown

```
"Move the selected field down in the order. Check
whether it is already at the bottom"
| elm oldIdx |
elm := fieldsPresenter selectionOrNil.
elm isNil ifTrue: [^nil].
oldIdx := fieldsPresenter selectionByIndex.
(oldIdx = fieldsPresenter model size) ifTrue: [^nil].
fieldsPresenter model removeAtIndex: oldIdx.
fieldsPresenter model add: elm afterIndex: oldIdx.
fieldsPresenter selection: elm.
```

The final button on the second page is to create the appropriate objects from the CSV records and add them to the right component type. Not only do we want to create them in the right component type, we also want to create them within the right root. Remember, we might have a root for IndyCar and a root for Formula One. Both maintain teams and drivers. Therefore, we should only be able to get into the import wizard if we know the root. Once we know the root, we can just ask the root to find within its children the right one that can hold teams or drivers. We will do that in the same way as we find out which class to use for the CSV import, namely through the #mode. In this case the root very much plays the role of the model, so if we open the import wizard with the root as its model, we can ask for the model whenever we need the root.

The RaceApplicationShell method below is also the method in which we add a menu command on a new menu, Import Data. The command should only be available if a component is selected.

RaceApplicationShell>>openCSVImport

```
ImportWizardShell showFor: componentsPresenter
    selection root
```

RaceApplicationShell>>queryCommand: aCommandQuery

```
(aCommandQuery command == #openCSVImport) ifTrue: [
    aCommandQuery isEnabled: (componentsPresenter
        selectionOrNil notNil)].
```

```
Shell subclass: #ImportWizardShell
    instanceVariableNames: 'mode filePresenter
    modePresenter samplePresenter varsPresenter
    fieldsPresenter root'
    classVariableNames: ''
    poolDictionaries: ''
```

ImportWizardShell class>>showFor: aRoot
```
    ^(self show) root: aRoot
```

ImportWizardShell>>modeComponent
```
    "Return the right application component class for the
    current mode setting"
    (mode == #team) ifTrue: [ ^TeamComponent ].
    (mode == #driver) ifTrue: [ ^DriverComponent ].
    ^nil
```

ImportWizardShell>>startImport
```
    "Create objects from the CSV records and add them to
    the application component"
    | component imported |
    component := self root children detect: [ : each | each
        isKindOf: self modeComponent ] ifNone: [nil].
    imported := component importItems: (self model
        createResult).
    MessageBox notify: (imported printString, ' ', mode,'s
        successfully imported').
    self view close.
```

This method leaves the responsibility for adding the imported object where it belongs, namely in the application component class. However, we can't make use of the normal #addItem, as that would open the dialog. Therefore we have to add a method #importItems: to both the TeamComponent and the DriverComponent class. Those classes are also responsible for validating the data. (Note that the TeamComponent class requires the same method but then with "each isKindOf: Team".

DriverComponent>>importItems: aCollection
```
    "Import a collection of Drivers in one go. Return the
    number of valid imports"
    | count |
    count := 0.
    aCollection do: [ :each |
        ((each isKindOf: Driver) and: [each name isEmpty
            not])
        ifTrue: [
            self items add: each.
            count := count + 1 ]].
    ^count
```

With the presenter class with all the behavior in place, we can start building the view. The most important step we have to take is putting a Wizard card container in the shell. This container is linked to the card layout manager. When we drop normal containers on this Wizard container, they all use the full space of the container; they are laid on top of each other. To lay out the fields within each container, we have to select the required container in the view hierarchy. Table 11.2 shows the hierarchy.

Table 11.2
Hierarchy of the ImportWizard-Shell Components

Component	Aspects
Shell.Default view	LayoutManager: aBorderLayout
CompositePresenter.Wizard Card Container	Arrangement: #center
CompositePresenter.Default view	Arrangement: 1
BooleanPresenter.Radio Button	Name: "team" Text: "&Team import"
BooleanPresenter.Radio Button	Name: "driver" Text: "&Driver import"
TextPresenter.Default view	Name: "filename"
PushButton.Push button	Command: #fileChooser Text: " ... "
PushButton.Push button	Command: #cancel Text: "Cancel"
PushButton.Push button	Command: #nextCard Text: "Next >&>"
CompositePresenter.Default view	Arrangement: 2
ListPresenter.Enhanced list view	Name: "sample" HasSortHeaders: false
Column	Text: "Column 1" GetContentsBlock: [:each | each at: 1]
Column	Text: "Column 2" GetContentsBlock: [:each | (each size > 1) ifTrue: [each at: 2]]
Column	Text: "Column 3" GetContentsBlock: [:each | (each size > 2) ifTrue: [each at: 3]]
Column	Text: "Column 4" GetContentsBlock: [:each | (each size > 3) ifTrue: [each at: 4]]

(Continued)

Table 11.2 (Continued)

Component	Aspects
Column	Text: "Column 5" GetContentsBlock: [:each | (each size > 4) ifTrue: [each at: 5]]
ListPresenter.Default view	Name: "variables"
ListPresenter.Default view	Name: "csvFields"
PushButton.Push button	Command: #copyField Text: "&Copy"
PushButton.Push button	Command: #removeField Text: "&Remove"
PushButton.Push button	Command: #fieldUp Text: "&Up"
PushButton.Push button	Command: #fieldDown Text: "&Down"
PushButton.Push button	Command: #previousCard Text: "& >> Back"
PushButton.Push button	Command: #cancel Text: "Cancel"
PushButton.Push button	Command: #startImport Text: "&Import"

11.2.3 Summary

In the above subsections we have investigated importing Comma Separated Value files. We built a generic solution that can be subclassed for any kind of object. As a user interface we created a wizard.

11.3 Importing from the Web

Contacting a Web site, reading and interpreting data, mapping the data to existing objects, and updating those objects with the imported data.

The importing function that we built in the previous section is ideal for bulk upload functions. The same structure could be used for entering the race results as well, but would mean that we first have to find the data, enter it in a CSV file and then import it. That would make our race screen redundant and the user would still have to enter the details. Better would be if we could read the information from the Web and from there fill in the race data, which can then be presented to the user through the race screen.

Unfortunately, Web pages do not follow a structured scheme like CSV files. However, as Web pages do use structures for tables, we can quite easily find the information we need. Web pages are typically formatted with HTML, which stands for Hypertext Markup Language. This markup language uses tags (or elements) for markup information. We can use those tags to find the information we need and write it in the correct place in our application. Of course this is not a very reliable method as the owner of the Web page might change the format which would make our upload fail. But as it is a good demonstration of how we can read information from the Web, we will build an example here.

11.3.1 *The HTML import model*

First we have to find Web pages which contain the data that we require. With permission from Formula1.com Limited, we can use their Web pages to read data for personal use. The structure of their race page URL is "http://www.formula1.com/races/racenewsYY/GP-NAME/XXXX.html". We have to dynamically replace the YY with the last two digits of the season. The GP-NAME is a list of names that they use which have to be mapped to our races and XXXX can be either the word "qualify" or the word "raceresults".

Extracting data from HTML pages.

Once we are connected, we can read the page into a stream. The next step is to find the information that we want to write into our application. As this differs per Web site, we have to build this specifically for the Web site that we are using. For that Web site, we can find the results table on the page by finding the tags <td class = "results">. These tags format the data that is written in the table. Just before the first tag, there is a table row tag, <tr>, which indicates the start of that row. The end of the row is indicated by </tr>. These rows can be interpreted in the same way as the records in the CSV files. Within rows, fields are separated with the <td> tags. We have to read the data until we find the </table> which marks the end of the table. From there, it is just a matter of extracting the data for each record and interpreting it so that we can map it to our data structure.

As we are following a similar approach to what we've done in the CSV import, and also have to use similar instance variables, we can make a superclass for both import types.

```
Object subclass: #DataImport
    instanceVariableNames: 'stream records'
    classVariableNames: ''
    poolDictionaries: ''
```

We can move the class method #on: from the CSVImport class to this superclass. The same goes for the instance methods #records and #stream:.

We move the CSVImport class to be a subclass of DataImport and remove the instance variables that we've defined in the superclass.

```
DataImport subclass: #CSVImport
    instanceVariableNames: 'mappings'
    classVariableNames: ''
    poolDictionaries: ''
```

As we have to write data to the race, we benefit from storing the race in an instance variable. This variable requires the standard accessors.

```
DataImport subclass: #HTMLImport
    instanceVariableNames: 'race'
    classVariableNames: ''
    poolDictionaries: ''
```

The tables for the race result and the qualification result are very similar, in the sense that the first column shows the position, the second the starting number, then the driver, the team, the time, and the average speed. The first sample below is from a qualifying page, the second from a race page.

```
<tr>
<td class = "results"><font size = 2>1</td>
<td class = "results"><font size = 2>3.</td>
<td class = "results"><font size = 2>Schumacher M</td>
<td class = "results"><font size = 2>Ferrari</td>
<td class = "results"><font size = 2>1'37&quot;397</td>
<td class = "results"><font size = 2>204.881</td>
</tr>
>
<tr>
<td class = "results"><font size = 2>1.</td>
<td class = "results"><font size = 2>3.</td>
<td class = "results"><font size = 2>Schumacher M</td>
<td class = "results"><font size = 2>Ferrari</td>
<td class = "results"><font size = 2>1h31'35&quot;271</td>
<td class = "results"><font size = 2>200.403</td>
</tr>
```

Based on this we can build a method that finds the records, like we did for the CSV files, and then split the records into fields, but first we have to build a method that can extract the table from the page. We use string searching as opposed to stream searching like we did with the CSV files, as Dolphin has a very fast searching primitive for strings. (In most other Smalltalks you will find that stream searching is faster than string searching, though.) For single character comparison, walking through a stream character by character is the easiest, but when you want to find a whole string, like a word or in our case a tag, the string comparison method is faster and easier.

SAVING AND IMPORTING THE RACE DATA

HTMLImport>>findDataSubstring
```
"This will search for the first data tag and from
there to the end of the table"
| str start end |
str := stream contents.
start := str indexOfSubCollection: self dataStartTag
    startingAt: 1.
end := str indexOfSubCollection: self dataEndTag
        startingAt: start.
^str midString: (end - start) from: start
```

The result of this can be split into records and fields.

HTMLImport>>findLinesIn: aString
```
"Split the string into an ordered collection of lines"
| lines start end |
lines := OrderedCollection new.
start := 1.
end := aString indexOfSubCollection: self recordEndTag
    startingAt: start.
[(end = 0) or: [start = 0]] whileFalse: [
    lines add: (aString midString: (end - start)
            from: start).
    start := aString indexOfSubCollection: self
            recordStartTag startingAt: end.
    end := aString indexOfSubCollection: self
            recordEndTag startingAt: (start+1).
    ].
^lines
```

HTMLImport>>findFieldsIn: aString
```
"Split the line into an ordered collection of fields"
| fields start end |
fields := OrderedCollection new.
start := 1.
end := aString indexOfSubCollection: self fieldEndTag
    startingAt: start.
[(end = 0) or: [start = 0]] whileFalse: [
    fields add: (aString midString: (end - start)
            from: start).
    start := aString indexOfSubCollection: self
            fieldStartTag startingAt: end.
    end := aString indexOfSubCollection: self
            fieldEndTag startingAt: (start+1).
    ].
^fields
```

In these methods we use start tag and end tag methods, which return the required tag.

HTMLImport>>dataStartTag
```
^'<td class = "results">'
```

HTMLImport>>dataEndTag
```
^'</table>'
```

HTMLImport>>recordStartTag
```
^'<tr>'
```

HTMLImport>>recordEndTag
```
^'</tr>'
```

HTMLImport>>fieldStartTag
```
^'<td class = "results">'
```

HTMLImport>>fieldEndTag
```
^'</td>'
```

We bring the #findLinesIn: method and #findFieldsIn: methods together in the following method, which writes the resulting ordered collection of ordered collections in the instance variable "records".

HTMLImport>>findRecordsIn: aString
```
"Extract records from a string and write the result in
the 'records' variable"
| lines linesWithFields |
records := OrderedCollection new.
lines := self findLinesIn: aString.
linesWithFields := lines collect: [ :line | | fields |
    fields := self findFieldsIn: line.
    fields collect: [ :field | self stripTags: field
        ] ].
records addAll: linesWithFields.
```

The #stripTags: method is required to remove any remaining tags from the field. This is a result of the way we extracted the fields from the lines, by just copying everything between the field start tag and the field end tag. Beware that this is not a very generic solution, as it does not cater for the situation where the characters "<" and ">" are used in the field value, nor does it cater for the situation where the field value is captured within a tag. But for our purpose it works.

HTMLImport>>stripTags: aString
```
"Strip everything in between (and including) $< and $>"
| input result |
input := ReadStream on: aString.
```

SAVING AND IMPORTING THE RACE DATA

```
result := WriteStream on: String new.
[ input atEnd ] whileFalse: [
    (input peek = $<) ifTrue: [
        [input peekFor: $>] whileFalse: [input
            next] ]
        ifFalse: [ result nextPut: input next].
    ].
^result contents
```

When we read the records, we need to map them to the starters in our race, so that we can set the result from the record onto the right starter.

HTMLImport>>mapStarterWith: aString

```
"Find the starter in the race for this record"
^race starters detect: [ :starter | starter raceCar
    startingNumber = (Integer fromString: aString) ]
    ifNone: [nil]
```

As we had to allow the driver to be changeable, we might have a different driver in the record from the one we have in the starter. In those situations we have to change the driver in the starter.

HTMLImport>>mapDriver: aString for: aStarter

```
"Check if the driver in the starter is the same as the
string. Otherwise change the starter's driver"
| name drivers driver |
(aStarter driver surname asLowercase = aString
    asLowercase)
        ifTrue: [ ^nil ].
"Schumacher test"
name := aStarter driver surname, ' ', (aStarter driver
    firstname at: 1) displayString.
(name asLowercase = aString asLowercase) ifTrue:
    [^nil].
"Really a different driver"
drivers := | self race component root allDrivers.
driver := drivers detect: [ :each | each surname
    asLowercase = aString asLowercase ] ifNone:
        [nil].
driver isNil ifFalse: [ ^aStarter driver: driver ].
driver := drivers detect: [ :each | name := each
    surname, ' ',
    (each firstname at: 1) displayString.
    (name asLowercase = aString asLowercase)]
ifNone: [nil].
driver isNil ifFalse: [ ^aStarter driver: driver ].
"Last resort"
^aStarter driver: '*** Unknown *** ', aString.
```

Now that we have the starter, we can set the qualification result and the race result based on the record. For the race result we record the finishing number and set the points. For the qualification result we have to convert the information from the HTML page into a Time instance. The easiest way is first to extract the numbers and then separate the minutes and milliseconds. When we extract the numbers, we make them into big numbers. As we know that the last five digits are the milliseconds and seconds, anything in front of them is the minutes. As the qualification is only on for an hour, we can safely assume that a qualification time will always be less than an hour. We can extract the minutes from the big number by using the #// message. This message divides by the argument and truncates the result. For the milliseconds we want to do the opposite, as we want just the remainder of the division. We can find that with the message #\\.

```
HTMLImport>>setRaceResult: aString for: aStarter
    | str result points |
    str := ReadStream on: aString.
    result := WriteStream on: String new.
    [str atEnd] whileFalse: [
        (str peek isDigit) ifTrue: [result nextPut: str
                next]
            ifFalse: [str next]
        ].
    result := Integer fromString: result contents.
    (result = 0) ifTrue: [^nil].
    points := race season pointsFor: result.
    aStarter raceResult: result; driverPoints: points;
        teamPoints: points.

HTMLImport>>setQualificationResult: aString for: aStarter
    | str result minutes milliseconds |
    str := ReadStream on: aString.
    result := ReadWriteStream on: String new.
    [str atEnd] whileFalse: [
        (str peek isDigit) ifTrue: [result nextPut: str
                next]
            ifFalse: [str next]
        ].
    result := Integer fromString: result contents.
    (result = 0) ifTrue: [^nil].
    minutes := result // 100000.
    milliseconds := (result \\ 100000) + (minutes * 60 *
        1000).
    ^aStarter qualificationResult: (Time fromMilliseconds:
        milliseconds).
```

We bring all these methods together into two methods, one for the qualification results and one for the race results. Once we've read the qualification result, we set the starting position.

HTMLImport>>readRaceDataFor: aRace
```
    "This method reads the data from the stream variable,
    converts it into records and sets the results of the
    race"
    | starter |
    race := aRace.
    self findRecordsIn: self findDataSubstring.
    records do: [ :record |
        starter := self mapStarterWith: (record at: 2).
        self mapDriver: (record at: 3) for: starter.
        self setRaceResult: (record at: 1) for: starter.
        ].
```

HTMLImport>>readQualificationDataFor: aRace
```
    "This method reads the data from the stream variable,
    converts it into records and sets the results of the
    race"
    | starter |
    race := aRace.
    self findRecordsIn: self findDataSubstring.
    records do: [ :record |
        starter := self mapStarterWith: (record at: 2).
        self mapDriver: (record at: 3) for: starter.
        self setQualificationResult: (record at: 5) for:
            starter.
        ].
    self race setStartingPosition.
```

11.3.2 *The Web data import wizard*

Now that we are able to convert the data and read it into our model, we have to build a screen from which the user can select a race and start reading the data. We will build a similar "wizard"-like form for it, even though it only has a single page. We will give the page a status bar showing the status of the data import. We will make the view look like Figure 11.5.

Testing an online connection and reading data from the Web. Using a status bar to show progression.

The Import Wizard presenter class is a subclass of the Shell class.

```
Shell subclass: #HTMLImportShell
    instanceVariableNames: 'seasonsPresenter
    racesPresenter importType root url'
    classVariableNames: ''
    poolDictionaries: ''
```

Figure 11.5
Results import wizard

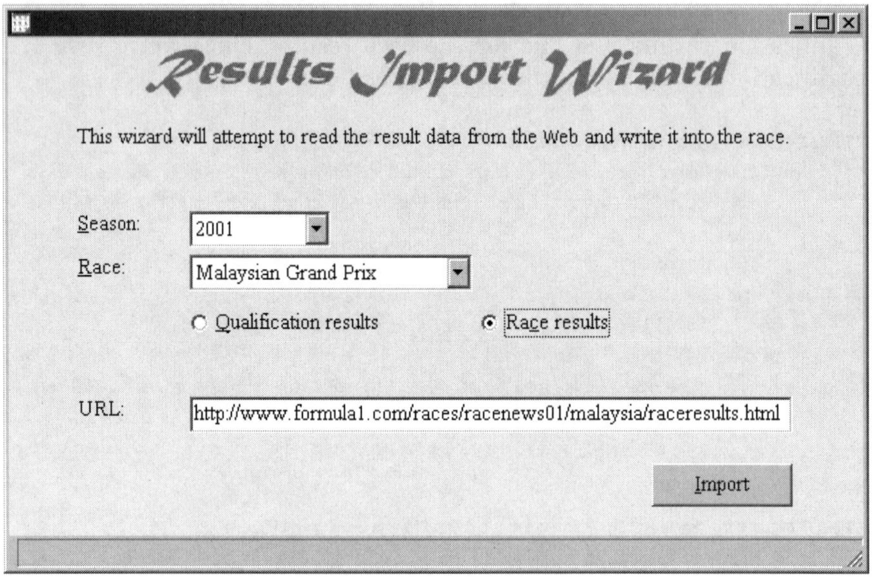

For the radio buttons we use the same technique that we saw in the previous chapter to choose between importing team data and driver data. We store the selection in the importType variable. For the root variable we can't use the same approach that we used in the CSV import, as we need the root to find the right seasons and races. Therefore, we have to have it available when we build the list of seasons, which is before opening the view. Therefore we make the root the model of the view, which makes the root available to the view right from the start. This also means that we have to open the view from within the RaceApplication with the #showOn: message, with the root as the argument. To call this message we add a menu option to our import menu.

```
RaceApplicationShell>>openHTMLImport
    HTMLImportShell showOn: componentsPresenter selection
        root

HTMLImportShell>>model: aRoot
    super model: aRoot.
    self root: aRoot.
    seasonsPresenter model: (ListModel on: self
        allSeasons).

HTMLImportShell>>createComponents
    super createComponents.
    seasonsPresenter := self add: ListPresenter new name:
        'seasons'.
```

```
    racesPresenter := self add: ListPresenter new name:
        'races'.
    self add: BooleanPresenter new name: 'qualification'.
    self add: BooleanPresenter new name: 'race'.
    self add: TextPresenter new name: 'url'.
    self add: TextPresenter new name: 'status'.

HTMLImportShell>>onViewOpened
    super onViewOpened.
    self qualifyMode: true.
    (self presenterNamed: 'qualification') model: (self
    aspectValue: #qualifyMode).
    (self presenterNamed: 'race') model: (self
        aspectValue: #raceMode).

HTMLImportShell>>allSeasons
    ^self root allSeasons asSortedCollection: [ :a :b |
        a name <= b name ]

HTMLImportShell>>qualifyMode
    ^(importType == #qualify)

HTMLImportShell>>qualifyMode: aBoolean
    aBoolean ifTrue: [self importType: #qualify].

HTMLImportShell>>raceMode
    ^(importType == #raceresults)

HTMLImportShell>>raceMode: aBoolean
    aBoolean ifTrue: [self importType: #raceresults].

HTMLImportShell>>importType
    ^importType

HTMLImportShell>>importType: aSymbol
    importType := aSymbol.
```

We can only select a race when we have a season, therefore we only enable the race drop-down when we have a season selected.

```
HTMLImportShell>>createSchematicWiring
    super createSchematicWiring.
    (self presenterNamed: 'seasons') when:
        #selectionChanged send: #buildRacesList
            to: self.

HTMLImportShell>>buildRacesList
    racesPresenter view enable.
    racesPresenter model: (ListModel on: self allRaces).
```

As soon as we have a selected race, we should have all the data to build the URL. However, the URL requires us to specify the race name as the Web site owners use it. Quite likely this differs from the name that we use. We can solve that by adding an importName. As that name is typically related to the circuit, we will add an instance variable to the circuit with its accessors.

```
MyModel subclass: #Circuit
    instanceVariableNames: 'location length lapRecord
    lapRecordDriver comment importName'
    classVariableNames: ''
    poolDictionaries: ''
```

The CircuitDialogPresenter and its view have to be modified so that it looks like Figure 11.6.

Now we can ask the circuit for the import name so that we can include it in the URL. But as we only know the race, we have to add a method to the Race class that picks up the importName from the circuit.

Figure 11.6
Circuit dialog with import name

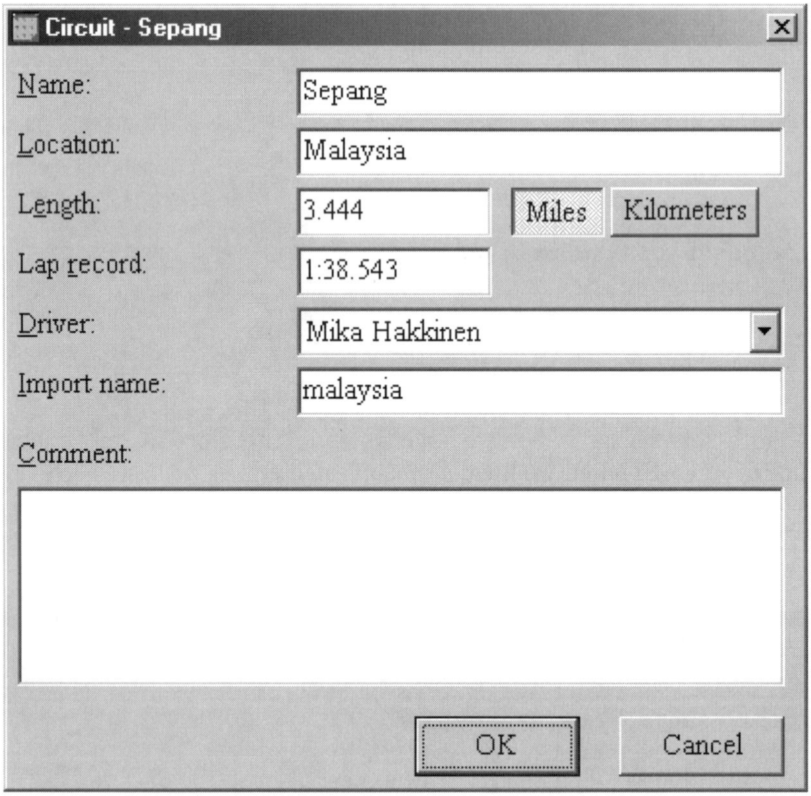

SAVING AND IMPORTING THE RACE DATA

```
Race>>importName
    ^self circuit importName

HTMLImportShell>>createSchematicWiring
    ...
    (self presenterNamed: 'races') when: #selectionChanged
        send: #buildURL to: self.

HTMLImportShell>>buildURL
    | string |
    string := 'http://www.formula1.com/races/racenews'.
    string := string, (seasonsPresenter selection name
        midString: 2 from: 3).
    string := string, '/', racesPresenter selection
        importName, '/', importType,'.html'.
    url := string.
    (self presenterNamed: 'url') value: url.
```

Now that we have the URL, we can try to connect and start the import. During the import we change the status through the several stages.

We use the IStream class here, which is a special COM interface class that can be used to read streams from the Internet. To check whether we have a connection, we make use of a standard windows DLL, wininet.dll. The class WinInetLibrary forms a wrapper around this class. When Dolphin is started, exactly one instance of this class is created. This instance can be accessed by sending the class the message #default.

```
HTMLImportShell>>startImport
    | stream import |
    self status: 'Attempting to connect'.
    (self connect) ifTrue: [
        stream := FileStream on: (IStream onURL: url)
            text: true.
        import := HTMLImport on: stream.
        self qualifyMode ifTrue: [
            self status: 'Reading qualification data'.
            import readQualificationDataFor:
                (racesPresenter selection)
                frameworkType: frameworkType.
            self status: 'Finished reading
                qualification data'].
        self raceMode ifTrue: [
            self status: 'Reading race data'.
```

```
                    import readRaceDataFor: (racesPresenter
                        selection) frameworkType:
                        frameworkType.
                    self status: 'Finished reading race
                        data'].
            ].
```

HTMLImportShell>>connect
```
    "Attempt to contact the URL"
    | isOnline |
    self status: 'Contacting ', url.
    "Prompt to go online"
    (isOnline := WinInetLibrary default ping: url)
        ifFalse: [
        self status: 'Could not connect to ', url.
        MessageBox notify: 'The Import Results Wizard
            requires a connection to the Internet.
            Either a connection is not available or
            the site could not be contacted.
            Please verify that your computer is online
            and press the Import button to try
            again.'.
        ^false ].
    ^isOnline
```

HTMLImportShell>>status: aString
```
    (self presenterNamed: 'status') value: aString.
    "(self presenterNamed: 'status') view update is
    private, therefore we use the local implementor which
    is not private."
    (self presenterNamed: 'status') view width: (self
        presenterNamed: 'status') view width
```

We need the last line to refresh the contents of the status bar. The status bar is quite different from the "normal" views in that it is redrawn by Windows, and Windows normally only does that when it has nothing else to do. Therefore we have to force that manually. The StatusOwnerDraw >> update does the job, but as it is a private method, we have to find a local implementor of that method.

After finishing the import, the user might want to make another selection. In those cases the status should be reset to an empty string.

HTMLImportShell>>resetStatus
```
    self status: ' '
```

HTMLImportShell>>importType: aSymbol
```
    ...
    self resetStatus.
```

Table 11.3

Hierarchy of the HTMLImportShell Components

Component	Aspects
Shell.Default view	LayoutManager: aBorderLayout
CompositePresenter.Default view	Arrangement: #center
ListPresenter.Drop down list	Name: "seasons"
ListPresenter.Drop down list	Name: "races" isEnabled: false
BooleanPresenter.Radio Button	Name: "qualification" Text: "&Qualification results"
BooleanPresenter.Radio Button	Name: "race" Text: "&Race results"
TextPresenter.Default view	Name: "R"
PushButton.Push button	Command: #startImport Text: "&Import"
Status.Status bar	arrangement: #south
Items add a StatusItem	Name: "status" GetImageBlock: nil

```
HTMLImportShell>>buildURL
    ...
    self resetStatus.
```

Apart from the status bar, the view doesn't have anything special on it. For the status bar we have to take a similar approach to what we did with the toolbars. We set the layout manager of the main shell to a border layout. The status bar can be put directly on the shell, together with a container. The container holds all the other presenters.

The status bar can contain multiple status fields. They are defined in a similar way to columns in a multi-column list.

Table 11.3 shows the complete hierarchy of the view.

11.3.3 *Summary*

In the above subsections we've extended our data import class to read HTML data from the Web. We learned how to test a connection and how to use the status bar at the bottom of the window.

11.4 XML data

In the previous two sections we have seen two ways of importing data from different data sources. Even though these work nicely in our application, in practice you are likely to come across data that is structured as XML data. XML data bears similarities to both of the above types of data, in the sense that it uses tags in a similar way to HTML pages, but the data is structured similar to CSV files, albeit more flexible. In XML each field has a tag identifying the field name and "records" can be built by nesting the fields. The qualification table from the above example could, for example, be structured as follows:

```
<Qualifications>
     <Qualification>
          <Place>1</Place>
          <StartingNumber>3.</StartingNumber>
          <Driver>Schumacher M.</Driver>
          <Team>Ferrari</Team>
          <Time>1'37"397</Time>
          <Speed>204.881</Speed>
     </Qualification>
     <Qualification>
          <Place>2</Place>
          <StartingNumber>1.</StartingNumber>
          <Driver>Hakkinen</Driver>
          <Team>McLaren</Team>
          <Time>1'37"860</Time>
          <Speed>203.912</Speed>
     </Qualification>
</Qualifications>
```

You can see that this structure is quite similar to the structure that we saw in the HTML pages. We can read through this structure by checking where a record begins and where a record ends. For the record itself we can check where the individual fields begin and end. As the fields all have named tags, we can store the values for each record in a dictionary, with the tag name as the key and the value as the dictionary value. In that way we can easily access the data and process it in our own objects. On top of XML being structured like this, XML makes use of definition documents (typically having an extension xsd), in which all the tags are described. This description can include the type definition, allowed values, documentation text, and so on. Based on such a definition document you can create your mapping even before you've read any XML document. The definition documents are also very usable when you are not at the receiving end, but at the sending end. In that case you have to create an XML document which you can check against the definition document.

In the previous two sections we created our own interface classes for the data that we wanted to read. As XML is becoming such an important standard, the current commercial version of Dolphin has a complete set of tools around the XML Document Object Model standard. This standard provides an application programming interface for XML documents (and HTML documents). This set of tools allows you to build interfaces to read and to write XML documents.

We won't go into detail about how to use these XML classes as that requires the commercial version of Dolphin Smalltalk.

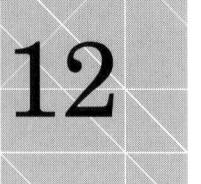

12 Application deployment

Now that we've finished the application, we typically want to make it available to other people. In most languages you would take all the files that you've been working on and compile them all together to make them into a single executable or an executable with a number of DLLs (Dynamic Link Libraries). In Smalltalk the deployment of an application is different, as all the code that you've been writing is already compiled and available in the image, together with the classes that came with the development environment and that you might have loaded from third parties. Therefore, if you want the application to be run, you just start your image. However, as your image also contains the development tools, you would not only breach your license if you just handed the whole image to your users, you would also give the user the ability to modify the application. This doesn't sound right for a good deployment strategy.

For Dolphin Smalltalk there are two ways to deploy applications, which are described in the sections below.

12.1 Making an executable

For making executables Object Arts has an additional tool available (which is not included in the version on the CD), called the Application Deployment Kit. This consists of a wizard that takes you through the necessary steps to create the executable. These steps are:

1 Strip the redundant classes. This step checks whether a class could possibly be used by the application. If not, the class is removed. The purpose of this step is to reduce the size of the executable. In this step the development tools are also removed.

2 Strip redundant methods. Of the remaining classes, every method is checked to see whether it could possibly be used by the application. As methods are sometimes used in an indirect way (for example with #perform:), this step can be a bit too optimistic and remove too much. To avoid this you can move those methods manually to a method category "must not strip".

3 Convert the image to an executable file. In this step the Dolphin.Exe file is merged with the image so that you end up with a single file from which the application can be started.

The executable file that results from the Application Deployment Kit cannot be run on its own, but requires the virtual machine (DolphinVMxxx.dll). On top of that, if you used the standard Dolphin icons like we have done in our application, you have to include the Dolphin resource library, DolphinDRxxx.dll. There are two more DLLs that are required in some specific cases; the DolphinCRxxx.dll is required when the application does runtime compilation of Smalltalk and the DolphinSureCrypto.dll is required if you make use of the cryptographic functions of a data validation system called DolphinSure (see also the next section).

The ADK comes with a license that grants you the right to deploy these DLLs with your applications to third parties as long as you strip the development tools from your applications before deployment.

12.2 Web deployment

In addition to the deployment as an executable, you can also create "applets" with Dolphin Smalltalk. Applets are typically small snippets of code that can run on their own. Applet deployment has become very popular through the Web, where the static HTML pages can be extended with rich functionality. In most cases these applets are written in Java as most Internet browsers come with the Java virtual machine that is required to run these applets. The Dolphin applets cannot run on a Java virtual machine, therefore when you deploy your application over the Web, your users have to get a Dolphin plug-in. This plug-in runs as the virtual machine for your applets. It also contains a compressed image with all the base classes except the development classes. Because of this and because the applet only downloads those classes that are needed when running it, your applets run as if the client has the full Dolphin environment.

Applets can be run in two ways: they can either be embedded within an HTML page or they can be hosted by the Internet browser. In the first case you define a rectangle within the HTML page in which the view will show itself, and in the second a child window of the browser will be opened for the view. The second option allows almost all the rich functionality, including resizing a form and menus which are not available in the first option. When you close the Web browser or move to a different page, the application window is automatically closed as the host is not available anymore.

Because of the richness that can be achieved by this method of applet deployment, you have to have a way to ensure that nobody can "break into" the application through the (public) Web and therefore gain access to the client PC. Dolphin has implemented a security system for this that can let the downloaded applet check itself against the source. To make use of this security system you have to obtain a "DolphinSure certificate". This certificate becomes part of the deployed application and is shown to the user when the applet is started. If you don't have a certificate, you can still deploy the application over the Web, but the user will be warned that the applet is not secured by a certificate.

The Web Deployment Kit is available as an additional tool (it is not included in the Dolphin version on the enclosed CD).

12.3 Summary

In this chapter we have discussed what is involved in deploying an application built in Dolphin Smalltalk. We have learned that there are two ways of deploying applications, you can either make "traditional" executables that can be run on PCs or you can create binary packages (applets) that can be embedded in an HTML page or hosted by an Internet browser.

Appendix A
Other Smalltalk resources

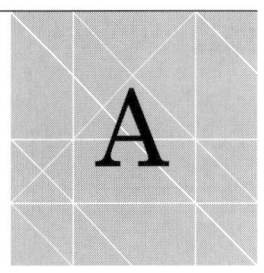

Smalltalk books

Goldberg, Adele and Robson, David (1989), *Smalltalk 80: The Language*. ISBM 0201136880, Addison-Wesley.

Lewis, Simon (1995). *The Art and Science of Smalltalk*. ISBN 0133713458, Prentice Hall.

Liu, Chamond (1996). *Smalltalk, Objects and Design*. ISBN 1884777279, Manning Publications Co, USA. Also published by Prentice Hall, ISBN 0132683350.

Sharp, Alec (1997). *Smalltalk by Example*. ISBN 0079130364, McGraw-Hill.

Beck, Kent (1997). *Smalltalk Best Practice Patterns*. ISBN 013476904X, Prentice Hall.

Other Books

Beck, Kent (2000). *Extreme Programming Explained*, 4th edn. ISBN 0201616416, Addison-Wesley.

Smalltalk on the Web

Dolphin Smalltalk specific

http://www.object-arts.com/Home.htm

Object Arts, the supplier of Dolphin Smalltalk.

http://www.object-arts.com/wiki/html/Dolphin/FrontPage.htm

Dolphin Wiki – containing loads of editable pages with additional information on Dolphin Smalltalk subjects.

News://comp.lang.smalltalk.dolphin

This is a Dolphin-specific public newsgroup with a friendly tone. In this newsgroup both beginners and experts can ask questions and help each other.

http://www.iandb.org.uk/

Ian Bartholomew is a long-time user of Dolphin Smalltalk. His Web site is full of useful information, extra tools, tutorials, and the newsgroup archive.

http://needle.anest.ufl.edu/anest4/bills/Smalltalk.htm

Bill Schwab – just like Ian Bartholomew, a long-time user of Dolphin Smalltalk. He has built a number of useful additions (goodies), one of which is DSDN, a tool to search through the Dolphin documentation, the newsgroup archives and the Wiki.

http://www.geocities.com/SiliconValley/Software/8887/index.html

This Web site, owned by David Gorisek, contains two tools specific to Dolphin Smalltalk: a multi-developer environment and an object database.

http://www.odellsoft.com/sunitbrowser/

A SUnit browser specific to Dolphin Smalltalk.

http://users.erols.com/dmacq/

A refactoring browser specific to Dolphin Smalltalk.

http://www.sirius.com/~lsumberg/PersonalMoney/Part1.htm

An extension to the Money tutorial from Object Arts.

General Smalltalk Web sites

http://st-www.cs.uiuc.edu/

The main Smalltalk Archives, a collection of pages about the history of Smalltalk, current versions, developments in the Smalltalk community, source code, and much more.

http://ansi-st-tests.sourceforge.net/SUnit.html

Smalltalk Unit Test Web site. Here you can find the basic Sunit test goodies for many different versions of Smalltalk. It also contains links to white papers on unit testing.

http://www.esug.org/

European Smalltalk User Group home page.

http://www.stic.org/

International Smalltalk Industry Council.

Appendix B
Overview of the main classes

This appendix gives an overview of the main classes in the base Dolphin system.

Object – The superclass of everything. All minimal behavior of an object of any subclass is defined in here.

Object subclass **AttributeDescriptor** (and subclasses) – These classes form the basis of the wrapping system used in MPV. See also ValueModel.

Object subclass: **Behavior** (and subclasses **ClassDescription**, **Class**, and **MetaClass**) – As classes themselves are also objects in Smalltalk, these classes are the classes of the individual classes. In these classes the individual classes are defined.

Object subclass: **BlockClosure** – Here the behavior of Blocks is defined.

Object subclass **Boolean** and subclasses **False** and **True** – Boolean itself isn't very interesting; the interesting classes are False and True. These both have only one instance; two of the very few reserved words in Smalltalk, false and true. In these classes you see the implementations of the messages #ifTrue:, ifFalse:, #and:, and #or:.

Object subclass: **Collection** and subclasses – Probably the most used classes, these are explained in more detail in Chapter 5.

ArrayedCollection subclass: **String** – Possibly to your surprise, the String class can be found in the Collection hierarchy. This means that many of the Collection methods can also be sent to a String. In addition, it has some typical String messages, like #midString:from:, #asLowercase, and #trimBlanks. You can use Windows formatting with the #formatWith: message. Comparison of Strings is case sensitive, so if you want to do case-insensitive comparison, you first have to either #uppercase them or #lowercase them.

String subclass: **Symbol** – Symbols are Strings that are unique within the system. This makes them very useful for keys in dictionaries. They are also used as message selectors.

SequencableCollection subclass: **Interval** – This collection isn't a real collection in the sense that it doesn't hold its elements, but it follows most of the main protocols for a collection. An interval has a starting number, an end number, and a step number. Intervals can be created on Integers by sending #to: to an integer. The standard step is 1. Intervals can also be created on other numbers, but then you need to define it as an explicit interval, like `Interval from: 0.01 to: 0.05 by: 0.01`.

Object subclass: **Color** – This class forms the interface to the Color system in Windows. You can use the full color capabilities of Windows through these classes, select the standard colors from the Windows system settings or define your own colors. You can set a color conveniently with the standard Windows ChooseColor dialog, implemented through the ColorDialog, `ColorDialog showModal`.

Object subclasses: **Command*** – We've used these classes frequently thoughout this book; whenever we wanted a command to be performed on a window, the definition of that command was an instance of the Command class. The CommandQuery class is used to enable/disable menu options and buttons on the windows through instances of the CommandPolicy class. The CommandDescription class is a support class of the Command class to hold additional information of a Command.

Object subclass: **ComparisonPolicy** – This class is used to define how objects can be compared.

Object subclass: **CompiledCode** – This class and subclasses give access to the compiled code in the image and externally.

Object subclass: **Compiler** – This class compiles the code when you evaluate an expression or accept a method.

Object subclasses: **DeadObject** and **DeafObject** – These classes are used to mark objects that can be garbage collected.

Object subclass: **DeferredValue** – This class can be used to send a long-lasting process to the background. It will fork the process at a low priority.

Object subclass: **Delay** – This class can be used to delay the processing for a specified amount of time.

Object subclass: **DocumentationManager** – With this class you can generate HTML documentation for any class.

Object subclasses: **DragDrop*** – These classes manage DragDrop events.

Object subclass: **Event** (and subclasses) – These classes form the interface to the event mechanism in Windows. They capture keyboard events, mouse events, and so on.

Object subclasses: **Exception*** – These classes form the exception mechanism for when Smalltalk comes across erroneous situations, like trying to send messages to objects that the objects don't understand or trying to do invalid things like division by zero.

Object subclasses: **External*** – These classes allow you to build interfaces with external systems like DLLs, executables, OLE-objects, COM-objects, and ActiveX objects.

Object subclass: **File** – This is the interface to the file system of Windows. A File object is basically a handle to the file.

Object subclass: **GraphicsTool** (and subclasses) – These are the tools/handles to whatever you can make visible on the screen.

Object subclass: **GUID** – Each class in the system has a GUID – a Globally Unique Identifier. Those GUIDs are objects of this class. This class is also able to interpret GUIDs from external objects, like COM-objects.

Object subclass: **HistoryList** – This class maintains a list of previous actions, so that you can implement the "back" and "forward" buttons.

Object subclass: **HtmlWriteStream** – This class allows you to write relatively basic HTML documents. It is used by the DocumentationManager. For more complicated HTML output this class can easily be extended.

Object subclass: **LayoutManager** (and subclasses) – These classes are used to manage the position of fields when views are resized. See Chapter 4.

Object subclass: **ListViewColumn** – These are the columns of a multi-column list.

Object subclass: **Locale** – This is the interface to the Windows Locale, where the number formats, currency symbols, and so on are defined. If you were building an international application, you could pick up the international settings and language from here and present the information accordingly.

Object subclass: **Magnitude** – Probably just behind Collection, the most widely used class. Magnitude itself is abstract, but the subclasses include the Number hierarchy, Point, Character, Date, and Time.

Magnitude subclass: **ArithmeticValue** – Abstract class holding the hierarchy of classes which allow arithmetic operations, like Numbers and Points.

Number subclass: **Float** – The Float class represents double precision (64-bit) floating point numbers.

Number subclass: **Fraction** – This class allows you to calculate with fractions without losing any precision, as a fraction is made up of two integers, the numerator and the denominator, which are maintained separately in the class.

Integer subclass: **SmallInteger** – This class holds the SmallIntegers as immediate objects. SmallIntegers range from –1,073,741,824 to 1,073,741,823. Integers outside this range are LargeIntegers, which are not held as immediate objects and are therefore slightly slower in use.

ArithmeticValue subclass: **Point** – A Point in Smalltalk is defined as two numbers with an @ in between. As the two numbers can be accessed separately, any calculation that can be done with the numbers can also be done with Points.

ArithmeticValue subclass: **Point3D** – A Point3D is basically a point with an added dimension. Looking at the implementation, you can see that implementing Point4D and other dimensions is very simple.

Magnitude subclass: **Association** – This is a rather peculiar class in this hierarchy. Association doesn't adhere to any of the mathematical protocols, except that it follows the comparison protocol.

Magnitude subclass: **Character** – Characters are immediate objects, just like Integers. Characters are in the Magnitude hierarchy for the same reason as Associations; they follow the comparison protocol. The Character class has many helpful methods, both on the class side, like #space, #tab, #cr, and #newPage, and on the instance side, like #asUppercase, #asLowercase, #isLetter, #isDigit, and #isVowel.

Magnitude subclass: **Date** – The Date class represents dates based on January 1, 1901. It allows calculations with dates by converting to days. Leap years are automatically taken into account. Dates can cooperate with Time instances, by converting the Date objects into Time objects.

Magnitude subclass: **Time** – The Time class is based around milliseconds. All calculations are done via conversion to milliseconds. See Chapter 7.

Object subclass: **MemoryManager** – This is a system class that maintains the allocated memory. One of its tasks is to manage the Garbage Collector.

Object subclass: **MenuItem** – Instances of this class are the items that are shown on a menu. The **CommandMenu** holds a CommandDescription.

Object subclass: **Message** – This is one of the examples where you can see that Smalltalk is defined in itself. Instances of the Message class are the messages that you send to other objects.

Object subclass: **MessageBox** – The MessageBox is the interface to the standard Windows message boxes. See Chapter 6.

Object subclass: **Model** – The Model class is an abstract class which is used as the superclass of application models following the Model-Presenter-View framework.

Model subclass: **AspectBuffer** – The AspectBuffer is used to keep a copy of the original object when working with Dialog windows. Modifications are made to the copy and when #apply is sent to the AspectBuffer, the modifications are sent to the original object.

Model subclass: **SmalltalkSystem** – This class gives the developer a view on the whole development system. It only has a single instance which can be accessed by sending #current to the class.

Model subclass: **TreeModelAbstract** and subclasses – These classes provide the Tree functionality. See Chapter 9.

Model subclass: **ValueModel** and subclasses – These classes form the wrappers around objects so that the objects have generalized accessors, #value and #value:. When changed, the ValueModel sends a notification to its dependants. This class forms part of the MPV framework.

Object subclass: **Mutex** – Mutex stands for Mutually Exclusive; this class manages mutually exclusive processes.

Object subclass: **ObjectRegistry** and subclasses – Some objects require registration, typically COM objects and other external objects. The registration is managed through these classes.

Object subclasses: **Package** and **PackageManager** – These classes represent the Packages and the PackageManager. There is only one PackageManager in the system.

Object subclass: **Presenter** – This is the abstract superclass of all presenters, both the composite presenters and the elementary presenters. It provides the basic protocols both for creation of the presenters and for showing the presenters' resources. It also provides the basic interface with the connected view.

Presenter subclass: **CompositePresenter** – This class is the abstract superclass of composite presenter subclasses.

CompositePresenter subclass: **Inspector** and subclasses – These are the presenter classes for the different Inspectors that can be opened on objects. Note that these presenters are shown in an InspectorShell.

CompositePresenter subclass: **Shell** – This forms the Windows shell for subpresenters. Instances of this class and subclasses have a Windows frame and a caption. The Shell also provides the generic command history functionality.

Shell subclass: **Dialog** – The Dialog provides a standard modal window on an AspectBuffer with OK/Cancel functionality.

Dialog subclass: **ValueDialog** – The ValueDialog forms the abstract superclass of Dialogs that present single ValueAspects.

ValueDialog subclass: **CommonDialog** and subclasses – These are standard Windows dialogs; BrowseFolderDialog, ColorDialog, FileOpenDialog, FileSaveDialog, FindDialog, FindReplaceDialog, FontDialog, and PrintDialog. They are typically opened with the message #showModal.

ValueDialog subclass: **ProgressDialog** – This dialog can be used to show a progress bar.

ValueDialog subclass: **Prompter** – This dialog is quite often used as an example of a simple dialog requesting information from the user. For example: Prompter prompt: "What is your name?".

Shell subclass: **DocumentShell** – The DocumentShell adds standard file handling to the Shell class, so that the model can be saved to a file or restored from a file.

DocumentShell subclass: **SmalltalkWorkspaceDocument** – This class represents the standard Smalltalk workspaces.

Shell subclass: **SmalltalkToolShell** – The subclasses of this class are the development tools like browsers, debuggers, inspectors, the view composer, and the system window.

Presenter subclass: **ListPresenter** – This an elementary presenter which forms the basis for all lists.

Presenter subclass: **ValuePresenter** – The subclasses of this abstract class are the elementary presenters that present single ValueAspects.

Object subclass: **ProcessorScheduler** – The sole instance of this class manages the processes. When adding a process to the ProcessorScheduler, the priority can be set to, for example, #userBackgroundPriority.

Object subclass: **Rectangle** – This gives a standard set of functionality for a Rectangle. This class can be used as a prototype for other frequently used shapes.

Object subclass: **Resource** – All views are stored as instances of this class's subclass **ViewResource**.

Object subclass: **RichText** – This class is able to convert text strings into RichText and vice versa.

Object subclass: **SearchPolicy** and subclasses – These are similar to the ComparisonPolicy class and subclasses with the difference that these have more widespread use. With the SearchPolicy you can set a standard search policy in a class. This is used, for example, in the Dictionary.

Object subclass: **SessionManager** and its subclass: **DevelopmentSessionManager** – The single instance of these classes represents the main process on the computer. They manage the startup and shutdown of the process, and know about things like the computer name.

Object subclass: **SharedQueue** – This class forms the shared queue for the Input State.

Object subclass: **Signal** and subclass: **NotificationSignal** – These classes form part of the exception handling.

Object subclass: **Sound** – This class forms the interface to the Windows sound handling.

Object subclass: **SourceManager** – This class handles the reading and writing to and from the source file and the changes file.

Object subclass: **StatusOwnerDraw** and its subclass: **StatusItem** – These two classes handle the contents of the status bar.

Object subclasses **STB*** – These classes handle the binary filing.

Object subclass: **Stream** and subclasses – These classes provide streaming functionality over collections.

PositionableStream subclass: **ReadStream** – This is a read-only stream, useful for running over a stream where you want to be sure that no modifications are made to the contents.

PositionableStream subclass: **WriteStream** – This stream does not allow reading, just writing.

WriteStream subclass: **ReadWriteStream** – This subclass adds the reading functionality to the WriteStream.

ReadWriteStream subclass: **FileStream** – The FileStream allows a File to be accessed as a Stream. The FileStream can be set to read only, write only and read-write. New files can be created automatically; information can be added at the end of an existing file or inserted at a specific point. FileStreams can be either over text files or over binary files.

Stream subclass: **Random** – The Random class provides four means of creating a stream of random numbers, the C function rand(), a Linear Congruential generator, a generator based on Lehmer's linear congruential method, and Park and Miller's "Minimum Standard" congruential generator.

Object subclass: **TestCoordinator** – This class is used by Object Arts to test all the classes that have a #test method on the class side.

Object subclass: **ToolbarItem** and subclasses – These classes handle the contents of the toolbars.

Object subclass: **TreeNode** – This class forms part of the tree-handling as described in Chapter 9.

Object subclass: **TypeConverter** and subclasses – These classes convert objects of a certain type into objects of different types and back if necessary. Typical use is between text and another type to convert the input of a text field into the required type. The reverse is used to convert objects of a certain type into text so that they can be displayed in a text box. See also Chapter 7.

Object subclass: **UndefinedObject** – The UndefinedObject class holds one instance, nil, which doesn't have any contents, and answers false or nil to virtually everything. Most of the methods are there to "undo" the superclass's implementation. One interesting method is #subclass: instanceVariableNames: classVariableNames: poolDictionaries:. This method allows you to create a class with superclass nil, which means that it is a root class!

Object subclass: **View** – This class is an abstract class and holds the hierarchy of the different classes of visible elements.

View subclass: **ContainerView** – This abstract class holds the hierarchy of composite views.

ContainerView subclass: **AbstractCardContainer** and subclasses – These classes provide the handling of tabbed views (**CardContainer**) or sequential views (**WizardCardContainer**).

ContainerView subclass: **ScrollingDecorator** – The ScrollingDecorator handles the horizontal and vertical scroll bars.

ContainerView subclass: **ShellView** and subclasses – these are the real containers of other views.

View subclass: **ControlView** and subclasses – The ControlView is the abstract superclass of the elementary view components.

View subclass: **DesktopView** – This view, which has a single instance, represents the desktop. This instance can, for example, be asked what the resolution is. It is also the container of all currently existing views, therefore you can send a command to all the views via this instance.

Nil subclass: **ProtoObject** – This is an abstract class that can be used as a basis for so-called "stub" classes, typically used in interfacing with another system.

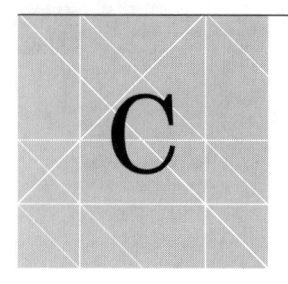

Appendix C
Additional tools

On top of the tools that we used throughout this book, Dolphin Smalltalk has a number of additional tools that are briefly described here.

The simple class browser

This is a simplified version of the CHB described in Section 3.1.1. It lacks some functionality in that it doesn't allow you to group the methods by protocol or by variable and it doesn't show you the first two columns in the method list (Figure C.1).

Figure C.1
The simple class browser

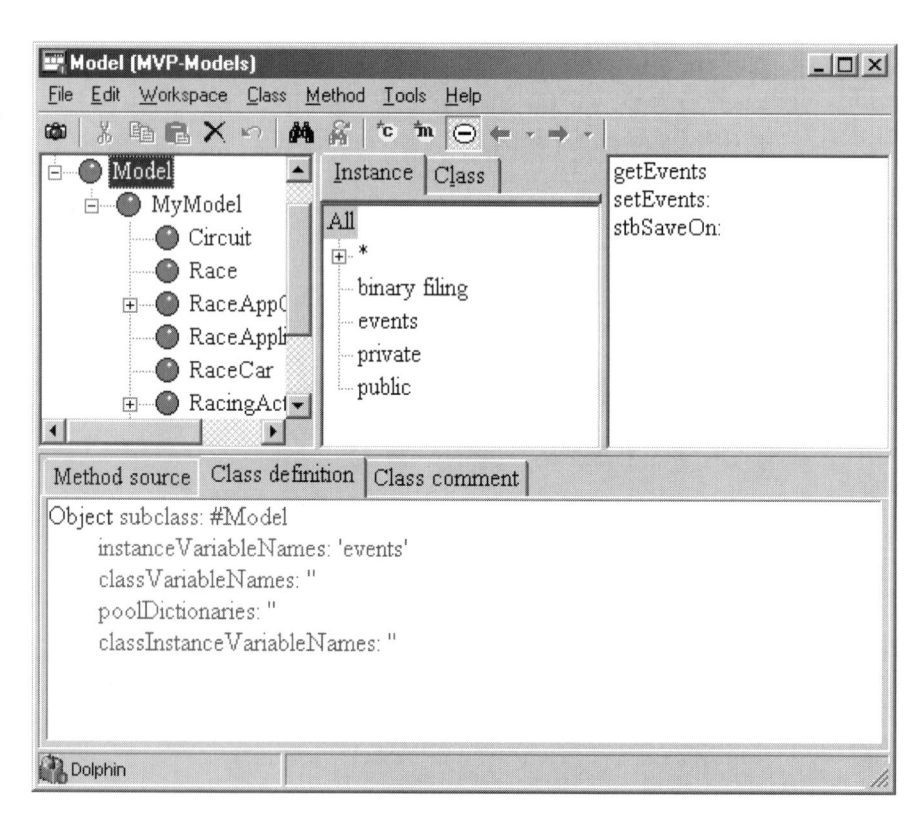

APPENDIX C   307

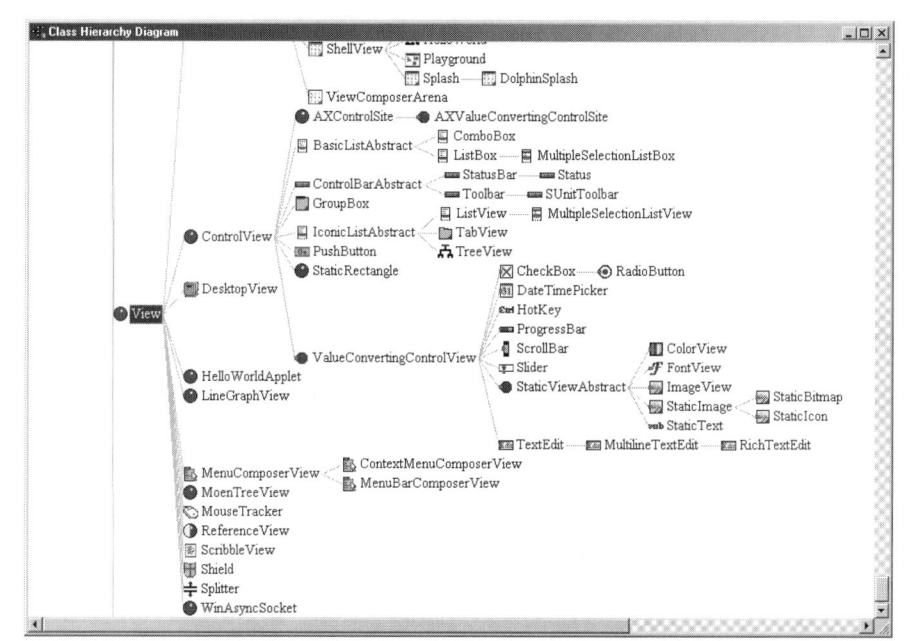

Figure C.2

The class hierarchy diagram

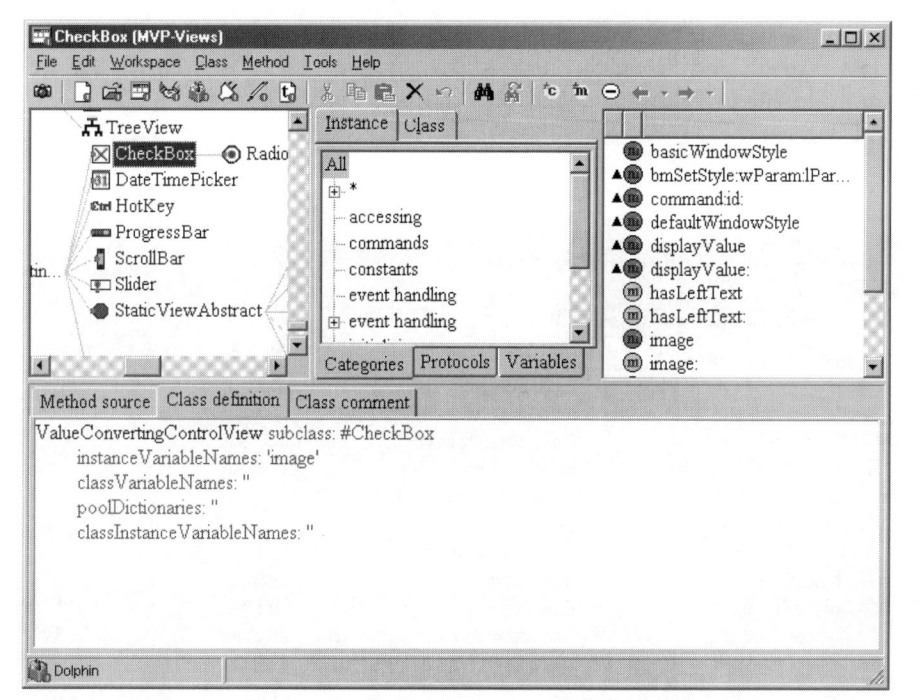

Figure C.3

The moen tree browser

The class hierarchy diagram

This tool shows you the whole hierarchy in a horizontal tree structure (a moen tree) (Figure C.2). It is an excellent navigation tool, especially if you have a large monitor. It is also a good tool to learn the hierarchy structure of the class hierarchy. From the moen tree you can select a class and then open a browser on it.

The moen tree browser

This is the same as the CHB with the difference that the class hierarchy is implemented through a moen tree, which means that you have to do more horizontal scrolling (Figure C.3).

The resource browser

The resource browser lists all the available resources (views) (Figure C.4). When you select one you can open a view composer on it.

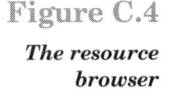

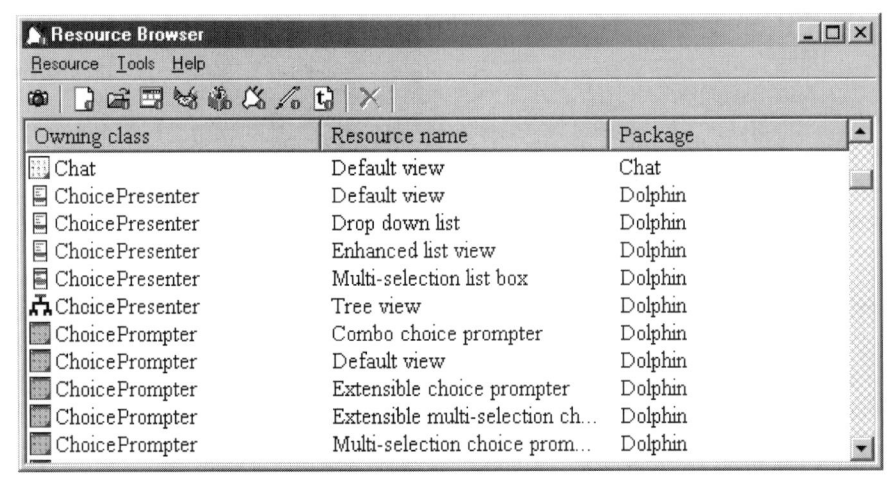

The pool dictionaries inspector

This inspector lists all available pool dictionaries (Figure C.5). Pool dictionaries are shared variables across the system. Here you can find, for example, the MS-Windows variables that are used in the system.

Figure C.4

The resource browser

Owning class	Resource name	Package
Chat	Default view	Chat
ChoicePresenter	Default view	Dolphin
ChoicePresenter	Drop down list	Dolphin
ChoicePresenter	Enhanced list view	Dolphin
ChoicePresenter	Multi-selection list box	Dolphin
ChoicePresenter	Tree view	Dolphin
ChoicePrompter	Combo choice prompter	Dolphin
ChoicePrompter	Default view	Dolphin
ChoicePrompter	Extensible choice prompter	Dolphin
ChoicePrompter	Extensible multi-selection ch...	Dolphin
ChoicePrompter	Multi-selection choice prom...	Dolphin

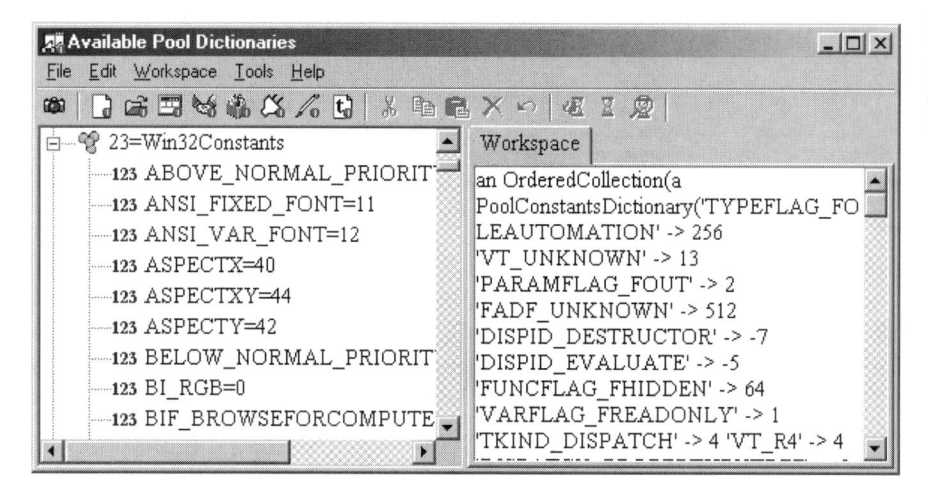

Figure C.5
The pool dictionaries inspector

The protocol browser

The protocol browser is the main maintenance window for Protocols (Figure C.6). Here you can create new protocols, define which messages belong to the protocol and which classes belong to the protocol.

Use of protocols and therefore the protocol browser is outside the scope of this book.

Dolphin Live Update

The Dolphin Live Update screen allows you to update your version of Dolphin Smalltalk with the latest patch level(s). Object Arts informs the users on a regular basis of new patches through the Dolphin Smalltalk newsgroup. The update requires an Internet connection.

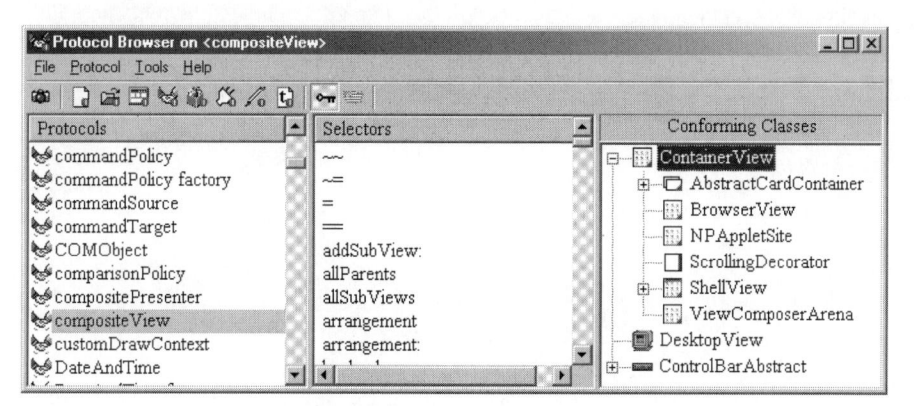

Figure C.6
The protocol browser

The ActiveX Component Wizard

The ActiveX Component Wizard allows you to install ActiveX components as part of your development environment.

Dolphin Options

The Dolphin Options window shows the default settings that are used in the different components of the Dolphin Smalltalk development environment (Figure C.7). One of these options is the standard font used throughout the system. When you double-click on the option, you can change it to the required value.

Figure C.7
The Dolphin Options window

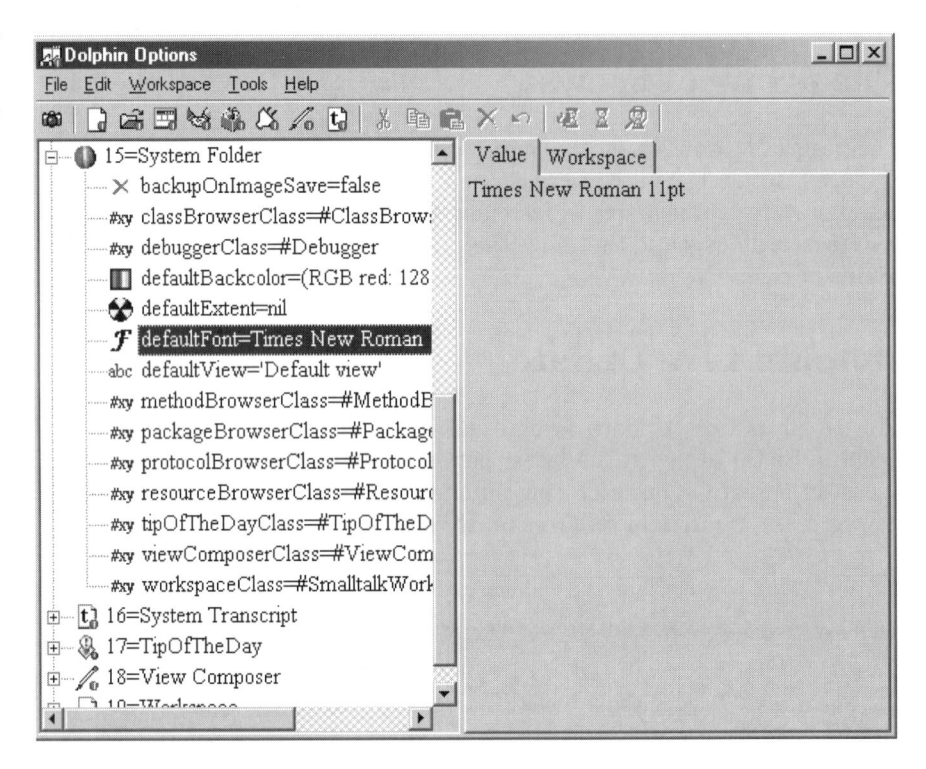

Appendix D
Date and Time field formatting

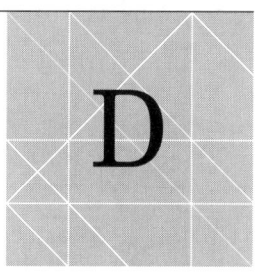

The following table, from the Microsoft documentation, shows the formatting possibilities for the Date and Time fields.

Element	Description
d	The one- or two-digit day
dd	The two-digit day. Single-digit day values are preceded by a zero.
ddd	The three-character weekday abbreviation.
dddd	The full weekday name.
M	The one- or two-digit month number.
MM	The two-digit month number. Single-digit values are preceded by a zero.
MMM	The three-character month abbreviation.
MMMM	The full month name.
yy	The last two digits of the year (that is, 1996 would be displayed as "96").
yyyy	The full year (that is, 1996 would be displayed as "1996").
h	The one- or two-digit hour in 12-hour format.
hh	The two-digit hour in 12-hour format. Single-digit values are preceded by a zero.
H	The one- or two-digit hour in 24-hour format.
HH	The two-digit hour in 24-hour format. Single-digit values are preceded by a zero.
m	The one- or two-digit minute.
mm	The two-digit minute. Single-digit values are preceded by a zero.
t	The one-letter AM/PM abbreviation (that is, AM is displayed as "A").
tt	The two-letter AM/PM abbreviation (that is, AM is displayed as "AM").

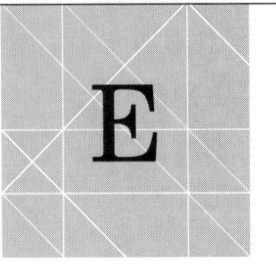

Appendix
The CD

On the CD you will find two installation files and a number of Dolphin Package files. The two installation files make use of the Microsoft Installer that comes with Microsoft Windows 2000 and Microsoft ME. For earlier versions of Microsoft Windows (Windows 95, Windows 98 and Windows NT 4) you require the appropriate Windows Installer, which you can download from the Microsoft Web site[1] or from the Object Arts Web site (http://www.object-arts.com/Downloads4.htm). If it isn't installed on your machine, you have to install it before you can install Dolphin Smalltalk.

Installing Dolphin Smalltalk

The file DolphinSmalltalkValueEdition.msi contains the Dolphin Smalltalk development system. Double-clicking on this file will install it on your machine. After installing it you will see an additional menu option on your Start menu; Dolphin Smalltalk 4.0. Within that menu you will see a shortcut to some text files and two Dolphin Smalltalk options, one of them called "Fresh install". In our case, after a new installation these two menu options do exactly the same, they create a working image. To make this working image you have to enter an unlock key. The unlock key for this book that allows you to use Dolphin Smalltalk has to be entered *exactly* as below:

1B6BQNU-XMKIEGJ-2IDELGI-YLV9QX

After entering this unlock key a fresh Dolphin Smalltalk image is created and opened. In addition, a Welcome screen is opened with some interesting examples.

Installing online help

The online help, called the Education Centre, also uses the Microsoft Installer which has to be installed on your computer. It runs on the Microsoft HTML Help engine. If it isn't installed as part of your operating system, then you can download it from the Object Arts Web site (http://www.object-arts.com/Downloads4.htm).

---

[1] Microsoft doesn't give permission to distribute these files on CD.

The chapter packages

The chapter packages contain the source code for the individual chapters. As some of the chapters rewrite code of the previous chapter, it wasn't possible to make the packages incremental. This means that before loading the package of a specific chapter, you have to uninstall the package of the previous chapter. If you forget, Dolphin will warn you that certain classes in the package already exist, therefore the new package cannot be loaded.

And finally ...

In the Application directory you will find the whole application as you would distribute it. The FormulaOne.exe file is a runtime executable of the application that is built in this book. To use the executable you have to have the virtual machine installed on your machine, which is the DolphinVM004.dll. As we are making use of the Dolphin icon resources, you have to have the DolphinDR004.dll in the same directory as the application file (the executable). The FormulaOne.dat file contains some of the Formula One race data that you should also be able to load on your application after finishing Chapter 11. The files Teams.csv and Drivers.csv contain comma separated data that can be imported with the CSV Import function which is built in Chapter 11.

Index

Note: Page numbers in **bold** indicate where a term has been defined in the text.

A
1-of-n variables   69–70
   presenting   70–1
AbstractCard Container class   **305**
abstract classes   **3**, **51**
   RacingActor   51–3
accessors   27–8, 164
   getters and setters   27–8
Action-Object model   186, 228
ActiveX   255
ActiveX Component Wizard   310
age calculation   60–1
A-Kind-Of (AKO) relationships   3
AllCircuits   228
AllDrivers   136, 226–8, 228
AllSeasons   238
AllTeams   133–4, 227
Apple   1
applets   293–4
application   17–20
Application Deployment Kit (Object Arts)   292–3
arguments   **2**, 9
ArithmeticValue class   **314**
Array   **90**, 92–3
   starting numbers   112–114, 116
ArrayedCollection class   297
AspectBuffer class   **301**
   Season component   100, 101
Association class   **300**
Attribute Descriptor class   **297**

B
Bag   **90**, 91–2
Bartholomew, Ian   207, 296
Beck, Kent   30, 128
Behavior class   29, **297**
bill-of-material (BOM) relationships   3
binary files   256
binary messages   **9**, 10
bitmaps, toolbar buttons   207
BlockClosure class   **297**
   error handling   129–31
blocks   **11**
Boolean class   **297**
booleans
   Driver component   69, 73–4
   radio buttons   73–5
breakpoints   123, 125–7
browsers   26
   class hierarchy browser (CHB)   23–6
     Team component   48
   package browser   47–8
   protocol browser   309
   resource browser   308
   simple class browser   306
   Web   293
buttons
   radio
     Driver component   74–7
     layout manager   72–4
     testing their behavior   71–4
   toolbar   201–7
     large buttons   206–7

C
Canvas class   240–1
capitalization   57–60
captions
   Driver component   83–5
   RaceCar component   134–5
CardContainer class   **305**
category grouping   24
CD   312–13
   CSV files   267
Changes file   **5–6**
Character class   **300**
Circuit class   142, 144
Circuit component   18, 141
   basic model   142–50
   global variables   225
   presenter and view   150–60
   Race component   162
CircuitComponent class   191
CircuitDialogPresenter   150–4, 157–60
   Web data import wizard   286
circuit length   142–4, 157–60
Class   **297**
ClassDescription   **297**
classes   **3**, 297–305
   comment   25–6, 27
   creating   26–31
   definition   25
class hierarchy browser (CHB)   23–6
   Team component   48
class hierarchy tree   23–4
class instance variables   264–8
Collection classes   90–3, **297**
   decision table   91
Color class   **298**
   graphs   241, 249–52
combo box   82
Command* classes   **298**
CommandDescription class   298
CommandMenu class   **301**
CommandPolicy class   298
CommandQuery class   298

315

INDEX

Comma Separated Value (CSV) files, importing 261–2
   data import wizard 268–76
   generic import class 262–8
comments 29
CommonDialog class **302**
ComparisonPolicy class **298**
CompiledCode class **298**
Compiler class **298**
complex objects 161–3
CompositePresenter class **302**
   subclasses 31, 302
      Team component 34
concatenation 56
containers 72–4
   Driver component 76
ContainerView class **305**
context menus 198–9
ControlView **305**
conversion methods 143–4, 156–60
Copy 100–4
cryptography 293
CSV (Comma Separated Value) files, importing 261–2
   data import wizard 268–76
   generic import class 262–8
CSVImport class 264–8, 271, 277
CSVImportDriver class 266–7
CSVImportTeam class 266–7

D

databases 255
DataImport class 277
data import wizard
   comma-separated data 268–76
   Web 283–9
DATE class 60
Date class **300**
   calculations 60–1
   CSV files 267
   Driver component 63–5, 67–8
   formatting possibilities 64–5, 311
DeadObject class **298**
DeafObject class **298**
debugger 122, 124–7
   as main coding tool 127–8
   RaceCar component 125–7
deepCopy 100–4
DeferredValue class **298**
definition documents, XML 289–91
Delay class **298**
dependants 66
deploying applications 292, 294
   making executables 292–3
   Web deployment 293–4
deprecated methods 25
DesktopView class **305**
DevelopmentSessionManager class 303
Dialog class 32, **302**
DialogView class 41
Dictionary **90**, 116–7
   RaceCar component 117–20
disabling menu commands 200–1
displaying expressions 9
DLLs (Dynamic Link Libraries) 292, 293
DocumentManager class **298**
DocumentShell class **302**
   file handling 32
   saving object data 256, 258, 259

Dolphin*.dll 6
Dolphin.chg 5
DolphinCRxxx.dll 293
DolphinDRxxx.dll 293
Dolphin.exe 6
Dolphin.img 5
Dolphin Live Update 309
Dolphin Options 45, 310
Dolphin resource library 293
Dolphin Smalltalk environment 4
   file setup 4–6
   Launcher 6–7
Dolphin.sml 5
DolphinSure 293, 294
DolphinSureCrypto.dll 293
DolphinVMxxx.dll 6, 293
DragDrop* classes **298**
Driver class 55–61
   association with RaceCar component 121
   MyModel class 96
Driver component 18, 50
   caption 83–5
   gender 68–83
   model 50–61
   picture 86–8
   presenter 61–3
   view 63–8
DriverComponent class 190, 274
DriverDialogPresenter class 61–4, 68
   caption 83–5
   fields 64
   gender 75–6, 78–9, 80–1
   picture 85–7
drivers
   ages 60–1, 67
   default 120
   names 55–60, 66–7
drop-down listboxes 55–60
   Driver component 81, 82
   results 228–9
Dynabook 1
Dynamic Link Libraries (DLLs) 292, 293

E

Education Centre 326
enabling menu commands 200–01
encapsulation **2**
   accessors 27
errors
   handling 13–14, 122–4
      RaceCar component 129–31
      Race component 177
   method list 25
evaluating expressions 9
Event class **299**
Exception* classes **299**
exception dialog 123, 128
executables, making 292–3
exit, saving data on 259–60
extensions to inherited behavior 3–4
External* classes **299**

F

False class **297**
field aspects 40
File class **299**
file-handling windows 32
File menu 256–8
file setup 4–6

INDEX

FileStream class **304**
Float class **300**
   overriding of inherited behavior 4
formatting standards 29
Formula1.com Limited 277
Fraction class **300**

G

garbage collector 22
getters 27–8, 94
   see also accessors
global variables 132–4, 225–8
Gorisek, David 296
graphical display of results 238–54
   information requirement analysis 239–40
   LineGraph view 240–7
   user-definable graph 246–54
GraphicsTool class **299**
GraphPresenter class 245–6
group boxes 71–2
   Driver component 77
GUID class **299**

H

Hello World example 16
help, installing online 312
HistoryList class **299**
HTML (Hypertext Markup Language) 277
   import model 277–83
   Web deployment 293–4
HTMLImport class 277–83
HTMLImportShell class 283–9
HtmlWriteStream class **297**

I

IdentityDictionary 115–16
Image file **5**, 6
ImagePresenter 87
importing
   comma-separated data 261–76
   from the Web 277–90
ImportWizardShell class 270–4
indexes
   score definition 93
   starting numbers 112–15
inheritance **3**
   abstract classes 51
   Driver component 51
   Model-Presenter-View (MPV) paradigm 26–7
initialization, lazy 165
inspector 12–13
Inspector class **302**
installing
   Dolphin Smalltalk 312
   online help 312
instance variables 2, **3**
   initialization 29
   Team component 27, 35
instances **3**
Integer class 300
   overriding of inherited behavior 4
Internet *see* Web
Interval class **298**
IStream class 287

J

Java 6, 293

K

keyword messages **9**, 10
Kilometer class 142–4, 156–60

L

labels 104–7
lap record 145–50, 153
LargeIntegers class 25, 300
large toolbar buttons 206–7
Launcher 6–7
LayoutManager class **399**
layout managers
   data import wizards 272, 289
   proportional 194–5
   radio buttons 72–4
   results 232–3, 253
   splitter bars 193–6
   toolbars 201
lazy initialization 165
Length 142–4
LineGraphView class 240–6
Lisa 1
ListModel class
   results 236
   Season component 102, 103
ListPresenter class 31, **303**
   results 236
list presenters
   Driver component 77–83
   RaceCar component 134–5
   Season component 96–7
ListView, multi-column 107–9
   dynamic resizing 236–7
ListViewColumn class **299**
Locale class **299**
LookupTable 115

M

Macintosh 1
Magnitude class **299**
   extensions to inherited behavior 4
   subclasses 300
maintenance
   race application 197–8, 207
      context menus and menu bars 198–9
      enabling and disabling commands 200–01
      methods 197–8
      toolbars 201–7
      virtual tree 216–9
   Race component 161, 166–7
   Team component 47–9
measurement units 142–9
MemoryManager class **300**–1
menu bars 199
menu composer 198
MenuItem class **301**
menus
   context 198–9
   enabling and disabling commands 200–1
   File 256–8
MessageBox class **301**
   error handling 128–31
Message class **301**
MessageNotUnderstood class 123, 127
messages
   binary **9**, 10
   combining multiple 15
   keyword **9**, 10

318 INDEX

messages (*continued*)
  order of evaluation   10–11
  #perform: 158
  #queryCommand: 200–1
  types   9–10
  unary   **9**, 10
MetaClass   **297**
methods   **2**
  defining   29
  deleting   54
  deprecated   25
  grouping   24
  list   24–5
  names   29
  primitive   25
  private   25
method source
  class hierarchy browser   25
  debugger   124
Microsoft look   44–6
Microsoft SQLServer   255
Mile class   142–4, 156–9
milliseconds
  lap record   145–50
  type converter   154–6
modal windows   32
Model class   **301**
  Team class   27
Model-Presenter-View (MPV) paradigm   19–20, 26–7, 32
  Driver component   67
  ValueAspectAdapters   34
  see also models; presenters; views
models   **19**
  Circuit   142–50
  Driver   50–61
  modifications   258–9
  Race   161–6
  RaceCar   110–22
  racing application   186–92
  Season   89–95
  Team   22–31
  see also Model-Presenter-View (MPV) paradigm
moen tree browser   307, 308
multi-column lists
  dynamic resizing   236–8
  Season component   104–9
  STBFiler   258
Mutex class   **301**
MyModel class   95, 226

N

newsgroup   295
NotificationSignal class   **303**
Number class
  extensions to inherited behavior   4
  overriding of inherited behavior   4
  subclasses   300

O

Object-Action model   186, 228
Object Arts
  Application Deployment Kit   292–3
  Dolphin Live Update   309–10
  ODBC package   255
  online help   312
  Web site   295
Object class   **297**
  subclasses   297–305

object databases   255
object-orientation (O-O)   1–2
  application   18
ObjectRegistry class   **301**
objects
  containing objects   14–15
  links between   110, 113
  names   95–7
  saving data   255–61
ODBC package   255
OLAP data cubes   255
Omnibase   255
online help, installing   312
Open DataBase Connectivity (ODBC) package   255
Oracle   255
OrderedCollection (OC)   **90**, 92–3, 112
  importing comma-separated data   261–3
  STBFiler   256
overriding of inherited behavior   3–4
  method list   24

P

package browser   48–9
Package class   **301**
PackageManager class   **301**
Palo Alto Research Center   1
parameters list   **124**, 127
parameter value   **124**–5, 126
parent-child relationships   3, 213–15
Pen class   242
pictures   85–8
Point3D class   **300**
Point class   **300**
polymorphism   **4**, 197
pool dictionaries inspector   308–9
PoolDictionary   91
PositionableStream class   304
Presenter class   **301**–2, 303
  Team   31
presenters   **19**–20
  Circuit   149, 150–60
  Driver   61–4
  modifications   256–8
  Race   166–79
  race application   192–3
  RaceCar   132–4
  results   231–3
  Season   97–9
  Team   31–5
  see also Model-Presenter-View (MPV) paradigm
primitive methods   25
private methods   25
ProcessorScheduler class   **303**
ProgressDialog class   **302**
Prompter class   **302**
proportional layout managers   194–5
protocol browser   309
protocol grouping   24
ProtoObject class   **305**
Published Aspect Inspector   37
  Team component   40

Q

qualification times   162

R

RaceAppComponent class   187–91
  global variables   225–6

INDEX

results 234
tree model 209, 222–4
RaceApplication class 187–8, 196
tree model 209–11, 216–19, 220
RaceApplicationShell class 192
data import wizards 273–4, 283
maintenance 197–8
results 234, 235, 236, 253
saving object data 256–8, 259–61
tree model 209–13
RaceCar class 110–12
RaceCar component 18, 110
error handling and debugger 122–32
global variables 225
model 110–22
presenter and view 132–40
virtual tree 220–3
RaceCarView class 134–40
Race class 163, 165–6
Web data import wizard 287
Race component 18, 161, 184
global variables 225–8
model 161–6
presenter and view 166–79
sorting the starters 179–84
virtual tree 220–3
RaceDialog 167–70
RaceShell 170–79
results 228–9
RacingActor class 51–3, 54
MyModel class 95
radio buttons
Driver component 74–7
layout manager 72–4
testing their behavior 71–2
Random class **304**
read-only fields 63
ReadStream class **304**
ReadWriteStream class **304**
Rectangle class **303**
refactoring 183
relational databases 255
resource browser 308
Resource class **303**
Resource toolbox 38, 39
Team component 40
results 230
collection 230–1
drop-down lists 228–9
graph 238–54
presenter 231–3
season's 230–9
return values 11–12
RichText class **303**
RootComponent class 212, 226

S

safe objects 2
saving object data 255–61
Schwab, Bill 296
score definition 93–5
Scribble 240
ScribbleView 240
ScrollingDecorator class **305**
SearchPolicy class **303**
Season class 89
association with RaceCar component 121
MyModel class 95
Race component 163–5

results 231
graphical display 239
starting numbers 112–16
Season component 18, 89
model 89–95
multi-column lists 104–19
object name 95–6
presenter and view 96–104
Race component 161–2
results 230–9
virtual tree 220–1, 224–5
SeasonComponent class 191
season-dependent components, integrating 208–54
SeasonDialogPresenter 97–9, 102–3, 105–7
SeasonGraphShell class 247
SeasonInstanceComponent 234, 253
SeasonResultPresenter class 232–3, 238
security system 293–4
selector **2**
SequenceableCollection class 298
SessionManager class 303
Set **90**, 92–3
graphical display of results 242
setters 27–8
see also accessors
SharedQueue class **303**
Sharp, Alec 84
Shell class **302**
HTMLImportShell class 284
race application presenter 192–3
RaceCar view 132, 134–7, 138–40
Race presenter 170–9
splitter bars 193–4
Team presenter 31–2
ShellView class **305**
Hello World example 16
shortcuts 43
radio buttons 71–2
Signal class **303**
simple class browser 306
SmallIntegers class **300**
Smalltalk Binary filing (STB) 256
Smalltalk language 1–4
SmalltalkSystem class **301**
SmalltalkToolShell class **302**
SmalltalkWorkspaceDocument class 259, **302**
sort blocks 94
SortedCollection (SC) **90**, 92–3
Race component 179–81
sorting the starters 179–84
Sound class **303**
Source file **5**
SourceManager class **303**
splitter bars 193–5
SQLServer 255
stack trace 123, **124**, 126
Starter class 163, 165
results 230–1
sorting 179–84
starting numbers 112–16
Static Text 38
status bars 283, 289
StatusItem class **303**
StatusOwnerDraw class **303**
STB (Smalltalk Binary filing) 256
STB* classes **303**
STBFiler 256, 258
STBInFiler 256

STBOutFiler 256
stepping commands 125, 126–7
    see also debugger
Stream class **304**
streams 58, 278
    importing comma-separated data 262, 264
String class **297**
    and Symbol class, difference between 70
strings
    HTML import model 279
    manipulation 56–8
subclasses 3–4
SUnit 30, 128
superclasses 3–4
Symbol class **297**
    and String class, difference between 69–70
system buttons 201–3
system transcript 8

T

tabs
    comma-separated data 261
    radio buttons 72, 83
    sequence setting 44–5
tab strip presented as buttons 71
Team class 26–31, 48
    association with RaceCar component 116–20
    modifications 53–5
    MyModel class 95
Team component 18, 21
    maintenance 47–9
    model 22–31
    presenter 31–5
    view 36–47
TeamComponent class 198, 274
TeamDialogPresenter class 32–3, 35, 48
    caption 85
temporary variables 57, 166
TestCoordinator class **304**
testing
    debugger 128
    Driver component 60–1, 66–8
    radio buttons 71–3
    Team component 30, 40, 42–3
text area 25–6
text files 255–6
TextPresenter class 38–9
Time class **300**
    formatting possibilities 65, 311
    lap record 145–50
    milliseconds type converter 154–5
ToolbarItem class **304**
toolbars 201–6
tooltips 201, 206
TreeDemo class 210–12
TreeModelAbstract class **301**
TreeModel class 209–10
TreeNode class **304**
TreePresenter class 31
trees 208–20
    adding branches 220–5
    virtual 208, 213–19
True class **297**
TypeConverter class **304**

U

unary messages **9**, 10
UndefinedObject class **304**–5

V

ValueAspectAdapters 34
ValueDialog class **302**
ValueModel class **301**
ValuePresenter class 31, **303**
variables
    1-of-n 70–1
        presenting 71
    assignment 12
    class instance 264–8
    global 133–4, 225–8
    grouping 24
    temporary 57, 166
View class **305**
view composer 36–8
view containers 37
view hierarchy 39
ViewResource class **303**
views **19**–20
    Circuit 150–4
    data import wizard 274
    Driver 63–8
    LineGraph 240–6
    modifications 256–8
    Race 166–79
    race application 192–6
    RaceCar 132, 134–7
    Season 99–100
    Team 36–47
    see also Model-Presenter-View (MPV) paradigm
virtual lists 105–7
virtual machine
    executables 293
    file setup 6
    Web deployment 293
virtual trees 208, 213–20

W

Web
    browsers 293
    deployment 293–4
    importing from the 276–91
WinInetLibrary class 287
WizardCardContainer class **305**
    results 235
wizards 268
    data import 268–76
    executables, making 292
workspace 7–8
World Wide Web see Web
WriteStream class **304**

X

Xerox 1
XML data 289–91
XML Document Object Model standard 290

Table 4.5

Sequence in which Dolphin Smalltalk opens a window

Method	Description
Presenter class ≫ showOn:	One of the many invocation methods to open a view.
Presenter class ≫ new	Here an instance of the presenter class is created.
Presenter ≫ initialize	Any initialization can be set here.
Presenter ≫ createComponents	This is where the subpresenters are created.
Presenter ≫ model:	Here you connect the model to the subpresenters.
Presenter ≫ createView:	This method creates the view by calling the method Presenter class ≫ #loadViewResource:inContext:.
Presenter ≫ view:	This method lets each subpresenter know which is its subview.
Presenter ≫ onViewAvailable	This allows you to modify aspects of subviews before opening the view. The presenter knows about the view, but the view itself is not yet connected.
Presenter ≫ connectView	Here the view is connected to the presenter and to the model. When the view connects to the model (through the View ≫ #model: method), the View ≫ #onModelChanged method is triggered.
Presenter ≫ onViewOpened	This is a trigger that allows you to insert methods that you want to run immediately before the view opens. It already exists in memory, but it is not yet drawn.
Presenter ≫ createSchematicwiring	This is where you connect the trigger wiring to the view.
View ≫ onViewOpened	This triggers the Presenter ≫ #viewOpened.
Presenter ≫ updateCaption	Set the caption when the view opens.
Presenter ≫ setInitialFocus	Set the cursor when the view opens.
View ≫ show	And finally, this makes the view visible.

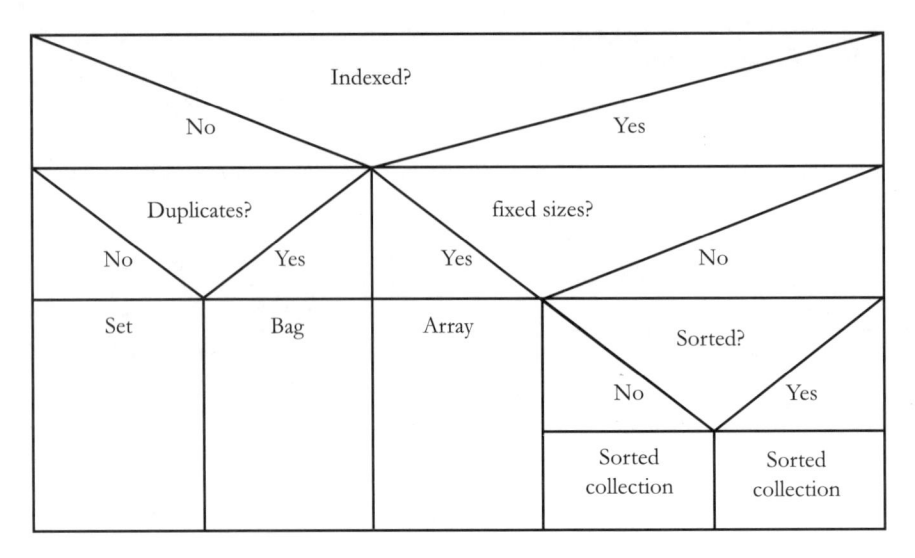

Figure 5.1

Collection decision table

Message	Set	Bag	Array	OC/SC
#at: index	✗	✗	element	element
#find: element	element	✗	✗	✗
#includes: element	boolean	boolean	boolean	boolean
Discriminators	[each | (each at: 1) # $D]			
#findFirst: discriminator #findLast: discriminator	✗	✗	index	index
#detect: discriminator	element	element	element	element
#select: discriminator #reject: discriminator	new set	new bag	new array	new oc/sc
Operational	[:each | Transcript cr; show: each, 'book']			
#do: operation	itself	itself	itself	itself
#collect: operation	new set	new bag	new array	new oc/sc
#inject: initialValue into: operation	result value	result value	result value	result value

Table 5.1

The most frequently used messages for the main collections